Preachers Present Arms

Preachers Present Arms

The Role of the American Churches and Clergy
in World Wars I and II, with Some Observations
on the War in Vietnam

by

Ray H. Abrams, Ph.D.

*Emeritus Associate Professor of Sociology
The University of Pennsylvania*

*War is a terrible trade;
But in the cause that is righteous
Sweet is the smell of powder. . . .*
—Miles Standish

WIPF & STOCK · Eugene, Oregon

Wipf and Stock Publishers
199 W 8th Ave, Suite 3
Eugene, OR 97401

Preachers Present Arms
The Role of the American Churches and Clergy in World War I and II
with Some Observations on the War in Vietnam
By Abrams, Ray H.
Copyright©1969 Herald Press
ISBN 13: 978-1-60608-935-4
Publication date 7/31/2009
Previously published by Herald Press, 1969

To
H. S. A.

ACKNOWLEDGMENTS

Grateful acknowledgment is made to the following publishers and individuals for their courtesy in granting permission to use quotations from materials on which they hold the copyright:

The Abingdon Press: *The Clean Sword* by Lynn Harold Hough; *America—Here and Over There* by Luther Wilson.

William C. Allen: *War! Behind the Smoke Screen.*

The American Academy of Political and Social Science: "The Churches and the Clergy in World War II," in *The Annals*, Vol. 256, March 1948

American Tract Society: *A Manual of Devotion for Soldiers and Sailors* by Judson Swift.

Association Press: *The Christian Witness in War* by E. I. Bosworth; *The Challenge of the Present Crisis* by Harry Emerson Fosdick; *Christian Ethics in the World War* by W. D. Mackenzie; *Practice of Friendship* by George Stewart, Jr., and Henry B. Wright; *Summary of World War Work* by the International Committee of the Y. M. C. A.; *Service with Fighting Men* by the Y. M. C. A.

Bernard Iddings Bell: *What Has God to Do With This War?*

Dodd, Mead and Company: *New Poems*, a poem, "The Illusion of War" by Richard Le Gallienne.

Doubleday, Doran and Company: *Is Preparedness for War Unchristian?* by L. G. Broughton; *Why Christianity Did Not Prevent the War* by Isaac J. Lansing; *The True Story of Woodrow Wilson* by David Lawrence; *Fighting for Faith* by George F. Pentecost; *One Hundred Per Cent Americanism*, edited by A. L. Squiers.

E. P. Dutton and Company: *The Price of Peace* by E. M. Stires.

The Federal Council of the Churches of Christ in America: *General War-Time Commission of the Churches, War-Time Agencies of the Churches.*

Houghton Mifflin Company: *Society at War* by Caroline E. Playne; *Militant America and Jesus Christ* by A. M. Rihbany.

Liveright Publishing Corporation: *The Conscientious Objector* by Walter G. Kellogg; *Spreading Germs of Hate* by George S. Viereck.

Alfred A. Knopf: *Propaganda Technique in the World War* by Harold D. Lasswell.

The Macmillan Company: *The Rise of American Civilization* by Charles A. and Mary R. Beard; *Labor Speaks for Itself on Religion*, edited by Jerome Davis; *Essays on Nationalism* by C. J. H. Hayes; *The Way to Life* by Henry C. King; *Patriotism and Religion* by Shailer Mathews.

Marshall Jones Company, and Horace J. Bridges: *As I Was Saying* by Horace J. Bridges.

Joseph Fort Newton: *The Sword of the Spirit.*

Daniel A. Poling: *Huts in Hell.*

Fleming H. Revell Company: *Conscience and Concessions* by A. W. Anthony; *German Atrocities* and *The Blot on the Kaiser's Scutcheon* by Newell Dwight Hillis; *President Wilson and the Moral Aims of the War*, edited by Frederick Lynch; *Moral Aims of the War*, edited by Walter Laidlaw; *What Did Jesus Really Teach About War?* by E. L. Pell; *The Church and the Great War* by Worth M. Tippy; *With the Y. M. C. A. in France* by H. C. Warren.

Round Table Press: For permission to reprint this work.

Charles Scribner's Sons: *Is Christianity Practicable?* by William Adams Brown; *Soldier Silhouettes* by W. L. Stidger; *Fighting for Peace* by Henry Van Dyke.

David Steele: *Papers and Essays for Churchmen.*

The Yale University Press: *In a Day of Social Rebuilding* by Henry Sloane Coffin; *War and Preaching* by John Kelman; *Religion and the War*, edited by E. L. Sneath.

The Viking Press: *Untimely Papers* by Randolph Bourne; *The Conscientious Objector in America* by Norman Thomas.

Joseph F. Wagner, Inc.: *War Addresses—from Catholic Pulpit and Platform.*

Willett, Clark and Company: *Leaves from the Notebook of a Tamed Cynic* by Reinhold Niebuhr.

Thankful acknowledgment is also made to the following magazines for granting permission to use quotations from their files:

The Advocate of Peace; The Atlantic Monthly; The Baptist Courier; The Biblical World (now *The Journal of Religion*); *The Catholic World; The Christian Century; The Christian Herald* (and Dr. A. E. Keigwin); *The Christian Register; The Churchman; The Congregationalist; The Federal Council Bulletin; Harper's Magazine; The Lutheran; The New Republic; The Outlook* (now *The New Outlook*); *The Presbyterian; Unity; The Watchman-Examiner; The Western Recorder; The World Tomorrow; Zion's Herald.*

TABLE OF CONTENTS

Chapter *Page*

I. THE CHURCHES OF AMERICA IN THE REVOLUTION, THE CIVIL, AND SPANISH-AMERICAN WARS   1
    The American Revolution
    The Civil War
    The Spanish-American War
    The Banishment of War by Resolutions

II. EUROPE STARTS A WAR AND AMERICA PREPARES   13
    War and Propaganda
    Beginnings of the Preparedness Movement
    The *Lusitania* Disaster
    The Churches Abandon Neutrality
    The Preparedness Bandwagon
    America Decides to Fight

III. THE HOLY WAR   49
    The Call to the Colors
    The Intellectuals
    Theology for War Time
    Christ and the Bayonet
    The Church and the State

IV. THE CHURCH AS SERVANT OF THE STATE   77
    Organizing for War
    Recruits and Liberty Bonds
    Campaigns on the Home Front
    Prohibition, Temperance, and Public Morals

Chapter

V. THE CHURCHES CONTRIBUTE TO WAR-TIME HYSTERIA 93
- The Atrocity Mongers
- The Kaiser as Beelzebub
- The Hun
- Hymns of Hate
- The German Plot
- Music and Patriotism
- Spy Hunting
- The Clergy Under Indictment

VI. THE CHURCHES INTERPRET THE FIRST AMENDMENT 125
- Free Speech, Ltd.
- The Pope's Peace Proposals
- The Pacifists
- When Conscience Is a Crime

VII. THE FEDERAL COUNCIL OF THE CHURCHES OF CHRIST IN AMERICA, 1917-18 143
- War and the Mind of Christ
- The Council and the Conscientious Objector
- The Brotherhood of Man

VIII. THE COLLAPSE OF THE PEACE SOCIETIES 159
- The World's Oldest Peace Society
- Peace Through Force
- Fighting for Peace

IX. THE Y. M. C. A. IN KHAKI 169
- The Red Triangle
- The Ministry of the Y. M. C. A.

Table of Contents

Chapter   Page

X. GROUPS OF IRRECONCILABLES — 177
    The People's Council
    Peace Programs in War Time
    The Russellites
    Friends of the Conscientious Objector
    Friends, Mennonites, and Dunkards

XI. THE NON-CONFORMIST CLERGY — 191
    The Iron Hand of the Hierarchy
    The Number of Pacifist Clergy
    Adventures in Non-conformity

XII. THE ESPIONAGE ACT, MOB VIOLENCE, AND THE CLERGY — 209
    Grist for the Espionage Acts
    Popular Justice

XIII. WAR BRINGS A REVIVAL OF RELIGION — 221
    The Return of the Lord
    The New Day
    Gold Stars

XIV. VICTORY AND POST-ARMISTICE DISILLUSIONMENT 227
    The Pre-Armistice Mind
    The Victory
    Disillusionment and Repentance

XV. CONCLUSION — 241

XVI. THE CHURCHES AND THE CLERGY IN WORLD WAR II — 259

XVII. CONCLUSION, 1968 — 275

NOTES AND REFERENCES — 293
BIBLIOGRAPHY — 313
INDEX — 323

INTRODUCTION

THE World War is fast disappearing down the horizon. Yet so tremendous was this social upheaval and so far-reaching, both in time and space, that the wisest of men are just now beginning to comprehend its ramifications and actual significance. Whatever keener insight and clearer judgment have been achieved are due, in part at least, to the great mass of first-hand materials for study which have arisen out of the war; to certain events since 1918; and to the perspective given by time and reflection.

The search for the truth about the war itself and the attempt to separate myth from fact have been carried on in a most determined manner since the day of the Armistice. Happily for the social scientists, many of the great men who helped put on the spectacle have made their confessions and written their memoirs. Secrets have been turned loose from the government archives. Professional propagandists have told us the inside story. Hence the *modus operandi* is a mystery no more.

However, of the myriads of books written about the World War, relatively few have been concerned with the integral relationship of the civilian population to the whole configuration of war. The part played by the citizens at home, while always of interest to the student of society, has seemed so lacking in the glamorousness of warfare that the battles on the various home fronts have received scant attention.

In the present work, I have chosen a group out of the civilian population, the clergy and the churches of the United States, and endeavored to indicate their place in the social pattern during the years 1914-18. In addition to portraying the attitudes and activities of these organizations and their leaders, I have sought to provide insight into the mechanisms of social control and into the causes for the various types of social and individual behavior manifested in the great melodrama enacted in those days.

Now a people at war cannot be organized from the ground up overnight, since a social organization is a most complex arrangement that has been in the process of development for millenniums. The origin of the habit patterns of a given society, in many instances, are traceable back into the mists of the past.

Some arranged pattern of human relationships is always necessary for the general welfare of the individuals in a society. Whatever the particular pattern may be, the various collective responses which have come to be regarded as obligatory and correct are standardized into folkways and mores. These are believed to be sacred.

The social ordering of individuals to make them conform to these accepted and authoritative standards of the group is brought about by means of social control over their behavior. They are conditioned from babyhood to respond in a certain fashion to certain stimuli or symbols. When standardized group behavior is deemed desirable or necessary in any particular—like monogamous marriage—all the institutions, the state, the school, the church, and the family, act as instruments of social control by teaching the children to regard this marriage pattern as true and sacred. Being thus habituated, relatively few adults will question monogamy or will have to be forced to continue in conformity to the approved pattern. Fear of public opinion and the law will suppress most of the deviations from the norm.

The actual methods of social control, as Professor Lumley points out, may be placed under two heads: the use of physical force and of symbols.

Obviously, if it were necessary to compel everyone by violence to accept the societal pattern, it could never be accomplished. The use of symbols, on the other hand, is much easier, more effective and enduring. The symbol may be a word, a phrase, an object or a song. It is a stimulus which because of previous association produces a certain type of response. The policeman represents the law which we have been taught to obey. The old homestead may be nothing more than some weather-beaten shingles and pieces of clapboard, but for those brought up under its roof it represents home, loved ones, and the sweetest memories of a lifetime. The cross to the Christian is more than mere wood. By association it has come to mean the Christian religion. The flag is a mere bit of cloth, but if the colors be arranged in a familiar way, and we have been taught to love it because it stands for our country, it will evoke an emotional response which we call patriotism. And these symbols which have an emotional setting are the most powerful of all in determining individual and thus group behavior.

Because the majority of individuals in a society have been conditioned to act in certain ways in the presence of specific symbols, most of which have a strong emotional tone, it is possible for authorities consciously to control the behavior of human beings by subjecting them to powerful stimuli or pressures, thus compelling them, often unconsciously, to act in the manner desired by those in power.

Hence, in a time of great social crisis, like a war, the government may practically control the total life of the mass of the population. Since a war in modern times cannot be carried on without the fullest cooperation of the majority of the citizens, the knowledge of the means of social control for those in charge of affairs is more important than ever before.

Faced with the problem of arousing the patriotic devotion of the nation, the leaders must convince the inhabitants of the necessity of the war, the wickedness of the enemy, and the righteousness of their own cause. These basic propositions are promoted by a form of social control known as propaganda. The news is presented in such a way as to arouse the fullest enthusiasm for the fight. When the life of the group is at stake or thought to be so, the majority of the members are welded into a solid mass, are more credulous than ordinarily, will believe practically everything they are told and do what they are commanded.

The propaganda artists, skilled in the knowledge of crowd psychology, manipulate the appropriate symbols which appeal to the prejudices, dreams, fears, sentiments, illusions, and hopes of the people. Then, as Professor Harold Lasswell has so well expressed it, "the collective egotism of a nation makes it possible to interpret the war as a struggle for the protection and propagation of its own high type of civilization."

Since of all the psychic stimulations to which a human being can be subjected war is the most powerful, all the basic emotions of fear, love, and hatred can easily be aroused. Soon the nation is welded into a practically complete unity, minor group differences are forgotten or laid aside, there is a sense of solidarity, a singleness of purpose and an ecstatic sense of being engaged on a mission, a crusade, worthy of the gods. The few who have entertained doubts or fears about the nation's holy cause will fear the terrific pressure of the group. Every available means of publicity will be used to exert this pressure. The newspapers will show that practically everyone is loyal and at the same time brand the objector as a traitor. A few stories of pacifists being beaten, tarred and feathered, or strung up by a rope will have the desired effect of intimidating other recalcitrants, and show that society is determined to suppress all opposition opinion.

In a war all institutions may be relied upon to cooperate in the struggle to save their particular type of civilization. The churches, particularly, take a prominent part. During the World War all of the countries involved witnessed this social phenomenon.

I have endeavored to show the role played by the churches and their leaders in the United States during the recent war: (1) How they reacted to the various societal forces, particularly the symbols and propaganda; and (2) in what manner the churches were used as agents of propaganda; and (3) their contribution to the winning of the war. Or the problem may be stated: "How did the forces of social control affect institutionalized religion and its leadership, and how did these religious institutions, in turn, serve as agents of social control?"

In order to gain the enlistment of the churches, it was but necessary to subject them to symbols which would elicit the most powerful response. Since God and country have nearly always been closely associated, as indeed they are in the inscription on the tomb of practically every Unknown Soldier in the world, the enlistment of God's people was not difficult to accomplish. In the preparedness era in this country, by the process of trial and error, there were discovered the symbols which appealed most strongly to the people at large and to the particular groups. By April, 1917, the formulæ were pretty well known. The church people, however, must not be thought of as being essentially different from the individuals outside the fold. Except in certain cases of isolated sacred societies, the church people belong to the same accessible secular society, possess, of course, the same psychic mechanisms, and are conditioned in their behavior patterns by the same major social factors which impinge upon the consciousness of all the members of society.

But there is an intimate psychological connection between patriotism and religion that is of the utmost importance. In the last two centuries, particularly since the French Revolution, as Professor Carlton J. H. Hayes has so convincingly shown, the rise of modern Nationalism has become a religion with its sacred scriptures, dogmas, ritual, propaganda, priests and devotees. It has in the absence of a national church in this country become a great unifying religious force for all the peoples of the nation. Protestants may disagree about the communion service and the mode of baptism, but not about their homage to the state. Moreover the ideology of Nationalism and religion grow out of the same social soil and make their appeal to the same emotions of fear, love, hatred and revenge, the longing for a satisfying object of worship, a need for fellowship in a common cause, and a sense of security.

The Christian religion, inheriting the forms of Judaism, also copied the concepts of politics for its theology—God as sovereign ruler giving the laws, demanding absolute obedience from his subjects, expiation for sin, and visiting punishment upon all his enemies. Hence the thought forms and the dialectic of the western state and Christianity are so closely related as to be, in some respects, almost identical.

The similarity of the symbols of Nationalism (as found in the United States, e.g.) and the religion of Christianity is at once apparent if they be placed in parallel columns:*

The flag	The cross
The Constitution and the Declaration of Independence	The Bible
Tradition of the fathers	Sacred tradition and theology
Patriotic slogans	Holy words and phrases
Patriotic songs	Hymns
Uniforms	Gowns, surplices, et.cetera.
Patriotic parades	Religious processions
Hero worship	Worship of saints
The sword	The sword of the spirit

It can readily be seen that the appeals to the citizens to wreak vengeance upon their enemies had only to be couched in holy phraseology to bring forth the desired responses from the church people. The Old Testament, with its war-god, Jahweh, the Holy Wars of the Israelites, the Imprecatory Psalms, and the Day of the Lord of Amos; the heathen in his blindness versus the Christian, the false versus the true gospel; the Christian crusades, the war hymns of the church; the example of Jesus driving out the money changers from the Temple and rebuking the Scribes and Pharisees; the sufferings of little innocent Serbia and Belgium, and the cross of Christ, the symbol of sacrifice for others and world redemption through the shedding of blood—

* For a full amplification of this theme, *vid.* C. J. H. Hayes, *Essays on Nationalism*, Macmillan, N. Y., 1926, chapter IV.

these and a hundred other symbols were utilized to take advantage of the religiously motivated individuals, while the awful struggle was painted as the Battle of Armageddon or the Holiest War of all the Ages. Thus were the Christian hosts mobilized for battle.

The resulting success of the Allied governments, including our own, in their skilful handling of propaganda, especially designed to appeal to the clergy and the church members, is proved in the remarkable support given the war by practically all the religious groups and the ministers in the United States.

In making a study of the effects of this propaganda on institutionalized religion * I have pursued the method of securing samples of attitudes verbalized or expressed in activity from a great variety of sources.

In presenting the results of this study, I have picked out the samples of opinions and activities which seemed representative and to bear light upon the particular topic under discussion. Most of the individuals who have been quoted are listed in *Who's Who in America*. I have taken it for granted that they were as influential and representative as others and that "the lesser lights would twinkle after." There have been some exceptions, but in all the research involved the rule has, in general, held true. The obscure preachers and editors of religious publications followed in the wake of their more illustrious brethren.

While at times the abundance of quotation may seem to be encyclopedic, I have taken this risk for two reasons. I have preferred, in many instances, to let the men speak for themselves for, if I had summarized these statements in my own words, the reader would in some cases accuse the present writer of extreme and unkind exaggeration. Again, the inclusion of a mere quotation or two as supporting evidence for some conclusions—like the almost universal sanction of the bayonet, for example— would be regarded by many a reader as showing an exceptional rather than a widespread point of view.

I have sought, as far as humanly possible, to be objective about both men and events. Whatever personalities may be introduced into the picture are purely for purposes of illustration. I am seeking to expose no one. And, neither do I regard any of

---

* While many sociologists prefer to restrict the use of the word *institution* to firmly entrenched group habits or mores, the term will be used in this book to denote both established customs and the organizations of human beings which serve to perpetuate these "institutions." The meaning in every case should be clear from the context.

the individuals as being insincere. For, insincerity, as commonly understood, is a psychological impossibility. The human mind must, of necessity, continue to believe in itself and thus can rationalize paradoxical situations without end.

In making the completion of this work possible I am indebted to many libraries, organizations, and editors for assistance rendered. I am also grateful for information received from an almost countless number of persons who, through interviews or correspondence, have given such splendid cooperation.

I wish to thank Drs. Carl Kelsey, J. P. Lichtenberger, and Stuart A. Rice of the Department of Sociology of the University of Pennsylvania for their reading of the manuscript and for helpful criticisms. I am deeply grateful to Professor Granville Hicks of the Rensselaer Polytechnic Institute for so generously placing at my disposal valuable material which he had already collected on the subject; for his excellent suggestions; and for his reading and criticizing the manuscript.

The author, however, is alone responsible for the presentation of the facts and the manner in which they have been interpreted.

RAY H. ABRAMS.

The University of Pennsylvania,
Philadelphia, Pennsylvania.

INTRODUCTION, 1969

Thirty-six years ago, when *Preachers Present Arms* was first published, America was in the middle of a Great Depression. Today, the country is not in an economic depression, but in a state of relative prosperity. Yet, there is a psychological state of deep despair over the conduct and dubious outcome of a small war being fought halfway around the world in Southeast Asia. Our prosperity is not dissolving our anxiety nor lessening the debate about this war which for several years has been our chief national concern and headache. It is costing us more than half of the national budget.

The stated reasons by the Establishment for the furthering and continuation of the present backing of the Saigon government, both militarily and politically, are well known and have been explained and discussed at great length over the years. The propaganda techniques are much the same as used in previous wars, the same old slogans and appeals (sometimes dressed up in new styles). The manipulation of the emotionally charged symbols to obtain national endorsement and unity in backing up the administration is being tried over and over again. These symbols include our sacred commitments to treaties, the defense of small nations from communist aggression (the bogeyman of communism has been of great service to the propagandists), the promoting of a free world, the domino theory (never permit the first domino to fall) the fear of the spread of communism if Hanoi wins, the fear of a take-over by China with a population of about 700,000,000 people (and their development of the atom bomb), our national honor, and so on. Phrases such as, "We are holding back the tidal wave of communism engulfing the world," and "We cannot let down our boys in Vietnam," are heard. This war, in common with other wars, has developed its own particular catch phrases, "timely" metaphors, basic philosophical assumptions and arguments on both sides. President Johnson, with a Texas background, naturally thought at times in terms of the frame of reference of the defense of the Alamo. Our battles in Vietnam likely reminded him of the historic stand on March 5, 1836.

The battle for men's minds goes on. In essence, the propaganda from the point of view of the administration is fundamentally based on loyalty to the state as one's greatest obligation. God is generally assumed to be on our side; thus there is no problem at this point. The President and his followers have insisted that we must present a show of national unity; otherwise the enemy will think that we are divided, weak, and timid. We, by all means, must present a united front, otherwise the U.S.A. will be embarrassed and hamstrung in its war and peace efforts. While dissent and criticism are invited in a true democracy, such as ours, we must be constructive in our comments and help the government to pursue the war to ultimate victory. Thus goes the party line. America has never lost a war and we do not intend to lose this one. Outstanding public leaders such as former President Eisenhower have publicly stated many times that "When you are in a war, you are in to win."

In April 1968 Eisenhower wrote under the title, "Let's Close Ranks on the Home Front":

> In a long life of service to my country, I have never encountered a situation more depressing than the present spectacle of an America deeply divided over a war in which we have committed so much in treasure, in honor, and in the lives of our young men. What has become of our courage? What has become of our loyalty to others? What has become of the noble concept of patriotism, which in former times of crisis has carried us through to victory and peace? If in the desperate days of World War II we had been torn by this kind of discord, I doubt that we and our allies could have won.

He deplores the critics of our military policy and the amateur strategists who proclaim, "We can never win the Vietnam War." He points out, "They are quoted endlessly, and, of course, their words give aid and comfort to the enemy and thus prolong the war."

The violent dissenters, the draft card burners, *et al* are shocking to our former President. "Their action is not honorable dissent. It is rebellion and it verges on treason."[1]

It is obvious that no one can draw the fine line between "honorable" and "dishonorable" dissent. Eisenhower is not talking about the old-time liberal dissent, but the more dramatic and extreme forms as indicated.

Yet, in the end, practically all forms of dissent point to a lack of national unity. Governments would probably be most happy if there were no dissent at all—in that case those responsible for running affairs would have a completely free hand, "a consummation devoutly to be wished" for those in charge of the national destiny.

Unfortunately, for those entrusted with the successful manipulation of those symbols of patriotism (as they see it), of loyalty and devotion to the cause, the objectives have proved most difficult to achieve. The responses have been often completely negative, if not met with a deluge of violent criticism and demonstrations. Numerous competent students have reminded us that this is about the most unpopular war in which we have ever been engaged. At any rate, there is every reason to believe that the opposition to this war has been more skillfully organized, more vocal and effective than in any of our previous struggles.

For the sake of a perspective, it might be well to take a brief glimpse at the nature of the internal opposition to some of our previous military operations. One can only generalize about the discontent. After the Revolution, John Adams estimated that about one third of the colonists were loyal to the Crown, one third were indifferent, and one third sided with the revolt.[2]

The War of 1812 was conducted with much discontent and bitterness particularly in the North, where the ships were rotting in the harbors and the British made forays at will. It was called, "Madison's Folly." At the Hartford Convention held in December 1814, there was a serious discussion about revising the Constitution and much talk about secession from the Union.

The Mexican War also had its opponents. Lincoln seriously questioned the war and risked his political career. James Russell Lowell wrote the Biglow Papers which voiced the strong sectionalism of Massachusetts in its opposition. Webster and Clay opposed the war. Whittier and other prominent writers joined them.

The dynamics of the Civil War were such that Lincoln had to face a great many scurrilous attacks on his reputation. The many Copperhead newspapers continued to flay the President and his generals. The speeches of Jefferson Davis were printed in full and those of Lincoln reduced to a paragraph or two, when it suited them. Draft riots persisted; southern sympathizers abounded, particularly in such states as Ohio and Illinois. Clement L. Vallandigham, representative in Congress from Ohio, was sentenced to prison because of his antiwar speeches. Lincoln commuted his sentence to banishment behind the Confederate lines. Vallandigham found his way to Canada and back to the United States and was nominated by his Peace Party to run for governor of Ohio. The detailed presentation of the opposition in the North to the Civil War would run into volumes.

As for World Wars I and II, it is sufficient to point out that there was a considerable amount of propaganda and pressure against the wars and our participation in them. It did not cramp the style of the government particularly, since public opinion was, for the most part, definitely on the side of complete prosecution.

In the light of what has transpired in the past, it should not be surprising that the same phenomena should take place in the present. There are always those individuals or organizations who, for one reason or another, do not go along with the Establishment. The social forces in the contemporary scene are many and varied, often in conflict with each other. There are several special reasons for the present antiwar sentiment.

First, a neo-isolationism has been growing steadily for several years. Among the causes are the expense of foreign aid, lack of many visible results, and a feeling that our attempts to run the world or parts of it have been a miserable failure. That it is much better to spend our money at home is the argument. The war in Vietnam is just one more illustration of pouring money down the drain.

Moreover, a new generation of youth has been reared on the philosophy of child rearing that has discounted authoritarian approaches and leaned to permissiveness *a la* the books of Dr. Benjamin Spock. (It should be noted that Dr. Spock has often been misquoted, misinterpreted, and sadly maligned.) The decline in the type of parental discipline characteristic of the past and the shift to the child-centered home have for millions of youngsters given them a God-given right to protest against their elders and secede from the world around them. Thus we have hippies, draft card burners, marchers, protesters, sit-ins, "pot" parties, and campus riots. These are comparatively new phenomena in our social order.

Since the Vietnam War is already unpopular, it is natural to reason, "Why go to war and die for an immoral cause?" These questions and affirmations of revolt are further reinforced by the parents who do not wish to see their male offspring shot in the rice paddies of Southeast Asia right on their own TV set or to learn from Uncle Sam some days later that this has happened. These same adults are paying for the war and are protesting the taxes, the billions that this struggle is costing us. Then consider the corruptness of the Saigon regime and the likelihood that the war is already a lost cause.

The propaganda against this war has been most effective. It has cast a long shadow of grave doubts on the worthiness of our cause. This has never been a holy or righteous war as many believed World Wars I and II to be. Hence, the government has never been able to fall back on a fundamental base line of agreement about the nature of the struggle as in past conflicts. Also, while wars cannot be conducted in the open, our government has run into a series of difficulties labeled for want of a better phrase, "the credibility gap."

Probably no war has been so thoroughly covered by so many mediums or debated by so many people. Those who have gone to Vietnam and either broadcast on the spot or given their reports upon their return are by no means in agreement about what is transpiring in Vietnam or the interpretation of events there. The oft repeated question, "What are the facts?" may sound sophisticated, but in reality it presumes the impossible and in this respect is naive. The social scientist queries, "What is a fact?" Certitude in the world of knowledge is most difficult of attainment.

Inevitably the public is confused and saddened. For the first time a major war has really been broadcast on television in a big way. Soldiers are seen in action. The dead and the dying are seen in our own living rooms. Where is the glory on the battlefield, Pickett's charge at Gettysburg, or the fight between the Constitution and Guerrière? The war is an endurance contest—Who can hold out the longest and do the most damage to the other side?

For the military, the progress of the war is measured in terms of a "body count" of the dead. Long ago the accuracy of this "count" was discredited. However, chalking up the figures on the blackboard is almost a daily exercise, as if this were even believed by the public. The thinking appears to run this wise—if, and when, we kill a sufficient number of the North Vietnamese and the Vietcong and the guerrillas, the war will be won.

One suspects, on the other hand, that *were* we actually, clearly, and demonstrably winning the war, and the enemy were visibly in retreat gradually being brought to his knees, the general attitude in this country would be strikingly different. A glorious victory, for the great bulk of the population, would be celebrated and result in a strengthened national ego. A negotiated peace on terms other than a total victory is difficult for most Americans to take. It appears, however, at the present writing, that our countrymen may have to compromise for that "just and lasting peace" for which they have been fighting.

The feeling that the war has arrived at a stalemate is widespread. For several years the dean of American columnists, Walter Lippmann, has been telling us that we can never win a land war in Asia. In spite of administration protests and unwillingness to admit other than victory, senators, congressmen, and leaders in public life are voicing openly these opinions.

"The Vietnam War has been a mistake, destroying something precious in the word America." This was the verdict of the editor of *Look* magazine, with a larger circulation than any other magazine of its type in the country.[3]

In the meanwhile pressures to get out of Asia have been strengthened by the growing realization (though denied by the administration) that we cannot successfully fight a war in Vietnam on the one hand and the war on poverty on the home front at the same time. The dollar is already seriously in danger. The burning of our cities, the increase in violence and irresponsible types of behavior, unless attended to and taken seriously, will lead to another civil war.

The *Zeitgeist* in the spring of 1968 was one of prevailing pessimism. There is a temporary lift in that hopes are centered in the peace conference being held in Paris. Otherwise the boasted American Way of Life (whatever that may mean) has brought disillusionment, confusion, despair, lack of focus, conflicts of interests, racial strife, anger, frustration, and lack of trust in the leadership at the highest levels. Faith in the democratic process is receiving severe and telling blows from many quarters, including our oldest and greatest universities.

The strongest and wealthiest nation on the earth with a population of about 200,000,000 has been stymied in its attempt to beat a tiny fifth rate power of about 17,000,000 people. Our national pride has been injured. What seemed so easy a few years ago, is now chalked off as a lost cause by men in the higher echelons in our society. The Pentagon and a few reporters argue that we are really winning the war (and it could be that we are) but a growing number of citizens are unimpressed.

Almost daily men are writing and expressing opinions about the war that often brought jail sentences in World War I. In a syndicated column from Paris, May 10, 1968, Arthur J. Domment stated: "If anything, it [the Vietnam War] has proved that half a million troops on the ground and bombs in the air are not the way to stop communism in Asia, something that any person with even a slight firsthand acquaintance with Asia and Asians could have told the State Department five years ago."[4]

Candidates for the office of President of the United States running in the primaries have been boasting to the audiences that they would end the war in Vietnam and there have been promises that if elected President, "I promise we shall never have another Vietnam." This is clear repudiation, not to mention other implications.

The clergy and the churches reflect the general national scene. They, too, are greatly divided. There is a wide spectrum of opinion among them. However, save for a few "hawkish" individuals such as the Reverend Carl McIntire, head of the Reformation Hour (an ardent and professional anticommunist), most of the clergy have been relatively temperate in their public pronouncements. There have been a few bellicose speeches by the men of the cloth, but not really sufficient in numbers to cast much weight in the balance of opinion. Quite a contrast to 1914-18 when hundreds of clergymen of prominence flayed the Kaiser and "all his ilk" and believed that by sheer word magic and oratory they could help to win the war against the Antichrist.

In the conclusion to this edition of *Preachers Present Arms* additional data will be presented to indicate some of the significant changes that have taken place in the churches and among the clergy in general since 1914-18 and a comparison with the present involvement in Southeast Asia.

I wish to express my deep appreciation to Dr. Grant M. Stoltzfus for his valuable assistance and encouragement in the preparation of the present edition of *Preachers Present Arms*. I am also greatly indebted to the Herald Press for its interest and publication at this time.

Ray H. Abrams

1 From the article, "Let's Close Ranks on the Home Front," Copyright by Dwight D. Eisenhower. Quotation used by permission of *The Reader's Digest*.

2 *The Columbia Encyclopedia* (New York: Columbia University Press, 1956), article, "Loyalists."

3 *Look*, Vol. 32, No. 10, May 14, 1968, p. 33.

4 *The Philadelphia Inquirer*, May 10, 1968.

CHAPTER I

THE CHURCHES OF AMERICA IN THE REVOLUTION, THE CIVIL, AND SPANISH-AMERICAN WARS

THE SOULDIERS POCKET BIBLE

Containing the most (if not all) those places contained in Holy Scripture which doe shew the qualifications of his inner man, that is a fit Souldier to fight the Lords Battels, both before he fight, in the fight, and after the fight.

> Part of the title page of *The Cromwellian Bible*, 1643.

CHAPTER I
THE CHURCHES OF AMERICA IN THE REVOLUTION, THE CIVIL, AND SPANISH-AMERICAN WARS

IN THE history of civilizations, from the earliest chronicles to the present day, two forces have ever been joined together in a dual alliance. They are war and religion. And, of all the great world religions, with the possible exception of Mohammedanism, none has been more devoted to Mars than has Christianity. Founded by one who was adored as "the lowly Nazarene," "The Prince of Peace," and "The Lamb of God," his followers have, nevertheless, when occasion demanded, pictured him as a mighty warrior in the forefront of battle. They have participated under his banner in the bloodiest wars known to man.

This allegiance between militarism and Christianity and the reliance of a government upon the forces of religion in time of war find many illustrations in the history of the United States of America. A consideration of the part taken by the clergymen and the churches in our leading wars shows that the government has been able to depend consistently upon organized religion for support.

In this chapter the role played by the churches and their leaders in the Revolution, the Civil, and the Spanish-American Wars will be summarized briefly with a view to providing an introduction and background to the understanding of the much fuller description which follows of the alliance of militarism and the disciples of Jesus in the great World War. As we shall see, the fighting parsons of 1917-18 had ample precedent for their belligerent conduct and ardent expressions of patriotic devotion in the manner in which their spiritual forefathers participated in the wars of this country in days gone by.

THE AMERICAN REVOLUTION

Revolutions do not spring up overnight. That is as true of the American Revolution of 1776 as of the Russian Revolution of 1917. Always the minds of a sufficient number of the people —and their emotions—must be ready for the change.

The American Revolution had been in the process for years prior to the actual Declaration of Independence. Among the many factors responsible for the open break with the mother country was one which is often overlooked—the doctrines preached from many of the colonial pulpits. Studies made of this period reveal that the clergy in New England, particularly, were responsible in large measure for the preparation of the soil in which the seeds of revolution could be sown.[1] They had long been educating the people with the vocabulary of native rights and liberty before 1776. Milton and Locke furnished them with abundant inspirational material, while Locke's doctrine of the "people's rights to choose their own rulers" was expounded from many a pulpit.[2]

"The alliance of the ministers with the leaders of the agitation against England was one reason for its success. . . . With a vocabulary enriched by the Bible they made resistance and at last independence and war a holy cause," says Alice Baldwin with reference to the clergy of New England.[3]

Professor William Warren Sweet concludes that "no church in the American Colonies had so large an influence in bringing on the war for Independence as had the Congregational."[4]

When the American Revolution started to express itself in ballistic fashion the religious forces and the spirit of rebellion with few exceptions united in the holy cause. Many of the clergy of New England served as "recruiting agents, chaplains, and fighters. . . ."[5] The sharp-tongued John Cleveland of Ipswich "is said to have preached his whole parish into the army and then to have gone himself."[6]

The Presbyterians also furnished a considerable percentage of the leaders of the Revolution.[7]

The other groups too were enthusiastic for the Revolution, the Baptists, the German Reformed, the Lutherans. George Washington congratulated the Baptists for the unanimity with which they had proved themselves the "firm friend of civil liberty," and promoted "our glorious Revolution."[8]

The famous Muhlenberg family guaranteed the support of the Lutherans,[9] and the Carrolls the Catholics. According to Archbishop Carroll, "Their [Catholic] blood flowed as freely, in proportion to their numbers, to cement the fabric of independence as that of any of their fellow citizens."[10]

The Quakers were divided.[11] The Mennonites for the most part did not take sides, but were loyal to the spirit of independence, while the Moravians, a non-resistant sect, suffered most, but also took the side of the Colonists.[12]

However, among those who stood by the Crown were notably the Episcopalians and Methodists, since they were more closely bound to the mother country by church ties and an overlapping ministry. The Episcopalians in New England were largely Loyalists; in other sections they suffered divisions. At the close of the Revolutionary War "no church was in so deplorable a condition as was the Anglican."[13] The Methodists were in a similar dilemma. John Wesley had classed John Hancock as a felon and called upon the Colonists to lay down their arms. Wesley's leadership and the influence of the many English Methodist missionaries in this country caused the majority of those in Methodism to side with the mother country.[14]

In concluding these observations on the churches in the Revolution, it should be noted that, in addition to the close relationship that existed between the Christian forces and the Colonial army, the predominately English culture of the Episcopalian and Methodist churches was the decisive factor in accounting for their strong emotional attachment to the mother country. And, in the World War, nearly a century and a half later, the Episcopalians, having maintained a close connection with the English church and traditions, were so conditioned that they inevitably thought of the English ideals and civilization as *par excellence* and the English people as on the side of right. It is not surprising, therefore, that they took the lead among religious groups in hastening our entrance into the war to save what they considered the true culture. Clergymen in other denominations, born in England and Canada, joined in this early movement. Loyalties grow out of the soil.

THE CIVIL WAR

In the Civil War the call to battle received unanimous support from the various denominations. The Methodists, Baptists, Congregationalists, Lutherans, Catholics, Moravians, German and Dutch Reformed, Old and New School Presbyterians tried to outdo each other in declaring their undying allegiance to the Federal Government.[15] Only in the Protestant Episcopal and Old School Presbyterian Churches were protests raised against the passage of patriotic resolutions and "even in these churches the protests represented but a small minority."[16]

The Methodists took great pride in their record of "one hundred per cent" loyalty. Abraham Lincoln sent them a letter to testify:

> Nobly sustained as the Government has been by all the Churches, I would utter nothing which might in the least appear

invidious against any. Yet without this, it may fairly be said that the Methodist Episcopal Church, not less devoted than the rest, is by its greater numbers the most important of all. It is no fault in others that the Methodist Episcopal Church sent more soldiers to the field, more nurses to the hospitals and more prayers to heaven than they! God bless the Methodist Churches! And blessed be God, who in this trial giveth us the churches.[17]

In the Confederacy, most of the churches supported the South. The Presbyterians, in session in 1862, were convinced that "this struggle is not alone for civil rights, and property and home, but for religion, for the church, for the Gospel."[18]

The Southern Baptist Convention in 1861 declared that every principle of religion and patriotism called upon them to resist invasion.[19]

The Protestant Episcopal Church, having never taken sides on the slavery question, had no pre-war hatreds, and hence, while divided during the war, easily reunited afterward.[20]

In 1863 the Confederate clergy addressed a communication to "Christians throughout the world," in which they protested against the high-handed methods of Lincoln who, "under the guise of philanthropy, and the pretext of doing good . . . would seek the approbation of mankind upon a war that promises to humanity only evil, and that continually."[21]

As the war progressed and the Southern armies receded, the Northern churches entered sections of the South and took possession of many Southern churches. This type of invasion met with the approval of the War Department which commanded the Federal generals to give over to Northern church boards and leaders all the churches in their areas "in which a loyal minister does not officiate."[22] The pretext which the Yankees gave for this invasion was that it was missionary work. The protests of the Rebels met with an appeal to Scripture: had not Jesus commanded his followers to go "into all the world and preach the gospel"?[23]

Not all the Northern churches, of course, participated in this enterprise, though large organizations like the American Baptist Mission Society reaped some of the benefits.[24] In 1864, the Missionary Board of the Methodist Episcopal Church appropriated $35,000 for this particular work and missionaries were sent to various places in the South.[25] President Lincoln did not approve of these attempts to convert the South to Christianity.[26]

A few of the clergy in the North were anti-Abolitionists. Henry J. Van Dyke, pastor of the First Presbyterian Church in Brooklyn, and a Jeffersonian Democrat, was opposed to the methods and doctrine of the Abolitionists. He believed that slavery was permitted by Divine Law, "not as the final destiny of the enslaved, but as an important and necessary process in their transition from heathenism to Christianity." Standing on the Scripture, he maintained that the Abolitionist who teaches that slavery is a sin thereby "blasphemes the name of God and His doctrine."[27] Dr. Van Dyke was several times threatened by mobs.

However, in the vast majority of cases, both North and South, patriotism became the religion of both pulpit and pew. On January 4, 1861, Henry W. Bellows, pastor of the All Souls Church, New York, and adviser to Abraham Lincoln, declared the contest one "between civilization and the barbarous institution of slavery." The North would go to war, if necessary, said he, in order "to save order and civilization."[28] R. L. Stanton, professor in the Theological Seminary of the Presbyterian Church, Danville, Kentucky, guaranteed that "God is in the contest" and "His strong right arm will give them [the Northern troops] victory." God, he urged, worked "through all policies, all men, all events, and reaches His ends infallibly and gloriously." Those who refused to support the war "were abhorred, both in earth and in heaven."[29]

Sermons preached in those days savored of bitterness and hatred. The Southern Baptist Convention complained: "We find churches and pastors of the North breathing out slaughter and clamoring for sanguinary hostilities with a fierceness which we have supposed impossible among the disciples of the Prince of Peace."[30]

Some of the clergy acted as emissaries of the Federal government. Henry Ward Beecher was asked to go to England in 1863 to propagandize that country to help in changing English opinion in favor of the North. Archbishop John Hughes of New York went to France in 1861, where he succeeded in giving the French people the Northern perspective on American affairs.[32] Bishop Matthew Simpson of the Methodist Episcopal Church, a close friend of Lincoln, toured the North during the war delivering a patriotic lecture entitled, "Our Country." This propaganda proved highly effective.[33]

THE SPANISH-AMERICAN WAR

In the war with Spain there seems to have been more of a division of opinion, but large numbers of the leaders in the pulpits joined in proclaiming the old slogans. On the first day of May, 1898, Henry Van Dyke,* in his church at Princeton, New Jersey, prefaced the observance of the Lord's Supper with the words: "We have prayed for peace. This prayer has been denied. Now we must pray for victory." Furthermore, "We have come as a nation to our Cross. It is *not* a Cross of Gold. . . . If we bear it in submission . . . it will be a ransom for the many, and a sign of peace for far-off generations."[34]

In Philadelphia, William H. Davis, pastor of the Church of the Redeemer in Germantown, preached that the history of Spain was one "in which the Councils of the devil had obtained" and added, "More righteous is this war than the war for independence . . . [and] the Civil War . . . because in this war we are fighting for the freedom of those who are bound to us by no other ties than those of common humanity. God bless our soldiers! God bless our sailors!"[35]

Ernest Howard Crosby, speaking shortly after such events, related:

> If you address a miscellaneous audience at the Cooper Institute in New York—an audience of some fifteen hundred, composed neither of blackguards nor gentlemen—and tell them as I have that war is a relic of barbarism which has no business to show itself at the beginning of the twentieth century, they will cheer you to the echo, and scarcely a man will be found to make a protest. I have also spoken to audiences of well-educated Christians and I have found them cold. Only once were my hearers unanimous against me without exception, and that was when I was invited to address a meeting of Protestants.[36]

The Banishment of War by Resolutions

In the years following the Spanish-American adventure the peace movement came to be exceedingly persuasive and thrived on popular support. "I doubt if any propaganda," explained John Dewey, "has ever been carried on with greater persistence or with greater success—so far as affecting feelings was concerned—than that for peace during the decade prior to 1914. The times were so ripe that the movement hardly had to be pushed."[37]

The various peace organizations waxed eloquent in denunciation of war and in proclaiming the golden dawn of a new era. Of the thirty-odd organizations working for that end, the American Peace Society was the oldest, tracing its ancestry back to 1815 through the New York Peace Society which was

---

* Son of the Henry Van Dyke referred to in the Civil War.

founded at that time. There were also branches of this organization in the majority of the states. The annual peace conferences started by Albert K. Smiley in 1895 at his hotel at Lake Mohonk in the Catskills, by 1910 had an attendance of 300 invited guests. But though popular these meetings were for the most part quite innocuous.[38] The World Peace Foundation took on an aggressive program, as did the Carnegie Endowment for International Peace which labored on behalf of international conciliation.

In February, 1914, the Church Peace Union was created with an endowment of $2,000,000 from Andrew Carnegie, who had said: "It is too bad that the churches cannot have some funds for peace work. They could really do more than any other institution in existence." The steel magnate acknowledged, "I have been feeling more and more that it is to the churches we must look for the bringing of peace."[39] At the same time so confident was Mr. Carnegie that universal peace was at hand that he incorporated into the deed of gift a provision that "if in the judgment of the trustees, the time shall come when peace is fully established, and no more need be done in that cause, the income of the grant may be spent for the alleviation of poverty or other good causes."[40]

Thus supplied with optimism, the organization, with a list of twenty-nine trustees, composed of some of the most prominent laymen and clergy from Protestant, Catholic, and Jewish faiths, added its prestige and money to the attempt to convert the world to abandon its age-old habit of resorting to war.

One of the avowed objects in the formation of the Federal Council of the Churches of Christ in America in 1908 was to further this cause of peace. In a preliminary conference in 1905, the Honorable Chief Justice Brewer had struck the popular note:

> Let us catch the sweet echoes of Bethlehem's song. . . . As against the war spirit, I invoke the spirit of the Master. As against the call for battleships I invoke the action of a United Church, and I am sure that a Federation of all the churches will soon make it plain that as for this nation there must be no longer war nor a getting ready for war.[41]

In 1912 the Federal Council called upon the Christian men and women of the nation "to rise at this time and demand that all nations learn again the first principles of the teachings of Jesus Christ, that membership in his kingdom should bind them together in mutual love and . . . that the thought of engaging with each other in deadly combat shall become abhorrent and impossible forever."[42]

Among the churches, if the tenor of the sermons, the denominational journals, and the proceedings of the annual ecclesiastical conventions may be taken as an index, the interest in peace was, in general, lukewarm up to about 1911. After this date the effect of the influences for peace began to be noticeable and arbitration of international disputes a popular theme.

Frederick Lynch, Secretary of the Church Peace Union (founded in 1914) and intimate friend of Andrew Carnegie, speaking at Lake Mohonk in 1912, thus appraised the force of the movement:

> Last year nearly every Protestant Church in the United States had something to say in favor of the arbitration treaties. The Federal Council created a commission on Peace and Arbitration, and connected with all its thousands of churches, had literally thousands of sermons preached and resolutions passed. The Protestant Churches of this nation have put themselves on record as favoring the unlimited arbitration of international disputes.[43]

Deluged with peace literature and resolutions against war and militarism by church organizations as well as the professional societies, this country seemed to peace-lovers the very nation chosen of God to bring in the millennium. Bryan had effected numerous arbitration treaties, and even the political parties lined up with the peace movement, for in 1912 both the Republicans and the Progressives approved the settlement of international controversies by peaceful means. The latter, under the forceful leadership of Colonel Roosevelt and Jane Addams, had lamented "the survival in our civilization of the barbaric system of warfare among nations" and asked for the settling of disputes by civil means.[44]

To Dr. Lynch the current scene was most pleasant. "It looks," said he, "as though this were going to be the age of treaties rather than the age of wars, the century of reason rather than the century of force. And every treaty is a golden band uniting the nations into one." Moreover, "the one word that is upon all men's lips today is the brotherhood of man."[45]

One plaintive note, the absence of European clergymen at European peace conferences in contrast to the interest shown by the American and English clerics, was the minor in an otherwise joyous song. "The state churches," claimed Dr. Lynch, "follow governments rather than lead them."[46]

With such assurances and confidence in the will to peace on

the part of the churches and the people of the United States, this most popular of all causes, widely endorsed by high respectability and low, came down to the summer of 1914. Among those traveling to Europe that season could be found a large number of churchmen bound for peace conferences on the Continent.

The World Peace Congress, scheduled to be held at Constance, August 2-5, barely got started ere it was compelled to adjourn to London under the difficulties encountered due to the troop mobilization and confiscation of trains.[47] The Twenty-first International Peace Congress was to take place at Vienna, September 15. The chairman of the honorary committee of the Congress was His Excellency, Leopold Count Berchtold, the Foreign Minister of the Imperial and Royal Government of Austria, who had been largely responsible for the framing and sending of the ultimatum to Serbia, July 23, 1914. This Peace Congress never met.[48] The other Peace Conference, planned by Catholics, was to have taken place at Liége, the very day of the German invasion.[49]

CHAPTER II

EUROPE STARTS A WAR AND AMERICA PREPARES

The truth about the war, when it is written, will please neither pacifist nor militarist; neither preacher nor business man; but it may help to set them free from errors long deluding.

       HENRY SEIDEL CANBY,
        Education by Violence, 1919.

CHAPTER II
EUROPE STARTS A WAR AND AMERICA PREPARES

War and Propaganda

IN THE halcyon days just prior to 1914, then, a glorious optimism pervaded the peace movement, and Americans in general believed a big war impossible. While the historians had followed the details of European struggles, alliances and intrigues, and the more astute had recognized that across the Atlantic was a powder mine ready to explode without a moment's notice, most of the pacifists seem to have been either ignorant of or to have ignored the realities of the situation.

When in the summer of 1914 war actually broke out in Europe, the religious groups and peace societies, in common with the majority of the American people, were astounded that such a catastrophe could come about so suddenly. The dream of perpetual peace soon vanished like a bubble and with it the cherished hopes built up through the years. Yet, at the same time, it was generally maintained that inasmuch as the United States was a thoroughgoing lover of peace, guided by a superior ethical code with forbade participation in the race in armaments and European Machiavellian machinations, we could never, therefore, be drawn into what was regarded as a disgraceful embroglio.

That this country abandoned its alleged neutrality and threw all its resources in on the side of the Entente is a matter of history. But why did America change her mind and decide to fight? Moreover, what social forces and social controls operated? What influences were brought to bear, and what were the processes of reasoning or wishing which led the churches to renounce their former pacific position and to accept in the manner of a convert the Allied legend of the "holy war" against Germany? What finally led the clergy and laymen to gird up their loins in the preparedness movement and pledge their very lives in the effort to crush the Germans?

In order to answer these questions let us outline, briefly, the various factors which combined to turn the tide of public opinion in this country.

As soon as the war started, the British, it will be remembered, quickly got control of the major avenues of news circulation that could be used to influence American opinion. The one cable from Germany to the United States was immediately cut and direct control of the others taken over by the British government. Bertrand Russell wrote: ". . . Allied propaganda, through British control of the cables, secured wider publicity than that of Germany, and achieved a notable success in winning the sympathy and ultimately the cooperation of the United States."[1]

The practice of searching the mails, the censorship of news at the source as well as in transit as authorized by the Defense of the Realm Act, or "Dora," gave the British practical control of all news that came to America. Hence, says C. Hartley Grattan, "Honest, unbiased news simply disappeared out of the American papers along about the middle of August, 1914."[2]

In the ensuing battle of propaganda and counter-propaganda for the control of American public opinion, Sir Gilbert Parker, who claims to have had charge of British propaganda in the United States during this period, has described his activities in rather frank fashion in *Harper's Magazine* for March, 1918.

> Perhaps here I may be permitted to say a few words concerning my own work since the beginning of the war. It is in a way a story by itself, but I feel justified in writing one or two paragraphs about it. Practically since the day war broke out between England and the Central Powers I became responsible for American publicity. I need hardly say that the scope of my department was very extensive and its activities widely ranged. Among the activities was a weekly report to the British Cabinet on the state of American opinion, and constant touch with the permanent correspondents of American newspapers in England. I also frequently arranged for important public men in England to act for us by interviews in American newspapers; and among these distinguished people were Mr. Lloyd George (the present Prime Minister), Viscount Grey, Mr. Balfour, Mr. Bonar Law, the Archbishop of Canterbury, Sir Edward Carson, Lord Robert Cecil, Mr. Walter Runciman (the Lord Chancellor), Mr. Austen Chamberlain, Lord Cromer, Will Crooks, Lord Curzon, Lord Gladstone, Lord Haldane, Mr. Henry James, Mr. John Redmond, Mr. Selfridge, Mr. Zangwill, Mrs. Humphrey Ward, and fully a hundred others.
>
> Among other things, we supplied three hundred and sixty newspapers in the smaller states of the United States with an English newspaper, which gives a weekly review and comment on the affairs of the war. We established connection with the man in the street through cinema pictures of the army and the navy, as well as through interviews, articles, pamphlets, etc.; and by letters in reply

to individual American critics, which were printed in the chief newspaper of the state in which they lived, and were copied in newspapers of other and neighboring states. We advised and stimulated many people to write articles; we utilized the friendly services and assistance of confidential friends; we had reports from Americans constantly, and established association, by personal correspondence, with influential and eminent people of every profession in the United States, beginning with university and college presidents, professors and scientific men, and running through all the ranges of the population. We asked our friends and correspondents to arrange for speeches, debates, and lectures by American citizens, but we did not encourage Britishers to go to America and preach the doctrine of entrance into the war. Besides an immense private correspondence with individuals, we had our documents and literature sent to great numbers of public libraries, Y. M. C. A. societies, universities, colleges, historical societies, clubs, and newspapers.

It is hardly necessary to say that the work was one of extreme difficulty and delicacy, but I was fortunate in having a wide acquaintance in the United States and in knowing that a great many people had read my books and were not prejudiced against me. . . .

Also, it should be remembered that the Society of Pilgrims, whose work of international unity cannot be overestimated, has played a part in promoting understanding between the two peoples, and the establishment of the American Officers' Club in Lord Leconfield's house in London with H.R.H. the Duke of Connaught as president, has done, and is doing, immense good. It should also be remembered that it was the Pilgrims' Society under the fine chairmanship of Mr. Henry Brittain, which took charge of the Hon. James Beck when he visited England in 1916, and gave him so good a chance to do great work for the cause of unity between the two nations. I am glad and proud to think that I had something to do with these arrangements which resulted in the Pilgrims taking Mr. Beck into their charge.[3]

Due to the influence of the British liberals and such writers as H. G. Wells, most of whom were opposed to the war at the outbreak, the legend of a "holy war" quickly arose. Within a few days after the entrance of Britain into the conflict, motives were adduced for participation that had never previously been thought of. Irene Cooper Willis, in her *England's Holy War,* demonstrates that "without Liberal opinion the war would never have been a Holy War."[4] But under their guidance it came to be interpreted in spiritual terms: "the war to end war," "to preserve civilization," et cetera.

A. G. Gardiner, in the London *Daily News* of August 8, coined phrases later to be familiar in American pulpits and newspaper editorials.

> . . . this is not a war of peoples, but of despots and diplomatists. It is, we may hope, the last supreme struggle of the old dispensation against the new. Let us be quite clear in our minds as to the real enemy. We have no quarrel with the German people. . . . No, it is not the people with whom we are at war. It is the tyranny which has held them in its vise, the tyranny of personal government armed with a mailed fist, the tyranny of a despotic rule, countersigned by the Krupps. . . . In this war we are engaged in fighting for the emancipation of Germany as well as for the liberties of Europe.[5]

H. G. Wells, prophet of the new era, proclaimed:

> Every sword that is drawn against Germany is a sword drawn for peace. . . . The victory of Germany will mean the permanent enthronement of the War God over all human affairs. The defeat of Germany may open up the way to disarmament and peace throughout the earth. . . . Never was war so righteous as war against Germany now.[6]

Mr. Wells furnished a good share of British propaganda to America in the pages of *Mr. Britling Sees It Through.* This book found its way into the pulpits throughout the land. Many of the prominent churchmen in England found time to write on the spiritual aims of the war, from the point of view of the Allies. Such a series, entitled *Papers for War Time,* was circulated widely in Great Britain and among religious people in the United States.

Thus it came about that through the medium of Sir Gilbert Parker's propaganda, which made particular use of the legend of the "holy war," and the measured assurances of British liberals and clergy, the ideal outline for later ecclesiastical reasoning in the United States came to be carefully prepared and almost unconsciously accepted.

The press and magazines in this country became thoroughly saturated with this Allied point of view. *The New Republic,* founded in 1914, had, as its avowed purpose, the educating of the liberals to the Allied approach.[7] The New York *World* and particularly the New York *Times* were against Germany. Even the Hearst papers, definitely anti-British and often accused of being pro-German, published two and one-half times more Allied material than pro-German.[8] The religious press swung into line, for the opinions of the editors as to the daily events and the aims of the belligerents were dependent, for the most part, upon the material that they saw in the daily papers and the magazines.

The reasons for the effectiveness of the Allied propaganda may be summed up in the words of an impartial historian, Professor Carlton J. H. Hayes: "Entente propaganda in the United States was even more general than that of the Teutons; it was also more adroit, more sympathetic, and more conformable to American prejudices and American wishes."[9]

The French story to the American people played up the name of Lafayette as a symbol of eternal friendship and the contribution of French culture to the world. In the estimation of Professor Harold D. Lasswell:

> The French propaganda was lucid and simple. Her retiring armies told a prima facie story of who had been prepared for the War (after the early cloud of false news had blown aside), and her chief propaganda was that of simple satanism. The Germans were never able to popularize so striking an epithet as "Hun" or "Boche" and their clumsy exhortations to hate or their sneering references to the "Allies" were much less powerful and invidious. The French vocabulary had powerful words like humanity and democracy, which reverberated with a tremendous clang abroad.[10]

The Germans, according to the admission of numerous authorities, like George Sylvester Viereck, editor of *The Fatherland*, were most inept at propaganda.[11] Further evidence of inefficiency is given by Count Von Bernstorff,[12] Count Czerin,[13] the Austrian Minister of Foreign Affairs during a part of the war, and Kaiser Wilhelm himself.[14] Those chiefly responsible for disseminating the doctrines of the Central Powers in America were Dr. Bernhard Dernberg, formerly Secretary of State for the colonies, who came officially as the representative of the Red Cross, and Dr. Heinrich Albert, attached to the Embassy as Commercial Attaché. George Sylvester Viereck, as editor of *The Fatherland*, was already at work before the German propaganda committee commenced operations through the establishment of the German Information Bureau. With the help of various Germans, news releases were sent out to over 500 papers. In December, 1914, Dr. William Bayard Hale, a former clergyman, who had been a journalist for many years as the literary editor of the New York *Times* and editor of the *World's Work*, was employed to prepare propaganda literature. He was a close friend of Woodrow Wilson.

However, for several reasons, the game of chess proved to be too hopeless. The Germans lost out in their attempt to convert public opinion in this country. Suffice it to say that the American people got the idea that the German people and the German government were two separate things, and that the German government was a menace to the world. The Hon. James M. Beck has been given credit for introducing such a clever distinction, but it is to be remembered that he was exposed to this critical reasoning while in England as a guest of the Pilgrims' Society. His legal analysis of the many-colored books, entitled *The Evidence in the Case,* demonstrated from an alleged unbiased point of view that the Allies had righteousness on their side. This book had a tremendous effect on opinion in the United States. Other works consumed by the public were telling exposures of German extremists, such as Bernhardi and Nietzsche, whose opinions were said to represent those of the German people. The government did not speak for the people but these writers and philosophers did! Later the German people and their government were merged into one in popular estimation.

The German propaganda, none too well received at the first, was ruined for further effectiveness by the sinking of the *Lusitania.* The finishing crash came with the exposure of the Zimmermann note—"the final debacle of German propaganda in the United States," repined Viereck.[15]

In the meanwhile Colonel Edward M. House and Walter Hines Page were arranging the diplomatic skids upon which their country was eventually to slide in on the side of Britain. And, Woodrow Wilson, at first speaking on behalf of absolute neutrality, finally succumbed completely to the Entente legend. Through Colonel House he had already committed himself to the Allies before the presidential election of 1916.[16]

On the economic side it should be noted that through a series of loans obtained from banks in the United States the Allied nations had borrowed from August 1, 1914, to January 1, 1917, the sum of $1,900 million, and Great Britain alone had overdrawn her credit by about $45,000,000.[17] On the other hand, the estimated financial stake which America had in German war finance was about $27,000,000, a comparatively insignificant figure.[18] "The disparity between our financial entanglements with Germany and with the Allies," comments C. Hartley Grattan, "hardly calls for more emphasis than this sentence: The lack of financial ties with them made it easier for America to contemplate going to war with the Central Powers."[19]*

BEGINNINGS OF THE PREPAREDNESS MOVEMENT

With the foregoing facts in mind, there will now be traced the manner in which the churches and the clergy were affected by the various social forces and group pressures operating in American life during the era of preparedness up to April, 1917.

In general, it may be said that throughout the nation the churches listened to Wilson's proclamation of neutrality with great respect and probably intended to carry it out to the letter. But a sustained neutrality under the circumstances was too much to expect. "Morally neutral the country never was," asserted John Dewey, "and probably the only stupid thing President Wilson did was to suppose, in his early proclamation, that it could be." [20]†

A reading of the files of the newspapers from various sections of the country reveals that it was in the great seaboard cities along the Atlantic coast that pro-Ally and preparedness sentiment first developed. The cities facing the Atlantic seemed much closer to the scenes of European strife than those inland. As late as February 15, 1917, the editor of the *Deseret Evening News*, leading newspaper in Salt Lake City (and owned and controlled by the Church of Jesus Christ of the Latter-Day Saints), had laughed at the fears expressed by a New York newspaper over our lack of preparedness.

---

* The effect of these loans on the bankers of this country may be estimated from the following: Thomas W. Lamont stated the position of the J. P. Morgan Company: "Those were the days when American citizens were being urged to remain neutral in action, in word, and even in thought. But our firm had never for one moment been neutral; we didn't know how to be. From the very start we did everything that we could to contribute to the cause of the Allies." (In the Anglo-American Number of the *Manchester Guardian*, January 27, 1920.) In like manner confessed Otto H. Kahn: ". . . those who, like myself, from the fateful August days of 1914 on, took their stand unequivocally with the Allied cause. . . ." (In a letter to *The American Monthly*, June, 1928.)

† Note, for instance, the statement of Ernest Milmore Stires, rector of St. Thomas's Church, New York. "The fact is that for more than two years before [the declaration of war] there had been no peace in our hearts or conscience. Millions had felt the dishonor and danger of moral neutrality. . . . We prayed. . . . God was merciful, the nation roused itself, resisted the moral anæsthetics administered by good but mistaken leaders, forced the issue . . . took the place long awaited for her on the field of honor." (E. M. Stires, *The Price of Peace*, Dutton, N. Y., 1919, p. 245.)

> Such invaders [says the *Deseret Evening News*] as in the past have found it possible to make a landing have found it pretty hard and altogether desirable to get out again. Germany is not likely now or at any other time to try the experiment, so that the fears of the woeful New Yorker may be largely discounted.

Thus in many respects the West remained relatively calm and undisturbed, while the pulse of the East nervously responded to every excitement. The churches, together with other institutions and groups, mirrored this effect of geographical distance so that in the East considerably more thought was given to the war than in the region beyond the Mississippi.

Hence, particularly in the Atlantic States, the first sound of the boom of guns created a sense of uneasiness and brought forth prayers for peace. The Federal Council of Churches, with headquarters in New York, requested President Wilson to set aside a day of prayer for peace, which he did, designating Sunday, October 4. Literature was sent out to 130,000 churches within the fold of the Council with the cooperation of the Church Peace Union. This included several prayers written by Bishop David Hummell Greer, William T. Manning and others, together with a "peace hymn" written by John Haynes Holmes.[21]

By the middle of August the Federal Council was sending out appeals to the churches of all the warring countries of Europe urging those people "having relatives in the armies to write them personal letters, exhorting them, whatever be the provocation of the enemy, to reduce in every way the horrors of war." [22]

The Jews held a big peace meeting in New York City on their New Year's, while various other groups blended their voices in the general demand for cessation of conflict.

Sunday, October 4, the day set aside by President Wilson for prayer, proved to be an unqualified success. The New York *Times* the following day featured the occasion on the front page: WHOLE NATION PRAYS FOR PEACE. Most of the clergy caught the spirit of the day, making strong appeals. Bishop William Lawrence of Massachusetts believed that "people were becoming convinced that war was wickedness, useless, and stupid."[23] Malcolm James MacLeod, of the Collegiate Church of St. Nicholas, New York, asked his hearers to "think of the dead boys today, the maimed and crippled. I don't care whether they are Germans, English or Russians. They are all their mothers' sons and the sacredness of human life is degraded. Worst of all is the moral degradation and the legacy of hate."[24]

The churches and Christianity had been well-nigh universally blamed for permitting the war to come about. Men thought that in some miraculous way the Christians should have prevented the holocaust, and because they did not Christianity was a complete failure. Charles W. Eliot expressed this idea when he said, ". . . for nineteen hundred years the ethics of Jesus of Nazareth have been in the world but have had no effect to prevent or even reduce the evils of war. . . ."[25] Numbers of the clergy seem to have expended the better part of their time endeavoring to meet this charge. They maintained that Christianity had actually never been tried. Yet a no inconsiderable number were inclined to agree with Dr. Eliot. "If the church were true to itself," lamented John Henry Jowett, of the Fifth Avenue Presbyterian Church, New York, "there would have been no more war today."[26]

Cardinal Farley, having just returned from Europe, spoke in St. Patrick's Cathedral, New York, on the first Sunday in October. He was reported as having absolved the Catholic Church from all responsibility and furnishing another version to account for the origin of the war.

> Had the people of Europe heeded the pleas of the late Pontiff [Pius X], had they heeded the teachings and warnings of the Church, they would not now be engaged in a bloody war. But they did not heed. Almost every nation in Europe was persecuting the Church, trampling on its rights, driving it unto the corners of the land. [He mentioned France, particularly, in this connection]. . . . And now they are paying the penalty. They are suffering for their sins against God.[27]

In the meanwhile the preparedness movement had loomed on the horizon as early as September, under the leadership of Theodore Roosevelt. In November, William Howard Taft had addressed a men's church club on behalf of increased armament.[28] About December 1, the American Defense Society and the National Security League were born. One of the sponsors of the latter organization and the main speaker at its birth was Major George Haven Putnam, publisher, strong Anglophile, and vice-president of the New York Peace Society. Putnam was already urging Americans to arm to resist the impending German invasion (presumably after the British defeat!),[29] as was Lyman Abbott, editor of *The Outlook,* and Congregational clergyman.[30]

Among those particularly active in the promotion of the National Security League were Solomon Stanwood Menken, the founder; Judge Alton B. Parker, Democratic candidate for president in 1908, vice-president of the American Peace Society and pro-Ally; James M. Beck; Robert Bacon of the Morgan firm; Myron T. Herrick, a Francophile; John Grier Hibben, president of Princeton, a clergyman and strongly pro-Ally; Theodore Roosevelt; Elihu Root of arbitration fame; Joseph H. Choate, famous barrister; and George Wharton Pepper, lawyer and prominent layman in the Protestant Episcopal Church.[81]

The League was supported principally by prominent Eastern capitalists, including J. P. Morgan, the Episcopalian, and John D. Rockefeller, eminent in Baptist circles.[82]

In addition to stumping the country for preparedness, the League was most convincing in its anti-pacifist campaign. It flooded the states with pamphlets warning us of the impending doom when Germany conquered the Allies. According to one observer:

> In the vocabulary of the League, the terms "German," "pro-German," "pacifist," "socialist," and "anti-Preparedness advocate" became synonymous and indistinguishable. One who favored the Allied cause was a patriotic American; one who favored the German side—nay, even one who sought to maintain a neutral position—was a "hyphenated American," "a dangerous alien," "a spy," a "traitor."[33]

Lyman Abbott, who said that he was a member of every peace society in the country, in a meeting held in Carnegie Hall, New York, under the auspices of the National Security League, argued that the League by its campaign for an increased army and navy "was the best peace society in the United States."[34]

Already some of the leaders of public opinion in the peace and religious circles were beginning to counsel against any peace move on the part of our government. Henry Van Dyke, Presbyterian clergyman and Minister to Holland, early in December strongly advised Wilson to refrain from any move in that direction,[35] while Andrew Carnegie, in the same letter in which he accepted appointment to the office of vice-president of the International Peace Forum, opposed any action for peace initiated by the United States. He was also glad the World Peace Congress had been called off.[36]

By Christmas of 1914 the line of battle between the Security League group and the pacifists had been pretty well drawn up, for in December the American League to Limit Armaments had been organized in New York City to combat the forces calling for increased defense. Those actively interested in this movement were Bishop David Hummell Greer, Oswald Garrison Villard, L. Hollingsworth Wood, Lillian D. Wald, Nicholas Murray Butler, Dean Frederick P. Keppel (later Third Assistant Secretary of War under Newton D. Baker), Percy Stickney Grant of the Church of the Ascension, New York, and William Pierson Merrill, minister the Brick Presbyterian Church, New York.[37]

This infant organization soon engaged the fire of the National Security League, which was intent upon utterly discrediting the pacifists. But Bishop Greer, who usually acted as spokesman, stood his ground. He was president of the Church Peace Union and interested in other peace organizations. He maintained that "peace will never be obtained by the use of force. The idea is all wrong." "The teaching of Christ, the manner of his life and of his death, were proof that he would be opposed to war."[38]

Another national defense movement, the American Legion, started about March 1, 1915. One of the sponsors was Major General Leonard Wood. Many of the clergy recommended the Legion in glowing terms, while multitudes from all over the East, at least, rushed in their applications for chaplaincies. An applicant from Peekskill, New York, B. C. Warren, pastor of the St. Paul's Methodist Episcopal Church, stated he could "ride, shoot, handle a spade, march or act as chaplain."[39]

Nicholas Murray Butler definitely opposed the formation of the Legion and added: "It would be just as important to organize for the prevention of earthquakes."[40] Bishop Greer accused General Wood of issuing propaganda on behalf of the Legion from army headquarters. Wood denied this and demanded an apology. The correspondence was released for the benefit of the readers of the New York *Times,* wherein Wood implied that he endorsed the Legion as a private citizen and not as an army officer.[41]

The Legion seems to have thrived on the publicity and continued to grow, for within six weeks the organization claimed forty thousand members. Theodore Roosevelt became the president, ably supported by Taft, Root and others. The advisory committee contained the names of Joseph H. Choate, George W. Wickersham, Senator Henry Cabot Lodge, Nicholas Longworth, William Allen White, and Harry Pratt Judson, president of the University of Chicago.[42]

In the spring of 1915, Theodore Roosevelt and General Wood boomed the preparedness campaign. General Wood toured the universities of the North, advocating bigger preparations for war. One of the visible results of this campaign was the establishment of the citizens' military training camps, so strongly recommended by John Grier Hibben.

But the peace societies were by no means inactive. They commended the President for the attitude which he had maintained. The New York Peace Society, however, committed itself to "a powerful navy as our national means of defense, but never for aggression."*

As early as January, 1915, the Church Peace Union sent out a questionnaire to ten thousand ministers of all denominations to discover their attitude on preparedness. The results of this were published on May 31, 1915. More than ninety-five per cent were opposed to any increase of armament at this time, while the large majority were in favor of Wilson's attitude.† The secretary of the Church Peace Union issued a statement, optimistic in tone:

> . . . the one thing that seems to have made the greatest impression on the minds of the ministers is the fact that where there has been no armament there has been no talk of war.
>
> These answers showed the ministers to be the most antimilitaristic who happened to be in Europe last summer. They are absolutely against the increased armaments propaganda.[48]

Nevertheless the state of alarm on the part of those interested in opposing the increase of armament was evident, for on March 1, the Church Peace Union sent out a letter, signed by Protestants, Catholics, and Jews, to all the churches and clergy of America. (For representatives of diverse faiths to send letters to the churches, which they had joined in signing, was a new venture.) The message read:

> Partisanship is adding fuel to fires of passion. Clergymen should allay prejudice not intensify it. Each of the warring nations believes in the justice of its cause. . . . In this calamitous hour, denunciation of either side assumes a superhuman knowledge of complex policies and purposes, imperils the influence of our government in promoting peace, aggravates a quarrel which we should help abate, creates dissensions among our own people, inflames a war spirit in America and gives force to the criticism that

---

* This statement in the New York *Times* (Jan. 8, 1915), was signed by Andrew Carnegie, George Kirchwey, Hamilton Holt, Frederick Lynch, George Foster Peabody, Oscar Straus, Stephen Wise, and George Haven Putnam.

† I have been unable to discover whether the majority of the answers to this questionnaire were received prior to or after the sinking of the *Lusitania*. Obviously, that fact has an important bearing on the interpretation to be placed upon the replies.

the Church has abdicated its sacred function as the maker of peace and concord.

. . . This is the time to prepare, not for war, but for peace.*

In the meanwhile the number of people of importance who had publicly committed themselves to the Allied cause continued to increase. By 1915 the British had composed a book of *Sixty American Opinions on the War.* "The object of this little book," modestly admitted the authors, "is to show how many friends we have in America." There were many more friends than those listed, to be sure, but at least one-half of the number given were people of wide influence. The names of certain clergymen found their way into the pages. In January, 1915, Frank Isley Paradise, rector of Grace Church, West Medford, Massachusetts, had said from his pulpit:

> At length, I do believe we shall catch the spirit of battle, and fling back the challenge of German nationalism. For we too have a conscious national destiny. The God of Israel has anointed us to champion the cause of the poor, the weak and the down-trodden. We too shall struggle for world power. It will be the helping and healing power of Christian civilization.[44]

Charles Henry Parkhurst, pastor of the Madison Square Presbyterian Church, New York, claimed he had been definitely anti-German since the beginning. Langdon Cheves Stewardson, formerly president of Hobart College, confessed, "As for myself, I am English heart and soul."[45]

THE LUSITANIA DISASTER

On May 7, 1915, at 2:15 p.m., the *Lusitania*, when just off the Irish coast, was struck by a torpedo from a German submarine and sank in eighteen minutes. One thousand fifty-four lives were lost of which one hundred and two were American. Upon receipt of the news of this tragedy, the American people did not immediately clamor for war, as is generally believed. They were too stunned to demand revenge at once. While men like Roose-

---

* The signers of this letter were twenty-nine in all: Peter Ainslee, Arthur Judson Brown, Francis E. Clark, James Cardinal Gibbons, Archbishop J. Glennon, Bishop David H. Greer, Frank O. Hall, Bishop E. R. Hendrix, Rabbi Emil G. Hirsch, Hamilton Holt, William I. Hull, Charles E. Jefferson, Frederick Lynch, Charles Macfarland, Marcus M. Marks, Shailer Mathews, Edwin D. Mead, William P. Merrill, John R. Mott, George A. Plimpton, Junius B. Remensnyder, Judge Henry W. Rogers, Robert E. Speer, Francis L. Stetson, James J. Walsh, Bishop Luther B. Wilson, Jenkin L. Jones, W. H. P. Faunce, Bishop William Lawrence. (New York *Times*, March 1, 1915.)

velt and Lodge, who had endeavored to stimulate more of the war spirit, now shouted their demands, and George W. Wickersham, bitterly anti-Wilson, called for fifty submarines,[46] the great majority of the citizens did not follow them.

> It is a singular thing [writes David Lawrence] that while a few people on the Eastern seaboard were clamoring for war, a careful examination of the editorials showed that out of a thousand compiled by telegraph in the three days after the *Lusitania* was sunk in May, 1915, less than one-half dozen indicated a belief that war should be declared. Opinion was almost unanimous that the situation called for diplomacy, and an effective expression of American feeling, with the hint, of course, that if satisfaction could not be secured the American people would be behind the President in whatever course he should formulate.[47]

The statement holds good for sermons preached all over the United States on the Sunday following the sinking of the British vessel. The New York *Times* of May 10 had an almost nation-wide survey of ministerial opinion. The religious sensibilities of the ministers were deeply shocked and they were horrified, but there seems to have been little call for reprisals. In New York, men like Bishop Greer believed that it was a "time for calmness, not words." John Haynes Holmes announced: "It is militarism that has committed this crime." Others followed. John Henry Jowett: "It is a colossal sin against God and it is premeditated murder." Henry Sloane Coffin: "Barbarism and civilization, clearly the issue." David James Burrell, of the Marble Collegiate Church: "I call it murder most foul." Malcolm James MacLeod: "Bloody murder, pure and simple." Leighton Parks of St. Bartholomew's placed Germany outside the pale of civilization. S. Parkes Cadman, of Brooklyn, and Charles Aubrey Eaton, of the Madison Avenue Baptist Church, both preparedness advocates, were guarded in their language. The act was "brutal and inhuman," exclaimed Dr. Cadman and we should prepare "to defend our threatened ideals." Dr. Eaton hinted that "America must not stand aside." It was some time later when Dr. Eaton attacked Wilson for not avenging the *Lusitania;* it should have been done, he said, "if it took ten million men, if our cities were laid in the dust and we were set back a hundred years."[48]

A. B. Moldenke, of St. Peter's Lutheran Church, one of the foremost places of worship for Germans in New York City, foresaw the possibility of war:

If the United States were to go to war against Germany with a just cause, German-Americans would go to war with their adopted country. Germans living here . . . will not fight it. If they cannot fight with it, they will be neutral.

In Cleveland, Ohio, Ferdinand Q. Blanchard, of the Euclid Avenue Congregational Church, demanded that the United States put an end to this "crime against civilization. . . . The hour for tolerant neutrality has passed." Frederick Keller, of the Evangelical Lutheran Church, held that since the passengers had been warned, "Germany is absolutely justified in sending to the bottom a boat which carried nearly one-half a million dollars worth of munitions of war."

In Chicago, an appeal was formulated on Saturday, May 8, in the Chicago *Press* signed by Lutheran clergymen calling upon the German pastors in the interest of "truth and justice" to call the attention of the congregations to the fact that "the German government had been forced by England to the horrible steps, and, according to international law, is not responsible for the loss of American life." One Lutheran pastor pointed out that the passengers had committed suicide. The English pulpits in Chicago did not hesitate to brand the act as "dastardly," "fiendish," and "barbarous."

According to the press report, as far as could be ascertained, not a single minister in the city of Milwaukee mentioned the *Lusitania* disaster. "The city is apparently so strongly German-American that the English preachers dare not aggravate the German-American parishioners by any reference to the affair; and the Germans realize the danger of the situation too well to start any controversy."

In Philadelphia, Russell Conwell called the sinking "murder in cold blood" and took occasion to commend Italy's action in preparing to enter the war with the Allies, saying, "It is the only Christian thing to do." In Washington most of the clergy urged restraint, while in Boston Bishop Lawrence protested but advised calm. Cortland R. Myers, of the Tremont Baptist Temple, termed the *Lusitania* affair the "most damnable chapter yet written. The German people have placed themselves in the same class with the African savages in the jungle." He continued, "the German government is in league with hell. But I offer my prayer that . . . America be saved from entrance in this world war."

The papers for weeks after the event devoted a generous amount of space to letters expressing opinions. The effect of the *Lusitania* was like cutting down through American public opinion with a knife and dividing it up into segments.

Among the clergy, those who had been inclined toward preparedness now became staunch advocates of an "arm to the teeth" policy. Lyman Abbott, for instance, demanded war: "When Sumter was fired on, Lincoln acted. He did not wait to deliberate beforehand."[49]

Wilson's letter to Germany seemed to meet the requirements, for it was greeted with notes and resolutions of approval from even the genuinely pacifist element in the churches. On the other hand the German-American group either defended the sinking of the *Lusitania* or generally remained silent. In Chicago a small group of German pastors walked out of a Methodist ministers' meeting when resolutions were adopted on the *Lusitania* tragedy.

Cardinal Gibbons, presumably speaking for many Catholics, took an objective view of the matter:

> It seems a terrible cost to sacrifice thousands of young men. . . . just because a few insist on taking a risk, for it is nothing but foolish for Americans to take the dare of traveling by ships that are in danger. Why should they court the danger? . . . A true lover of America should sacrifice personal whims when the honor and peace of the nation hangs in the balance. It seems like asking too much to expect the country to stand up and fight just because a few are over-daring.[50]

THE CHURCHES ABANDON NEUTRALITY

Those major trends and cleavages of opinion which had developed among the denominational groups and religious personalities during the ten months since the beginning of the war cannot be adequately comprehended without taking into consideration an additional factor—the national origins and connections of the clergy and the churches.

Many of the men of English birth, like Drs. Cadman,* Manning,† William Carter and G. Ashton Oldham, and Canadians, like Walter Laidlaw, and Charles A. Eaton (who also had close relatives in the conflict), had taken the side of England and had come out definitely against Germany and for a stiff program of preparedness in the United States.

---

* Cadman's love of his native land may be inferred from the following appraisal of the glories of English civilization: "From Alfred the Great to the present war, can you find anything in the history of mankind comparable with the story of this little island?" (A. L. Squiers, Ed., *One Hundred Per Cent American*, Doran, N. Y., 1918, p. 62.)

† It has only been in recent years that Dr. Manning has incorporated the fact of his English birth in *Who's Who in America*.

The strong Scotch-Presbyterians and Wesleyan Methodists leaned, naturally, toward Great Britain. The Irish Catholics, to a great extent, were not in sympathy with the aims of England.

Among the denominations, the Protestant Episcopal Church in this country, since its founding, has been a thoroughly English organization, having many ties that bind it to the mother church in England. Its clergy are constantly passing back and forth between the two countries. It is generally appraised as the church of society, it maintains an air of aristocracy, and has within its ranks those who parade their titles and English connections. Many of the priests were sympathetic with the philosophy of the leisure class. At the time of the war numerous wealthy bankers, like the Morgans, either belonged to this church or had Episcopalian associations. Hence, with a few notable exceptions, the Episcopalian clergy, steeped in English tradition and culture, and, in general, on the side of the vested interests, simply acted in accord with the conditioning and habit-patterns already well established. Moreover, the Episcopalians, more than any others, have been traditionally tied up with various military organizations and patriotic orders, either through chaplains or social affiliations.

The Baptists, Congregationalists, Unitarians, Universalists, and Methodists, all with English origins and backgrounds, retained their sympathies with the mother country. The Unitarians in the United States, as was also the case in England, provided more than a proportionate number of pacifist ministers.

The Dunkards and the Mennonites, with a pacifist inheritance of a rugged variety, together with, in many instances, a German ancestry and heritage, had a double reason for indifference if not actual hostility to preparedness.

German sympathies dominated the various Lutheran groups. Composed to a great extent of members attached to Teutonic culture, the idea of war against the Fatherland was abhorrent. The Allies were held directly or indirectly responsible for the conflict at arms and all its accompanying horrors. The Lutherans varied in their policies all the way from "watchful waiting" to active dissemination of pro-German propaganda.*

---

* Among the Germans, particularly in the Middle West, the German propaganda did its work with telling effect. "While British propaganda re-echoed from many Episcopalian pulpits, the Germans found their support mainly in the Lutheran churches, where in many cases the German language persisted. It was not necessary to subsidize the elements represented by these groups. They were naturally pro-German, but propaganda stiffened their backbone and made their leaders more militant." (G. S. Viereck, *Spreading Germs of Hate*, Horace Liveright, N. Y., 1930, p. 46.)

While many of the Catholics were of Irish descent and had no love for England, the protests against the British which arose from them seems not to have been voiced through the churches but through the various Irish and Irish-American societies. The Catholics before the days of April, 1917, were, in their pulpit utterances, loyal to the President, and refrained, apparently, from the type of criticism so prevalent among the Protestant churches.

The Jews, divided into numerous groups of national origins, in the early days presented a complexity of attitudes. But they were in a delicate situation. They could not afford to be classed as disloyal and become victims of persecution by the anti-Semitic Americans. Rabbi Stephen S. Wise, against preparedness and radically opposed to war, reversed his position as soon as war was declared and equaled the most enthusiastic Gentiles in his enthusiasm for war aims. Many other Jewish clerics had been in line before.

The pacifist elements, represented by the peace societies and the Society of Friends, together with such men as Bishop Greer, John Haynes Holmes, William P. Merrill, Charles E. Jefferson, Robert E. Speer, Henry W. Pinkham, Charles A. Dole, Jenkin L. Jones, Frederick Lynch, and others, withstood the mounting pressure of public opinion. But the great body of the clergy, waiting to discover which way the tide of public opinion would flow, were beginning to succumb to the subtleties of Allied propaganda and the tactics of the defense societies and Security and Navy Leagues.

The Preparedness Bandwagon

As has been indicated, the sinking of the *Lusitania* greatly strengthened the cause of the Entente in this country. On Memorial Day, 1915, the trend of sympathy for the Allies and for an increased armament was very noticeable.

The first week in June, E. Ellsworth Shumaker, speaking before the West Side Y. M. C. A., New York, is reported to have made this significant statement:

> How many of us secretly prayed that Italy would enter the war? I know that I did. Let us put an end to our hypocrisy or pretended neutrality now. Dr. Newell Dwight Hillis, after a correspondence with more than five hundred persons, has reached the conclusion that nineteen out of every twenty people in this country are for the Allies. Let us say that the ideals for which England and France are fighting are the ideals of freedom for which our forefathers bled. About those ideals we can never be neutral.

Our getting into the war might prove to be the greatest step we could possibly take on behalf of peace.[51]

Certainly the sinking of the *Lusitania* gave the preparedness proponents an argument that hitherto had been lacking. Here at last was the actual proof that Germany was a menace to America. The National Security League now called on the clergy to back up and bless the efforts of the organization. The clergy of New York City were requested by the League to preach on preparedness July 4. The response was gratifying, though there were a few protests by Frederick Lynch and the American League to Limit Armaments.

Further evidence of the trend of opinion may be adduced from the results of a questionnaire sent out in the fall of 1915 by *The Continent* of Chicago to the ministers of the country. An overwhelming majority declared themselves in favor of preparedness. About the same time a vote in Brooklyn, "embracing ministers in something like twenty denominations, showed one hundred and fifty-one in favor of preparedness, while six qualified their approval and only fourteen were opposed."[52] Charles A. Eaton, through the pages of *The Independent*, gave assurances that "this war is the greatest blessing that has ever fallen on mankind since the German Reformation."[53]

As appropriate for the celebration of Thanksgiving, 1915, the Conference Committee on National Preparedness, representing most of the preparedness organizations, under the chairmanship of Henry A. Wise Wood, urged the ministers again to talk upon the popular theme of the day—military preparedness. There were a few objections to this proposal led by William P. Merrill, who informed the militarists that such a topic for a Thanksgiving message was "repugnant to good taste and proper religious sentiment."[54]

The summary of the mood of Thanksgiving pulpit oratory was given out by the *Times*:

> Sermons by New York preachers on Thanksgiving Day this year were unlike Thanksgiving sermons that New York congregations ever heard before. . . . Throughout the sermons there was an almost universal note in favor of military preparedness. The exception was at the Broadway Tabernacle [Charles E. Jefferson].[55]

The *Times* exaggerated the unanimity of opinion, for there were other ministers in the city opposed to preparedness at this time. Yet it is a fair indication of the growing sentiment on the part of the church representatives in favor of an increased army and navy.

The year 1916 was characterized by mass meetings, debates on preparedness, and the crystallization of public opinion.

Theodore Roosevelt, an outstanding figure during this period, already proficient in castigating pacifists and hyphen-Americans, now converted an increasing number of the disciples of the Prince of Peace to his point of view. Roosevelt's effect upon the churchmen varied, but among certain elements it seems to have been quite profound. They admired and envied his crusading spirit, his roaring pronunciamentos, and were captured by his evident sincerity. The ex-President's descriptive adjectives of pacifists added color to his speeches and soon enriched the vocabularies of the preparedness clergy, who also turned to labeling the more timid ones "cravens, cowards, poltroons, and eunuchs." And now in the early days of 1916, the sage of Sagamore Hill charged, "the professional pacifists are at best an unlovely set of men, and, taken as a whole, are probably the most undesirable citizens that this country contains."[56]

At a meeting of the Methodist Social Union in New York City in April, 1916, the retiring president, W. R. Comfort, was cheered when in an address he lauded Roosevelt, the main speaker of the evening. Roosevelt, in turn, was vociferously applauded for his attack on Wilson and the hyphenates.[57]

Another event, however, reveals the antagonism of the German-Americans. At a dinner of the Lutheran Society in New York, John A. Haas, president of Muhlenberg College, Allentown, Pennsylvania, upbraided the Colonel for his militarism. At the mention of Roosevelt's name the audience hooted.[58]

Meanwhile the Allied propaganda increased in power. In Cleveland, Ohio, in February, William H. Hubbell, pastor of the Second Presbyterian Church, in the campaign conducted by the Cleveland *Leader,* was urging Bible students to give dimes for a battleship. Other ministers also supported the project.[59]

Upon the appointment of Newton D. Baker to the position of Secretary of War, Charles LeRoy Goodell, of St. Paul's Methodist Church, New York, opposed Baker because he was a "peace at any price pacifist."[60]

John Grier Hibben, writing for the American Defense Society, on the subject of our lack of preparedness, exclaimed that if the program for adequate national defense were not pushed the boys would be "led to slaughter like cattle to the shambles." He further pleaded: "Let us brand as a traitor whoever lives in our midst, enjoying the protection and prosperity of our country, and yet dares to express by word or by deed the spirit of hyphenated loyalty. There is . . . no place and no quarter for traitors."[61]

George R. Van de Water, rector of St. Andrew's, New York, who had been chaplain of the 71st Regiment during the Spanish-American War, explained: "I am a preacher, and it is my duty to pray for peace but it is just as much so to prepare for war, if necessary."[62] Dr. Manning now announced: "Preparedness will command peace,"[63] and Frank M. Goodchild of the Central Baptist, New York, lamented: "This country knew which side was right and so did President Wilson . . . but he didn't act."[64] William Carter, of the Throop Avenue Presbyterian, New York, formerly a secretary for a peace organization, was, in a debate with Dr. Merrill, maintaining that the pacifist was "too intellectually arrogant, too cocksure of himself."[65]

A Baptist clergyman, Leonard G. Broughton of Tennessee, wrote a book, *Is Preparedness for War Unchristian?* For the first six months after August, 1914, he had been pastor of Christian Church, Westminster Bridge, London, and hence could speak from "personal knowledge":

> I believe [he said] that preparedness as at present interpreted in this country is distinctly Christian, and in keeping with the highest principles of American statesmanship. And that a man, however sincere he may be, who sets himself against it, is not the friend of his country. I am in a position to know from firsthand observation, that if England and France had been prepared, Europe would now be at peace. It was because they were so thoroughly unprepared that the present war was precipitated.[66]

Among the Jews, Rabbi Samuel Schulman of Temple Beth-El, New York, could see no "contradiction between promoting peace and preparedness." His position is an excellent example of the phenomenon of ethnocentrism:

> I hold that America has a great trust for humanity. It is a nation that, for the first time in the world's history, has organized itself, not on the basis of race, nor on the basis of creed, but on the basis of the recognition of the rights of men and the dignity of our common humanity. It . . . has a destiny as a teacher to the world which is greater and more prophetic than that of any other people on earth.[67]

While Roosevelt was influencing his fellow patriots on an emotional level, Charles W. Eliot, President-Emeritus of Harvard, prominent Unitarian layman, and "perhaps the most highly respected of American educators," wrote a series of letters to the New York *Times* in the early days of the war, condemning Germany and expounding the concept that the Allies were thoroughly righteous in their fight for liberty and democracy. He soon proposed a naval alliance with the saviors of civilization for the sake of defense and world peace. "Have the American people," he asked, "no duty toward the support of public liberty, justice, and humanity in the world outside of their own borders?" [68]

"The prestige of Dr. Eliot's name," estimates C. Hartley Grattan, "must have led hundreds to accept these ideas as truth." [69]

William Howard Taft, another prominent Unitarian layman, was also exceedingly influential. In February, he gave the principal address to the annual meeting of Rockefeller's Bible Class, in New York, and spoke in favor of a large army and navy. Charles M. Schwab of the Bethlehem Steel Corporation was on hand and jovially endorsed these proposals, though he reminded the members of the Bible Class that this was not because of any personal interest in armament.* [70]

President Wilson, who had opposed preparedness in his message to Congress in December, 1914, was beginning to change his mind by July, 1915. The preparedness parades staged all over the country by the National Security League were interpreted by his secretary, Joseph P. Tumulty, as a Republican demonstration. Hence, when a parade was announced for Washington, Tumulty arranged for the President to lead it. This political stroke put Wilson in "command of the forces in this country demanding preparedness." [71] In November, 1915, in his speech before the Manhattan Club of New York, Wilson came out definitely for preparedness. On December 7, in his message to Congress, the program of increased military preparations, drawn up by the Secretary of War, Garrison, was endorsed, and by January, 1916, Wilson was touring the country, speaking on behalf of increased defenses.

The friends of peace and the anti-preparedness movement lost their chief support when the President went over to the other side. On April 6, a mass meeting packed Carnegie Hall, New York, to listen to speakers criticize the Wilson program.

---

* For Mr. Schwab's agreement with Lord Kitchener, pledging, in 1914, the products of Bethlehem Steel to the Allies for five years, *vid.* C. H. Grattan, *Why We Fought*, Vanguard, N. Y., 1929, p. 138. John Moody says the agreement made Bethlehem Steel "one of the strongest industrial allies of the British Government." (Moody, *Masters of Capital*, New Haven, 1919, p. 168.)

During this period of our history the American Union Against Militarism strove to prevent the ever-increasing militarization of the American mind. Stephen S. Wise toured the Middle West endeavoring to uproot the seeds sown by Wilson and the National Security League speakers.

In the winter of 1916, Walter Laidlaw, executive secretary of the New York Federation of Churches, sent out a questionnaire to a thousand clergymen, the results of which were given in a preliminary report in March. This showed 151 in favor of preparedness and fourteen opposed.[72] A week later, Frederick Lynch exhibited the results of a petition against preparedness circulated by the Church Peace Union. Fifty clergymen had signed by that time and signatures were still coming in.*

The Church Peace Union petitions and pamphlets, appealing to the clergy to help defeat certain "organized and determined efforts to stampede the nation," caused no little annoyance to some of them. On March 27 there appeared in the New York *Times* a lengthy epistle signed by eighty-three ministers of varying degrees of prominence, in which it was declared without equivocation that they were all opposed to the appeal of the Church Peace Union and were for preparedness. It was affirmed that the program might better be left to the government and the ministers fulfil their duties "by earnest prayer and spiritual counsel, and our duty as patriots by abstaining from profitless addresses to the government." †

An event six weeks later, Saturday, May 13, received their unqualified approval, for on that day occurred a preparedness parade for which New York had been getting ready for many weeks. It was reported that 125,863 loyal patriots were in line in a parade that continued for twelve hours. The clergy of the great city showed their colors. "Clergy a Notable Division,"

---

* Walter Laidlaw objected to Lynch's questionnaire inasmuch as it had not been circulated indiscriminately, but he did not explain why only 165 out of 1,000 had answered his own questionnaire. The list furnished by Lynch at that time is of interest for purposes of future reference. Some of the names were: Peter Ainslie, Charles F. Dole, Washington Gladden, Bishop Greer, Frank Oliver Hall, John Haynes Holmes, Charles E. Jefferson, Arthur C. McGiffert, Henry N. MacCracken, William P. Merrill, John Herman Randall, Junius B. Remensnyder, Gaylord S. White, Stephen S. Wise, Howard C. Robbins, Cornelius Woelfkin. (New York *Times,* March 13, 1916.)

† A partial list of the signers (most of whom were Episcopalians) reveals a representation from all denominations: George William Douglas, W. T. Manning, Milo H. Gates, C. L. Slattery, Ernest M. Stires, W. N. Guthrie, Herbert Shipman, George R. Van de Water, Percy S. Grant, G. Ashton Oldham, C. K. Gilbert, W. L. Bevan, Alexander G. Cummins, Walter Laidlaw, S. Parkes Cadman, Avery A. Shaw, William Carter, Charles L. Goodell, Worth M. Tippy, David G. Wylie, Nehemiah Boynton, Cornelius Woelfkin.

the press reported. The Division contained 130 divines. The officers representing the various denominations were: Herbert Shipman, David James Burrell, James N. Connelly, Charles A. Eaton, William H. Morgan, Lewis T. Reed, Joseph Silverman and W. Merle-Smith.[73]

The next day being Sunday, most of the ministers appear to have commented on the events of the day preceding. According to the press, Dr. Merle-Smith exclaimed, "I am glad that the ministry of the Presbyterian Church is not pacifist. . . . Of the Presbyterian clergy invited to march only six sent word that it would be against their scruples to do so. The great body of the Presbyterian Church is arrayed on the side of preparedness in fighting unrighteousness, injustice and all forms of evil and vice."[74] Frank Hall of the Church of the Divine Paternity (Universalist), who had signed many peace petitions, thought Jesus would have approved of the parade "but would have been saddened by the necessity of it."[75] Rabbi Wise regretted the demonstration: "Are we to enter the armament gamble, in which every nation loses and hell alone is victorious?"[76]

But after such an exhibition of militaristic enthusiasm Dr. Manning was still not satisfied. In a long letter to the *Times*, May 29, he wrote: "Our moral sense as a nation is dulled. Morally we have lost our way. Our present lack of national spirit is due also in part to a vast amount of well-meant but mistaken and misleading and really unchristian teaching about peace."

A few months later he was preaching on the glories of military training. "I advocate it because of its moral and spiritual values. It will give us needed discipline. . . . It will tend to make our young men better Americans, better citizens, and better Christians."[77]

In connection with the advocacy of military training it is enlightening to note the correlation between the office of chaplain in military and patriotic organizations and enthusiasm for preparedness. This is particularly true among the Episcopalians. A few of the militant clergy holding chaplaincies at this time or in the Spanish-American War were: George W. Douglas, William T. Manning, Milo H. Gates, Ernest M. Stires, George R. Van de Water, S. Parkes Cadman, William Carter and Herbert Shipman.*

---

* In July, 1916, our trouble on the Mexican border diverted attention somewhat from Europe but gave the repressed military urges an opportunity to find partial expression. S. Parkes Cadman and Herbert Shipman went down as chaplains. By November Dr. Cadman was reported as being in favor of

The general advocacy of war in the East had grown to such proportions that the editor of *The Advocate of Peace* was soon to observe that "the Christian Church is now 'blessing' the war which it did nothing to prevent. There are other evidences that it is now planning to exploit the tragedy of it for its own interest." [78]

In the midst of the war talk, pro and con, the presidential election of 1916 took on more than average significance for certain interests and nationality groups in this country. Although the United States was not at war with Germany, the German-Americans were already much despised by the "one hundred per cent" Americans led by Roosevelt. Then "when the presidential election of 1916 approached, the rivalry between the two parties for the 'hyphen vote' reached a climax." [79] This hyphen vote was to a certain extent under the control of the Lutheran clergymen. The Lutherans hoped to put a strict neutral in the White House. Wilson was accused of being pro-British in numerous meetings of the Lutheran clergymen called to consider the subject.[80] Various rumors spread about the bids made by candidates for the cooperation of these ministers. The Chicago *Journal* accused Charles Evans Hughes, the Republican candidate, of giving pledges to them at a secret meeting of German Lutheran ministers at Milwaukee.[81] Lutheran divines wrote letters to the press urging the election of Hughes.

The cross-currents of propaganda defeated Hughes for president.[82] Wilson's campaign managers had painted their candidate as a pacifist—"He kept us out of war." This slogan was calculated to win over the German-American electorate. (Though Wilson and some of his associates had tried to put us into the war before this they did not hesitate to use the keeping of their country out of war as a battle-cry.) The peaceful inclinations of William Jennings Bryan added weight. He spoke with tremendous effect in the Middle West and emphasized this phase of the President's record almost to the exclusion of everything else. Only one state in which Bryan spoke went Republican.[83]

When the election results were finally tabulated it was discovered that the German-Americans had not supported Hughes but Wilson. Some blamed Roosevelt for this. Hughes and Roosevelt had been "too thick." Hughes had lost both Mil-

---

having "eleven million men ready to defend our borders at any moment." (New York *Times*, November 14, 1916.)

Dr. Shipman, chaplain at West Point, 1896-1905, died in March, 1930, and was buried with full military honors in the "Arlington" of the Military Academy reserved for cadets and graduates, such an exception having been granted for only one other civilian. (New York *Times*, May 27, 1930.)

waukee and St. Louis. The American Union Against Militarism, analyzing the vote, declared that "The hyphen vote was practically a myth," and that President Wilson's re-election was "due primarily to the fighting pacifist sentiment in the United States." [84]

Whatever interpretation one may choose to place upon the results of the election of 1916, it may be safely inferred that the majority of the citizens of the United States at that time were in favor of keeping out of the European War.

With the election over, Europe again became the center of attention. No sooner had the excitement of electing a president died down than news came of the so-called Belgium deportations. Such atrocities damned the Germans in the eyes of the clergy even more than the sinking of the *Lusitania,* though several of the Lutherans, including Dr. Moldenke of St. Paul's, New York, defended Germany and blamed Belgium. A huge mass meeting was arranged at Carnegie Hall, December 18, to protest against the treatment of the Belgians. Dr. Manning presided, while James M. Beck, Alton B. Parker, and Elihu Root fanned the flames of hatred and fury against Germany. Telegrams were received from Roosevelt, Joseph H. Choate and Archbishop Ireland. An appeal from Cardinal Mercier added to the intensity of feeling.[85]

On November 29, the United States government protested officially on the grounds that the deportations were illegal and inhuman and embarrassing to the work of the Belgian Relief Committee.[86]

At the same time Wilson had been endeavoring to conduct peace negotiations to bring about the end of the war. Calling for an avowal of the respective views of the belligerents "as to the terms upon which the war might be concluded . . . ," the nations were informed:

> He [the President] takes the liberty of calling attention to the fact that the objects which the statesmen of the belligerents on both sides have in mind in this war are virtually the same, as stated in general terms to their own people and to the world. . . .
>
> In the measures to be taken to secure the future peace of the world the people and Government of the United States are as vitally and directly interested as the Governments now at war. . . .[87]

The inference by President Wilson that Germany and the Allies were on the same moral plane caused the King of England, when he heard the news, to break down and weep.[88]

AMERICA DECIDES TO FIGHT

In the midst of the President's efforts to bring about peace in Europe there was released to the press a significant document on January 1, 1917, by George Wharton Pepper. It was a virtual protest to the Christians of America against "any attempt to promote a premature peace in Europe." The press release contained the signatures of notable Christians from all over the United States. Peace propaganda was deplored. There must be a permanent peace in Europe but ". . . to clamor for the ending of the present war without insuring the vindication of truth, justice and honor is not to seek peace, but to sow disaster." Referring to the unsettled issues of Belgium, the *Lusitania,* Serbia, et cetera (but not to the British violation of American rights on the high seas), the document further stated:

> The just God who withheld not His son from the cross, would not look with favor upon a people who put their fear of pain and death, their dread of suffering and loss, their concern for conquest and ease above the holy claims of righteousness and justice, and freedom, and mercy and truth. . . . The memory of all the saints and martyrs cries out against such backsliding of mankind. Sad is our lot if we have forgotten how to die for a holy cause.*

This rather unusual manifesto to the people of the United States received the able backing of several religious journals, including *The Churchman,* whose editor, while asserting that "the follower of Jesus is essentially a pacifist," nevertheless believed the activities of the Church Peace Union were lacking in "discerning statesmanship." It was "inevitable," therefore, that "some such pronouncement should be provoked." [89]

Hamilton Holt, the editor of *The Independent,* sized up the situation in an entirely different light. He not only regarded the appeal as a "grave mistake," but as "a movement to halt all peace discussion and to flout the efforts of the President of the United States, and the neutral governments of Europe," who

---

* Some of the sixty-five signers were: Bishops Cleland K. Nelson and Joseph F. Berry, Lyman Abbott, George Wharton Pepper, John Grier Hibben, Charles L. Bonaparte, Bishop Philip M. Rhinelander, Winston Churchill, Henry C. King, Bishop Thomas F. Gaylor, Gifford Pinchot, Bishop William Lawrence, William T. Ellis, William A. Sunday, Henry Bond, Richard C. Cabot, Harry Emerson Fosdick, James M. Speers, Alexander MacColl, William J. Schiefflin, Bishop Charles P. Anderson, Eben E. Olcott, Charles R. Brown, William R. Moody, Newell Dwight Hillis, George R. Rutledge, William C. Bitting, George A. Gordon, A. Z. Conrad, Cornelius E. H. Patten, George W. Coleman, W. T. Manning, Walter Laidlaw, S. Parkes Cadman, Charles H. Brent, John Timothy Stone.

were trying to substitute "reason for armed conflict." Holt also insisted that the public would certainly believe that the signers were advising "their brethren in Europe to continue to slaughter one another" on the presumption that the "ravage of Belgium" and other deeds could "only be atoned by blood."[90]

The Church Peace Union did not take the "insult" lying down. A conference was called which included members of the executive committee of the World Alliance of the Churches and of the Commission of International Justice and Goodwill of the Federal Council. Their statement, under the circumstances, seems quite mild. The signers, over 400 in number,* wished it to be known that they took an "open stand with those who labor for the establishment of a lasting peace upon the foundations of righteousness," and they believed in a league of nations and a world court.

Inasmuch as all groups believed in "a lasting peace upon the foundations of righteousness," the preparedness and jingo elements could scarcely disagree with the Church Peace Union, on that point at least.

The failure of the President to bring about peace through negotiation did not end his attempts to terminate the war. On January 22, he made one of the most famous speeches of his life to the Senate of the United States on "Peace Without Victory." Either because it was misunderstood or the people did not believe in this type of solution, the speech was followed by evidences of disapproval in which many of the prominent clergy joined. The even-tempered English clergyman, John Henry Jowett, who had been keeping his sentiments in the background, wrote a letter in which he disagreed with Wilson: "A settlement which left the victory of the Allied cause uncertain would have no permanency."[91]

The pacifists took new courage. Dr. Lynch praised the President and told of church groups that applauded him for his message. "We are glad," said he, that "our name appears with those latter groups rather than with those who call for a fight to the finish."[92] Jenkin Lloyd Jones, editor of *Unity*, wired Wilson, "You have dared where press, pulpit, legislators, and cabinets have halted. God's blessing be with you."[93]

---

* A few of the signers were: Bishop Greer, W. P. Merrill, W. H. P. Faunce, Nehemiah Boynton, Francis E. Clark, Howard A. Bridgman, Bishop Luther B. Wilson, Charles S. Macfarland, Frederick Lynch, Henry Sloane Coffin, Arthur J. Brown, Charles E. Jefferson, Charles Stelzle, James I. Vance, Hamilton Holt, Howard C. Robbins, Frank O. Hall, Percy S. Grant, J. Howard Melish, Frank Mason North, Stephen S. Wise. (*Christian Work*, Vol. CII, No. 4 (January 27, 1917), p. 102.)

The moves on behalf of peace did not dampen the ardor of the preparedness wing, however. George Haven Putnam, still a vice-president of the New York Peace Society, and now president of the American Rights League, protested, in a speech delivered in the Mt. Morris Baptist Church, New York, against our slackness: "We ought to be helping England and France and Belgium now. They are fighting for civilization. It is our fight." [94] The League counted among its members Talcott Williams, Lyman Abbott, Agnes Repplier, Professor William Gardner Hale, Randolph H. McKim, and "other clear-headed, far-sighted, patriotic Americans." Their proclamation of February 12 preceded Congressional action: "The acts of war have been consummated. . . . It is no longer a question as to whether there shall be war with Germany. There is war with Germany." [95]

All of these patriotic organizations, clamoring for war, were ever assured of the assistance of some of the clergy as well as members of the peace societies. At this time Dr. McKim again analyzed the situation facing the nation. As far back as May, 1915, he had put the pacifists on the horns of the dilemma: "I do not hesitate to say if it [the "instinct" for self-defense] really were in conflict with the Christian religion we could not accept the Christian religion as a divine revelation." [96] A few months later he was convinced that "the name American citizen no longer commands the respect it once did." [97] By Thanksgiving, 1916, he was practically urging the United States to make war upon Germany.[98]

The hopes of the patriots were clearly approaching a realization when, on February 3, 1917, diplomatic relations were severed between the United States and Germany. Then the stock market immediately took a sharp turn upward, the bankers and brokers, according to some authorities, being for the war.[99] The break with Germany, due among other things, to the resumption of submarine warfare on the part of the Teutons, seems to have met with the approval of practically all of the clergy, even of those who had been most peaceful. Pleas for universal military training were heard far and near.[100]

In anticipation of coming events, G. Ashton Oldham, rector of St. Luke's Episcopal Church, New York, held a big military service on February 4. The choir marched in behind an immense American flag. National airs were sung. Dr. Oldham is reported to have set the example of patriotic consecration: "I, for one, am ready to lay down my life if my country needs it, for the rights of humanity and what I believe to be the cause of God." [101]

The pacifists were now getting ready for their last stand. On the night of February 3, William Jennings Bryan, speaking to a crowd of five thousand or more in New York City, was cheered when he avowed that the United States would not "get down and wallow in the mire of human blood." [102] Out of this meeting, the Emergency Peace Federation, sponsored by several peace organizations, took tangible form. In the next three months it raised over $76,000 for its work.[103] Its Keep-Us-Out-of-the-War Committee put on large meetings in New York City, some in connection with the Socialist-Labor Party.

In Washington, an Emergency Peace Federation Committee was formed, while in Chicago, long an active peace center under the inspiration of Jane Addams and Louis Lochner, the pacifists began to take steps calculated to prevent our engaging in war.

On February 12, a large delegation of pacifists encamped at Washington. Meetings were staged and conferences with Congressmen in between. David Lawrence wrote to the New York *Evening Post:* "Somehow, the pacifists got a better reception than their most enthusiastic followers have believed was possible in the national capital." [104]

Emergency Peace Federations sprang up in various cities from coast to coast. The clearing house for all peace societies at 70 Fifth Avenue, New York City, was sending out telegrams every night advising one hundred peace societies what to do the next day.

A group of peace workers in New York, under the chairmanship of Frederick Lynch, passed resolutions stating that the conference stood "unalterably against war . . . not only as a general principle, but in this present crisis as well." [105]

On April 2, the national capital became again the scene of mass meetings both for and against a declaration of war against Germany. The Emergency Peace Federation with three thousand pacifists in attendance from practically every state in the Union passed resolutions of loyalty but asked for a referendum before a declaration of war was made. The newspapers, in general, ridiculed the reluctance to wage war and attempted to discredit totally the benighted peace workers by publishing observations of reporters to the effect that most of the pacifists had queer looks and strong German accents. Two special trains of anti-pacifists had come down from New York, with a special delegation of ministers, all calculated to combat the evil influence of the peacemakers.

The efforts of the pacifist organizations tended to further the antagonism of the war element among the clergy. Dr. Eaton wanted to know "who are these people [of the Emergency Peace Federation] imposing on simple half-baked women, making their husbands hang their heads in shame?" [106] Malcolm J. MacLeod couldn't believe that if Jesus were living in the present he would be a pacifist: "I believe there are times when to be a pacifist is to be perilously near being a traitor." [107]

George A. Gordon of the Old South Church, Boston, achieved quite a reputation for his sermon, "Was Jesus a Pacifist?" In this he pointed out the absurdity of conferring such a label upon the Master.[108] Henry Winn Pinkham, minister to the Unitarian Church of Melrose, Massachusetts, asked Dr. Gordon, "Did Jesus kill anybody in order to redeem the world?" Pinkham continued:

> Somehow, it does not seem easy to conceive the Savior as the . . . inspirer, helper and friend of the soldier as he rushes to stick his bayonet into the guts of a brother man. . . . Somehow the Christian heart shudders—mine does at any rate, if not Dr. Gordon's—at the thought of Jesus clad in khaki, with a bomb in his hand, or turning the crank of a machine-gun to spatter wounds and death among his fellow men.[109]

Resolutions read at Tremont Temple, Boston, read:

> . . . we repudiate indignantly the utterances and criticisms of certain so-called pacifists, . . . who, whether consciously or unconsciously, acting in behalf of Kaiserism, are seeking by an insidious propaganda to divide American sentiment.

William Harman Van Allen, rector of the Parish of the Advent, Boston, after reading the resolutions, said that he had never done anything "more befitting a Christian on the Lord's Day." [110]

While the anti-war groups were concentrating their efforts to keep their country out of the European conflict, others, equally determined, were intent upon stirring up the war spirit of patriotism to push America in. The New York Federation of Churches issued an appeal on war, Sunday, March 11. The churches which responded approved of war by a vote of 158 to 52, and agreed

> that the President will be justified in recommending to Congress the most extreme measures, . . . and that it is our duty and that of all loyal citizens to tender immediately to the government all the service of which we severally and collectively are able.[111]

A statement sent out by Bishop Lawrence and widely endorsed made a "demand" that the President be ready for any emergency and "to lead the people to defend at all costs the integrity of the nation."[112]

The first week in March, the Massachusetts Clerical Association (Episcopalian) had already endorsed war.[113]

Isaac Massey Haldeman, who had been pastor of the First Baptist Church in New York since 1884, and leader among the pre-millenarians, expressed deep regret over the country's lack of military preparations:

> Today, as a nation, we are shamelessly and criminally unprepared; and, if tomorrow our sons, our brothers and the splendid youth of America should be called to war, they would be sent forth as sheep to the slaughter; nor will history forgive or forget the crime of it.[114]

The governor of Connecticut, active in the work of the Baptist Church, took it for granted that the church was now the loyal servant of the state and requested the churches "to gather a census of the State's war material in men."[115]

On the day before the declaration of war, Cardinal Gibbons, who had changed his viewpoint considerably since 1915, now prayed for the success of our arms as well as peace and advised:

> Above all else we must be loyal to our country. . . . There should be no hesitancy on the part of able-bodied men in answering the call that has gone forth to man the ships that protect our shores. I hope Catholic young men will step up and take their places in the front ranks. They should obey whatever our Congress decides is for the good of the country.[116]

S. Parkes Cadman, who had long been branding the acts of the Kaiser as those of "a devil incarnate," was asked at one of his meetings at the Bedford Y. M. C. A. what should be done when Ambassador James W. Gerard returned from Germany. "Prepare! Prepare! Prepare!"[117] he shouted. Now when war was declared he was endorsing one of the doctrines of Mohammed by saying, according to the New York *Times,* "If a man dies in battle giving God glory and in the service of his country, he dies well."[118]

While it is evident that a considerable number of the clergy were ready for the young men of this country to shoulder muskets on April 6, the day that Congress declared war, a good-sized minority were not immediately prepared to accept the dogma, *Vox populi, vox dei.*

Among the people at large there were indications of lack of enthusiasm for the war. John Kenneth Turner in his *Shall It Be Again?* states that the majority of the people in America were against war at that time. If a popular referendum had been submitted the chances are that it would have been voted down in April, 1917.

To summarize the preparedness era, it may well be said that America, idealistic and comfortably naive in 1914, was called upon overnight to grow up and render a balanced judgment upon events of diplomacy and war completely beyond her grasp or power to understand. In an attempt to place responsibility for the European conflagration, she, of necessity, had to weigh and sift an overwhelming mass of the most confusing kind of evidence, and was subjected to no little annoyance in the bargain.

In this national experience there were various reactions on the part of both groups and leading personalities, varying from the utmost alarm and call to arms to a flight from the reality of the war itself. Yet it can be said that the various forces at work in those years had prepared the minds of the American people, even though they were somewhat reluctant, to what seemed to be the inevitable.

The cumulative effect of all the stimuli could no longer be resisted. The power of propaganda, the economic interests linked up with the security leagues and the defense societies which led in the fight for an increased armament, the influence of the geographical location on the preparedness movement, the effect of the sinking of the *Lusitania* and other vessels, the atrocity stories, the Zimmermann note and the renewal of Germany's submarine warfare, the tremendous influence of leaders with national prestige like Roosevelt, Taft, Eliot, Root—all of these and other pressures could not be withstood forever. In addition to the effect of all this on the churches and their leaders, institutionalized religion made its contribution both for war and for peace and thus added to the sum total of the stimuli to which the citizens of the United States were subjected and obliged to react from August, 1914, to April, 1917.

Fundamentally, however, the outcome of those two and one-half years was decided by the forces of propaganda, including, of course, the control of the sources and the agencies for the dissemination of news. Ultimately public opinion was controlled by the press. That the Allied propaganda proved to be the most effective was in the main due to the common cultural heritage, a common language and literature, of the English and the majority of the American people.

In such exciting times the critical powers are held in abeyance. The appeal is to sentiments and powerful emotions and not to cold logic. Since "words and visible symbols are the most powerful instruments of suggestion in human behavior,"[119] the leaders were shrewd enough to use words and phrases, pictures, flags and other paraphernalia that appealed to emotional attitudes, thus bringing about the desired modes of behavior.

Boys on the farms of Iowa and Kansas, who had never been within a thousand miles of the ocean, were soon ready and eager to fight even for the freedom of the seas, because the phrase was associated with our early American naval tradition, particularly the War of 1812.

CHAPTER III
THE HOLY WAR

IDEALISM

"It is neither a travesty nor exaggeration to call this war on the part of America, a truly Holy War."
>HENRY CHURCHILL KING,
>*President, Oberlin College.*

President Wilson and the Moral Aims of the War, (edited by Frederick Lynch) p. 71.

"The man who is disloyal to the flag is disloyal to Christianity; the State must be obeyed under pain of incurring the guilt of mutiny against God."
>JOHN E. WICKHAM,
>*Superior of the New York Apostolic Fathers.*

New York *Times*, Dec. 3, 1917.

"We must keep the flag and the Cross together, for they are both working for the same ends."
>JAMES I. VANCE, *Minister,*
>*The First Presbyterian Church, Nashville, Tennessee.*

The Christian Century, Sept. 20, 1917.

REALISM

The Instruction of Junior Officers

"We've got to teach these men to be mean, they must look mean, act mean, because they are going against a dirty enemy, an enemy that recognizes no sportsmanship, but who uses every means in his power to kill —in order to combat that spirit we've got to make our men just a little bit more proficient in the art of killing than they are, we've got to put the spirit of kill in our men, and so put the fear of Christ in the Germans. . . ."
>REGINALD BARLOW,
>*Major 302nd Infantry, Camp Devens, Mass., Sept. 28, 1917.*

Quoted in *The Outook,* Oct. 10, 1917.

CHAPTER III
THE HOLY WAR

THE CALL TO THE COLORS

IMMEDIATELY following the severance of diplomatic relations with Germany, with the sending home of Count Von Bernstorff, the churches held patriotic services, passed resolutions promising to support the President to the limit. Many urged war at once. By the time Congress got around to carrying out these desires, one looks in vain for protests. All the church organizations and nationalistic groups vied with each other in flowery resolutions of patriotism—the Jews, the Catholics, the Protestants, the various Irish, German, Lutheran societies and the Mormons.

The Methodists of New England, assembled, pledged themselves "and all that we have—our fortunes, our lives, our prayers, and our sacred honor—to the cause of our country, in this, her critical hour of peril and need,"[1] while the presidents of three Lutheran bodies* sent out a call to the members to prove their loyalty to the President and Congress.[2]

George Richmond Grose, Methodist clergyman and president of DePauw University, gave advice to the students to "Keep cool, do the duty nearest at hand." Five companies of men were in training on the campus. "The administration and faculty . . . have backed enthusiastically all enlistments."[3] It should be noted, however, that DePauw retained its Department of German with full teaching staff during the war.

As an indication of the immediate effect of the call to the colors on the representatives of Christendom, consider events in a metropolis far removed from the Atlantic coast, Salt Lake City, Utah, on the eve of the declaration of war. It is to be

---

* Less than a month before our entrance into the war, Charles F. Oehler, president of the Evangelical Lutheran Synod of California, wrote: ". . . England, so history teaches us, loves no country but England. English militarism exceeds the militarism of any other two countries, and it indeed fights the militarism of other nations now in this present World War for the sole purpose of coming out of this struggle the undisputed ruler of the earth, on the Continent and on the seas. . . .

"It would be a great pity and the greatest mistake America has ever made if our great Republic would lend its aid and give its money, means and blood to aid a foreign power in the accomplishing of its own selfish purposes." (Letter to the *Survey*, Vol. 37, No. 23 (March 10, 1917), p. 675.)

remembered that the Mormon city had remained comparatively unaffected by the preparedness sentiment. Yet, on April 1, a majority of the churches were presented with handsome new silk American flags, which were used in appropriate flag-raising services. The rector of St. Paul's Episcopal Church announced:

> The church will be loyal, not only by word from the pulpit, but in the sending forth of her sons as in past days, a sacrifice upon the altar of the nation, if occasion demands. . . . Patriotism may be an old-fashioned sentiment; nevertheless, the three greatest words in our language are God and Home and Country.[4]

P. A. Simpkin, of the Phillips Congregational Church, believed that the Christian church had the duty "of preaching the sacred obligation of national love and sacrifice, for patriotism is a part of religion. . . . It is an hour in which to urge on youth its duty."[5] E. J. Magor, of the Iliff Methodist Episcopal Church, was assured that a call to arms might be the command of Christ.[6] The other members of the cloth were soon expressing the same mystical idea. The Baptists under the leadership of C. B. Allen heard that they were "fighting this enemy of the world, and when the smoke of battle lifts I doubt not we shall see that God has called us to the throne for such an hour as this."[7] The Central Christian Church heard words of praise and comfort by its pastor, Chester A. Snyder, on "The Militant Mother." "One great sacrifice of the day," the preacher reminded them, "was the surrendering by those mothers of their sons to fight for humanity under the Stars and the Stripes."[8]

The eighty-seventh Annual Conference of the Latter-Day Saints, in session when war was declared, and appraised as "the most impressive conference ever held," listened to avowals of loyalty by the leaders. Elder Stephen L. Richards affirmed:

> There is no more loyal people to the government of the United States than the Church of Jesus Christ of the Latter-Day Saints. . . . There should be no more loyal people from border to border of the United States and in all its possessions than are the members of the Church of Jesus Christ of the Latter-Day Saints.[9]

Elder Jack spoke to the mothers: "When we fight we fight to conquer; and let me say to these mothers whose sons may have to go to war, when we fight we will conquer by the power of God."[10]

THE INTELLECTUALS

When a nation in modern times engages in war it cannot hope to succeed without the backing of the great majority of the common people, and particularly necessary is it to have the support of the intellectuals.

What is more, the rise of the spirit of nationalism has so completely transcended all other psychic stimulations that any nation may now rest secure in the experience that it can always count on the citizens, high and low, to support its warfare. This thesis, as far as the upper classes and leaders are concerned, is well maintained by Julien Benda in what he calls *La Trahison des Clercs* (*The Treason of the Intellectuals*). The intellectuals, having lost the tradition of the love of abstract truth and justice, have descended to the marketplace and become absorbed in "political passions," despising those who are freed from popular impulses.[11] That is what happened in every country engaged in the World War. The *clercs* gave the war its passionate spiritual significance and drive. As in England, the liberals in the United States led the procession in manufacturing slogans for the war and providing the philosophy of history. Woodrow Wilson, outshining them all in preaching and exhortation, furnished the key for placing the war on a holy plane—to make the world safe for democracy.

The New Republic, always pro-British, while deploring the hatred, welcomed the war with outstretched arms: "Participation by the United States in the war will have one result in which all good Americans can rejoice without misgivings. It will help enormously to remove misunderstanding between the Canadian and the American nations and to lay an indispensable foundation for their future cooperation." Canada would have been ashamed of us, according to the editor, if we had not entered the war.[12] That attitude was quite typical of the liberal group in this country, with a few exceptions, of course.

Randolph Bourne, grieved over the "intellectual strabismus" of John Dewey,[13] wrote:

> They [the intellectuals] are now completely asserting that it was they who effectively willed the war against the dim perceptions of the American democratic masses. A war deliberately by the intellectuals! A calm moral verdict arrived at after a penetrating study of inexorable facts.[14]

Under the direction of George Creel, the Committee on Public Information took charge of propaganda, ably supported by the liberals. Learned historians, economists, sociologists, and philosophers succumbed to what Charles A. Beard has called "The Story for Babes"—the Allied propaganda or mythology of Entente righteousness and virtue against Germanic diabolism, with all the falsification of history to support this legend. So convinced were these professors that they turned out hundreds of pamphlets and articles for George Creel and the Security Leagues for the purpose of educating the masses to the Allied point of view.[15]

While this analysis is concerned primarily with the churches and the clergy, it is to be remembered that other groups and individuals were affected as deeply by the *Zeitgeist*. If the most noted social scientists, who had spent all their days in scholarly research and in critical analysis and judgment of world events, lost possession of their reasoning faculties, it is not surprising that the most intelligent of the clergy, as well as the lesser lights, did likewise.

In fact, cold intelligence seems to have had relatively little chance in those days. People were guided by their emotional reactions and those were basically the same for all men. Radicals, liberals, conservatives, atheists, infidels, agnostics, advanced theologians, modernists, and fundamentalists, all alike were swept off their feet by the mass movement. The war was heartily endorsed and scriptural reasons furnished by representatives of such extreme points of view as Isaac Haldeman and Frank M. Goodchild, premillenarians and defenders of the faith on the one hand, and such heretics within the Baptist fold as Dean Shailer Mathews of the Divinity School of the University of Chicago, and Harry Emerson Fosdick of the Union Theological Seminary, New York, on the other.

What happened to the pacifists who were so opposed to war in the preparedness era? Most of them also succumbed. Rabbi Stephen S. Wise, who had scolded the war-like clergy and called the preparedness movement "unchristian," now lost his detachment and led in the cry for the "slaughter of the Boche." In his estimation the Germans should be made to pay to the uttermost farthing.[16] Frank Oliver Hall who had "preached for peace and worked for peace for thirty years" was soon calling for a fight to the finish and asking men and women to serve their country "to the last penny in their purses and the last drop of blood in their veins."[17]

Frederick Lynch, one of the founders of the Church Peace Union, and editor of *Christian Work*, was one of the most ardent peace men in America, if not in the world. In 1915 he had recommended the "excommunication" of "every man that takes up the sword."[18] He worked against our entrance into the war up to the very last. But once in the fray he was calling the Germans "Huns" and "baby-killers" with gusto.[19] The president of the

Church Peace Union, Bishop David Hummell Greer of the Cathedral of St. John the Divine, New York, after some mental and spiritual struggle, came around to thanking God for the two great nations, England and America, "standing hand in hand, shoulder to shoulder in the great crusade against tyranny and aggression."[20]

There were scores of other notables who became converted in various degrees to the "holy war" aims of the Allies. Dr. Lynch said that out of his wide acquaintance with peace men he could think of "hardly a dozen out of hundreds" who were not loyally supporting the war.[21] A list of the converts would include Charles E. Jefferson, Robert E. Speer, John R. Mott, Howard A. Bridgman, editor of *The Congregationalist*, J. Howard Melish, Charles F. Aked, Charles W. Wendte, Bishop Benjamin Brewster of Maine, Rabbi Louis L. Mann, Algernon Crapsey, and Frank Crane. Both William Jennings Bryan and Clarence Darrow had been pacifists but during the war period each came out wholeheartedly for the fight to the finish. Their speeches sound so much alike that for all practical purposes they are interchangeable.[22]

THEOLOGY FOR WAR TIME

How did the molders of religious opinions in the churches justify our entrance into the war? This question has been answered in part, for, as we have seen, the process of rationalization of the struggle in terms of light versus darkness, virtue versus sin, humanity versus autocracy, civilization versus chaos and God versus the devil had been going on in many a pulpit for at least two years prior to April, 1917. The legend of the "holy war," concocted in England, had grown to be almost universally accepted by the idealists in the churches over here. America had now entered the holy crusade on the side of the Allies. Nothing was more natural than for Randolph H. McKim to proclaim from his pulpit in Washington that

> It is God who has summoned us to this war. It is his war we are fighting. . . . This conflict is indeed a crusade. The greatest in history—the holiest. It is in the profoundest and truest sense a Holy War. . . . Yes, it is Christ, the King of Righteousness, who calls us to grapple in deadly strife with this unholy and blasphemous power [Germany].[23]

On the eve of the declaration of war William E. Barton, famous Lincolniana scholar, preached to his congregation in the First Congregational Church, Oak Park, Illinois, on "The Heritage of Humanity." After quoting from German works he announced:

> I place here on the pulpit these four books, Treitschke, Nietzsche, Bernhardi, Clausewitz. . . . I say deliberately that the great question now to be settled in the present war is whether the future is to be dominated by the ideals of these four books, or this other one, the Holy Bible, the Gospel of Jesus Christ.[24]

Since America, in common with the Allies, was fighting a "defensive war," with no desire for territorial reward (the secret treaties came to light later), it was relatively easy to raise the discussion to a high ethical plane, and rationalize to the limit of one's ability.

This psychological phenomenon has been well expressed by Professor Harold Lasswell:

> The churches of practically every description can be relied upon to bless a popular war, and to see in it an opportunity for the triumph of whatever godly design they choose to further. Some care must, of course, be exercised to facilitate the transition from the condemnation of wars in general, which is a traditional attitude on the part of the Christian sects, to the praise of a particular war. This may be expedited by securing suitable interpretations of the war very early in the conflict by conspicuous clericals; the lesser lights twinkle after.[25]

Having had the advantages of the "suitable interpretations" already provided by the British intellectuals and clergy, together with much reflection and discussion in this country about the war in the thirty-two months prior to our entrance, the leaders now set to work to provide the philosophical basis and theological interpretation of the war to the minutest detail.

It was clear that Germany had willed and deliberately started the war. She had been eagerly waiting and praying for *Der Tag* for about half a century. The writings of Bernhardi and others proved her utter contempt for the other nations and the brutal nature of her people. Consistent with her ideals of fifty years she had invaded Belgium, committed unmentionable atrocities and violated without shame every principle of civilization.

But civilization was the creation and the expression of Christianity. The destruction of one meant the annihilation of the other. Since civilization now hung in the balance, Christianity was thereby fighting for her life. God would not stand by and countenance such a catastrophe. America had been chosen as his loyal servant to take the leading part in punishing the ruthless Germans and to save Christianity. Thus with such a divine calling victory would be ours. The fight for righteousness, justice, liberty and to make the world safe for democracy simply meant defending the principles for which Christ himself had died. Hence the war itself was a holy war to promote the Kingdom of God upon earth. To give one's life for his country was to give it for God and His Kingdom. God and country became synonymous.

Joseph Fort Newton, leaving the Church of the Divine Paternity, New York, to accept the call from the City Temple, London, had carried with him an American flag presented in an appropriate farewell service by Frank Oliver Hall to "entwine it with the British." Dr. Newton, theologian and mystic, expressed his convictions:

> Think it all through, and at bottom, the war is religious. If our enemies are right, our religion is wrong, our faith a fiction, our philosophy false—yes, justice a dream, and righteousness a delusion. Then might is right, the battle is to the strongest and the race to the swiftest, and the more ruthless and unscrupulous we are the better. By the same token, if our religion is right, if God is a reality, and the order of the world is moral, our enemies are wrong! The very stars in their courses are against them. . . .[26]

Samuel McCrea Cavert, assistant secretary of the General War-Time Commission of the Churches, saw in America's participation in the war a profound "missionary enterprise as the moral equivalent of war."

> In the last analysis the ultimate issues of the war are moral and religious. It is simply to say that we are in the war because we believe that thereby we are somehow serving God—taking a step in the direction of a society that is more in accord with his will and the spirit and principles of Jesus Christ. For, whatever may have been the origins of the war, it is rapidly becoming clearer every day that it is now developed into a conflict between forces that make for the coming of the Kingdom of God and forces that oppose it. Hence when as Christians we give our support to the cause now presented by the war, we are simply doing, in a restricted way, a small part of what as "good soldiers of Jesus Christ" we are all the while aiming to do.[27]

James A. Francis (Baptist) of California put it succinctly, "I look upon the enlistment of an American soldier as I do on the departure of a missionary for Burma."[28]

In a full-page appeal for missionary funds the prudential committee and officers of the American Board of the Congregationalists declared the aims of the war and those which the American Board held for a century were quite identical, that "our soldiers and sailors are preparing 'The Way of the Lord.' They are 'making straight in the desert the highway for our God.' . . . *We Must Win the War to Win the World.*"[29]

William B. Meyers, at the Park and Down Congregational Church, Wollaston, Massachusetts, had predicted in October, 1914, that we would be inevitably drawn into the conflict on the side of the Allies, and now "if we have sinned," said Dr. Meyers, "it is in not going in sooner." As for the use of force, after all, "between the sword and sermon is only a matter of degree, and one can be as redemptive as the other."[30]

Another contribution came through the pen of Bishop Charles H. Brent of the Philippines, who, having just returned from the French battlefront in May, 1917, believed that on the fate of France "depended the fate of the world." The Bishop thus described the issue: "We are fighting for the rights of personality. . . . In the old days wars were fought for territory, and, in so far as they were thus fought they placed property above human life. . . . This is very far from being a 'capitalistic war.' It is a war of the plain people."[31]

The announcement came from Frank Mason North, president of the Federal Council of the Churches of Christ in America, that ". . . the stir of the breath of God is upon the common people of the world. . . . The war for righteousness will be won! Let the Church do her part."[32]

Moreover, to the clerical mind, in a righteous war, the chances of the enemy's winning are nil. God himself would never permit it. "Germany cannot succeed. Do you know why?" asked George R. Van de Water. "Because there is a God in the Heavens. And there is truth waiting in the world for triumph."[33] As Isaac J. Lansing phrased it, "beyond all doubt our pure motives and purposes have received upon them the divine sanction. God could not express himself in antagonism to what we are doing."[34]

Yet, at the same time, it will be remembered, the Kaiser and the German people were accused of blasphemy because of their boasted familiarity with God as expressed in the phrases, *Me und Gott* and *Gott mit uns.*

Among all peoples, no matter how far advanced in civilization or religious thought, in time of great social upheaval, like a war, God takes on added importance. His blessing is asked upon every enterprise and soon He is blessing every activity. The Christian, while repudiating the doctrine of henotheism, always conceives of God as being on his side and in time of war he, of course, cannot imagine that Jehovah would listen to the prayers of the unrepentant enemy. The Germans and the Allies were alike in this respect. Each side believed it had the monopoly on God and emphasized the usual spiritual interpretation of history—the Chosen People, with a divine destiny being carried out under the ægis of the Almighty.

When *The New Republic,* though thoroughly patriotic, had suggested that God had nothing to do with the conflagration, this frank refusal to accept the theory of the divine calling of the nation and the spiritual significance of battle met with rebukes. Bernard Iddings Bell, socialist and popular college preacher, dean of St. Paul's Cathedral Church, Fond du Lac, Wisconsin, aide to the Senior Chaplain, Great Lakes Naval Training Station, now warden of St. Stephen's College, Annandale-on-the-Hudson, answered *The New Republic*:

> This article is written in the certainty that God, the Almighty, the Eternal, the Triune, whom we Christians worship as revealed to the whole world in the Incarnation of the Son, the God-Man, is the most powerful, the most active, and the most important of all who are influencing the war. . . . He is delaying victory to either side in the deadlock until men shall comprehend that the war is being waged between spiritual principles and vital philosophies rather than between mere armed forces. This He is doing until men shall be ready for such a victory as is won by humble hearts and souls lifted up to Him, to His everlasting laws, to His divine love.[35]

In the doctrine that God was in the struggle of the nations, there was the inseparable corollary that Jesus Christ as His only begotten Son must also be present. In this assurance, Bishop Edwin Holt Hughes, of the Methodist Episcopal Church, concurred: "God pity us if we are not going to have God's Son in this war! . . . God's Son must be with our young men or there is not much hope for them. We are agents of God, and we are charged with the duty of keeping the sons of our homes in the war in the comradeship of the Son of God."[36]

Another Methodist bishop, Luther B. Wilson, a trustee of the Church Peace Union, wrote that "German autocracy was seeking to drive its dagger into the heart of the world's democracy," and urged that men and women fall in line and make a forward march singing, "As He died to make men holy let us die to make men free!"[37]

In this Crusade against the powers of darkness, it was necessary to convince the mothers and fathers who were making a sacrifice that they were not offering up their sons to Baal. So, it was reasoned, the soldiers, in fighting, found salvation itself. "They who offer up their lives for a high ideal of justice and humanity walk side by side with the world's Savior and King," assured Ernest M. Stires of St. Thomas's Church, New York. Moreover, he argued, their training as troops is but

> the preparation for the higher level to which they will climb on the consecrated fields of France, where the baptism of fire will cleanse and inspire. This is no dream of a visionary. . . . The calm judgment of reasonable leaders declares that invaluable results have already been gained, and that vastly greater results are not far away.
> They will find God. They will discover their souls.[38]

For Dr. Stires the war made soldiers Christian in a way that all the preaching of nearly two thousand years had failed to accomplish. The historian, he believed, would record when the war ended, "the very faces of the victorious soldiers were ennobled by the beauty of the ideals for which they fought." [39]

Roosevelt had said, in the summer of 1915, "A mother who is not willing to raise her boy to be a soldier, is not fit for citizenship."[40] Abraham Mitrie Rihbany, of the Unitarian Fellowship, placed the matter on a higher plane: "I want every American mother who has a son at the front to feel that the precious gift she has given to the nation has been offered not upon the altar of Moloch but upon the altar of Christ and of the sacred duty which every man owes to mankind."[41]

William L. Stidger, pastor of the First Methodist Episcopal Church of San Jose, California, truck driver for the Y. M. C. A. in France, furnished the results of his observations in a book (put together in forty-eight hours), *Soldier Silhouettes,* written for "but one object . . . to give the father and mother, the brother and sister, the wife and child and friend of the boys 'over there' an accurate heart picture." "No boy," wrote Dr. Stidger, "goes through the hell of fire and suffering and wounds that he does not come out newborn. The old man is gone from him, and a new man is born in him. That is the great eternal compensation of war and suffering."[42]

The dogma that life in the trenches produced a glorious revival in the lives of the boys was a popular theme with the ministers back home as well as those who sent back reports from the front. The idealistic books of Coningsby Dawson (*The Glory of the Trenches*), Thomas Tiplady (*Soul of the Soldier*), Donald

Hankey (*A Student in Arms*), et al., popularized this conception, since these men were fighters and were thought to know what they were talking about. Some ministers and lecturers specialized in the subject of the "Religion of the Trenches." John Kelman, pastor of the St. George's United Free Church, Edinburgh, Scotland, visited America during the war, delivered the Lyman Beecher lectures on preaching at Yale, and convinced thousands of the heights of spiritual living in the muck and mire of the fields of Flanders. "It is for us to interpret to them [the soldiers] the meaning of their own experience," quoth the preacher. "Without knowing it, they are bearing in their bodies the marks of the Lord Jesus."[43]

Catholics, too, were certain of their faith. After collecting volumes of statistics on the subject it could be stated, "not one clear case appears in all the reports and letters in which a Catholic soldier has been unsettled in his belief in God by the war." In fact the Catholic boys were "not puzzled as non-Catholics are by God's allowing war."[44] Their faith had been increased and not diminished by the war, both American and British chaplains testified to that.

Confronted with the necessity of every Sunday facing a congregation composed of Christians, spiritually troubled and anxious about not only the physical well-being but the spiritual aspects of the lives of their sons, ministers were under compulsion to reenforce the hopes and faith of the fathers and mothers, the brothers and sisters, wives and sweethearts. What else could they have preached other than that the boys in the trenches had found God? To have remained silent or to have pointed out the spiritually devastating effect of warfare would have cost them their leadership and their jobs. The churches demanded ministers who gave comfort and dogmatic assurance, and they received it, for clergy and laity alike could not continue to believe in the orthodox God and face reality—the possibility of their sons going to war for a holy cause and losing their faith in God on the way. The psychological factors at work were, of course, extremely powerful. The churches and the Y. M. C. A., the Catholic and Jewish organizations sensed this great spiritual need and tried to meet it.

Dr. Fosdick, in view of the anxiety, pictured the splendid spiritual leadership of the American troops, and, concerning General Pershing and his associates, said: "No army in the history of the world ever went out under such a company of Christian gentlemen as ours."[45]

In order to bolster up the faith of the boys at the front,

various societies published tracts and manuals of devotion. The American Tract Society published a *Manual of Devotion for Soldiers and Sailors,* written by Judson Swift, with an introduction by Theodore Roosevelt.

The soldier was taught to say: "Surely I have a right to be proud, and I am proud, to love my country and to thank God that He made me a citizen of the greatest nation upon the earth. . . ." Then he learned that he would rather die in the service of his country than "to possess all the gold that the world holds." Before going into the "storm and hail of shot and shell" the youth was taught to pray to Jehovah: "My God and Father, I rejoice that Thou art the God of battles, and that Thou hast ever been a defender of Thy people. . . ." After the victory, the gallant warrior was instructed to give thanks: "Thy right hand is become glorious in power. Thy right hand hath dashed in pieces the enemy. . . . Grant us strength to go forward and continue to us Thy blessed protection and deliverance." For the sailors and marines an equally appropriate prayer was provided: "Keep our ship in safety, and give victory to our fleet over the enemy. . . ."

In the event of being taken prisoner, the unfortunate Christian warrior might repeat:

> Deliver me from cruel and unhuman treatment. Give my captors a better mind and a better heart. Grant me, I beseech Thee, wisdom and strength and courage, that I may meet without fear whatever awaits me, . . . open the prison door and proclaim liberty for the captives and evermore will I praise Thee through Christ my Redeemer.[46]

To ask men to enlist in a "holy war" meant that the interpreters of the mind of Christ had to convince their followers that Jesus was not a pacifist, that he approved of the war and that he would fight himself, if he were here upon earth.

There were theologians who justified the Crusade but tried not to lean too heavily upon Jesus for Scriptural support. Dr. Fosdick, for instance, frankly said:

> The Master never faced in his own experience . . . a national problem such as Belgium met when the Prussians crossed the border. . . . The fact is that Jesus did not directly face our modern questions about war; they were not his problems, and to press a legalistic interpretation of special texts, as though they were, is a misuse of the gospel.[47]

Nevertheless, Dr. Fosdick proceeded to show how angry Jesus became on certain occasions, and was practically certain that he would support the Allies.[48] Nearly a year after the Armistice he was saying, "I have no use for a man who has not, for four years now, been angry underneath."[49]

On the other hand, Dr. Henry Churchill King, the president of Oberlin College, escaped the dilemma by assigning to Jesus a unique mission which made

> certain particular courses proper for him that would not be proper for us, . . . and other courses not only proper but obligatory upon us that would not have been proper for him [such as works of reform]. At the same time these clear implications of his fundamental teaching it would not only be permissible but obligatory that his disciples should later undertake.
>
> It is clear from this point of view, therefore, why we cannot conceive of Jesus as a soldier or military commander. As Dr. George Adam Smith has pointed out, we should have like difficulty in conceiving him in many callings in which his disciples are rightfully engaged.[50]

In contrast to Dr. King's point of view—placing Jesus outside the realm of battle, or, as in the case of Dr. Fosdick, refusing to use the proof-text method (but using it indirectly), most of the theologians had no difficulty whatsoever in placing Jesus in the very forefront of the thickest fighting leading his troops on to victory.

Was Jesus a pacifist? In answer to that critical question J. Wesley Johnston, of the John Street Methodist Episcopal Church, New York, affirmed: "Christ was the greatest fighter the world has ever seen." He was "the Lion of the Tribe of Judah," and "surely every believer in Christ . . . will unsheathe his sword and gladly give his life . . . to help win the fight against the forces of cruelty, abomination and hell."[51]

Edward Leigh Pell, of Richmond, Virginia, wrote: "We will fight pacifism not only because it is contrary to the teachings of Christ, but because its whole tendency is to make a yellow streak where you want a man." "Jesus was just as truly a fighter as Moses, Joshua, David, Washington, Lee or the fighting parsons of the gold-fever days in the far West." "The fact that Jesus never used it [physical force] proves nothing except that he never needed it . . . he had higher forces."

Dr. Pell then related a typical story, apparently calculated to move his hearers to action. It is about the wife of one Jones, alone on a stormy night with a brutal gang of ruffians attacking the house. A rescue party dashes to save her:

For the love of God—quick! Fire!

Heavens! the brute has caught her in his arms. Shoot through that window! Quick! For the love of God—quick!

It is all over. There is blood on the bed. There is blood on our hands. There is blood everywhere.

There are three men lying dead on the floor. Horror of horrors! And we are Christians!

Yes, we are Christians! And we have done our duty. We have laid pretty Jones' wife [sic] upon her bed, for she has fainted. . . . And there is not a trace of hate or vengeance in our hearts. "Praise the Lord," says Wilkins, who is a Methodist. "I feel like singing the doxology," whispers Watson devoutly. . . . "Amen!" say we all.[52]

This parable proved that Christians should wage righteous warfare to kill the Germans, the thugs about to rape civilization as they had ravaged Belgium.

There were, of course, plenty of texts and incidents to support the view that Christ could be a mighty warrior. There was the driving out of the money-changers. There was the injunction, "Render unto Cæsar, the things that are Cæsar's." Furthermore, since Jesus of Nazareth had never come out with his opinion about war as had General Sherman, his very silence seemed to give consent.

But the texts that were being used by the pacifists to justify their position had either to be proved spurious or shown to have been misinterpreted. This task of explaining away the favorite pacifist texts of the New Testament turned out to be simply a matter of exegesis. A text, for instance, that presented difficulties was the command to turn the other cheek. Dr. Pell insisted Jesus "could not have meant it literally, for the Master always practiced what he preached and you know he never turned the other cheek."[53]

Dr. Rihbany, who had come to this country from Syria, the land of his birth, with but nine cents in his pocket with which to start his career in America, prided himself, because of his Oriental birth and background, upon understanding the mind of Christ. He explained that the so-called pacifistic utterances of Jesus about turning the other cheek were not to be taken literally for "the letter killeth." At the time of the trial when the officer struck him, Jesus did not remain silent. *"Jesus did not turn the other cheek to the brutish smiter*: he *protested* against the injustice and his protest is one of our noblest assets" (John 18:22). (Italics in the original.)[54]

On the other hand, when Jesus was spat upon by the mob (Matt. 27:3), he offered no protest since it could not have availed anything to have remonstrated.

> Nor could one reasonably expect a person like Jesus turning upon a mad mob and engaging in a fist fight. We could not imagine even men who waged great wars, as Pericles, Marcus Aurelius and Abraham Lincoln, doing such a thing. So Jesus stood in sublime and dignified silence before his assailants.[55]

Jesus was "no anarchist," warned Lyman Abbott in explaining why Jesus told Peter to put up his sword in the Garden of Gethsemane. "By this rebuke of Peter he sanctioned the right of the police officers to use force in the execution of the law." And, by inference, the right of the Allies to force Germany, the criminal, to obey international law.[56]

Dr. Rihbany harmonized all the conflicting texts to portray Jesus as favoring the use of the sword. He claimed that the utterance of Jesus, "They that take the sword shall perish with the sword" (Matt. 26:52), was "seized upon by the pacifists to convert America to pacifism with the authority of Christ." But the pacifist exegesis of the text was incorrect, for "in these words Jesus speaks of the eternal law of retribution, and plainly justifies the taking of the sword against those who would use it in wars of aggression. . . . By taking up arms against those who would subdue . . . other peoples by the sword, America is proving the truth of this Scriptural saying."[57]

A prominent Methodist clergyman, Lynn Harold Hough, professor at Garrett Biblical Institute, and after the war president of Northwestern University, wrote a book entitled *The Clean Sword*. In this treatise the author sought to prove "the Bible is not pacifistic literature,"[58] that the use of the sword for high ideals, such as the Allies exemplified, was a duty. "A sword defending order and law and virtue and civilization has a right to appeal to Him for approval and support. The author of the book of Revelation pictures Him with a two-edged sword in his mouth. . . ."[59]

Harold Bell Wright, one time clergyman in the Christian (Disciples) Church, specialist in themes dealing with Christianity in a modern setting, writing for the *American Magazine*, certified that: "a thirty-centimeter gun may voice the edict of God as truly as the notes of a cooing dove. . . . The sword of America is the sword of Jesus."[60]

W. Douglas Mackenzie, president of Hartford Theological

Seminary, after surveying the demands for righteousness in the teachings of Jesus, concluded that

> . . . nowhere has the Sermon on the Mount, the embodiment of the Spirit of Christ, exercised more visible and amazing power than in the matter of war.
> . . . this war, when carried by the Allies and America to the right issue, will be another proof of the divine power of the Sermon on the Mount.[61]

For Professor Ernest De Witt Burton, head of the Department of New Testament Literature and Interpretation in the Divinity School of the University of Chicago, the correct interpretation of our war aims lay in the meaning of the application of the Golden Rule:

> In particular we may contend that it is really in the interest of the German people that the German armies shall be defeated, and the people themselves released from the domination of those false ideals which have been industriously bred into them for forty years and more.
> For the sake of France . . . England . . . Europe and Asia and Africa, for the sake of the unborn generations of Americans, . . . it was for all these and in obedience to the Golden Rule itself that we went to war.[62]

Howard A. Bridgman, editor of *The Congregationalist,* agreed with Professor Burton in that if he "were a madman who had already killed helpless women and children," he should want himself to be killed before he did further harm. The German leaders, with all their "duplicity, inhumanity and lust for power," if they saw it as did Dr. Bridgman, "would be glad to have America enter the war against Germany."[63]

While these masters in the interpretation of the Holy Scriptures were listing the Sermon on the Mount among the great war documents, ministers were being jailed for quoting texts from it and taking portions of the New Testament too seriously. In Boston, when the Association to Abolish War decided to circulate the Sermon on the Mount in a printed pamphlet without comment, an agent of the Department of Justice warned against its distribution.[64]

Howbeit, in the estimation of many, if this religious classic were properly explained in the light of Jesus' full teaching, no difficulty need be experienced. In fact, it was Edward Increase Bosworth, Congregational minister and dean of Oberlin College, who decided that, while "to take life in hate is a dreadful deed," the taking of life in war might be Christian:

> The Christian soldier in friendship wounds the enemy. In friendship he kills the enemy. In friendship he receives the wound of the enemy. He keeps his friendly heart while the enemy is killing him. His heart never consigns the enemy to hell. He never hates. After he has wounded the enemy he hurries to his side at the earliest possible moment with all the friendly ministration possible . . . with an invincible hope that sometime . . . he and his enemy shall find common ground . . . in some great enterprise of God.[65]

CHRIST AND THE BAYONET

Though the majority of the clergy were probably reluctant to go as far as Dr. Bosworth and contend that one could pray for his enemy and show manifestation of love while in the act of throwing hand grenades, there were some who courageously attempted to face the issue. Take, for instance, the use of the one weapon of warfare which seemed more hideous and barbarous than all the others—the bayonet. To ignore its use Christians could not; defend it they ultimately must; glorify it they frequently did.

A Y. M. C. A. physical director, A. E. Marriott of Camp Sevier, supplied the soldiers with an "invaluable little manual" on *Hand-to-Hand Fighting*. The chief points of attack were minutely explained:

> Eyes. Never miss an opportunity to destroy the eyes of the enemy. In all head holds use the finger on the eyes. They are the most delicate points in the body and easy to reach. The eye can easily be removed with the finger.[66]

George W. Downs, speaking in the Asbury Methodist Episcopal Church in Pittsburgh, in November, 1917, regretted that he was not at the front. He explained how he felt about the matter. His "blood boiled" when he heard men say "their religion forbids the killing of men with guns and bayonets." He is also reported to have declared: "I would have gone over the top with other Americans, I would have driven my bayonet into the throat or the eye or the stomach of the Huns without the slightest hesitation and my conscience would not have bothered me in the least."[67]

According to the Boston *Herald*, Herbert S. Johnson,* pastor

---

* Graduate of the Army War College, 1923. (*Who's Who in America*.)

of the Warren Avenue Baptist Church of that city, likewise contributed to the education of the church people on the technique of bayoneting the enemy. Pointing to the location of his vital organs, he explained: "Three inches are not enough, seven inches are too many and twelve inches are more than too many, for while you are pulling out the bayonet you are losing the opportunity to drive it into another man five inches."[68]

Albert C. Dieffenbach, editor of *The Christian Register* (Unitarian), was proud of the part that Jesus would play in the war. In an editorial he wrote:

> As Christians, of course, we say Christ approves [of the war]. But would he fight and kill? . . . There is not an opportunity to deal death to the enemy that he would shirk from or delay in seizing! He would take bayonet and grenade and bomb and rifle and do the work of deadliness against that which is the most deadly enemy of his Father's kingdom in a thousand years. . . . That is the inexorable truth about Jesus Christ and this war; and we rejoice to say it.[69]

The American Peace Society also acknowledged the fitness of the bayonet. Through the official journal, *The Advocate of Peace,* the editor advised its use on benevolent and cultural grounds: "We [America] must help in the bayoneting of a normally decent German soldier in order to free him from a tyranny which he at present accepts as his chosen form of government."[70]

The ideal under these circumstances would have been the complete extermination of the German people to free them from the shackles of their form of government. This point of view, expressed or implied a thousand times in a variety of ways, was the same philosophy condemned in the Germans, namely, the forcibly imposing of one's own culture upon another people because of its avowed superiority.

Some timid souls back home objected to the use of the bayonet on the ground that it was demoralizing. But, contended John Kelman, "it does not brutalize," for "they [the soldiers], doing it under the fierce compulsion of a sense of duty, suffered no such deterioration. . . . It seems to be motive and not deed that counts in permanent moral consequences."[71] One gets the impression from reading the work of Dr. Kelman on *War and Preaching* that the danger of moral deterioration from the use of profanity was far greater than that which might come from the effect of killing one's fellows.

The testimony of chaplains and "Y" men corroborated the uneasiness soldiers felt at the thought of having to use the bayonet. Daniel A. Poling, overseas on special service, had taken note of it,[72] while James M. Stifler of the First Baptist Church, Evanston, Illinois, religious director for the "Y" at Camp Dodge, had witnessed the change that came over every company "after their first few lessons at bayonet practice."[73]

But the masterpiece of the defense of the Christian bayonet was published under the guidance of the Y. M. C. A. The process of reasoning that glorified all details of warfare and ascribed to them a high spiritual significance, with values in character building, reached its perfection in a book, *The Practice of Friendship*, by George Stewart, Jr., Lieutenant, Infantry, U. S. A., and Henry B. Wright, Camp Director of Religious Work, Army Y. M. C. A. Dr. Wright was a professor in the Yale Divinity School. "The American nation," wrote the authors, ". . . is engaged at this very hour in an attempt . . . to Christianize *every phase* of a righteous war waged to save the very life of democracy." (Italics mine.)[74] That they did not evade the issue of Christianizing every phase of the war may be understood from the following. It is an excellent example of the ability of the human mind under compulsion to reconcile contradictory ideas and rationalize them into a supposedly consistent working philosophy.

To the raw recruit "inevitably there comes a day of testing—a day when men's souls are tried as by fire—the first day of the bayonet drill, when men charge over the embankment and into a trench to drive their bayonets into straw dummies made to imitate human bodies with wooden frames inside to represent bones. . . ." Then:

> Sick at heart and haunted by uncertainty, your lad and my lad stand on the night of that initial experience at the parting of the ways of fatalism and faith. It was for just such an hour as this that you and I came to army camps. . . .
> But in the hour of soul crisis the Secretary can turn and say with quiet certainty to your lad and my lad, "I would not enter this work till I could see Jesus himself sighting down a gun barrel and running a bayonet through an enemy's body. At first I shrank from associating Jesus with the bayonet and essayed to place in His hands the sword the use of which He himself sanctioned. But soon I reflected that the sword, which is today only an article of adornment, was in His day the most terrible weapon of mutilation and destruction known and that the modern bayonet is no more dreadful an implement since it is simply the sword attached to the rifle. Then it was that I saw Heaven open and beheld One faithful and true. He was no longer mounted on a white horse, to be sure, nor arrayed in a white garment sprinkled with blood nor was

He armed with a sharp sword to smite. Rather I discerned through clouds of gas and smoke One on foot arrayed in a garb of olive drab which was stained with blood and mire, and in His hands a bayonet sword attached to a rifle. He asked no man to go where He would not go. He did not lead His men up to the painful and bloody tasks which are the climax of every battle charge, to disappear just as the disagreeable deed had to be done and thus shift the responsibility on others. He stood in the center of the line and the very front in the thickest of the fight and these quiet words of assurance from His lips put courage into every heart and strength into every arm of those in the hosts which followed Him, 'Lo I am with you alway, even unto the end'. . . ." I would not enter the war work till I was sure of this vision and heard these words. But with them came peace and power I had never known before.[75]

As to whether the minister should be expected to participate in the shedding of blood on the battlefield, which had been justified for the ordinary soldier, there were at least two conflicting points of view. Francis Greenwood Peabody of Harvard University, author of *Jesus Christ and the Social Question,* for instance, objected to the exemption of ministers and divinity students from the draft, pointing to the example of the French clergy in the battle line.[76] Julius Walter Atwood, Bishop of Arizona (Episcopal), supported the war but said he was thankful that "this country and the Church are one in the maintaining of the principle that those who serve at the altar must come there with clean hands on which there is no stain of blood."[77]

The Church and the State

In addition to the demands upon the clerical minds to bless the "holy war" and all the instruments of terror as but the necessities to carry out the will of God, a further problem presented itself in the reconciling of the separate functions of church and state.

In America, the boast among the Protestants that we had a complete separation of church and state, while a bit of pleasant fiction before the war, broke down completely after April, 1917. This fact, however, seems never to have been recognized, or admitted at least, by any of the various religious groups.

Those who defended the use of the church machinery for the carrying out of the will of the state thought of it as purely a voluntary performance. The church was not bowing to the will of the state but was of its own accord pledging its loyalty to the state to help the good fight in which the nation was involved.* God being on the side of the Allied army, American Christians, therefore, were, in reality, fighting God's battles—against Thor and Wodin.

There had been several methods and attempts at reconciling the obvious rivalry between the church and the state, the conflict between loyalty to Jesus and obedience to the nation. But of all ways the frank admission of the dual system of ethics, one for the state and another for the church, was abhorrent to American theologians. That the individual Christian and the Christian nation should have two standards of ethics or codes of morals had been proposed by several German philosophers as a way out of the admitted difficulty. Frederick Naumann, for example, unhesitatingly took that position. He was the son and the grandson of Lutheran pastors in Germany, and for many years a Lutheran minister himself, an authority on Mitteleuropa, and a member of the Reichstag. He was an enthusiastic admirer of Jesus. Yet, he confessed his inability to reconcile the religion of Jesus with the code of conduct required by the state. Because his point of view was so scorned by American ministers, who in practice accepted it, I give several paragraphs from his *Briefe über Religion:*

> The Gospel is one of the standards of our life, but not the only standard. Not our entire morality is rooted in the Gospel, but only a part of it. Besides the Gospel there are demands of power and right without which human society cannot exist. I myself, at least, do not know how to help myself in the conflict between Christianity and the other tasks of life save by the attempt to recognize the limits of Christianity. That is difficult, but it is better than the oppression of half truths which I have had to bear.

> The state rests upon entirely different impulses and instincts from those which are cultivated by Jesus. . . . All constructions which attempt to explain the state from brotherly love to our neighbor are, considered historically, so much empty talk. . . . The state forms part of the struggle for existence, a cuirass which grows out of the body of the tortoise, a set of teeth which the nation creates for itself, a compound of human wills, of soldiers and

---

* William E. Barton phrased the idea: "The German theory is of a state existing by divine right, and its will personified in the person of its sovereign wherein the individual must subordinate his conscience and obey. The American theory is that the state expresses the will and the conscience of a free and sovereign people. There are two irreconcilable principles." (Sermon, *The Moral Meanings of the War,* p. 8—a pamphlet.)

prisons. This compound is, in all its harshness, the prerequisite of culture. And it found its pattern form in Rome not in Nazareth.

How am I to say that Bismarck's preparations for the Schleswig-Holstein War were a service in the Kingdom of Jesus Christ? I cannot manage to do so. Yet, all the same, I admire these preparations. It does not occur to me to lament them. Not every doing of one's duty is Christian. Bismarck did his duty, for his avocation was the cultivation of power. But such a duty and its fulfilment are not directly an imitation of Christ.

Hence we do not consult Jesus, when we are concerned with things which belong to the domain of the construction of the state and of Political Economy.[78]

Such a philosophy as that held by Naumann was thoroughly repudiated by all the clergy in this country. Dr. Fosdick, looking back over the war period from the hillside of 1919, held this philosophy to be altogether reprehensible and responsible for German atrocities and wickedness.[79]

From the realistic approach, however, the only difference between Frederick Naumann and the average American prelate or theologian was this: The Prussian frankly admitted that he was unable to reconcile the "conflict between Christianity and the other tasks of life." The Americans, to whom dual ethics was inconceivable, upheld the preservation of their state as the highest good—since it embodied the defense of what they termed civilization and the preservation of Christianity in terms of righteousness, justice and freedom. The ethics of the state, therefore, were the necessities of the hour. The end ("to make the world safe for democracy") justified the means. It was the "war to end war." Every vital design and act of the United States government at war was called Christian. Acts of devotion and loyalty to the country were the highest expression of the Christlike life. Hence, the ethics of Jesus became the ethics of the state.

"We are fighting not only for our country, and for the democracy . . . of the world, . . . but for the Kingdom of God," said George F. Pentecost, pastor of the Bethany Presbyterian Church, Philadelphia. And with a clear sense of logic he pointed out that "if this is God's war we should have Christian soldiers to fight it." He could not "draw any line between

Christianity and patriotism. . . . The two go together." "The Church of Christ itself must enter the war"—and "every Presbyterian Church should be a recruiting station."[80]

The Lutherans, schooled in the philosophy of the all powerful state, readily acknowledged the supremacy of the government and the duty of all to obey its commands. The editor of *The Lutheran* put the case in this wise:

> The church has the right to plead with a free people that war be avoided. . . . But when war is declared, it must keep silent. It must submit to the powers that be. The church is subject to the state in the temporal sphere just as every citizen must be . . . it must say, "I submit to the authority of the powers that be." The church may be called upon to suffer for her convictions, but it may never be a rebel.[81]

For the Catholics, no difficulty presented itself. In a book of *War Addresses—from Catholic Pulpit and Platform,* compiled chiefly for its value as a witness to Catholic patriotism and loyalty, may be found speeches reflecting the "true Catholic sentiment and effort in supporting the American cause in this war." His Eminence John Cardinal Farley declared: "The Catholic Church has put all the power of its great organization at the service of the United States in this crisis simply because we Catholics are citizens of the United States. . . . As Catholics in America we owe unswerving allegiance to the government of America, and it is our sacred duty to answer with alacrity every demand our country makes upon our loyalty and devotion."[82] James Cardinal Gibbons, in a military mass at Camp Meade, told the soldiers: "Remember such wounds as you may receive will be honorable. You will be proud of them and will boast of them and will want to show them in years to come. Go forth to battle and victory, and God be with you."[83] Archbishop Ireland, speaking to new recruits in St. Paul, Minnesota, assured them: "You are the privileged ones, because you are permitted to make the highest sacrifice; to offer, if necessary, your very lives on the altar of your country."[84]

The Catholic philosophy may be summarized in the words of Bishop William T. Russell of Charleston, South Carolina:

> God is the author of every just government, and is its sanction. From him all powers derive their authority. . . . The President and Congress rule by this divine right . . . the citizen is bound to uphold the authority of the state in obeying its laws and by defending it if need be with his life against an unjust attack.[85]

It is difficult to discover any essential difference between the above outspoken points of view of the Lutherans and Catholics drilled in discipline and obedience and that expressed by representatives of sects noted for their liberalism and freedom granted to the individual conscience. William Douglas Mackenzie, Congregationalist, for instance, in his work on *Christian Ethics in the World War,* proceeds to expound the metaphysics for war time and condemn the German philosophy of the supremacy of the state. The state in a defensive war, Dr. Mackenzie pointed out, was

> simply carrying out to the limit of its power the duty inherent in its nature, the essential task for which, in the will of God and in the nature of man's life, it was created. . . .
> While the use of force is essential to the functions of the state . . . it is fatal to the church. Force and sacrifice are both methods of God. . . . In human society as a whole their operation has become assigned to two different institutions. The same men must, or ought to, live and work wholeheartedly in each. . . . And the result is that we must serve the state with its use of force, and the church with its use of sacrifice.[86]

While, of course, the church does not wage war itself, her members as citizens in the state owe fullest allegiance to their government. Dr. Mackenzie by that differentiation sought to escape the dilemma of the allegiance of the church to the state. But every page of his book dealing with the problem contains the clear implication that the voice of the church should support the government in the war. It approved of the action of the state. The church thereby became part and parcel of the war system.

In concluding these observations, it may be said that, no matter what may have been the metaphysical notions about the relationship that the church bore to the government during the war, the facts show the "complete enlistment of the church in the service of the state as a new phase in the historic struggle between the two."[87] The proof of this statement will be established later in a consideration of the activities of the churches and their attitude toward various phases of the conflict.

In the meanwhile, the extent to which the propaganda and the legend of the "holy war" had reached into the towns and hamlets and unto the children in all the homes of America may be deduced from the results of a questionnaire given out to the grade pupils of Marshalltown, Iowa, asking, "How Can I Help to Win the War?" a partial list of the answers were printed in *Religious Education,* receiving, apparently, the editorial approval:

    I can invent patents for fighting.
    I can pray God every night that we may win in this war.
    I can feed my dog nothing but what would be thrown away.
    I can help grandma so she can find time to teach mama to knit.
    I can darn my stockings as soon as there is a tiny hole, so it won't get larger.
    I can depend wholly upon God.[88]

CHAPTER IV

THE CHURCH AS SERVANT OF THE STATE

GENERAL HEADQUARTERS
AMERICAN EXPEDITIONARY FORCES

France, March 4, 1918.

To the Young People
of the Churches of America:

I am glad to have the opportunity of sending you greetings and hearty approval of the concerted support the church forces of the country, through you, are giving the government. The great active moral influence of the churches of America cannot fail to add power to the nation.

Yours sincerely,

(Signed) JOHN J. PERSHING.

To Dr. Daniel A. Poling
American Y. M. C. A.
12 Rue d'Aggresslau,
Paris, France.

CHAPTER IV
THE CHURCH AS SERVANT OF THE STATE

Organizing for War

ALL religious organizations came to acquire new importance in the eyes of the government directly after the war began. Here were vast agencies for propaganda of all sorts—for stimulating patriotism and the spirit of sacrifice, for the selling and buying of Liberty Bonds, conserving the food supply, recruiting, keeping up the morale of the people at home and the spirit of the troops in the camps and at the front, suppressing subversive propaganda, and promoting a feeling of brotherly love toward the Allies.

The churches not only became willing agents for these important tasks, but felt for the most part flattered that the government took them into partnership. The clergy, who were honored with government positions, writing pamphlets, making speeches over the country, or four-minute ones between acts at the theatres, positions as chaplains, special agents for commissions, or as secret agents, all had an increased prestige, both real and imaginary.

The immensity of the cause, the outlet in strenuous denunciation of the foe, the revival of the idea of hell fire and brimstone (in this case the Germans being the sinners) gave the pulpit new life and vigor. The members of the clergy, as of other talkative professions, depend in large measure for a living "upon their capacity to arouse an emotional response in the breasts of their clientele. When the public is all warmed up to fight, the clerical who treats the matter coldly is committing suicide, just as is the writer or the promoter."[1] The clergy, in general, in their eagerness to depict sin and to reform the world, are always prepared for a crusade against Satan and the powers of darkness. During the war, the Kaiser took the form of His Satanic Majesty—the incarnation of evil. Audiences applauded with ecstasy the thought of his hanging. During 1917-18 Billy Sunday was at his best. "If you turn hell upside down," said he, "you will find 'Made in Germany' stamped on the bottom."

The churches assumed a unity of purpose hitherto unknown

in religious annals. Denominational distinctions were lost sight of. What the churches had failed to accomplish in the furtherance of church unity in half a century of virtual peace came about almost overnight in a united effort to help kill the Germans and thereby promote the best interests of the Kingdom of God.

The leaders lost no time in getting thoroughly organized on a war-time basis. Within twenty-four hours after the declaration of war, the Federal Council of the Churches of Christ in America laid plans for the fullest cooperation. At a special meeting in Washington, May 8-9, 1917, this organization met in joint session with representatives from The Home Missions Council, The Foreign Missions Conference of North America, The Federation of Women's Boards of Foreign Missions of the United States, The Council of Women for Home Missions, The International Committee of the Young Men's Christian Association, The National Board of the Young Women's Christian Association, The American Bible Society, and The World Alliance for Promoting International Friendship Through the Churches! No less than thirty-five different religious bodies engaged in war work were represented.[2]

The group proclaimed the utmost loyalty and cooperation with the forces of the government: "We are here to pledge both support and allegiance in unstinted measure."[3]

By September 20, the General War-Time Commission of the Churches saw organization—"a body of one hundred persons chosen from the different religious agencies which are dealing in direct and responsible ways with the new problems which the war has raised."[4] This high-powered machine aimed to cooperate with the War Commission of the Roman Catholic Church and agencies of the Jews in "matters of common concern." The roll of members of the great Commission, with the various sub-committees, is impressive, not only for men of eminence, but also for the number who had led in the preparedness movement, and those who during the war made the front pages for their patriotism.[5] The chairman, Robert E. Speer, however, was rated in National Security League circles as a dangerous pacifist. William Adams Brown of Union Theological Seminary, the chief secretary of the Commission, in an address delivered in Oxford University, England, had perceived values in the war as far back as October 18, 1914.[6]*

---

* But in 1916, Dr. Brown had lamented that "the Christians within each [nation] are found heart and soul in support of their respective governments not only in the physical struggle in which they are engaged but what is more

A mere outline of the activities of the organization would fill several chapters. A record of them would require volumes. The Commission served as a clearing house of information. There were over twenty-five committees on every possible topic and for every conceivable emergency. Its work included the appointment of chaplains, "reenforcing the efforts of the government to maintain a high moral standard in the army," "providing for the religious and moral welfare of the workers in communities engaged in the manufacture of munitions of war and in the shipbuilding industry," "stimulating local churches to mobilize their resources for war-time tasks," "arranging for an exchange of ministerial service by the ministers of America and those of Great Britain and other Allied countries," et cetera.[7] The Commission raised and had spent over $300,000 when the war ended. And it should be remembered that all of the major denominations had independent war work commissions. With all this organization and unprecedented cooperation there was but one object— to win the war. The hundreds of pamphlets and literally tons upon tons of literature bore ample testimony to the unswerving convictions of the churches.[8]

The Roman Catholic Church, organized for similar service under the National Catholic War Council, directed by fourteen archbishops and with Cardinal Gibbons as president, demonstrated an equal devotion to the cause. The loyalty of the Catholic hierarchy and people may be inferred from the pledge of allegiance made by representatives of the church in April, 1917:

> Inspired neither by hate nor fear, but by the holy sentiments of truest patriotic fervor and zeal, we stand ready, we and all the flock committed to our keeping, to cooperate in every possible way with our President and our national government, to the end that the great and holy cause of liberty may triumph. . . . Our people now, as ever, will rise as one man to serve the nation. Our priests and consecrated women will, once again, as in every former trial of our country, win by their bravery, their heroism, and their service, new admiration and approval. . . .[9]

The Jews coordinated their work under the Jewish Welfare Board, with various affiliating organizations, sixteen all told.[10]

Recruits and Liberty Bonds

The patriotism, the willingness to do anything to further the aims of the government are demonstrated by the warmth of re-

---

significant, in their interpretation of the moral issues at stake." (W. A. Brown, *Is Christianity Practicable?* Scribner's, New York, 1916, pp. 4-5.)

sponse which every call from Washington received. "Requests of the government," rejoiced Worth M. Tippy, a secretary of the Federal Council, "are in a class by themselves. They constitute a privilege and an opportunity for service which cannot be denied."[11]

Many of the churches went much further than they were asked. They became recruiting stations for the enlistment of troops. Burris Jenkins, pastor of the Linwood Boulevard Christian Church, Kansas City, Missouri, before war was declared made eloquent appeals for men who would volunteer when war actually came.* The Plymouth Congregational Church of Brooklyn, shepherded by Newell Dwight Hillis, passed a resolution before the commencement of hostilities that "in the event of war both the church building and the services of the regiment [of church members] will be offered to the government."[12] Charles Aubrey Eaton, of the Madison Avenue Baptist Church, New York, offered to turn over his parish to the government to be used as a recruiting station, army and navy officers being invited to take charge. Women in the congregation were asked to assist in making up a census of the men in the neighborhood of military age.[13]

John Timothy Stone, of the Fourth Presbyterian Church, Chicago, wrote of an unhappy youth who drifted into a church service on Good Friday night *before* America had entered the European strife. The minister preached on war. He told how Canada and Australia had so nobly responded to the call of duty but "we had held off!" "Men," pleaded the clergyman, "you can enlist even if your country has not called you." Then he prayed, "[Lord] send sons from this church this night to the ranks of enlistment, and may this crucifixion night lead us to the cross on fields of France to save the world for whom Christ died."

At the close of the service, the restless young man came up and thanked the minister and added: "I'm going to enlist in the morning."

"What a manly face the young man had; what a grasp to his hand. . . . The pastor looked . . . into his face to thank God for the power to preach."

The strange young man went to Toronto and enlisted. In June, 1919, after a Sunday morning service he had returned to

---

* Out of an audience of "17,000 noisy patriots" at the mass meeting, 73 volunteered. (*The Christian Century*, Vol. XXXIV, No. 14, April 5, 1917, p. 17.)

thank the preacher. "That Good Friday sermon not only sent me to France, but it found my soul."[14]

The paramount duty of enlisting was emphasized by Billy Sunday: "The man who breaks all the rules but at last dies fighting in the trenches is better than you Godforsaken mutts who won't enlist."[15]

Lyman Abbott recommended that, "in this hour every Christian Church should be a recruiting office for the Kingdom of God. . . . The Christian Church and the Christian ministry should hear the voice of the Master saying, 'I have come not to send peace but a sword.' And they should lead Christ's followers forth, his cross on their hearts, his sword in their hands. . . ."[16]

The New York Federation of Churches asked the pastors to request the women in their congregations to assist in the statewide military census and suggested that the churches be used as registration places.[17]

In such a time of national crisis the ministers welcomed suggestions and material for sermons. To fill this need, Ozora S. Davis, president of the Chicago Theological Seminary, wrote a series of articles, *Preaching in a World at War;* these later appeared in a book. This work was the best of its kind and contained references to passages in all the inspiring war literature. Dr. Davis, however, was careful to point out the insidious weakness of such pacifist books as *New Wars for Old* written by John Haynes Holmes, and advised that there were "certain responsibilities for the guidance of the people" that would "demand that a preacher shall support the nation in its struggle" or "retire from the pulpit."[18]

In selling Liberty Bonds the clergy were indispensable. Every Liberty Loan campaign met with the joyous cooperation of the ecclesiastical leadership. Liberty Loan Sundays were announced by the government, extensive literature being sent out to all the ministers of the nation in advance. Sermons were to be preached and members urged to buy to the limit. When clergymen failed to preach these sermons or distribute literature sent by the authorities, their congregations suspected them of pro-German infection, the ministers received calls from Federal agents, mobs came with tar and feathers, and court machinery ground out sentences.

The Federal Council of Churches, which would have been the logical organization to have prepared the literature for the clergy, was deemed "too pacifistic" in some of its utterances for the officials in charge of the Publicity Division of the Liberty

Loan campaign. They chose instead Walter Laidlaw, executive secretary of the New York Federation of Churches, who, pro-Ally since 1914, had long been active in the preparedness campaigns prior to April, 1917, and in the anti-pacifist activities. He prepared the pamphlets for the first and second Liberty Loan campaigns issued by the Treasury department.

Dr. Laidlaw packed these pamphlets full of appropriate sermonic suggestions, illustrations, proof-texts, and outlines. Most of the material was of the quality evidently calculated to stir up righteous hate against Germany for starting the war, for perpetrating the "rape of Belgium," and furthering her Pan-Germanic ambitions.[19]

These canned sermon helps, while welcome in the study of many a parson, did not meet with universal approval. Jenkin Lloyd Jones, editor of *Unity*, for instance, objected particularly to this type of propaganda, accusing Dr. Laidlaw of

> perversion of history, a profanation of the sanctities which breeds disgust. When the United States will stoop to this charlatanry in religion, it provokes only the contempt of the real minister who resents the implication that he needs government aid in his pulpit ministrations.[20]

Preparations for the third Liberty Loan extended to vast and elaborate proportions. In order to put the propaganda over in the churches, the clergy were gathered for instruction and stimulation in various key cities over the land. In New York an all-day affair took place, April 4, 1918, under the auspices of the National Committee on the Churches and the Moral Aims of the War. The project had the backing of the publicity committee of the Liberty Loan organization of the second Federal Reserve district, all the details being arranged by Dr. Laidlaw. The clergy turned out en masse.

John Henry Jowett struck the keynote of the session: "There can be no kind of . . . nesting agreement, between the dove of peace and the present German eagle. . . . The first thing we have to do is to win the war by vanquishing a militant, intolerant and intolerable autocracy."[21]

A Polish countess, having been an eyewitness to some barbarities, told of horrible atrocities and of little girls raped by German soldiers. Henry Morgenthau unfolded the plight of Armenia, Sir George Adam Smith expressed the gratitude of Great Britain that the United States and the mother country were fighting side by side for God and the Kingdom. Guy Emerson, publicity director for the Liberty Loans, acknowledged that the campaigns could not be put across "without the cooperation of the church."

In order to facilitate further propaganda for the loans, a "beautiful piece of typical church music entitled, 'The Liberty Anthem' had been prepared with the request that on Liberty Loan Sunday the congregations gather on the sidewalk" and sing the anthem and "The Star-Spangled Banner."

The government had also arranged a striking pantomime to be staged by the children of the Sunday school. Then cards were prepared showing on one side "General Allenby entering Jerusalem on foot, and on the other the contrasting entry of the Germans into Belgium." These cards were for distribution to the children, so they would "go home and ask questions. . . . We want this loan talked about in the homes."[22]

The proportions of the sermonic material for the clergy to use with the third Liberty Loan greatly exceeded the other two. The members of the cloth were told that the churches had prepared public opinion long before so that "President Wilson could take the course he did a year ago"—*i.e.,* openly advise war against Germany. The clergy had helped to save the nation and were given the cheering words: "The kind of patriotism you have is the kind the nation needs. The ideals actuating your lives . . . are the ideals the people need. The conviction that a Holy God reigns . . . needs only to be freshened."[23]

Albert Bushnell Hart of Harvard reminded them of the glorious tradition of the "church militant in America" with her fighting parsons in all the wars. Nearly forty clergymen of all denominations and sects joined in their testimony to prove that the militancy of the parsons and the churches had not abated, that their loyalty to the Kingdom of God and the state could not be doubted. The following are a few excerpts:

> Oh! Church members, let us wake out of our sleep, and brush the haze of moral and spiritual inertia from our eyes. . . .
> . . . We fight *because* we are Christians and we will win *because* we are Christians.
> —Charles A. Eaton, Madison Avenue Baptist, New York.

> The Liberty Loan . . . is a consecration of our money to a sacred cause.
> —John Henry Jowett, Fifth Avenue Presbyterian, New York.

> Every dollar and every service given to Uncle Sam for his army is a gift to missions.
> —John M. MacInnis, South Presbyterian, Syracuse.

When we support this war we follow Him [the Great Peacemaker]. We deny Him if we refuse.

—John Francis Morgan, Claremont Presbyterian, Jersey City.

The man who does not see that our cause is right, and that our defeat would mean the exalting of crime, of despotism, of conscienceless brutality, is a man whose soul is darkened either by ignorance or blindness to the realities of the moral order. It is as plain as the light of day that our Republic now is engaged upon no less a task than the ransoming of humanity.

—Wm. L. Sullivan, All Souls' Unitarian, New York.

I would have the members of the churches, Christian and Jewish, alike, stand foremost among the citizens of America furthering the high war aims of our nation.

—Rabbi Stephen S. Wise, Free Synagogue, New York.

In this Liberty Loan we are in no small measure achieving the aspirations of this government and the commands of this Gospel.

—V. G. A. Tressler, President General Synod of the Lutheran Church in the U. S. A.

Under the influence of this high-pressure salesmanship the church people gave liberally. According to the reports by the Federal Council they were "eagerly responding" in "putting the Liberty Loan over the top."[24] How much money the various denominations contributed to the support of the Liberty Loans can never be determined, since few of them subscribed as church bodies. The Bishops of the Methodist Episcopal Church, when they called on the church to give to the third Loan, pledged that their members would give $80,000,000.[25] The Mormons pledged $750,000 for the first four Loans.[26]

When the fourth Liberty Loan was launched, September 27, 1918, religious journals donated pages of space to advertising the sale of the bonds. One appeared in *Christian Work* for October 12, covering a full page.[27] At the top were the words:

KILL THE HUN
KILL HIS HOPE

and in the middle of the advertisement a picture of a bayonet and a one hundred dollar liberty bond. Beneath these emblems appeared the reminder:

BAYONET AND BOND
—BOTH KILL!

One kills the Hun, the other kills his hope. . . .
Buy U. S. Government Bonds, Fourth Liberty Loan.

In the city of Philadelphia the bankers made a direct appeal to all the churches and their members to secure additional subscriptions "amounting to fifty million dollars and upwards." In a full page advertisement in the newspapers quotas were assigned to the respective church bodies:

Baptist	$7,000,000.00
Catholics	17,000,000.00
Episcopalians	10,000,000.00
Jewish	3,000,000.00
Lutheran	4,000,000.00
Methodist Episcopal	10,000,000.00
Presbyterian	10,000,000.00

And other denominations in proportion.

Constitute yourselves church members of Philadelphia, a Conscience Committee to increase your own subscriptions, and to secure an increase among your confreres, for God, for country and humanity.[28] *

Campaigns on the Home Front

The American people suddenly discovered during the war that they were the most wasteful of all the inhabitants of earth. The food which they threw away would feed the Allied armies, at least so it was ordinarily believed. Thus the government started a campaign to make them food-conscious by the use of various devices chiefly remembered as the "wheatless" and "meatless" days. The Committee on Food Conservation at Washington enlisted the churches in a nation-wide hook-up. In a no uncertain tone they were given to understand that they "should

---

* As an illustration of the pressure brought to bear upon citizens to buy Liberty Bonds the following is of interest. It is a full page advertisement (one of a series) which appeared in the Arkansas *Gazette*, Little Rock, Arkansas, Sunday, April 14, 1918:

SLACKER

* * *

Any man or woman in this town, who does not take all the Liberty Bonds that he or she possibly can buy, is in exactly the same class with those wretched creatures of feeble brain and feeble spine, those cowards we call "SLACKERS."

Such men and women . . . are not fit to associate with Real Americans. Such men and women are not fit to live in this community, or anywhere else in America. They are not fit to live at all.

* * *

Such men and women are *yellow to the core.*

This space donated by
Beal-Burrow Dry Goods Company
as part of its contribution toward winning the war.

(Sixty-four firms were listed as contributing to advertising for the Third Liberty Loan)

be in the forefront of the work."²⁹ Home pledge cards having been distributed, weekly reports of food saved by the church folk were asked for.

Howard B. Grose, editor of *Missions* (Baptist), represented the conference of editors of the religious press at the Food Administration Headquarters. For several months he furnished the news concerning the work of the Food Administration to more than seven hundred papers and periodicals, including the Catholic, Protestant and Jewish press, "which took copy from the same source with utmost harmony and cooperation."³⁰ Dr. Grose, following the precedent set by the Liberty Loan sermonic material, gave the clergy similar pamphlets containing sermon texts, outlines, with patriotic suggestions. "Civilization is at stake," the editor wrote, and "to win the war we must practice food substitution and saving as a part of our religious and patriotic duty."³¹

The principle of frugality inculcated by the Puritan forefathers now served a patriotic purpose. The pulpits throughout the land called upon loyal members of the congregations to feed their children "more potatoes" as the editor of *Unity* ironically expressed it, so there would be "more bread for the fighters going to the war fronts to assist civilization."³²

The same ideas were carried out in the campaigns by the government for its multitudinous purposes and on behalf of the Red Cross. It has been officially calculated that 1,564,850 letters urging support of the Red Cross were mailed by the government agencies to clergymen alone between May 15, 1917, and June 20, 1918.³³ The Committee on Public Information, through its chairman, George Creel, thanked the church people and organizations for the magnificent support they had given official requests from Washington and said "the desire to cooperate has nowhere been manifested more splendidly than in the work of the religious bodies within the nation. . . . The leader in religious bodies has an opportunity to disseminate information and to arouse the interest to serve the . . . nation."³⁴

"The Germans," said Mr. Creel recently, "spread the report that the pastors of the United States received orders from me about the sermons they were to preach, and that I had spies in every church to see that these orders were obeyed. This was absolutely untrue."³⁵ One can readily perceive how the impression got abroad that the government wrote the sermons for the clergy to use, but the sending out of spies to insure patriotic sermons would have been like carrying coals to Newcastle.

In urging a full-time war program upon the churches, the

Federal Council took a leading part. The President, Frank Mason North, saw no excuse for the church which,

> with the nation under arms for the very principles of righteousness and good-will for which the church stands and for which its Lord gave himself in the agony of the Cross, does not promptly, effectively and sacrificially mobilize all its resources for high achievement both in arms and in the devotion of its moral and spiritual energy.[36]

To impress fully the inhabitants of the hinterland with the worthiness of the cause, a committee under the General War-Time Commission was organized to carry the message of responsibility to the local church, with Worth M. Tippy, as executive secretary. In the centers of war-time industries increased forces of religious workers undertook to care for the new workingmen and their families, the local churches being mobilized into a War Council to keep up the morale of the workers. In order that these mushroom war production communities might have the proper understanding of the spiritual significance of the items in which they were engaged in manufacturing—arms, ammunition, shrapnel, and barbed wire—Liberty Churches became established where ministers could gather the polyglot population together.[37]

Out in the great open spaces, a rural secretary, Edmund deS. Brunner, carried on an extensive campaign under the guidance of a Committee on Rural Fields. He had the cooperation of three thousand ministers who spoke before farmers' institutes and "councils of defense." A war standard of efficiency for the rural churches, designed to "lift up" the conditions of country life, set the pace for the backward communities. Churches achieving the mark of their high calling were named "Rural Liberty Churches." This program received the welcome and support of the Secretary of Agriculture.[38]

Dr. Brunner interpreted war aims to farmers by dealing with the economic realities of life on the farm. The war was not only righteous, but its outcome would affect the farmer's pocketbook. Denying that we were fighting for profits, he nevertheless pointed out that had we not entered the war we would have lost our prosperity, no treaty would have been sacred, and there would have been a lower standard of living. Such a state of affairs would have impaired the country church, "for with these losses would have come the anguish of unsatisfied living and the nerve strain of living close to the dead-line of poverty." Therefore, said Dr. Brunner, "the country church should and must get into the war." [39]

In an effort to spread further the light into the agricultural districts, the government asked the committee on rural work to hold a series of state conferences, bringing together the religious leaders of the states with the leaders of the state colleges of agriculture, the county agents, et cetera. In these conferences the plan of community organization worked out by the Council of National Defense was to be presented and coordinated with those of the Department of Agriculture, the Bureau of Education and the churches.[40]

Gifford Pinchot headed up the Commission on the Church and Country Life which concentrated on the war problem in Ohio. Some idea of the thoroughgoing alliance of church and state there may be derived from the following news item:

> The Ohio Rural Life Association, through its executive secretary, the Rev. Chas. O. Gill, will be used by the Ohio Branch of the Council of National Defense to carry the messages of patriotism to the villages and open country where no other medium is available. Mr. Gill, in his capacity as Secretary of the Federal Council's Commission on the Church and Country Life, has made a thorough survey of the counties of Southwestern Ohio, which revealed a general apathy among the farmers toward the war. It is believed that a campaign of patriotic education carried on through the ministers of local churches is the best means of overcoming this condition. . . .[41]

But in all maneuvers to build up the rural and blighted areas of the states, the inhabitants were reminded, and this in a pamphlet issued by the Committee on War Time Work in the Local Church: "Should the need arise the farmer must not and will not shirk from the great sacrifice—the giving of his sons to the army and navy of his country."[42]

Prohibition, Temperance, and Public Morals

The ideal of church cooperation, sacrificing for missions, salvation through faith and works, loyalty to God and the brotherhood of man, were all now connected with the campaign to win the war. Practically all the major slogans of the churches that had been found effective in promoting the Kingdom prior to 1917 were now turned to the direct advantage of the government.

The campaign for temperance, which had been waged in this country for half a century or more, now marched under the title,

Strengthen America Campaign, conducted in favor of national prohibition under the guidance of Charles Stelzle. The committee admitted that "naturally much emphasis was laid upon the importance of national prohibition as a war measure." * "Liquor Problem Dealt with by Federal Council as a Menace to National Success in War," ran the headline to an article in the official *Bulletin*.[43] The prohibition movement was now pushed not primarily on a health basis but because the nation needed sober workers in the munition factories, and sober farmers to produce grain for food. A poster issued by the United Committee on War Temperance Activities in the Army and Navy read:

IN CAREFUL TESTS SHARPSHOOTERS MADE 3 TIMES
AS MANY ERRORS AFTER TAKING A FEW DRINKS.[44]

Another campaign—against venereal disease and immorality —based its main arguments in this country and in England on the ground that laxity in sexual relations would lower the morale of the soldiers. A fight for purity of life in order to "beat the Germans," came to be the dominant motive. Humanitarian and moral ideals were secondary.[45]

Bishop Lawrence, making an impassioned plea in this campaign, said:

> Moral questions are involved, of course, questions of purity, of family, of integrity, of the sacredness of womanhood and of childhood, chivalry and honor. These, however, are not my concern tonight; nor are they at this time the concern of the masses of our people who are building up the army; the vital question is that of keeping our men fit to fight and so to win the war.[46]

That the churches and their leaders could play an indispensable part in propagandizing the nation they themselves amply demonstrated. For them the plans and the wishes of the government were paramount. The Federal Council, through Dr. Tippy, polled the country by asking a representative clergyman in each city to report on the "prevailing position of the clergy" in his particular city. The answers showed that almost to a man the Protestant clergy of the country were urging the "vigorous prosecution" of the war. "Not a single instance of disloyalty was cited." Among the German Lutherans there reigned

---

* The Episcopalians in the diocese of New York, after some difficulty, put through a resolution to support national prohibition for the period of the war. (*The Churchman*, Vol. CXVI, No. 21, November 24, 1917, p. 653.)

loyalty and no obstructionism. The pastors who opposed our entrance into the conflict were now doing their part in "seeing it through." Many pastors voluntarily reported the "active earnest war work" of Catholic priests and the Negro clergy.[47]

In the Presbytery of New York, out of a total of 184 ordained ministers, 75 were in the active pastorate, and 31 out of the 75 had given up their pastorates "for some form of war service." The conclusion drawn is significant:

> An average of 41 per cent of the pastors of one denomination in the nation's chief city engaged in active war work, and about 42 per cent of these in service abroad, is a record of which any community might be proud.[48]

In the foregoing account a few illustrations have been used to show what the churches meant by "cooperation with the government."

CHAPTER V

THE CHURCHES CONTRIBUTE TO WAR-TIME HYSTERIA

Nathaniel Hawthorne, speaking of Matthew Maule, one of the victims of the witchcraft delirium in New England, wrote: "He was one of the martyrs to that terrible delusion, which should teach us, among its other morals, that the influential classes, and those who take upon themselves to be leaders of the people, are fully liable to all the passionate error that has ever characterized the maddest mob. Clergymen, judges, statesmen—the wisest, calmest, holiest persons of their days—stood in the inner circle round about the gallows, loudest to applaud the work of blood, latest to confess themselves miserably deceived."

From *The House of the Seven Gables*.

CHAPTER V
THE CHURCHES CONTRIBUTE TO WAR-TIME HYSTERIA

The Atrocity Mongers

THE American people are particularly susceptible to fads and fashions. Their history shows them also to be victims of successive waves of emotion and hysteria—witchcraft delirium, revivalism, Ku Kluxism, the Yellow Peril, and the Red Menace. In this respect the record of the war years serves as a perfect gold mine of facts for those interested in the study of crowd psychology. That, in general, there is no limit to the gullibility of the public when under severe emotional stress seems amply to have been proved.

The governments, each bent upon representing the enemy as in league with the devil, stopped at nothing to support this theory of Satanism. The Germans, while the victims of many of the same types of atrocities as the Allies claimed to be, were either not clever enough in using these stories as propaganda material or they overlooked their chances altogether.*

The Allied atrocity tales, designed to play upon the sympathies of the populace, became unusually valuable in working up the moral indignation and righteous wrath of church congregations. Many churchmen were so thoroughly indoctrinated that even today, though most of the stories have been proved to be absolutely false,[1] they still believe what they read in the newspapers fifteen years ago.†

---

* The execution in Brussels of the English nurse, Edith Cavell, by the Germans came to be regarded as one of the major evidences of Hun brutality by the peoples in the Allied countries, due to the skilful use made of the story for purposes of propaganda. Shortly after the event, the French executed two German nurses under about the same circumstances. The Prussian officer in charge of propaganda work, when asked why he had not used this fact as propaganda against the Allies, said: "What? Protest? The French had a perfect right to shoot them!" (H. D. Lasswell, *Propaganda Technique in the World War*, Knopf, N. Y., 1927, p. 32.)

† The famous Bryce report about the German atrocities in Belgium, because of Bryce's high standing, was received as gospel in this country as well as in England. While subsequent investigations show that Bryce was mistaken, his report is still quoted as authoritative.

So clever was the propaganda that the most astute and levelheaded citizen believed everything he heard.* The average individual, including the ecclesiastical leaders, necessarily formed judgments, moral and factual, based on controlled evidence. Hence this withholding of information and supplying false news reports by the governments made it almost impossible for the molders of religious opinion to pass on any ethical judgments other than those which their governments wished them to make.

The atrocity propaganda was manipulated by the Allies with much adroitness in the United States. Numerous mass meetings to protest against the inhumanity of Germany were held in various sections of the country long before we entered the war. Thus the mind of the public was prepared. After April, 1917, the tales of outrages multiplied in number and magnitude. Public speakers found an abundance of material with which to arouse the emotions of an audience.

Such tales to be highly effective must be vitally related to the basic emotional drives—the love of parents for their child (hence the Belgian children with their hands cut off), or the sex drive, the strongest of all. Thus the most useful and powerful stories were concerned with women and sex. Hearing about the wholesale raping of Belgian women would arouse horror, anger, desire for revenge, but would, nevertheless, have an irresistible fascination by appealing to the imagination and stimulating the sex urge.

Moreover, any platform man who had a list of "new" stories, of several varieties, of course, had a distinct advantage over the individual who had to give them second-hand. The career of Newell Dwight Hillis, minister to the Plymouth Congregational Church of Brooklyn, will long be remembered in this connection.

To comprehend Dr. Hillis's war-time fervor, it will be necessary for a moment to go back to the beginning of the European conflagration. The pastor had traveled much in Europe, and had a wide acquaintance with the various political, social and economic factors in the several countries. For five years he had been lecturing on the genius of the German people and what could be learned from "The New Germany." He was rated as one of the most popular platform lecturers in the United States.

On the first Sunday in October, 1914, his sermon on the war indicated a degree of objectivity. "The prevailing impression in

---

* *The Appeal to Reason,* a Socialist journal run by E. Haldeman-Julius, skeptic, became *The New Appeal,* abandoning reason completely and becoming equally credulous with the believers.

New York," he said, "is that the Kaiser is to blame for the present war. I do not believe this to be the case." He then proceeded to extol the virtues of Wilhelm II.[2]

On the succeeding Sabbaths in the fall of 1914, he continued with the series of "Studies of the Great War." And, although these seemed to be neutral in their outlook, in reality, though admitting that France and Russia had interests at stake in the war, they revealed the beginning of his belief in the sole guilt theory.[3] By Christmas, Dr. Hillis had definitely changed his mind about the whole affair, had openly condemned German militarism, and had withdrawn his lecture on "The New Germany" from the lecture bureau.[4]

A few days later he exposed from his pulpit a "certain German professor at Harvard" (whom everybody recognized as Hugo Munsterberg), for having written an attack on the United States in an unsigned article in *The Atlantic Monthly*, under the title, "A Letter to Uncle Sam." This article had appeared three years before. Professor Munsterberg at once denied any connection with the authorship. Ellery Sedgwick, the editor, wrote to the New York *Times* to explain that the article in question had been written by a British imperialist.[5]

From the foregoing incident and an abundance of other data at hand, several characteristics of Dr. Hillis are clearly revealed. He seems to have been in the habit of at times forming conclusions unwarranted from a study of the facts. Explain it psychologically as one will, Dr. Hillis on many occasions did not weigh evidence with any degree of detachment.*

---

* Further instances of false statements made by Dr. Hillis may be mentioned. On page 125 of his *German Atrocities* occurs the following: "When General Grant found one of his aides chuckling over the news of a defeat of Sheridan, Grant court-martialed the man, found him guilty, shot him at daybreak—an example to be commended with reference to any man who vilifies Great Britain or France with his lips or pen."

A Cincinnati lawyer, M. G. Heintz (to whom I am indebted for the information), inquired of Dr. Hillis for his authority. Dr. Hillis, after several inquiries from Mr. Heintz, finally said it was General King, now dead. Meanwhile, inquiries from General J. Warren Keifer of Springfield, Ohio, the only surviving Major General of the Civil War (in 1927), and the Adjutant General's office revealed there is no record of such an occurrence. Mr. Heintz refers to Dr. Hillis's statement about General Grant as "an historical atrocity."

If the reader be interested in another incident see " An Open Letter to Dr. Hillis by George Creel," in *Harper's Weekly*, May 29, 1915 (Vol. 60, No. 3049, pp. 509-10). This is an exposure of gross misstatements of fact in connection with the Colorado Mining Strike made by Dr. Hillis in an address, "The Real Issue of the War in Colorado: A Straight Sermon to Young Men." Dr. Hillis had made the assertion that he had "investigated" the situation in Colorado and was therefore fully qualified to speak on the subject.

In 1915, however, the Brooklyn clergyman's work was impaired. He became involved in law suits connected with some bad investments which he had made in lumber deals. These legal difficulties continued for several years.[6] In the meantime he confessed the error of his ways, financial and ethical, breaking down in his pulpit with tears of remorse as he asked the forgiveness of his people.[7] Though his congregation manifested a gracious spirit and various ministers' conferences expressed their sympathy, nevertheless the confidence which people had reposed in Dr. Hillis was badly shaken.

The entrance of America into the war created an opportunity for him to repair his damaged reputation by plunging into patriotic activity. The terrific drive with which he entered into the spirit of the war, and the manner in which he damned the Germans made the enthusiasms of the War Department seem relatively lukewarm. Whether Dr. Hillis's efforts were a compensation for a feeling of guilt, we may leave to the psychoanalysts to determine. In any event, among the countless clergymen in the United States who gave themselves to the cause of calling upon the Almighty to doom the Germans to an eternity of hell fire, Dr. Hillis outdid them all. His reputation, which had dropped below par, now rose to its former heights.

At the beginning of 1917 he was begging for war and upbraiding the administration for its "dilly-dallying." He suggested that for the symbol of the eagle on the American flag, there be substituted a tortoise and under it inscribed the words from the first chapter of Genesis, "God made every creeping thing." [8] Incongruous as it may seem, in the same sermon his congregation heard: "Descended from a family of Quakers and reared by a father who practiced and taught the doctrine of non-resistance, I am in principle a Quaker and deeply sympathize with the pacifist movement."

Yet, his estimate of the German soldier had dropped to the level where he could call them "mad dogs," "insane men," "rattlesnakes," and "hyenas." "All civilization," he said, "must unite to kill the mad dog."[9] Dr. Hillis by this time had succeeded in building up such a reputation for himself that Theodore Roosevelt, in anticipation of leading a regiment in France, wrote: "I would rather have Dr. Hillis as chaplain than any other man I know."[10]

The American Bankers Association, quick to perceive what the oratorical ability of Dr. Hillis could accomplish in the sale of Liberty Bonds, called upon him to assist in the first campaign.[11] So pleased were the bankers that several of them sent him to

Europe during the summer of 1917 to gather first-hand information about German atrocities.[12]

Thus prepared for the second Liberty Loan drive, Dr. Hillis spoke 400 times in 162 cities. These lectures were put together in a little book, *German Atrocities,* with several photographs of alleged atrocities added for the benefit of the reader.

Doubtless thousands of people over the land can vividly recall a typical lecture on the war by this prominent clergyman. It is time to begin. Dr. Hillis and Lawrence Chamberlain, a banker, appear on the platform. The minister of the gospel begins his lecture, in which he promises to tell the truth about the war and to give his hearers the inside information about the atrocities perpetrated by the German soldiers. The stories are all from authentic sources. He pulls out from his pocket a token about the size of a silver dollar and made of aluminum. One of these, he tells his audience, is given to every German soldier. Then the speaker reads the inscription:

> I, the Kaiser of Germany, declare herewith on the authority committed to me by God Almighty, that the bearer of this token is permitted to commit any crime he may desire, and I, the Kaiser of Germany, will take upon myself the responsibility for such crime and to answer to God for the same.[13]

Now Dr. Hillis commences to tell about the crimes of these men, fiendish devils they are, who drink human blood out of their enemies' skulls, who commit murder and rape as pastimes, with crimes upon women as their specialty. He points to several dozen pictures of these atrocities (which had previously been tacked around the edge of the platform), telling the members of the audience that they can come up later to see the photographic evidence for themselves. Cameras do not lie. Having secured this pornographic effect, the lecturer proceeds. "Why do the German soldiers cut off the breasts of French and Belgian girls?" he asks. Here's the secret. A syphilitic German soldier is refused access to the German camp women, because the disease communicated to her would spread to other German soldiers and thus wipe out the Kaiser's army. "And if he uses one of these girls, he will be shot like a dog." Therefore,

> the soldier that has this foul disease must stay away from the camp women on peril of his life. Under this restriction the syphilitic soldier has but one chance, namely, to capture a Belgian or French girl; but using this girl means contaminating her. To

save his own life, therefore, when the syphilitic German has used a French or Belgian girl, he cuts off her breasts as a warning to the next German soldier.[14]

And yet, announces Dr. Hillis, sadly, "the worst atrocities cannot be named," or "can only be mentioned by men to men in whispered tones."[15]

Whether the citizens, as they listened to these tales of barbarism, reached into their pockets to give their last dollar to the Liberty Loan, or whether they even gave more liberally than they would have under the oratorical spell of a less authoritative speaker, cannot be determined. If appeals to sadistic impulses and libidinous desire were sufficient, the patriotism and the liberality of the 400 audiences must have known no bounds.

In these towns he showed the courage of his convictions by continuing to lecture in the face of "black hand letters" threatening to "blow his head off."[16] In Mishawaka, Indiana, according to the report, he had been carefully "surrounded by Secret Service men and local police officers."[17]

After a successful season of lecturing, the summer of 1918 again found Dr. Hillis in Europe, collecting fresh material for another series of lectures, which were published under the title, *The Blot on the Kaiser's Scutcheon*. In this series, the author outdid his former style. Some of the chapter headings are suggestive: "The Judas Among the Nations"; "The Black Soul of the Hun"; "Polygamy and the Collapse of the Family in Germany"; "The German Sniper Behind the Crucifix"; "Must German Men Be Exterminated?"

These lectures were received, apparently, as enthusiastically as the first series. Many testimonials were volunteered in the religious press from fellow-clergymen who had heard Dr. Hillis's report when he first returned from abroad. George Thomas Dowling wrote *The Churchman* to express his gratification at the "wholly authenticated" report from evidence "which could permit no question or from official records or affidavits preserved in government archives."[18]

Christian Work and *The Christian Century* published a number of Dr. Hillis's atrocity stories for him.[19] In fact, *Chrisitan Work* recommended that its readers write to the Committee on Public Information in Washington for a copy of *German War Practices*.[20] In the issue of September 29, 1917, appeared the headline, "An Announcement Extraordinary." Newell Dwight Hillis would contribute twenty articles to appear "exclusively in *Christian*

Work."* Proclaimed the editor: "They bid fair to be the literary sensation of the year."²¹

Yet, Dr. Hillis, though the outstanding example among the atrocity mongers, did not stand alone. There were thousands like him who believed and repeated the same stories. That they did not measure up to the minister from Brooklyn was merely because they lacked the subtle understanding of crowd psychology, the necessary technique, or the oratorical ability to sway the war-crazed multitudes.

There was, for example, Bishop William Alfred Quayle, who offered a contribution in the pages of *The Northwestern Christian Advocate:*

> We are not at war with the . . . Junkers . . . not Prussianism, not the Kaiser. . . . The German people is what we are at war with. . . . [They] have been conducting murder, not war. Hold fast to that. . . . The new atrocity story which appeared this week was spraying prisoners with burning oil. This is Germany's most recent jest. It makes them laugh so. . . .
>
> Germany has ravished the women of Belgium, Serbia, Roumania, Poland, Armenia. Germany murdered the passengers of the *Lusitania*. . . . Germany has poisoned wells, crucified inhabitants and soldiers, burned people in their houses, and this by system. Germany has denatured men and boys, has wantonly defaced the living and the dying and the dead. An eye-witness tells of seeing women dead at a table with their tongues nailed to the table and left to die. . . . Germany has disclosed neither decency nor honor from the day it started war, nor has a single voice in Germany to date been lifted up against the orgies of ruthlessness which burn the soul sick and which institute the chief barbarity of history . . . and to climax its horrid crimes Germany has inflicted compulsory polygamy on the virgins of its own land.²²

Speaking before the Republican Club of New York, George R. Van de Water confided:

> I could tell you things that have been told me by those who know. Consistent with their philosophy, and according to their kind of courage, they [the Germans] can stretch a nude mother in the style of crucifixion and hold her baby before her dying eyes, in order to scare a community into submission. That is a fact.²³

The list of such speakers, who more or less regularly used this type of illustration, could be added to *ad infinitum*. Echoed

---

* The series was practically identical with much of the material in *German Atrocities*, the more frightful stories being omitted.

and re-echoed, their reverberation was heard long after the Armistice. In September, 1919, Dr. Fosdick, though not given to relaying such stories, was asking:

> How could they [the Germans], calling upon God, do the cruel, bestial things that they have done? . . . The official cruelties, the U-boat war, the sack of Belgium, the deportations, the slave systems, the wholesale murders in Northern France, the massacres of the Armenians—how could the Germans, bone of our bone, and blood of our blood, calling upon God, perpetrate cruelties like that?[24]

Religious hatred against the Germans had achieved such a degree of intensity that any word which appeared to tone down the prevailingly hostile attitude was condemned as blasphemous and unpatriotic. Klaus Olandt of Montrose, New Jersey, in June, 1918, told of some of his pleasant experiences as a worker in German prison camps, whereupon he suffered a vote of censure passed by his hearers, the members of the General Synod of the Reformed Church in America, in session at Asbury Park, New Jersey. The speaker, introducing the motion of censure, called Mr. Olandt "a traitor." "Such talk," said he, "poisons the minds of the people and might cause them to doubt the stories of cruelty and barbarity that have been so well authenticated by American officials."[25]

At about the time the newspapers, the clergy and the four-minute orators were relaying their vivid accounts of atrocities to the public, fifty service men were brought over from France to aid as speakers in a Liberty Loan campaign. One of these, a sergeant, gave what purported to be first-hand descriptions:

> The Germans gave poisoned candy to the children to eat and hand grenades for them to play with. They show glee at the children's dying writhings and laugh aloud when the grenades explode. I saw one American boy about seventeen years old, who had been captured by the Germans, come back to our trenches. He had cotton in and about his ears. I asked someone what the cotton was for. "The Germans cut off his ears and sent him back to tell us they want to fight men," was the answer. They feed Americans tuberculosis germs.[26]

This sounded like the truth in the light of what the Americans had been hearing from press and pulpit. Yet General Pershing recalled the sergeant to France:

> As there is no foundation whatever in fact for such statements based on any experience we have had, I recommend that this ser-

geant, if the statements quoted above were made by him, be immediately returned for duty here, and that the statements be contradicted.[27]

The atrocity mongers heightened a conviction which had already assumed the sacredness and proportions of religious dogma, namely, that the Germans were solely guilty for starting the war. Clothed in the sanctity of historical authority, historians of first rank, having succumbed to the strain of their emotions, pointed the accusing finger at the Central Powers. They forgot much of the European history they had learned and taught prior to 1914.[28]

Professor Bang's famous work, *Hurrah and Hallelujah,* containing the supernationalistic speeches of German scholars and clergymen, convinced the Christians in this country that German Christianity was a spurious brand and therefore to be driven from the face of the earth. E. Hershey Sneath, professor of the Philosophy of Religion and Religious Education at Yale, explained:

> When the nation of Martin Luther, including not only the docile masses but the spiritually enslaved clergy and servile university professors, among whom may be numbered such religious leaders as Harnack, can accept and pray for the success of the war program of a ruler who regards himself to be the vicegerent of the Almighty, cooperating with him . . . approving the vices of hell as though they were the virtues of heaven—this nominally Christian nation is either guilty of awful blasphemy or it has lost its vision of an ethical God. . . . "*Gott mit uns*" is a God that is asked and believed to cooperate in the most damnable atrocities the human mind ever conceived in order to further low national aims.[29]

THE KAISER AS BEELZEBUB

A skilled propaganda artist knows that the enemy must be painted as black as possible, that the responsibility for trying to wreck the world must be placed upon his shoulders, and the masses must be convinced that historians will never revise the present judgment. As Bishop William F. Anderson of the Methodist Episcopal Church stated it: "The question as to the responsibility and the forgiveableness of this world disaster is a closed book to the people of this country, as it will be the judgment of history and all future generations."[30]

Dean Charles Reynolds Brown of Yale Divinity School also rendered a sweeping verdict: "There was only one nation on earth which really desired the war and was thoroughly prepared for the war, and in those fateful July days of 1914 did everything in her power to bring on the war."[31]

In addition to fastening the guilt upon Germany, the theory proved popular that the autocratic emperor, Kaiser Wilhelm, was the real culprit. Moreover, the Kaiser's religion, pagan and not Christian, accounted for his total inability to think of anyone save himself and Germany. This phenomenon, George Holley Gilbert, Congregational minister and theologian, analyzed in the pages of *The Biblical World:*

> . . . the strangest paradox of all is the fact that the man who is chiefly responsible for this infinite calamity to the world is the Constitutional head of the Christian Church of Prussia and regards himself as the chosen instrument of God in all the work of his life.
>
> . . . in the Kaiser's thought God is especially useful in war and is especially interested in German wars. . . .
>
> This thought of divine favoritism looks strange indeed in the light of the twentieth century. We expect to find it among uncivilized peoples; it is part of the narrow intellectual outlook of barbarians; but here it appears in a modern European sovereign who is proud of his culture and constant in his claim to the Christian name.
>
> . . . [we] have good reason to regard a thoroughly militarized Christianity, like that of the Kaiser, as the lowest and most harmful religion ever developed on earth.[32]

The Kaiser, thus chosen as the scapegoat, fitted into the picture admirably, while, to change the metaphor, millions of otherwise quite logically minded Americans, came to believe that Wilhelm was His Satanic Majesty, incarnate. "If the Kaiser is a Christian then the devil in hell is a Christian"[33] and "I am an atheist,"[34] announced Cortland R. Myers, of the Baptist Temple, Brooklyn.

The stereotype in the cartoons, depicting the Kaiser as Mephistopheles, harmonized with popular conceptions, while helping in turn to create them. In comparison to this gentleman, "Nero was a sanctified angel," confirmed I. Manley Sharp.[35]

The concern over the Kaiser's immortal destiny led to various serious proposals. The chancellor of Syracuse University, James R. Day, at the opening session of the university in the fall of 1918, told the assembled students that it was "religious to hate the Kaiser," since the Bible taught us "to hate the devil and all his works." "It would be a blessing," said Dr. Day, "if we could turn the beast of Berlin over to God and say, 'Lord, inflict violent wrath upon this creature'."[36]

W. W. Bustard, pastor of John D. Rockefeller's parish, phrased it quite succinctly: "To hell with the Kaiser."[37]

As a practical suggestion for incarceration on this mundane sphere, William E. Barton of Oak Park, Illinois,[38] and Robert S. MacArthur of the Baptist Temple, Boston, recommended complete banishment to St. Helena.[39]

The universal obsession properly to label and dispose of Wilhelm II so affected the minds of the men of the cloth that some of the manifestations of indignation bordered on symptoms of paranoia. James H. Maurer, President of the Pennsylvania State Federation of Labor, testifies to the following incidents which took place in Harrisburg, Pennsylvania.

> I have seen on the public square a giant head of the Kaiser, and clergymen in their ministerial garb outbidding each other to buy a spike, which they proudly drove into the Kaiser's skull.
>
> The local papers of Harrisburg, Pennsylvania, in 1918, devoted more than a column to interviews with the city's clergymen as to what they would do with the Kaiser if he were their prisoner. Some said, "Hang him by the thumbs and let him starve"; others said, "Bury him up to his neck and then place food and water in sight"; others, more bloodthirsty, said, "Hang him by his thumbs and cut pieces out of his body day after day until he was either dead or until there were no more pieces of flesh to cut out." Of all that expressed themselves, only one said, "Judge not, that ye be not judged."[40]

The fact that a section of the Treaty of Versailles calls for the trial of the German Emperor is proof enough that the Allied governments responded to a widespread popular indignation in favor of a public execution—a hatred created to a large extent by the ministers and the churches for whom "flaying the Kaiser" became a popular pastime.

The German leaders were generally accredited with almost if not quite equal guilt with their chieftain. "This ilk of pirates and murderers,"[41] *Zion's Herald* preferred to call them, while Henry Van Dyke became famous for his "Potsdam Gang" theory:

> I knew that the Predatory Potsdam gang had chosen and forced the war in order to realize their robber dream of Pan-Germanism. I knew that they were pushing it with unheard-of atrocity in Belgium and Northern France, in Poland and Serbia and Armenia. I knew that they had challenged the whole world of peace-loving nations. I knew that America belonged to the imperiled world. I knew that there could be no secure labor and no quiet sleep in any land so long as the Potsdam Werewolf was at large.[42]

THE HUN

The fine distinction between the German rulers and the German people, presumably introduced to this country by James M. Beck, and emphasized over and over again by Woodrow Wilson, was soon forgotten. While in the minds of a few the early device of allocating responsibility to the Kaiser and the Junkers persisted, the entire German people finally came under one indictment.

Francis Peabody described them as "untamed barbarians and maritime murderers,"[43] while Charles Carroll Albertson, of the Lafayette Avenue Presbyterian Church, Brooklyn, exclaimed that Germany was "a whole nation suffering from moral strabismus." [44]

William A. (Billy) Sunday paraphrased the idea:

> I tell you it is Bill against Woodrow, Germany against America, Hell against Heaven. . . . Either you are loyal or you are not, you are either a patriot or a black-hearted traitor. . . . All this talk about not fighting the German people is a lot of bunk. They say that we are fighting for an ideal. Well, if we are we will have to knock down the German people to get it over.[45]

Among the contributions to an understanding of the intricacies of the case, one given by the official War Committee of the Chapel of the Comforter, New York, illustrates the processes of the human mind when it attempts to explain the culture pattern of an opposing civilization:

> There is no peasant in the world so brutal as the German (and now a soldier). He would remain a beast. Himself a slave he is filled with the belief that, because a German, he is entitled to treat the men and women of other races as if they were animals beneath him. In this respect also, therefore, he is one heart and mind with his superiors, who, with an intelligence which he, of course, does not possess, planned to enslave the world.[46]

In the contest against these allegedly brutal German peasants and their leaders, the masses of the people in America showed how successfully they had been indoctrinated by a nationalistic and provincial education in our schools. The citizens, young and old, had but the vaguest notions of comparative government, but they did understand that all others were inferior to our own. American democracy, founded upon the greatest and wisest document struck off from the brain of man, the Constitution, must, therefore be the best and in the Providence of God survive all others. This was not a reasoned judgment, of course, but the result of an emotional attachment to a symbol which they had been taught to worship since childhood by all the institutions of the nation, the state, the church, the school and the press.

Whatever lingering doubts there may have been about the sacredness of democracy were dispelled in time of war by the heightened emotional response to symbols of our country—the flag, national anthems, familiar slogans, the pictures of great patriots and the appeal to the "instinct" of self-preservation.

The above phenomenon, naturally, was not confined to America, but was a characteristic of all countries that had come under the spell of nationalism.

Now this form of egotism, while occasionally causing international friction, is generally held to be a normal condition of affairs in time of peace; in time of war for the enemy peoples to display their love of country becomes unpardonable. Hence the German Kaiser and his subjects were condemned for adherence to their chosen form of government and particular cultural set-up and for believing that God was in favor of their institutions.

On the other hand, due to previous habituation, accentuated by the neurotic fervor of 1917-18, all patriotic Americans fully accepted the dogma of ethnocentrism and held to the religious tenet that God favored democracy, our particular brand actually representing His chosen form of government. Robert A. Ashworth, pastor of the First Baptist Church of Milwaukee, in explaining "God and the Democratic Movement," showed very definitely that democracy was "more than a form of government." It was Dr. Ashworth's "conviction that democracy is founded in the nature of man and is therefore the divine order of society. On that conviction is based our confidence in its ultimate triumph."[47] The German government, in challenging this principle thereby challenged God's plan for the universe.

With such a basic theory, the desire for revenge and the vindication of God's plan naturally knew no bounds. It was impossible to believe that a just God would not avenge the murderous course of Germany by visiting His holy wrath upon the Central Powers. "'Vengeance is mine,' saith the Lord, . . . 'I will repay,'" became in revised translation, "'Vengeance is mine,' saith the Lord, . . . 'the Allies will repay.'"

"God is, must be a Righteous God on the side of the Allies. . . . God is helping the Allies to win," wrote William W. Davis, assistant pastor of the Little Church Around the Corner, New York.[48] "The real reason for the war," in the opinion of Bishop Richard J. Cooke, of the Methodist Episcopal Church of Helena,

Montana, "was to vindicate God Almighty against the brutal philosophy of damned men."[49] The chaplain of Columbia College said: "We are dealing with a criminal brought to book and unrepentant. . . . How to treat Germany is a problem of penology."[50]

It seemed impossible in those days that Germany could ever be admitted to the family of nations again. Certainly not save as a dire sinner, repentant and pleading for mercy and forgiveness. The average clergyman, well fortified historically and ethically, by Old Testament accounts of the visitation of God's wrath upon wicked nations, knew what penalties Jehovah should heap upon the Germans for their defiance of the Almighty.

In protesting against the Pope's peace proposals, *The Congregationalist* contemplated the tragedy of "a distinct lowering of the ideals of public justice for the whole world should Germany escape without repentance as well as punishment for its unprovoked aggression and cruelty."[51]

In keeping with the spirit of the times and in order to keep perpetually before the minds of the people the spectacle of German spiritual bankruptcy, various schemes were proposed. William H. Van Allen suggested: "On that bright May day two years ago, anti-Christ revealed himself as he is, when fourteen hundred lost their lives in the *Lusitania*. . . . Let us see to it that this day be remembered so long as a Hohenzollern lives."[52]

Dr. Hillis maintained:

> When the war is over, every stone in the cathedral of Cologne should be marked. German prisoners should be made to pull these stones apart, German cars be made to transport every stone to Louvain and German hands made to set up the cathedral in Louvain or Arras.[53]

Among the sundry devices to punish Germany the boycott met with tremendous approval. On Easter Sunday, 1918, Malcolm J. MacLeod made a proposal to his congregation:

> Is Germany going to win in this war and go unpunished? . . . Is hell, after all, going to come off victorious? . . . I want to say that I never expect until Germany officially repents to purchase another article made in Germany, if I know it. I should like to circulate a pledge to that effect.[54]

Mark Allison Matthews, pastor of the First Presbyterian Church of Seattle, Washington, with a membership of over 7,500 (said to be the largest of the denomination in the world), came forward with a similar proposal. He wished to court-martial and shoot "any merchant or any person, a citizen of this government or of any Allied government, who buys an article in Germany for the next one hundred years." During that time Germany was to "remain in isolation, in sackcloth and ashes, cut off from the commercial confidence of the world."[55]

Samuel Hardin Church, President of the Carnegie Institute, believed that we should "show Germany by one hundred years of social and commercial ostracism that her crime is beyond forgiveness until her children's children beg for it with contrite hearts."[56]

With all of this Dr. Hillis thoroughly agreed, but made a more ingenious proposal in his book, *The Blot on the Kaiser's Scutcheon.*

> Society has organized itself against the rattlesnake and the yellow fever. Shepherds have entered into a conspiracy to exterminate the wolves. The Boards of Health are planning to wipe out typhoid, cholera, and the black plague. Not otherwise, lovers of their fellow-man have finally become perfectly hopeless with reference to the German people. They have no more relation to the civilization of 1918 than an orang-outang, a gorilla, a Judas, a hyena, a thumbscrew, or a scalping knife in the hands of a savage. These brutes must be cast out of society. . . . We know that Tacitus said nearly two thousand years ago that "the German treats women with cruelty, tortures his enemies, and associates kindness with weakness." But nineteen hundred years of education have not changed the German one whit. . . . In utter despair, therefore, statesmen, generals, diplomats, editors are now talking about the duty of simply exterminating the German people. There will shortly be held a meeting of surgeons in this country. A copy of the preliminary call lies before me. The plan to be discussed is based upon the Indiana State law. The law authorizes a State Board of Surgeons to use upon the person of confirmed criminals and hopeless idiots the new painless method of sterilizing the men. These surgeons are preparing to advocate the calling of a world conference to consider the sterilization of 10,000,000 German soldiers and the segregation of the women, that when this generation of Germans goes, civilized cities, states and races may be rid of this awful cancer that must be cut clean out of the body of society.[57]

HYMNS OF HATE

While all these special penalties were being talked over, a serious dispute arose among Christians as to whether, in the light of the New Testament, the Germans ought to be forgiven. Cruel invectives were directed at those individuals who persisted in peace-time notions about loving and forgiving one's enemies. A letter written to *The Congregationalist* by Sydney Strong, of the Queen Anne Congregational Church of Seattle, advised forgiveness and not hatred.[58] Subscribers objected. One Henry W. Broughton, M.D., demanded that the Department of Justice "should be warned of a man who inculcates the opposite view." "He is dangerous," said Dr. Broughton, and was persuaded that "a discussion of this matter of forgiveness of enemies at this critical time, is inopportune."[59]

The editor of *The Outlook,* Lyman Abbott, went further by saying:

> But I cannot pray for the Predatory Potsdam Gang, "Father, forgive them for they know not what they do," because that it is not true. . . . I do not hate the Predatory Potsdam Gang because it is my enemy; . . . I hate it because it is a robber, a murderer, a destroyer of homes, a pillager of churches, a violater of women. I do well to hate it.[60]

It should be recorded, however, that the campaign of hatred did not proceed unimpeded. There was a tiny, if ineffective minority of prominent clergymen and editors of religious journals who, though thoroughly committed to the war, counseled against demonstrations of wrath. Charles Frederick Aked, Dr. Fosdick, Bishop Greer and Dr. Jefferson, and a few others come to mind. Yet the hydra-headed monster, once let loose, could not be rechained. Many who admonished against the fire and brimstone theology, continued to relate atrocity stories in order to arouse the moral indignation of their congregations, or point out the obvious lesson of the type of education prevailing in Germany. This approach, followed by a final plea against hatred, could not offset the damage already done.

Moreover, those who attempted to conserve some of the energy spent by Christians in denunciation of the foe and sublimate or direct it against some of the evils at home, usually came to grief. Consider the case of Robert E. Speer, secretary of the Presbyterian Board of Foreign Missions, and chairman of the General War-Time Commission of the Churches. In February, 1918, he addressed a meeting of the Y. M. C. A. at Columbia University. It had not been his intention to talk upon the war, but rather to call attention to some of our own national sins— broken treaties, labor conditions, and race prejudice. As a nation, he said, we had, in fact, condemned Germany for some things of which we also were guilty.[61] Though Dr. Speer was no pacifist, had fully justified our part in the struggle for democracy (and later brought forth a book affirming his hearty backing of the war),[62] all this was lost sight of. Anathemas were heaped upon his head for weeks in the columns of the New York *Times*, in which for the most part the controversy was waged. "The speech was insidiously corrupting";[63] Dr. Speer was a "pro-German pacifist";[64] a "little cousin of LaFollette."[65]

The religious press all but unanimously rendered a verdict against Dr. Speer. The editor of *The Congregationalist*, Howard Allen Bridgman, who had opposed the war himself up to March, 1917, wrote editorially:

> The implication was that Germany was hardly more guilty than the other nations. It is for such excessive emphasis on our national shortcomings and for failure to recognize the unprecedented and colossal wickedness of Germany that Dr. Speer's critics take him to task, and we think justly.[66]

More than three months after the address in question, the editors were continuing to discuss the subject. Curtis Lee Laws, editor of *The Watchman-Examiner* (Baptist), pointed out Dr. Speer's lack of perspective and his forlorn attempt at "a balanced, judicial, philosophical discussion of the question of war." "We are now in a righteous war," Dr. Laws reminded Dr. Speer, "let further discussion be postponed until the war is over."[67]

The Y. M. C. A., through Fletcher S. Brockman, Associate General Secretary, did not believe that Dr. Speer was guilty of "pacifist utterances," since he had always been known for "his sympathy for and support of the Allies." And, assured Mr. Brockman, "the Y. M. C. A. stands for winning the war. . . . No known pacifists have ever been or will be used as speakers or workers."[68]

Dr. Speer remonstrated against the misconstruction so generally placed upon his speech, yet his statement, "I believe that it is a righteous and necessary war," scarcely availed him.[69] C. P. Fagnani, professor at Union Theological Seminary, warned the students at the Seminary against such insidious propaganda: "Any meetings that pro-Germans could attend with satisfaction are not such as loyal Americans . . . can consistently lend countenance to."[70]*

Surveying the American scene in the early winter of 1918, the government seems to have become alarmed. In an official communication issued to its 20,000 four-minute men, they were

---

* Dr. Fagnani at the Lake Mohonk Conference in 1903 had affirmed: "It is because God is back of the Quaker principles that the Quaker principles are destined to become universal." (Report of the Ninth Annual Meeting of the Lake Mohonk Conference on International Arbitration, 1903, p. 69.)

urged to eliminate "hymns of hate" and appeals to emotion: "Not an appeal to emotionalism, but an appeal to the emotions through conviction by statement of facts secures true converts, converts who when once convinced, remain convinced."[71]

But the hymns of hate went on. Perhaps Billy Sunday excelled others, both in originality and choice of words. He used to pray to the Almighty "to guide the next gunner who sights a U-boat so that his aim will be true." Believing that hell was the "basis on which Christianity is built," he had early composed a "Who's Who of Hell," listing Jezebel, Diderot, Voltaire, John Stuart Mill, Leo Tolstoi, et cetera, and the "Kaiser and his ilk," as citizens of that inferno of the damned.[72]

In pleading for men to give to the third Liberty Loan fund, Mr. Sunday reminded them:

> Our little trouble with Spain was a coon hunt as compared with this scrap we have on hand with that bunch of pretzel-chewing, sauerkraut spawn of blood-thirsty Huns. . . . We can win, we must win. We shall win, so dig down deep and let us fill Uncle Sam's bank vault high with our money and help send a shiver down the crooked spine of the Hohenzollerns who are dancing on the thin, thin crust of Hell and thus help the guns of the army and navy to dig their graves; then the world can live in peace.[73]

Throwing down the gauntlet to the Germans, he shrieked, with a voice cracked from the strain of overwork: "I today . . . declare war against Hell and all its commissaries and all its cohorts. You can't shoot your cursed kulture and your damnable Hohenzollernism down our throats. You can't spit on the Stars and Stripes."[74]*

While the phraseology of Mr. Sunday may be regarded as exceptional, the demand for retaliation was general. A prominent Roman Catholic, J. Hartley Manners, wrote in a pamphlet: "Let all the peoples of the Allied countries hate the Hun and hate him with a will to victory. Let that doctrine of Hate be

---

* During the war, Mr. Sunday held revivals in practically all the big cities in the United States. After a ten weeks' campaign in Chicago, he departed with 49,165 converts added to the fold. When the number of converts who actually came into the churches was tabulated it was discovered, for example, in the Presbyterian Church, 32 churches reported 109 members received. If the same proportion prevailed in the other churches reporting, the total number of accessions was 325, *i.e.*, 325 out of 49,165 expectations.

The results were so thoroughly disappointing that a vote of censure was passed by the Chicago Presbytery where Mr. Sunday held his membership. (*Unity*, Vol. 82, No. 5, Oct. 10, 1918, p. 52.) It is to be noted that Mr. Sunday was censured, not for lack of decorum or language unbecoming to a clergyman, but for lack of final results.

spread until it reaches to the smallest towns in the United States. . . . In His name I pray you hate the Hun."[75] Speaking to workmen in a shipyard, Charles A. Eaton pleaded that they "put hell into every rivet" they drove, all the while remembering that they "were sending it to the bloomin' Kaiser."[76]

The leader of the Chicago Ethical Culture Society, the Unitarian clergyman, Horace Bridges, pointed out, in a letter to *The Atlantic Monthly*, the "Duty of Hatred." This, in his judgment, was "an imperative of conscience prescribing resentment, as unconditional as the very law of love itself."[77] Dr. Fosdick wrote to the editor to say that, in spite of Dr. Bridges' mode of expression which sounded like hate, Dr. Bridges nevertheless had been talking about "love" all the time.[78]

This paradoxical relationship between love and hatred baffled many minds, but not those on the War Committee of the Chapel of the Comforter in New York. In a lengthy dissertation on the subject, they strove to show that "to love is to hate. Those who do not hate, do not love. Those who love Christ with passion love His spirit. . . . and, therefore, they hate with unquenchable hatred His enemies."[79]

In contrast to the foregoing are the words of a young soldier, Colonel Whittlesey of the Lost Battalion, who received the highest military decoration possible for the United States government to bestow. At a mass meeting at the 69th Regiment Armory, New York City, he, appearing in plain civilian dress, said: "Our men are not coming back hating Germans. No man who has been in the line facing the Germans will bear any malice toward them. I know that if any American infantryman met the Kaiser on the road he would be willing to share his hardtack with him. This is not false sentiment."[80]

A civilian population, seeking vengeance on an enemy at least three thousand miles distant from its coast line, cannot be expected to put up with a sense of frustration. It will seek to find an enemy near at hand. The highly emotionalized group attitude found a perfect substitute at home in the German-Americans. They had been discovered before April, 1917, of course, but after the declaration of war they could openly be hunted, tracked down and treated as traitors. Far-seeing men had perceived that this would be so and some of them in the churches, like Dr. Jefferson and Dr. Lynch, and the Bishops of the Methodist Episcopal Church, had warned against it. But their voices were lost in the tumult as men followed Theodore Roosevelt, who long before had outlawed the "hyphenates" and now, in time of war, heaped abuse upon this minority group.

From France, George A. Griffith (Episcopalian) of Baltimore, wrote that if he were in America:

> I should do my best to have put to death any Boche in America or any so-called American who would apologize in any way for what the Boche has done. . . . Loathe the Boche, preach against him—work against him—ostracize him socially and commercially. Take no chances—even though his reputation for loyalty has been a long-standing one. The leopard cannot change his spots—neither can the Boche lose his horns.[81]

Further information was volunteered by one who signed himself "a city pastor" in the pages of *The Outlook:* "The German as I have known him in church is not a spiritually minded person."[82]

The ministers not only saw danger in the presence of the German-Americans, but evil in everything that savored of a German accent. All was part of a vast network of Hun propaganda in this country—the higher criticism, the doctrine of evolution, the teachings of Germany, and the methods of education.

> . . . let us be true patriots and fight to its death the new German theology apostasy in America. Let us tear down from our universities, theological seminaries and churches this poisonous serpent that has stealthily coiled its slimy form around our modern life and with one voice declare that America shall be holy, pure and free. Exit bastard new German religious apostasy, and enter spirit of brotherhood, love, and power.[83]

That was the indictment made by George W. McPherson, Presbyterian minister, and re-echoed a thousand times in the same phraseology. David Hugh Jones of Evanston, Illinois, also a Presbyterian, said that "German rationalism had found its way into America," the people had lost their faith because of it, and the theological seminaries had been harboring the monster for years.[84] Many Presbyterians and Baptists particularly sensed this as a part of the general plot to undermine America's faith in God.

Isaac J. Lansing, in his *Why Christianity Did Not Prevent the War,* contended that "Germany led the world in accepting this general doctrine of atheistic evolution," and that German education in this country was in reality German propaganda.[85*]

The editor of *Zion's Herald,* in estimating the values to come from the war, subscribed to the belief that "one good thing to

---

* The use of the word "kindergarten" was objected to by some ecclesiastics, while others went so far as to urge the abolition of the institution on account of its German origin. (The *Presbyterian,* Vol. 88, No. 35, Aug. 29, 1918, p. 7.)

come out of the war" would be "the liberation of religious thought from the thraldom of Germany." [86]

The clergy who had received a part of their training in Germany knew for the most part that all the eloquence directed against the German theology was misapplied, yet the defenders of the German approach were few. However, Dean Shailer Mathews, of the University of Chicago, well known for his patriotism and work with the National Security League, did not go back on his training in Biblical interpretation:

> Every champion of reaction and obscurantism declares that the war is the outcome of German higher criticism. . . . Nothing could be more absurd. The theology of the Kaiser is not the theology of the modern theological world.[87]

THE GERMAN PLOT

Another count in the indictment against the Germans gradually took form. It was discovered that they had been plotting for years to undermine the morals and integrity of Americans, preparing the way for the downfall of our government for the inclusion of America in the Pan-Germanic scheme, when the Kaiser and his troops would land in Boston and New York, and thence march across the hinterland to San Francisco.

Once aroused to the realities and dangers of the situation, the pastors exposed the details of the vast plot, seeing evidences of its machinations in the German museum at Harvard, the German names of towns, and the use of Wagner's Wedding March.

Poultney Bigelow, former bosom friend of the Kaiser, at this time repudiated the Emperor (he has since the war apologized) and ferreted out the signs of the German plot to enslave the world. The clergy passed on the results of his researches. Dr. Lansing, for instance, agreed with Mr. Bigelow:

> And then the exchange professors, and the visit of Prince Henry and the Germanic Museum at Harvard, and the statue of Frederick the Great for Washington . . . and all the while the great General Staff of Berlin was feverishly at work preparing plans for an invasion of America on the Belgium-Rumanian plan.[88]

In contemplation of the impending Teutonic invasion from across the seas, Herbert S. Johnson, of the Warren Avenue Baptist Church, Boston, prophesied:

> I can see the time coming, when, unless we cease the camouflage, a strong man can't make his way through the streets of Bos-

ton because of the debris of a German bombardment. I can see the time when our women will be attacked by German soldiers, as the women of Belgium and France have been.[89]

The use of the German language, of course, came also to be very obnoxious.

SPEAK THE AMERICAN LANGUAGE

IF you don't know it—learn it.
    you don't like it—move out.

The above sign greeted all the citizens of a certain Kansas town during the war.[90] The use of the German tongue was prohibited by law in the public schools in fourteen states of the Union. Under the guidance of their State Councils of Defense, Iowa and Washington prohibited its use entirely. Iowa forbade the use of any foreign language in a public meeting.[91] This policy of banning the language in which the enemy carried on its conversation did not meet with the approval of the U. S. Commissioner of Education, P. P. Claxton.[92] His opinions, however, were ground under the heels of the various defense societies, defense councils, and security leagues. The American Defense Society, for instance, proposed:

> We can make war on the Hun language, and we will. Any language which produces a people of ruthless conquistadors, such as now exists in Germany, is not a fit language to teach to clean and pure American boys and girls, and the most ordinary principles of self-defense demand that it be eliminated. . . . Loyal men cannot permit the teaching of an enemy language.[93]

Clergymen in abundance joined in this crusade.

The campaign against German-language newspapers proceeded in much the same fashion. Samuel Hardin Church saw no possible excuse for their existence and recommended that the government "suspend all German language newspapers for the period of the war."[94] Cornelius Woelfkin, pastor of the Fifth Avenue Baptist Church, New York, took the same position.[95]*

Music and Patriotism

Martial airs are to patriotism what hymns are to religion. War stimulates the use of both to an unusual degree, since they serve

---

* A bill was proposed in Congress by Representative Smith of Michigan to strike out all German names of towns in the United States. (New York *Times*, June 2, 1918.)

to express, as perhaps no other medium can, the patriotic and religious fervor, the aspirations, hopes, joys, convictions, and faith of a people in the ultimate triumph of their cause.

Julia Ward Howe's *The Battle Hymn of the Republic,* the favorite lyric of the Civil War, became again a popular hymn during the late trial at arms. In order to bring it up to date, Henry Van Dyke, a chaplain in the navy at the time, wrote an additional stanza for the use of the Navy Department Commission on Training Camp Activities to be sung by the sailors in the Naval Training Stations.

> We have heard the cry of anguish,
> From the victims of the Hun,
> And we know our country's peril
> If the war-lord's will is done.
> We will fight for world-wide freedom
> Till the victory is won.
> For God is marching on.[96]

To this 1918 expression of the Spirit of the '60's Florence Howe Hall, the daughter of Julia Ward Howe, saw objections,[97] while the editor of the New York *Times* agreed by saying: "He [Dr. Van Dyke] would not thank anybody for editing, or even for improving his own poems."[98]

There was an intense desire to express the peculiar relationship between national patriotism and the war songs of the church. Special hymn books were called for. The Fleming H. Revell Co., publishers, attempted to fill the need, requesting William P. Merrill of the Brick Presbyterian Church, New York, to compile the collection of the mighty war hymns of the church. A note from the publishers asked, "Could your church make a better moderate investment for fostering patriotism?"[99]*

In those tense and trying days, German music had the reputation of being as dangerous as dynamite,† while the playing of "The Star-Spangled Banner" was regarded as the proper and effective prophylactic against any virus from musical propaganda.

---

* Clarence A. Barbour, president of Rochester Theological Seminary, now president of Brown University, edited a special war hymn book for the Y. M. C. A., and Louis F. Benson one for the Presbyterians under the title: *For God and Country.*

† The American Defense Society proposed the ban of German music as "one of the most dangerous forms of German propaganda, because it appeals to the emotions and has power to sway an audience as nothing else can." (New York *Tribune,* March 3, 1918.) The All-Allies Anti-German League formed in New York March 11, 1919, tried "to put a stop to the attempts to soften American hearts toward Germany by the production of German operas and music." (New York *World,* March 12, 1919.)

When the announcement came out that the Boston Symphony Orchestra intended to play in Carnegie Hall, New York, under the direction of Karl Muck, a small uprising occurred, led by Mrs. William Jay, assisted by Dr. Manning, then engaged as a volunteer chaplain at Camp Upton. Dr. Muck, a naturalized Swiss citizen since 1881, had been in Boston since 1912. His record, as far as the Department of Justice was concerned, seems to have been clear.[100] Yet, Dr. Manning proceeded to ring the alarum:

> While our boys, fighting at the front in our defense, are being assailed by liquid fire, poison gas . . . it is not fitting nor decent for us at concerts . . . to give countenance and support to the avowed friends and upholders of the Kaiser."[101]

Major Henry Lee Higginson, sponsor for the orchestra, stood by Dr. Muck. A crowd packed Carnegie Hall.

Dr. Hillis, in his desire to root out every source of anti-American influence, singled out Fritz Kreisler, the celebrated Austrian violinist. Despite the fact that it was well known that Mr. Kreisler had been wounded and honorably discharged from the Austrian army some time before the United States entered the war, Dr. Hillis, from his pulpit in Brooklyn, charged:

> What shall be said about men who enter into business with Muck and Kreisler? It is well known that Kreisler is an Austrian captain; that to obtain his release he entered into an agreement to send back to his home government a large percentage of his income. An Austrian gun costs approximately $20. Every night that Kreisler is paid $1000 Austria can buy fifty rifles with which Germany can kill our boys.[102]

Mr. Kreisler, who had canceled his American tour the same day that Dr. Hillis preached against him, demanded a retraction for what he called a "cowardly, irresponsible and unethical attack."[103] As a matter of fact the violinist had been for three years "the sole and unique support of seventeen British, Russian, French and Italian artists and their entire families who found themselves stranded and utterly destitute in Austria at the outbreak of the war."[104] All his vouchers for money sent abroad had been approved at Washington.[105] Dr. Hillis, of course, could very easily have secured this information.

Spy Hunting

The psychic drives that produce the phenomena of the Inquisition, burning of witches, Watch and Ward Societies, in time of war find expression and release in spy hunting. The tendency to pry into other people's affairs, inhibited in times of peace by social conventions, knew few restrictions in the years 1917-18. Countless thousands of self-righteous citizens indulged in the sport, and while the number of the clergy and laymen who took active part in the ferreting out of dangerous citizens will never be known, they must have been legion. There was not a community that did not have some of its citizens under surveillance by some self-appointed or semi-official representative of the government. The defense societies, and citizens protective leagues took the widest liberties in these activities. Ministers joined the spy-hunting societies and served as agents for espionage.

The American Protective League, for instance, was a purely volunteer organization of citizens as an auxiliary to the Department of Justice, assisting in slacker raids and ferreting out of spies. Its membership has been rated at 2,250,000, with branches of the organizations in every city and town of any size in the United States. Upwards of 3,000,000 investigations were conducted for the Bureau of Investigation of the Department of Justice, the Provost Marshal General's office, et cetera.[106] When the war came to a close, Attorney General Gregory issued a statement to the members of the League. The full text is suggestive of the days of the Inquisition in Spain. The American Protective League's influence during the war had been "a powerful deterrent of enemy and disloyal activities," he said, since these enemies knew "the eyes and ears of a great organization auxiliary to the government" were on every hand. The Attorney General wished to have the full benefit of these operations continued; thus he urged them to keep on with their espionage tactics, since "illegal activities harmful to the public morale during the discussion of peace terms must be watched for and reported."[107] However, something subsequently transpired, for on December 19, 1918, the national directors of the League issued an order for its dissolution, effective February 1, 1919. The order was a complete admission of the dangers of such an organization: "In such a time there is no place for organized citizen espionage. It is contrary to the spirit of democracy. It is dangerous in its tendencies and so might well be disastrous in its results."[108]

Various organizations of this type operating under the name of patriotism during the war numbered more than a hundred. There was one called the Anti-Yellow Dog League, announced as "an unofficial auxiliary of the Department of Justice." Boys of ten years of age and over were eligible for membership. They went out in search of disloyalists. They claimed to have one thousand branches all over the United States. Brooklyn alone had six, with several hundred boys in active service.[109]

While one may now laugh at the manifestations of hysteria and the attempts of millions of private citizens, including children, to make the world safe for democracy by means of a gigantic spy-hunting system, it is to be remembered that the public officials, the leaders of public opinion, and the newspapers created a state of panic and terror among the American people. After the war got under way, the press carried thousands upon thousands of stories of alleged spy activities. Most of these cases were pure figments of the imagination. Yet the effect was the same as if they had been true. Speakers, likewise, fearful of the "boring from within," reiterated warnings from the platforms.

The result was obvious. People were literally crazed with fear. Hence extreme measures were advocated. Samuel Hardin Church told an immense Philadelphia audience that, "we should demand that every German spy and propagandist shall be shot. . . ." Senator La Follette, he claimed, "ought to be expelled from the United States Senate as a public nuisance."[110]

With the picture in nearly everyone's mind of the enemy within the gates, the church leaders undertook to lead in saving their country in the war on the "home front." That they were intensely interested in aiding and abetting the general movement to extricate and expose the alleged spies may be proved from three sources. First, there is an almost complete silence, or certainly no condemnation of these witch-hunting endeavors. Second, testimony and confessions come to the present writer of ministers who belonged to these organizations, and of church members who "had their eyes peeled" to discover some new evidence that would lead to the exposure of "suspect" members of the congregation. Third, the public declarations of prominent leaders in the churches show that they supported this wholesale espionage system.

In Philadelphia, March, 1918, the Methodist clergy, assembled in "warlike mood," passed a resolution which was unanimously adopted and sent to the government by the four hundred ministers present, "amid cheering and patriotic enthusiasm." "We urge," said they, "the speedy enactment of a law which will mete out to German propagandists and traitorous Americans the full penalty of spies."[111]

Bishop Theodore S. Henderson of Detroit, addressing a Methodist Conference at Atlantic City in March, 1918, lamented the slackness on the part of the church to live up to its duty:

> It is a perfect tragedy that the Christian Church has been so slow to realize its possibilities. . . .
> We have other duties to perform. Every one should immediately get in touch with our War Council, should you find anybody of pro-German tendencies in your community. Let us locate, eliminate, and exterminate every pro-German in this country."[112]

Charles A. Eaton had been appointed chairman of the National Service Section of the Emergency Fleet Corporation, in which capacity he went about the country inspiring the toilers in the shipyards to increased production. At the submarine works in Newark, New Jersey, he counseled: "When he [the spy] comes sneaking around with a bomb, don't say 'Let us pray,' but take him out there on the marsh and tie him down and place the bomb on his chest. Light it and stand off and watch him blow to his Kaiser—to Hell! Be regular he-men."[113]

On his return from his tour over the States, this same pastor of the Madison Avenue Baptist Church said:

> Out on the Pacific Coast the men have what they call the Rail Committee. This is formed of workmen and is charged with seeing that every hand in the yards is one hundred per cent American and on the job eight hours a day, six days a week. In a yard at Seattle, the Rail Committee has an iron pipe which is called the Liberty Rail. It is kept near the blacksmith's forge. When a workman utters a disloyal sentiment, fails to buy bonds or war-savings stamps, or in other ways proves that he is lukewarm, the Rail Committee waits on him. The Liberty Rail is heated at the forge, and the disloyal workman is ridden about the yards on the hot rail. At one time, I was told, there were twelve men in a Seattle hospital recovering from Liberty Rail rides.[114]

Dr. Cadman gave instructions to enable his hearers to detect signs of disloyalty:

> And be increasingly watchful because this espionage to which we are subject exists everywhere. It employs the courtesan and the pervert. It seduces the unwary. . . . It cripples our ships so that they have to return to port. It burns and blows up our factories and supplies. . . . The Secret Service of the United States has done us unexampled service. But it should be the determination of every citizen to expose and confound these knaves and their tricks. And when you detect these reptilian movements, report them and see to it that they are squelched.[115]

Henry Van Dyke issued warnings:

> It is by law, civil in time of peace, martial in time of war, that the . . . republic must be protected. . . .
> Any inhabitant of this country who puts destructive material into the machinery of the ships which are carrying our brave boys across the ocean to serve under the flag is a constructive murderer and a traitor. He should face a traitor's doom. Shooting would be too good for him. If convicted, he should be hung without delay. The same thing is true of every American who puts destructive material into the minds of our American citizens, urging them to be disloyal or recalcitrant, persuading them to evade or resist the call which our country has made for the service of all its people in the defense of its rights and its honor.
> A man who by speech or action endeavors to impede America's efficiency in this righteous war should be judged by the law, and, if convicted, promptly executed.[116]

Dr. Van Dyke was, therefore, asking the death penalty for items, including obstruction of recruiting, and "sedition"—a more severe penalty than the law itself provided. He seems also to have had the impression that the whole country was under martial law simply because the United States was at war, an opinion not in accord with the facts.

The summary of the net results of all the spy hunting has well been given by the historians, Charles A. and Mary R. Beard:

> And yet when all these immense inquisitorial activities were sifted down to the very bottom, only two conclusions of significance remained. The first is that not a single first-class German spy or revolutionary workingman was caught and convicted of an overt act designed to give direct aid or comfort to the enemy. The second is that . . . the occasion of the war which called for patriotic duties was seized by emotional conservatives as an opportunity to blacken the character of persons whose opinions they feared or hated.[117]

THE CLERGY UNDER INDICTMENT

Judging from the foregoing delineation of clerical loyalty and enthusiastic devotion to the nation's cause, and the amount of energy the ministers must have consumed in watching over the patriotic and spiritual health of the United States during those days, he would be a rash critic indeed who could discover signs that the ministers were slackers. Howbeit, such a critic did appear in the person of Joseph H. Odell,* who, through the pages of *The Atlantic Monthly,* in February, 1918, under the title "Peter Sat by the Fire Warming Himself," administered the whip lash to his clerical brethren.

> Thoughtful men and women are asking what became of the spiritual leadership of America during those thirty-two months when Europe and parts of Asia were passing through Gehenna. What prelate or bishop or ecclesiastical dignitary essayed the work of spiritual interpretation? . . .

He then laid the blame upon the preachers for the whole present world situation. "The Kaiser is what he is because the preachers are what they are." They, with their German theology, had taken all the supernatural element out of the Bible under the inspiration of the Kaiser himself.

> It is the most damnable circle of atheistic conspiracy that the ages have known. Nevertheless, the preachers of America . . . never uttered an indictment loud enough to cause the male members of the churches to foozle a drive in their Sunday morning foursome at the country club.

An indictment so devastating needed an answer. It was forthcoming from the pen of George Parkin Atwater, rector of the Church of the Savior, Akron, Ohio.

> *The complete representative of the American Church in France is the United States Army overseas* [Italics are Dr. Atwater's]. Yes, an army, with its cannon and rifles and machine-guns, and its instruments of destruction. The Church, militant, sent, morally equipped, strengthened and encouraged, approved and blessed, by the Church at home. The army today is the Church in action, transforming the will of the Church into deeds, expressing the moral judgment of the Church into smashing blows. Its worship has its vigil in the trenches, and its fasts and feasts; its prayers are in acts, and its choir is the crash of cannon and the thrilling ripple of machine guns.
>
> Do you think, Mr. Odell, that if the Church as a whole had opposed war, or had sat by the fire warming itself, the nation could have put the army overseas without draft riots? No, from the beginning the Church was patriotic and loyal. . . .
>
> And the clergy and the Church of our nation spoke and spoke

---

* Dean Charles Reynolds Brown of Yale described Dr. Odell as "as Englishman who for several years has now been vacillating between the ministry and secular journalism, but is now the pastor of a small church in northern New York." (E. H. Sneath (Ed.) *Religion and the War,* Yale University Press, New Haven, 1918, p. 11.) Dr. Odell was pastor of the First Presbyterian Church, Troy, N. Y., and for ten years Chaplain of the 13th Pennsylvania Infantry.

with power. Hot, flaying, excoriating, scarifying words of righteousness, indignation and anger have poured forth from our pulpits. . . .[118]

Dr. Atwater's reply to the critical Odell found favor. Even *The Outlook*, for whom Dr. Odell served as war correspondent on the western front, sided with the churches, and listed among the "interpreters of the war" Archbishop Ireland, Drs. Manning, Gammon, Hillis, Cadman, Fosdick, Luther Wilson, and Van Dyke.[119] *The Congregationalist* added to the list Dean Hodges, Dean Brown, Drs. King of Oberlin and Gordon of Boston, and wondered "if in this connection Mr. Odell has happened to see anything from the pen of Dr. Newell Dwight Hillis bearing on this subject."[120]

Nevertheless Dr. Odell was not left alone. Dr. Cadman wrote to *The Congregationalist*, "I have re-read Mr. Odell's article and I am still convinced that he has a case."[121] George R. Van de Water, addressing the Republican Club in New York, recommended the article to the laymen for patriotic reading. Said he: "I felt as if my skin had been taken off my body and I was being larruped with it. Buy a copy and read it."[122]

Following this excitement the editor of *The Christian Register*, Albert C. Dieffenbach, upbraided the editors of the religious press for not doing their duty by their country:

> What is wrong with many of our contemporaries of the so-called religious press? Why do they not mightily declare their passion to win the war? . . . Our leaders must talk about the war and their passion to help win the war, and not about even Jesus Christ in such wise as to divert them from their duty. . . . Only once in a hundred times does either speaker or writer go to the center and soul of the business and utter a ringing challenge to win the war for God and Christ and mankind. . . . There is nothing to our hand and soul now and for months to come but the conquest of a race lusting to wrest freedom from us. Hear this, ye editors, and gird up the loins of your mind.[123]

The evidence on the war-time hysteria, as it affected the ecclesiastical hierarchy, leads to the conclusion that the church leaders, in spite of their priestly claim to depth of spiritual insight and knowledge of ethical values, displayed no such superior quality of moral judgment as has been assumed. At least, their speeches and conduct differed in no wise from the mass of the people whom they had undertaken to lead. The clergy were swept from their moorings in exactly the same way as were many of those untutored minds who made no pretensions to holiness or loving one's neighbor or knowledge of God's will.

CHAPTER VI

THE CHURCHES INTERPRET THE FIRST AMENDMENT

Democracy is not going to suffer from this temporary restriction [of free speech] and a little rest will prove wholesome to the tongue.

The Churchman, September 22, 1917.

CHAPTER VI
THE CHURCHES INTERPRET THE FIRST AMENDMENT

Free Speech, Ltd.

THE first casualty of war is free speech. Since the end to be attained supersedes all other values and motives, the right to life, liberty and the pursuit of happiness, freedom of speech and of the press, the right of peaceful assemblage and the right to petition the government for a redress of grievances —all are secondary.[1] The very abstractness of these rights permits their suppression to be accomplished with comparative ease. The crowd itself frequently goes much further in the denial of liberty than the forces of the official government. In the late war for the salvation of democracy this phenomenon was particularly noticeable. Democracy suffered most from her saviors.

The Protestant churches had been proud of their fight for religious and civil liberty in this country, and some of them, particularly the Baptist, Congregationalist and Unitarian groups, gloried in the right of the individual believer to worship God and interpret the Bible according to the dictates of his own conscience. During the war they were confronted with the necessity of repudiating their traditional ideals.* Farsighted individuals in the Federal Council of Churches saw that this would be so. And, in an effort to throw up a bulwark against the mounting tide, a resolution was passed by that body during the very first days of the war, reminding the churches that "the abuse of free speech is not as dangerous as its suppression and nothing

---

* What opposition existed to the restrictions of free speech came from a few radical ministers and religious publications like *Unity* and *The World Tomorrow*. In May, 1917, a few protesting voices were heard in the wilderness. Walter H. Macpherson, preaching in Joliet, Illinois, stated: "There should be freedom of speech and freedom of the press. Down at Washington, according to reports, they are attempting to put over a gag law, a law that will abridge the rights of the press and throttle the voice of the platform. I protest against this action, and I want to say that the day free speech is denied this platform I will go to jail." (*Unity*, Vol. 79, No. 16, June 14, 1917, p. 28.) As will be pointed out later, numbers of ministers did go to jail, though, as far as I can discover, Mr. Macpherson was not among them.

should be permitted to destroy the dearly bought right of freedom of conscience."[2]

Yet, when the Espionage Act of June 15, 1917, and its amendment of May 16, 1918, generally referred to as the Sedition Act, were passed they met with no particular opposition from the religious forces, though both of these acts affected the right of conscience, the interpretation of the Scripture, even its distribution, and fundamentally all talk in favor of peace.

Practical nullification of the Bill of Rights was made easy partly because of the manner in which the press throughout the country frightened the populace by constantly carrying highly colored and exaggerated stories of German plots, activities of spies, disloyal utterances, impending sedition trials, activities of the I. W. W. and all the other reputed enemies within the gates. The mass of people, worked up to a state of hysteria, believed the most absurd stories and resorted to lynch law and mob violence to preserve the social solidarity against the common foe.

Correspondents wrote of manifestations of paranoia in every section. One of them testified:

> I am amazed . . . at the hysteria and fanaticism which is pervading the country in every direction. The least word said against existing conditions and tendencies leads to arrest and condemnation. . . . It grows worse every day. . . . Has the world gone mad? . . . Few know what they mean by being Christians; they follow the crowd belief, even the professors in the universities and theological schools do the same.[3]

With the conviction that free speech does not mean "license," the religious press and pulpit repudiated or reinterpreted ancient liberties. The editor of *The Watchman-Examiner* estimated:

> Between the soldier in the trenches who turns his weapons upon his comrades and the man at home who makes his tongue a weapon against the whole-hearted and determined prosecution of the war, there is little to choose. Each is a traitor, no matter what plane he occupies or by what name he is called.[4]

John A. Ryan, liberal Catholic leader, expressed the basic philosophy of war time. The war being a just one the citizen "cannot reasonably complain if the government restricts his freedom of speech for the sake of the prosecution of the war. The authorities are justified . . . in preventing obstructive criticism."[5]

The emphasis upon loyalty and obedience by the Catholic

Church perhaps accounts for its particular impatience with critics. His Eminence, John Cardinal Farley, explained:

> Criticism of the government irritates me. I consider it little short of treason. Self-constituted critics are in fact disloyal, and even those whose duty it is to express disapproval should be extremely sparing in their use of this power.
>
> Every citizen of this nation, no matter what his private opinion or his political leanings, should support the President and his advisers to the limit of his ability.[6]

Cardinal Farley expressed very well the nation-wide feeling against various types of slackers and disloyalists. Fear of minority propaganda and activities, as in the case of the I. W. W., for instance, haunted men and women a thousand miles removed from the place of their reputed operations. In the summer of 1917 raids against these workers were made in many sections of the United States,[7] thus thrusting the I. W. W. into the limelight of publicity and intensifying the hatred against them.

Mark A. Matthews demanded: "By the power of Almighty God . . . autocracy shall be crushed and the damnable enemies, like the I. W. W., at home and abroad shall be forever chained."[8] Billy Sunday agreed: "And down, I say, with the slackers, and down with this God-forsaken crew of I. W. W's. What have they ever done I want to know. I'll be darned if some of them wouldn't face a firing squad at sunrise if I was running things. . . ."[9]

The editor of *Zion's Herald* said there was "no place in America" for any person who was not an "out and out supporter of the government,"[10] and hoped that the round-up of the I. W. W. would "bring an end to their nefarious propaganda."[11] This same journal, calling upon all the churches for "absolute loyalty to the government," since "America must be the land of patriots today," referred to Alexander Berkman and Emma Goldman as "despicable self-confessed anarchists."[12] *The Christian Register,* with other journals, thoroughly approved the arrest of Mrs. Rose Pastor Stokes, whose offense consisted in writing in a letter, "I am for the people and the government is for the profiteers."[13]

The editor of *The Outlook* disapproved, in those days, of all lack of conformity. He approved the dismissal of Professors Dana and Cattell from Columbia University,[14] the suppression of the *Masses*,[15] showed that La Follette was a disgrace to the Senate and Wisconsin,[16] declared that the pacifists had no right of assemblage,[17] and that with the aid of the Espionage and Sedition Acts, "if prosecuting officers now do their duty, there will be less excuse for lynch law as an evidence of patriotic Americanism."[18]

Shailer Mathews went so far as to say that organized socialism in America had turned itself into "anti-Americanism" (the Socialists were divided in their attitude toward the war), and that although "the bolsheviki may be sincere, the German Socialist of America is disloyal."[19]

While Joseph T. Cashman, field secretary for the National Security League, is reported to have toured the country with the proposal that there is "just one remedy" for men of "Scott Nearing's ilk" (*i.e.*, La Follette, et al.), "that is the firing squad just before dawn,"[20] Bishop Luther B. Wilson rejoiced that the legislature of Wisconsin had lifted up La Follette to "the scorn of civilization," and recommended that all men of his stamp be placed in jail.[21]

Disloyal utterances came, in time, to include the slightest criticism of anything pertaining to the war. In those days it was a crime, in Minnesota at least, to discourage women from knitting socks by the remark, "No soldier ever sees those socks." This statement might reach the ears of soldiers or men on the point of enlisting or being drafted and thus discourage them or lower their morale.[22] Men were sent to prison for criticizing the Red Cross and the Y. M. C. A., and for proposing the making of peace with Germany.[23]

In these repressive measures to insure the success of our arms, the clergy in general concurred.

THE POPE'S PEACE PROPOSALS

When, in the summer of 1917, the Pope issued new peace proposals, practically all of the Protestants looked upon them with suspicion. To begin with, as *The Churchman* phrased it, "Unfortunately the papacy has a long political history," and the so-called papal detachment was, therefore, not to be trusted.[24] Dr. Lynch, in the pages of *Christian Work,* practically told the Pope that he had no sense of justice, for His Holiness did not seem to realize that the blame for the damages of the war were to be laid "at the door of one nation." [25] Alva Taylor, professor in the Bible College of Missouri, prominent layman in the Church of the Disciples of Christ, and one of the contributing editors to *The Christian Century,* reminded his readers that the Pope's peace proposals sounded "suspiciously Austrian," and "Austria is the fairest political jewel in his political diadem."[26] Bishop Richard J. Cooke of Helena, Montana, warned his fellows to give no credence to any peace pleas, "even though they came from the Vatican."²⁷

Thus, as far as Protestantism was concerned, the proposals only served to entrench the mass of the churches more firmly in the desire to see "peace with victory."

The Catholics seem to have been rather cautious in committing themselves. *The Catholic World* knew that the fact that the message of His Holiness had been written in Latin would give it added weight and prestige. Cardinal Gibbons gave assurances that the Pope was actuated by lofty motives,²⁸ while *America* (Catholic) of New York City, took a more advanced position. "His Holiness," said this Catholic journal, "has set morality over against ruthless, brute force, and challenged men to choose between them." The nation that refuses to hearken to such a call "writes itself down not as a vindicator of justice, but as a monster lustful of men's blood." Because radicalism was "advancing by leaps and bounds," *America* urged the nations of the world to pay particular attention to the Pope's message, since, if the war continued, Socialism would take possession of all the warring countries.²⁹

The Pacifists

The Roman pontiff's peace proposals were unpopular among Protestants not merely because he represented the Roman Catholic Church. All talk of the possibility or the desirability of peace without first completely crushing Germany was rapidly coming to be suspect. The peace talkers had already been discredited as they came to be labeled unworthy citizens and secret spies of Prussianism, and now as the war moved on the deep-dyed German plot to ruin the world was seen operating through all efforts at conciliation. The sentiments of millions of people were expressed in the words of Dr. Lansing that "all the movements for peace have come either from the Germans or their bloodless tools, the pacifists."³⁰

At a patriotic meeting at Carnegie Hall, in March, 1918, in honor of the Archbishop of York, Dr. Manning announced:

> Whoever now talks of peace is no real friend of peace nor true friend of freedom, no loyal son of America. Our danger today is not from the Germans in the trenches, but from the so-called pacifists, the American bolsheviki, who are seeking by peace talk to break down the morale of our fighting men. We want no talk of negotiation, or indemnity, no restatement of war aims; we have only one war aim, the complete and decisive overthrow of the

Prussian military machine, its crushing defeat on the field of battle. Till then any talk of peace is dangerous or thinly disguised treason.[31]

That pacifism had any legitimate connection with sound Christianity was believed impossible even by the expert interpreters of the Gospels. Benjamin Wisner Bacon of the Yale Divinity School, a leading exponent of the rational approach to the interpretation of the New Testament, taught that all forms of peace propaganda should be "justly and properly repressed by the government as a war-time measure." He reprimanded John Haynes Holmes for writing the book, *New Wars for Old* (published back in 1916), because it gave "concrete and tangible form to that interpretation of the teaching of Jesus which we regard as misleading and dangerous." And Dr. Bacon pointed out:

> Recently the government itself has given warning against this type of pacifist propaganda; and there is only too much reason to believe that (quite without the intention or knowledge of its authors) those eminent pacifists, the Potsdam Conspirators, have made large financial contributions to its success.[32]

Eventually distinctions which may have formerly existed in people's minds between the various shades of opposition to the war broke down altogether. The terms, "pacifists," "conscientious objectors," "cowards," and "traitors," all came to be interchangeable. H. N. Coudon, chaplain of the House of Representatives, prayed: "Good Lord, deliver us from the hyphenated American, the pro-German, the spy, the slacker, and all who would retard the prosecution of the war for human rights, human happiness, in the establishment of a permanent world wide peace, for Christ's sake, Amen."[33]

Bishop Samuel Fallows of the Reformed Episcopal Church, Chicago diocese, an old Civil War veteran, used the language of '61 and called the peacemakers "copperheads and well-nigh traitors."[34] Frank Gunsaulus, a fellow Chicago clergyman, concurred in this opinion.[35] James Wesley Johnston advised treatment for them: "Either expulsion from the country or internment until the war ends."[36]

In Philadelphia, David M. Steele, rector of the fashionable Episcopalian Church of St. Luke's Epiphany, called attention to the "feeble selfishness of these people and the fallacy of what they have been pluming themselves upon as their peculiar virtue." The vast majority of these zealots, he certified, "made pacifism a screen for cowardice, for indifference and greed."[37]

James Samuel Stone, rector of St. James's Church, Chicago,

gave it as his opinion that the pacifist was the "most despicable and craven creature that crawls the earth," and that the word, "pacifist" was "the most disgraceful word in the English language."[38]

In March, 1918, the pastor of the First Baptist Church of Cleveland, Ohio, is said to have warned that, "Anybody who advocates peace now is disloyal. . . . A slacker, a Boche and a trench rat we are told are the three things that a British soldier hates. Add to the list the pacifist and you will have an evenly balanced quartet from the American point of view."[39]

The problem of arguing the pacifist out of court could not be met, however, on purely emotional grounds. This Dr. Fosdick recognized when he attempted to distinguish between terms which he regarded as often confused: "Even Jesus did not bless the peaceful; he blessed the peace-makers; and peace-making in any human relationship may any day involve resort to force."[40]

Dean Shailer Mathews admitted that the pacifist was right when he claimed that "war is unchristian," but maintained that he was mistaken in claiming that "all participation in war is unchristian." "The truth of this paradox is apparent when opposition to war becomes opposition to *a* war. For an American to refuse to share in the present war, to oppose preparation for war, to induce men to avoid draft, and to attack all forms of military preparation of national defense, is not Christian."[41]

A wide range of quotations illustrating anti-pacifist attitudes has been given to show how general was the state of agitated mentality. The feeling toward the conscientious objectors was even more intense. The pacifists and conscientious objectors were outlawed, not merely because they interfered with the fullest promotion of the war, but for deeper psychological reasons.

Despite loud acclaims of holy war aims among the clergy, there are evidences that numbers of even the most loyal of them were, at times, in doubt as to whether Jesus would approve of war. This mental conflict, in some cases, could not be resolved and it produced extreme personality disorganization. The individuals who were successful in their adjustments were of several varieties but for our purpose may be divided into two classes. In the first may be placed those whose misgivings were conscious and well known to themselves. They suffered, now and then, from what is often termed a "guilty conscience." But these doubts were suppressed back into the unconscious for a number of reasons—fear of social ostracism, loss of position, et cetera. The other class consists of those with whom this conflict of ideas about the war was carried on beneath the surface of the mind, and was, therefore, not a conscious process. These ministers were not aware of entertaining doubts about the holiness of the allied cause, for these doubts were repressed by the censor of the mind before they could get to the surface.

Nevertheless, with both classes of individuals, in numerous instances, these tabued ideas, having gotten by the censor, reappeared into consciousness in a form acceptable to the individual personality. The psychological device by which this process is carried on is well known in psychoanalysis under the terms "disguise," "mask," "rationalization," and "defense mechanism."

In the type of cases under discussion the mechanism is often referred to as "projection." Projection has been defined as "criticism leveled at others" that "is often an attack which applies more aptly to ourselves, but which, rather than endure, we deflect toward some innocent person or toward some guilty goat."[42]

Certain members of the clergy now recognize that, in their condemnation of the attitudes displayed by the pacifists and the conscientious objectors, they were actually denouncing as unpatriotic ideas with which they themselves frequently sympathized in secret. The unconscious motivation leading to the loud protests was not to squelch the objectors but to suppress their own doubts, misgivings, and lack of patriotism. Y. M. C. A. workers have told me of secretaries who were in the habit of going down to the "pen" in which the conscientious objectors (men taken in the draft who refused to fight) were confined in the camps, and then gaze at them in awe and wonder. The next day some of these same secretaries would utter violent pronouncements against the recalcitrants.

When Conscience Is a Crime

In the large group of objectors to the war were the men known as the conscientious objectors or "C. O.'s". According to the report of the War Department, "only 3,989 out of a grand total of 2,810,296 inducted men made any claim in camp for exemption from any form of military service as conscientious objectors on religious or other grounds."[43] This does not include various other objectors, such as the men sentenced to prison by the civil courts under the draft law for refusal to register or take a medical examination. Nor does it include the men in this class who never came before the courts, nor the 363,022 estimated by the government who evaded the draft.[44] (The total number was later cut down below this.)

Of these 3,989 conscientious objectors in camps, 1,300 " 'originally accepted or were assigned to non-combatant service'; 1,200 were furloughed to agriculture and 99 to the Friends Reconstruction Unit, while 450 were sent to prison by courts-martial. The remainder were still in camp when the Armistice was signed."[45] This means that all but 450 objectors who went to camp found some service acceptable to them and the government.

Which denominations furnished the objectors? Most of these men came from the smaller sects. It is an interesting fact that the larger denominations produced a mere handful of C. O.'s. There were two or three Catholics who objected on religious grounds, and one Jew on that basis.[46] Out of about 360 religious objectors court-martialed and sentenced, 138 were Mennonites.*

It is not my purpose to tell the story of the brutal treatment received by these men. That has been done quite thoroughly by others.[47] The aim here is to describe the attitudes manifested toward them by the Christian leaders and the churches.

This scattered band of approximately 4,000 men received so much attention from the secular and the religious press, the churches and the pulpits of the land, that the reader of the chronicles of that period is easily led into thinking that at least one million men refused to fight on grounds of conscience.

The fear that these disloyal and "yellow cowards" would destroy the beautiful story of the "holy war," undermine the faith of the people in the righteousness and sacred aims of the Allies, and set a bad example to others, led vast numbers of Christians to revile them. As Caroline E. Playne, in her *Society at War*, a psychological study of the life and conduct of English people during the late hostilities, has well expressed the current attitude, "it was alarming that these few thousands should put the millions in the wrong. . . . The romantic picture of the Captains and the Kings leading the battle array and striking terror in the aggressor's soul was marred when miserable con-

---

* The following list is furnished by Prof. J. G. Evert of Tabor College, Hillsboro, Kansas. (*Vid.* Norman Thomas, *The Conscientious Objector in America*, Huebsch, N. Y., 1923, p. 48.)

Mennonites	138	Molokans	6
International Bible Students	27	Apostolic Faith	4
Dunkards (Brethren)	24	House of David	4
Church of God (Holiness)	17	Plymouth Brethren	3
Church of Christ	17	Christadelphian	1
Quakers (Friends)	13	River Brethren	1
Seventh Day Adventists	11	Independent Christians	80
Pentecostal Faith	13		

scientious objectors, blots in the background, indicated that the amazing fine procession was but a vain show, a primitive appeal on behalf of a fanatical ideal. To the Captains and the Kings it appeared that the only course was to clear away these wretches. In some countries they were cleared off the face of the earth."[48]

Within a few weeks after the declaration of war in this country a questionnaire was sent out under the auspices of the Church Peace Union by Dr. Lynch to several hundred of the most esteemed clergy and laity, to ascertain what, in their estimation, were the best methods of dealing with the C. O.[49] A majority of the replies favored alternate service. Dozens of them savored of that bitterness against the objectors which was characteristic of attitudes developed a year later. Absolutists and political objectors, on grounds other than religious, did not register in the clerical and lay minds as being worthy of consideration. And men exempt from military service because they possessed an ordination certificate subscribed to doctrines of special privilege for themselves, yet said it was unthinkable that exemptions be granted those who were religious objectors but not members of the cloth.

The replies from famous bishops, some of whom were against any exemption for the C. O.'s, classing them as "cowards," "sentimentalists," and "anarchists," indicate that the bishops, in general, were most uncompromising. One Southern Episcopal bishop said: "The real conscientious objector is unbalanced. True Christian Churchmen are dying for Christ." While individual answers to this questionnaire cannot be quoted, due to its private nature, the attitude of many of the prominent leaders toward the C. O. is by no means a secret. Sooner or later a considerable number expressed themselves in print.

The Suffragan Bishop of Pennsylvania, Thomas James Garland, thought the attitude of the objectors deplorable:

> I have read about the conscientious objectors. My friends, it is a disgrace to apply the word conscientious to men who hold back when it is their duty to array themselves on the side of righteousness. The man who will not risk his life to fight against the evil might of Germany has an undeveloped conscience. He is a shirker.[50]

Bishop Luther B. Wilson remarked: "It is but brazen effrontery for a little group in such a nation as this to claim the monopoly on conscience, and where the claim is expressed it is folly upon the part of the majority to recognize it."[51]

The answer which Bishop Richard J. Cooke of Montana had given to Dr. Lynch, he himself released to the press. He maintained that the whole question of the conscientious objector was not a "church question at all." It had no relation to religious freedom and was "a state question," belonging entirely "to the domain of government." Then he upbraided the objectors who would not "suffer one hour of agony nor endure a pin prick for their country." The bishop advised: "Let him be deprived forever of all benefits of war, of all political and social and civil rights."[52]

The conscientious objector was characterized by George W. Downs as "a man who uses his religion to cloak a yellow streak." And when he had delivered his message to the congregation of the Asbury Methodist Episcopal Church of Pittsburgh, against pacifists, slackers, and conscientious objectors, it was reported that "men and women came to him, some in tears, some in righteous wrath against shirkers, to shake his hand and tell him how he had touched their hearts."[53]

Alfred Williams Anthony, executive secretary of the Home Missions Council, declared that, in the present conflict, "If I did not fight, I should brand myself as a coward and worse than a coward, as lacking in manly and Christian qualities." [54]

According to the *Living Church*, "Quakerism is sixteen hundred years too late to be entitled to the epithet Christian,"[55] while Dr. Parkhurst, editor of *Zion's Herald,* said, "God's employment of war as a means of dispensing with useless and harmful material is too conspicuous a feature of Scripture to allow standing room to Quakers and men of quaking disposition."[56]

In a sermon devoted to "The Treatment of Conscientious Objectors," George William Douglas, senior canon of the Cathedral of St. John the Divine, stated that many of them were "wolves in sheep's clothing." "From the religious standpoint," said he, the thing to do is to leave them to "the selective draft of God." Since our democracy had determined by a majority vote to enter the war the time for debate was passed. Not to submit was to "forswear his country altogether." Dr. Douglas believed that the objector was encouraging the Germans "in their war for the religious, moral, social and political standards of the Hun," and the C. O. should be obliged to wear "conspicuously on his breast a button with the letters 'C. O.' " [57] (For this last suggestion Dr. Douglas acknowledged his indebtedness to Dr. Fagnani of Union Theological Seminary.)

The editor of the *Baptist Courier,* Greenville, South Carolina, with what seemed to many irrefutable logic, exposed the complete inconsistency of all C. O.'s who were not absolutists.

> Noncombatant service is as certainly war service as combatant service, and if it is done patriotically, it shares in the dreadful work of killing. The man who does the shooting is morally not one whit more responsible for the work of his bullet than his noncombatant co-partner. Everyone sees this except the religious objector whose conscience has been cross-eyed into a scruple. . . . President Wilson [in dealing with the C. O.'s] was not trying to safeguard a great religious right. He was merely dealing with a practical situation in which he had to handle a bunch of cranks. His problem was exactly that of the keeper of a hospital for the insane where he must give the lunatics something to do and at the same time please their cranky brains.[58]

Horace James Bridges, Unitarian clergyman and leader of the Chicago Ethical Culture Society, perceived a "lamentable" situation in that no one was "ready to give a reasoned answer to the conscientious objector." Whereupon, Dr. Bridges wrote such an admirable answer, in October, 1917, that the Secretary of War requested a copy for his own use.

His argument is that since we are living in a democracy, with the right of protest, those who did not in time of peace speak out against the military powers of the government, if they rebel in time of war against the "proper exercise of the powers of Congress, are not only revolutionaries. They are also, in the exact sense of that term, traitors, in that . . . they are giving aid to the enemies of the country." Furthermore:

> *There is no ethical difference between making a surgical bandage for a wounded man, or knitting a trench helmet for a soldier, or growing corn to feed those who in any way are serving it, and killing an enemy with one's own hands, in the field or at sea.* Now every one of us, willy-nilly is in some way or other contributing to the maintenance and success of the armed forces of the United States. . . .
> If any one of you buys a Liberty Bond (as I hereby most heartily urge you to do), please remember that in doing so you are taking human life. If you think that you are not, and that the soldier who does kill incurs a moral taint that you escape, you are only deluding yourself.[59]

In those days statements in favor of the objectors or exposing their cruel treatment in prison had great difficulty in getting by the editor's blue pencils. Yet, attacks upon them, stories of their insincerity or stories of converted C. O.'s called for prominent space. The well-known case of Alvin C. York, from a little mountain church in Tennessee, called in the draft and stating that he was a conscientious objector, and his subsequent conversion "to the light" by appropriate Scripture verses quoted by his commanding officer became current coin. York's story and famous war record appeared on the front pages of all the leading dailies.

In the training camps, where the conscientious objectors were imprisoned, and where face-to-face situations with Christian leaders prevailed, the objectors received little, if any, sympathy.

A letter from one objector stated:

> I think it was a most common experience of conscientious objectors that their most bitter and intolerant enemies in the army were the chaplains and the Y. M. C. A. men . . . and they [the objectors] found that they were less understood and more contemptuously despised by these men than even by veteran soldiers who made no profession of allegiance to the principles of Jesus.[60]

Other objectors have furnished similar testimony.[61]

When John Timothy Stone became chaplain in charge of religious activities at Camp Grant, he tried to convert all the conscientious objectors confined there into accepting military service. The camp in which he thus labored had the reputation of being "one of the worst in the country in its treatment of objectors." [62] *

Practically all efforts on behalf of these men came through a few organizations like the National Civil Liberties Bureau, The Bureau of Legal Advice, The League for Democratic Control, The Fellowship of Reconciliation, and The Friends' Service Committee, all of which were interested in securing full legal

---

* An excellent illustration of the ingenuity exercised in describing conscientious objectors, which at the same time shows popular feeling, is to be found in the Camp Sherman Base Hospital *Journal*, January 25, 1919:

"When the Creator had made all good things, it seemed there was still some dirty work to do, so He made the beasts and the reptiles, and the poisonous insects; and when He had finished He still had some old scraps left over that were too bad to be put into the Rattlesnake, the Hyena, the Scorpion, and the Skunk, so he put all these together, covered it with suspicion, wrapped it with jealousy, marked it with a yellow streak, and called it a *Conscientious Objector*.

"This product was so fearful to contemplate that He had to make something to counteract it, so He took a sunbeam, put into it the heart of a child, the brain of a man, wrapped it in civic pride, covered it with brotherly love, made it a believer in equality and justice, a worker for and supporter of every good thing in the community, and called it an *American Soldier*. And ever since mortal man has had the privilege of choosing his associates. Let us all remember this in civil life."

rights for the objectors, and protested against the brutalities to which they were being subjected in many of the camps and prisons.

In these enterprises and appeals the churches and the clergy, save in a few instances, would take no part. A letter sent, October 26, 1917, to the Civil Liberties Bureau* by the Brotherhood of St. Andrew (Episcopalian) in reply to an appeal, indicates the maximum of courage displayed by the powerful denominations. On account of the "delicate nature of the inquiry" they could not mention the matter of the alleged brutalities imposed upon objectors confined in the camps to the resident secretaries but the Brotherhood would seek information through the field secretaries.[63]

Norman Thomas, active on behalf of more humane treatment for these religious objectors and political prisoners, states:

> The writer can testify from his personal experience that it was easier to talk with military officials and representatives of the War Department on this subject than with the high officials of the Christian church. . . .
>
> The average churchman was a romantic patriot and a complete sentimentalist. He was neither willing to investigate nor to accept the result of others' investigations of the conditions in military prisons.[64]

Another competent observer, William C. Allen, says:

> . . . so far as I know during the continuance of the war hardly any organization or statesman, preacher, church body, or periodical except Friends (Quakers) publicly lifted a voice of protest against the brutality then existing, or on behalf of liberty of conscience, in America. One church paper, *The Herald of Gospel Liberty*, told the story written by me, and, to its honor, the *Literary Digest* published it. America, while the war was on, was relatively careless as compared with the many public protests made in England.[65]

When in January, 1918, the Civil Liberties Bureau endeavored to arrange a conference with Christian leaders and liberals, Frederick Lynch, the secretary of the Church Peace Union, wrote that his organization had taken no action whatsoever in the matter of the conscientious objectors. However, he expressed himself as being opposed to the treatment they were receiving and that the committee might so inform the Secretary of War, Mr.

---

* The name of this organization is now The American Civil Liberties Union.

Baker. But he concluded with a caution not to publish his letter to the papers "because of certain relations which I bear to the administration at present."[66]

After the Armistice, further attempts to get cooperation in order to try to force the government to give up its "barbaric treatment" of religious and political prisoners met with small response from the clergy. L. Hollingsworth Wood, a Quaker and an attorney, as chairman of the Civil Liberties Bureau, wrote to a Boston minister:

> Worse, however, than the failure to penetrate the military mind is the absolute deafness of the ears of the clergy, who, the moment they hear these men are conscientious objectors, immediately take the position that they are without the pale of human relationships and will do nothing unless requested to do so by the War Department. It is one of the most terrifying evidences of the utter spinelessness of the supposed Christian leaders of our spiritual life that I have ever witnessed. . . .
> Unfortunately the Carnegie Foundation . . . is tied hand and foot by the fear of public criticism.[67]

At about the same time, W. G. Simpson, a pacifist minister connected with the Bureau, wrote:

> Our attempts to get action through the Church have been rather discouraging. The War Department and agents of the Department have seemed more stirred by our revelations of conditions in military camps and prisons than a great many of the clergy.[68]

A few clergymen interested to the extent of coming out and risking their reputations (some admit they had little to lose!) include such men as Norman Thomas, John Haynes Holmes, Jenkin Lloyd Jones, John Nevin Sayre, Bishop Paul Jones, Sidney Strong, Henry W. Pinkham, Judah Magnes, and such Quakers as Rufus Jones, Wilbur Thomas, and Edward W. Evans. There were a few others but not many.*

The contrast to the lack of interest in the objectors in America is the great amount of attention they received by notable English churchmen and laymen who worked in behalf of the C. O. Such a list would include Professor Gilbert Murray, Arnold Bennett, Jerome K. Jerome, Commander Josiah Wedgwood, Lords Parmoor, Morley, and Cecil, Robert Bridges, Arthur Hen-

---

* Another phase of the subject will be considered in further chapters in a study of the Federal Council, and such small groups as the Dunkards and Mennonites and Friends.

derson, Robert Smillie, George Lansbury, Bishops of Winchester, Oxford, and Lincoln, Dr. Clifford, Archbishop of Canterbury, Lord Bryce and others.[69]

Various memorials of protest were presented to Parliament from time to time, one on December 14, 1917, signed by 19 bishops and 200 clergy and influential laymen of the Established Church.[70]

Another contrast which is quite apparent is that between what has been described as the "condescending attitude" of the clerics, who rated the objectors as insincere and deserving of no consideration, and the realistic approach of the War Department. On June 1, 1918, a Board of Inquiry was set up by the Secretary of War to investigate cases of objectors that had not already been disposed of. The chairman of that Board, Major Walter Guest Kellogg, stated:

> Prior to my detail on the Board of Inquiry. . . . Although I had never set eyes on a conscientious objector, I firmly believed that they were as a class shirkers and cowards.
>
> My first trip as a member of the Board upset most of my ideas regarding the objector. I began to see him in a new light. And an examination of over eight hundred objectors in twenty widely distributed military camps and posts has convinced me that they are as a rule, sincere—cowards and shirkers, in the commonly accepted sense, they are not.[71]

CHAPTER VII

THE FEDERAL COUNCIL OF THE CHURCHES OF CHRIST IN AMERICA, 1917-18

Every office of the government with a war message to deliver appealed to the ministers first of all.

> From an advertisement by the Interchurch World Movement, March, 1920.

CHAPTER VII
THE FEDERAL COUNCIL OF THE CHURCHES OF CHRIST IN AMERICA, 1917-18

WAR AND THE MIND OF CHRIST

THE Federal Council of the Churches of Christ in America is, in several respects, the most important religious organization in this country. Its war-time policies and activities are, therefore, of immense significance. Representing about thirty of the Protestant denominations, the Federal Council had power and prestige. It occupied a unique and strategic position in its ability to sense the trend of religious thought and at the same time help to mold public opinion. The organization served as one of the great mediums through which the United States government was able to make its war propaganda effective.

With the declaration of war the Federal Council immediately registered a statement pledging its loyalty to the government, and at subsequent sessions of the annual meeting in Washington, D. C., the delegates listened to persuasive patriotic orations and passed resolutions assuring the country that the churches of the nation were heart and soul in the conflict and were gathering "their forces together at the start." [1]

"We abhor war," the members declared, "but since, in spite of every effort, war has come, we are grateful that the ends to which we are committed are such as we can approve." "What now is the mission of the church in this hour of crisis?" they asked, and answered, "It is to bring all that is done or planned in the nation's name to the test of the mind of Christ." [2]

The actual process involved in submitting "all that is done or planned in the nation's name to the test of the mind of Christ" was, in reality, never complicated. The government went ahead with its plans, preparing as best it could for days ahead, without consulting "the mind of Christ." The churches, as we have seen, simply followed with the proper blessing. The fact that the government had not submitted the declaration of war to Christ's approval, or to vote of his disciples or the people of the nation, never created any difficulty. Even among the Reformed Presbyterians (Covenanters) who lamented the lack of an amendment to the Constitution declaring this a Christian nation and "Jesus Christ as Lord of all," there was, nevertheless, an unqualified approval of the war and pride in its participation.[3]

One discovers this same attitude of approval all through the major churches of Christendom. While there was some slight criticism of the manner in which chaplains had been appointed and of the division of labor among the troops by the church organizations, there were no audible complaints of government policies from the Federal Council, save in minor detail. In this connection I am reminded of an editorial in a small denominational paper on the Pacific Coast. "If we have any doubts and fears at any time [about the war] it were wiser to mention them only to God in supplication."[4]

Yet, phrases used to describe the close relationship existing between Christian teachings and war, such as "the defense of Christianity," "the will of God," and "the mind of Christ," served a useful purpose. They helped many minds to bridge the gap between the days of peace and the enterprise of war. In the Federal Council itself, the joint committee on The Moral Aims of the War, according to its own estimate, did valiant service "in educating the people of the United States in these moral aims and of lifting their minds to their high level. No higher service could have been rendered. . . ."[5]

Its campaign for the education of the nation, undertaken "in conjunction with the Speaking Division of the Committee of Public Information" (George Creel's bureau), achieved notable success. The entire country through these efforts heard about the "moral aims of the war." Meetings were held in over three hundred cities, making a total of six hundred and forty-nine meetings in all. Through these meetings 33,334 ministers were reached. The attendance at the major meetings, and secondary meetings and institutes was over 800,000.[6]

One of the aims of the committee was: "To win the war against autocracy and to make the world safe for democracy and democracy safe for the world."[7] And in May, 1917, the Federal Council had declared itself in bold language on behalf of safeguarding civil and religious freedom. "Even in the strain of war," the churches were reminded, "the abuse of free speech is not as dangerous as its suppression."[8] Yet some months later a committee of the Federal Council urged: "Will not ministers speak out against the spirit of fault-finding as they speak out against slander?"[9] In time of war fault-finding is usually interpreted as being an abuse of the right of free speech.

The Council and the Conscientious Objector

The Federal Council also made a promising declaration in favor of conscience: ". . . nothing should be permitted to destroy the dearly bought right of freedom of conscience." [10] This resolution, put through in the early days by men like Harry Ward, who saw what lay ahead, has been described by Norman Thomas, who had many contacts with the Council during the war, as

> . . . from the beginning a scrap of paper, and neither the Federal Council nor the General War Time Commission of the Churches gave any aggressive or effective help during the days when a small body of liberals was struggling for a more humane treatment of conscientious objectors and other political prisoners.[11]

At the request of the Council, the National Lutheran Commission for Soldiers and Sailors Welfare "undertook to minister spiritually to the aliens and war prisoners interned in detention camps and war prisons." At this important task the commission accomplished its mission "both to the satisfaction of the government and the comfort and welfare of the aliens and prisoners." [12]

Although the rights of conscience were to have been safeguarded by the Council, nothing seems to have been accomplished. The organization, concerned about interned aliens and prisoners of war, their spiritual condition and the business of keeping up their morale, failed to offer any assistance to other prisoners incarcerated for being conscientious objectors. Whatever ministrations were carried out to this latter group by church people came from the Friends, the Dunkards, and Mennonites, who organized committees not only to visit the objectors in the camps and the prisons, but to check up on any complaints of unfair treatment received by them. So far as possible, all these situations needing adjustment were investigated in person by members of the committees.[13]

In June, 1917, the Civil Liberties Bureau, anxious to secure the full legal rights for all objectors in the draft, requested the Federal Council (1) to call the attention of the War Department to the existing situation and the likelihood that the men would be dealt with unfairly, (2) "to stand ready to give friendly help" to the objectors, and (3) "to create the proper atmosphere in the church, and by means of the church throughout the country" help to solve the "problem of the individual involved." [14]

Dr. Macfarland, speaking for the Federal Council, refused to cooperate with the Civil Liberties Bureau or to carry out the above suggestions. He explained that his organization had to "act in a representative capacity." It had to be "very careful to consider the psychology of the people" which it represented.[15]

Toward the end of the war, investigations carried on by the Civil Liberties Bureau and other groups into brutalities perpetrated against objectors brought to light tortures being inflicted comparable to practices of the church in the Middle Ages.[16] The Federal Council's aid in alleviating this unnecessary suffering was sought in vain, for the officials of the organization did not wish to be connected in any way with such a radical organization as the Civil Liberties Bureau. Furthermore the accounts of prison regime were believed to be highly exaggerated or not true at all. Finally, when pressure came from other quarters, the General War-Time Commission, in October, 1918, appointed a committee to investigate.

This committee, apparently, had difficulty in getting under way. The caution exercised may be judged by the following succession of events and exchange of letters. The Civil Liberties Bureau had called attention of the denominational War Time Commissions to the plight of the C. O.'s. The executive secretary of the Episcopalian Commission, Henry B. Washburn, in reply, wrote to the Civil Liberties Bureau on November 9:

> I have talked with Dr. Atkinson [of the investigating committee of the General War-Time Commission] over the telephone, and he assures me that thorough work is being done. He also assures me that the authorities at the War Department are thoroughly conversant with the situation.[17]

On November 15, W. G. Simpson, of the Civil Liberties Bureau, informed Dr. Washburn:

> . . . You said Dr. Atkinson assured you that the Committee of the General War-Time Commission was attending to the situation adequately. I am sorry to have to advise you that at the time of my most recent information they had held no conference either with Professor McCrea or with Judge Mack, nor do I believe that they have as yet sent the letter which they promised to write Secretary Baker. At any rate I was to have received a copy of it as soon as the letter went out, and that has never arrived.
> I am a minister of the church myself, but so often when I think of it, I can only hang my head.[18]

On November 18, Dr. Atkinson, Chairman of the National Service Committee of the Congregational Churches and a member of the Advisory Committee of the General War-Time Commission, wrote to Mr. Simpson:

> Since I saw you the other day, Professor Brown and I had a conference with Professor R. C. McCrea and Judge Mack. At the suggestion of the former, our committee has agreed to go to Washington and present the matter, which we discussed, directly to Secretary Baker. Professor McCrea has agreed to arrange an interview for us. . . .[19]

The same day Mr. Simpson received a letter from Dr. Washburn:

> The Christian Church is not uninterested in your problem, but at least I, as a representative, am not willing to take any steps until I know the facts. I hope that you realize that I have no other point of view than yours, and that you are naturally somewhat biased in your opinion. This is no reflection on your honesty but simply human.[20]

Gaylord White and Dr. Atkinson called upon General Munson and Professor McCrea, November 25. Dr. Atkinson wrote:

> General Munson promised to send immediately an Inspector out to Fort Leavenworth, so I think the abuses that are evidently so flagrant will be remedied.[21]

There the matter rested. In the meanwhile a few liberals were endeavoring to get the actual facts before the public.*

---

* The difficulties involved in getting the War Department to act may be gathered from the following: The Civil Liberties Bureau and the New York Bureau of Legal Advice had been complaining to Secretary Baker for months about the mistreatment of religious and political prisoners in various prisons. On September 3, 1918, Secretary Keppel wrote to L. Hollingsworth Wood of the Civil Liberties Bureau that he had just visited Fort Leavenworth and ". . . there are none of them [C. O.'s] in solitary confinement." (C. L., Vol. XXIX, p. 57.) On September 18, after the protesting organization had attempted some publicity and insisted that inhuman treatment was going on despite denials, Secretary Keppel wrote, ". . . in my judgment the activities of the Civil Liberties Bureau at the present time are a distinct hindrance and in no way a help in carrying these matters to a satisfactory conclusion." (C. L., Vol. XXIX, p. 66.) Then, in October, solitary confinement and brutal treatment was accorded many of the prisoners, including some Molokans. (Norman Thomas, *op. cit.*, pp 189 ff.)

On October 2, Secretary Keppel sent a letter to L. Hollingsworth Wood, Norman Thomas, John Haynes Holmes, and John Lovejoy Elliott, all working for the improvement of treatment of the objectors. These conscientious objectors, said Mr. Keppel, were making others fight the battles of the nation and ". . . this manifestation of supreme selfishness—far from awakening in you any feelings of resentment or abhorrence—is to your mind as it should be. . . . Gentlemen of your undoubted talents and ability might find better employment than that of directing your efforts and energies toward the protection of men

As late as November 20, Secretary Baker was quoted in the New York *World* as saying:

> I have visited Fort Leavenworth and my own investigation does not justify the allegations. I saw nothing but evidences of the most wholesome and sane discipline.[22]

Nevertheless, on December 6, enough pressure had been brought to bear to compel the War Department to abandon manacling. The official order is a frank admission of the use of such a practice.

> Fastening of prisoners to the bars of cells will no more be used as a mode of punishment. This and milder devices have been effective in the past in breaking the wilful or stubborn opposition of prisoners of the usual military type, who would not submit to the work requirements of the barracks. . . . But during recent months, with the influx of political prisoners to disciplinary barracks, particularly at Leavenworth, extremity of attitude on the part of this new type of prisoner has at times led to extremity of discipline, as provided by military regulations. . . .[23]

In December, the New York *World* came out with the first story to be given wide circulation about conditions in Leavenworth. Soon others, including the *Public Ledger*, conservative Philadelphia journal, in an editorial, called for an investigation:

> If any branch of the government's military activities calls for an instant investigation, it is certainly the treatment accorded the "C. O.'s" in the military prisons to which they have been sent by courts-martial. Even if half the allegations contained in complaints concerning the prisoners of this type . . . are true, the conditions demand instant correction and those responsible therefor summarily punished. . . .
>
> [They have been] kept for days in dark cells and forced for weeks to subsist under physical conditions which the law would not permit in the case of animals.
>
> * * *
>
> There is abundant reason to believe, in the severity of the sentences permitted to be imposed by army courts-martial, that there

---

who—we cannot blink the fact—are essentially enemies of your country. And may I add a word of caution and warning that, while you may with impunity address the officers of the government on this present subject, any activity on your part . . . directed to the encouragement of these political objectors in standing out against the draft officers or camp authorities, will inevitably expose you to the penalties which the law has prescribed for such conduct?" (C. L., Vol. XXIX, p. 96 ff.)

Future developments proved that the contentions of the Civil Liberties Bureau were correct. The members of the Federal Council, of course, were naive in their acceptance of the statements of the government at face value.

is lacking in the military mind that sense of fitness and of humanity which is in accordance with the age in which we live. . . .
. . . Torture has no place in the penology of the day, and least of all in the service which prides itself on its patriotism.[24]

It will be recalled that one of the liberals who took part in the preparedness movement and supported the war was Percy Stickney Grant of the Church of the Ascension, New York. Yet, all during the war he conducted his open forum where all sides could be heard. His belief in freedom of speech and conscience never became eclipsed by his enthusiasm for victory. He was one of the first to agitate for humanitarian treatment of political prisoners, a mass meeting to protest against the treatment of these men in Federal Military Prisons being held at his church, December 5, 1918.

In contrast to the activities and protests by a few individuals and organizations on behalf of the objectors, the record of the Federal Council and its commissions is silent. There is no instance of a public protest from the organization. Its private protests have been noted. In March, 1919, months after the major fight for humane treatment of objectors had passed, the committee appointed to investigate made its report, which was adopted. The War Department was exonerated, and it was recommended that those

> imprisoned conscientious objectors who are beyond question sincere should be granted amnesty at the time of the signing of the Treaty of Peace. . . . To punish them further in times of peace would set an unwholesome precedent in a nation that has always emphasized the principle of the freedom of the individual conscience.[25]

Arguing from such a major premise, why should the Federal Council have believed in punishment for the objectors in time of war?

There have been many critics of the Federal Council's attitude toward the objectors. It was John Haynes Holmes who was the most outspoken:

> As one who knows something about the inside history of the relationship of the Federal Council to the problem of the conscientious objectors, I charge the men at the head of this body with cowardice and hypocrisy. They are guilty of the final indecency—that of doing late and in security, as though of their own accord, what they refused to do at some cost, when the honor and lives of men were hanging in the balance. And these are they

who take the name of Him who "set his face toward Jerusalem," and carried his cross to Calvary!

Throughout the period of the war, these churches, with shocking unanimity, prostituted themselves to the work of hate. That they should have opposed the war was not to be expected. . . . As a matter of fact the churches rivaled the security leagues and national defense councils in the fell business of fostering hate, sowing bitterness and persecuting non-conformity. There was not an atrocity against the soul of man, not a blasphemy against the Holy Spirit of God, of which they were not guilty. And, now in a very few weeks, we shall behold these same churches, with their smug priests and laymen, coming forth in the security of a peaceful world, to talk again of tolerance, the free conscience, justice and love. . . .[26]

In answer to this accusation, Dr. Macfarland, the general secretary of the Federal Council, referred to the famous resolution made by the Council on behalf of conscience in May, 1917, and the work of the special committee already described.[27] Under the circumstances there was not much more that he could say.

The Brotherhood of Man

The surrender of the Federal Council to the government's program may be further appreciated by an inquiry into some of its other operations.

In order to acquaint the churches and the general public with the nature of its work, the organization started to publish the *Federal Council Bulletin* in January, 1918, under the direction of Charles Stelzle. Ninety-nine per cent of the space in the new publication was given over to the war activities of the various organizations connected with the Council and the war enterprises of the main body itself. The paper served as another admirable medium of propaganda for the government. Pastors, for instance, were advised to "organize War Savings Clubs among the children and young people of the Sunday School and . . . to stimulate the buying of Liberty Bonds." The clergy were told that they "must now take up each new Liberty Loan, each new Red Cross campaign, every effort of the government, and lift it up as an offering from the soul of the people."[28]

Frank Mason North, president of the Council, announced: "There is room for a good strong word for a church which was not geared up for the war. Some day someone will speak that word."[29]

Various schemes devised to promote the spirit of international brotherhood with the Allies came into effect. French chaplains welcomed into this country found their pictures in practically all the religious periodicals and in many of the daily papers. The reader of the *Federal Council Bulletin* could learn that the Protestant strength of the world had been dealt a terrific blow in the loss suffered by the French Protestants by the annexation of Alsace and Lorraine. They had lost "just one-fourth" of their church members.[80]

In the summer of 1918, Dr. Macfarland carried for the Federal Council "the message of the Christians in America to the French and Allied Armies." The messages handed to M. Clemenceau and also to Marshal Foch read:

> ... In the presence of God, we stand with you in solemn league and covenant, until the last Teutonic heel shall cease to desecrate this sacred soil, until again the unsullied lilies shall bloom in all their glory in the fields of France. Upon this frontier of freedom, which is not a mere line of trenches, but is a spiritual border, marking the line between honor and dishonor, between justice and wrong, our voices shall mingle. "They shall not pass." Here we stand together ... and if God wills, to die together. ...
>
> (Signed) FRANK MASON NORTH
> (Pres. of the Federal Council)
> JAMES I. VANCE
> (Chr. Executive Committee)
> ALBERT G. LAWSON
> (Chr. Administrative Committee) [81]

Similar messages were delivered to King Albert of Belgium and General Pershing.

The actual extent of the feeling of international brotherhood may be estimated from the attitude shown by the Council to a proposed conference of prayer to be held in Sweden.

Back in May, 1917, the Federal Council had admonished the churches of their duty to "purge our own hearts," and "to testify to our fellow-Christians in every land, most of all to those from whom for the time being we are estranged, our consciousness of unbroken unity in Christ."[82] The men of the cloth were reminded that it was "the time of times" to emphasize the international aspects of Christianity, "for unless there be more of brotherhood in the world after the war there will be less of the spirit of God. In such a day we dare not worship any national deity."[83]

The time was not far distant when the Federal Council would have the opportunity to apply the "international aspects of Christianity" to a concrete situation. On December 14, 1917, a conference of religious leaders from neutral countries was held in Upsala, Sweden, the call having been issued by Archbishop Söderblom and the Bishops of Denmark and Norway. This meeting resulted in plans for an international conference to be held in Scandinavia, April 14, 1918. The announcement explained:

> Representatives from both neutral and belligerent countries have received invitations, with the understanding that careful arrangements be made so that representatives from the various belligerent countries will not meet, publicly or privately. Sectional meetings will be held between neutrals and representatives of one side and the question of a general meeting will arise only after complete unanimity has been established with regard to the subjects composed in the agenda and on the assumption that both parties wish for such a general meeting.[34]

The invitation was very carefully worded and the list of topics proposed for discussion were non-partisan and non-political.

On April 4, some time after the unique proposal from Scandinavia had been received, the World Alliance for International Friendship Through the Churches, the organization through which the invitation had come to America,[35] held its annual meeting at the Broadway Tabernacle in New York. According to the official report, "the program from beginning to end was a militant clarion call to action and duty."[36] Henry Churchill King reaffirmed that this body was "heart and soul back of the government in waging righteous war which the enemies of democracy, justice and truth enforced upon the world."[37]

There was no response to the invitation to join in the spirit of reconciliation and brotherhood with fellow-Christians in Sweden. (The date of the proposed conference had been postponed, so there was still ample time.) The Federal Council, through its administrative committee, some time later reported that "it was agreed that it was not advisable to take definite action on the matter at this time."[38] By June 13, when someone had protested against this negative policy, the committee announced it was "awaiting further information."[39]

The reluctance of the Federal Council and allied organizations seems to have been greatly influenced by the French attitude and reply to the Scandinavian invitation. The editor of the *Federal Council Bulletin* pronounced the refusal sent by the French Protestant Federation to Stockholm an "inspiring message." A portion of the French refusal is given herewith:

> At the very hour when we are protected by our heroic fighters we cannot harbor the thought of going, in the shelter of their bodies, to engage in discussion, even indirect . . . with other men whose soldiers fight against our sons and brothers and who still occupy portions of the sacred soil of our country. That act, to many of our fellow-Christians and to us ourselves, would deserve a name which we do not wish to write in a letter addressed by Christians to other Christians.[40]

The official declaration of the Federal Council, while not as flowery in its expression of nationalism, held to the same thesis.[41]

Additional basic reasons for refusal to join in the conference were forthcoming. Dr. Macfarland, who had been in France investigating the motives which prompted the call for such a meeting, upon his return to this country gave to the press some of the results of his researches. He "felt quite sure that there have been efforts emanating from Germany to influence the churches of both warring and neutral countries," and what was deemed even more unpardonable, the churches of Germany were "clearly supporting with undivided strength the German power."[42]

Dr. Macfarland's information, practically all of which came from French sources and was accepted by him and the Federal Council, shows that both French and Americans believed the proposed Stockholm Conference was being engineered in part at least by German Christians for the purpose of breaking down the will to victory and the morale of the Allies.* If German Christians would show their sincerity, let them repudiate their government. That was the answer of the French and the Americans.

In England, it was reported, the Congregational Union had agreed to send delegates, and the British Branch of the Universal Church Alliance and the Society of Friends formally accepted the invitation. The British delegates were refused passports by their government.[43] The editors of *The World Tomorrow* saw in the willingness of the British group to attend, as con-

---

* I am also reliably informed that Archbishop Söderblom and the others who had issued the call to prayer were suspected of being pro-German. This belief was another factor back of the refusal to attend.

trasted with the refusal of the American, "further evidence of that bolder, truer Christian faith of our British brethren."[44]*

The war being over, another attempt was made to secure the cooperation of the American churches in a conference. The Federal Council of Evangelical Free Churches in Sweden sent out a communication to all the "Free Churches in the belligerent countries participating in the great war," for the purpose of "urging on all Christians the importance of reconciliation with one another in entire forgetfulness of hatreds engendered by the war."[45]

The administrative committee of the Federal Council in this country, in its report of this new proposal, doubted the wisdom of attempting to arrange for such a conference "at just this time," inasmuch as "it might be deemed impolitic and unadvisable by the official Peace Conference."[46]

The Federal Council's war record provides examples of the conflict which inevitably arises when a church body commits itself to a set of abstract ideals and at the same time wholeheartedly endorses the social order or political policies which are in almost complete contradiction. The Council, having declared in favor of freedom of speech, the right of conscience, the brotherhood of man, and prayer for the country's enemies, had also pledged its support to the state in the prosecution of the war to the finish. Many of its secretaries and men connected with the various war-time commissions were actively engaged in work for the government. Moreover, the financial support for the organization came from prominent business men and the patriotic

---

* Late in 1917 the British Council for Promoting an International Christian Meeting had proposed a conference similar to the one to be held in Sweden, of belligerents and neutrals to meet in prayer together. (*The New World* [later *The World Tomorrow*], Vol. I, No. 1, Jan., 1918, p. 21.) In Aug., 1918, to carry out its purpose, a meeting was held in Oxford, where it was resolved to keep on working toward the international meeting. Churches represented at the Conference were: Church of England, Eastern Orthodox, Church of Sweden, Dutch Reformed, Wesleyan Methodist, Congregational, Primitive Methodist, Unitarian, Baptists, Society of Friends. (*The World Tomorrow*, Vol. I, No. 10, Oct., 1918, pp. 245-246.)

The Socialists in England held a notable Inter-Allied Conference early in 1918. A statement of the aims of the Conference was transmitted to the Socialists of the Central Powers, together with conditions of peace which were believed to conform "with the principles of Socialist and international justice." The Conference hoped that the statement would meet with the approval of all Socialists and those in the Central Powers would "join without delay in a joint effort of the International, which has now become more than ever the best and the most certain instrument of democracy and peace." The Britishers regretted there were no delegates present from American Labor and Socialist organizations. (*The New Republic*, Vol. 14, No. 177, March 23, 1918, pp. 225-227, and Part Two.)

church bodies which it represented. The state, the business interests, and the religious denominations which the Council was supposed to represent were interested in but one thing— the winning of the war. They were naturally opposed to seeing the idealistic pronouncements of the Federal Council carried out in practice.

When faced with the situations which have been described, suppose the organization had defended the conscientious objectors after the draft had gone into operation, or had made moves to send delegates to the proposed conference in Sweden. What would have been the result? Its prestige with Washington would have been forfeited and the organization investigated by the Department of Justice. The financial support would have ceased, for business men and the churches demanded totality of allegiance to the flag.

That is not to say that the various policies of the Federal Council were all consciously framed with an eye to the favor of the government or to the means of economic support. It does mean, however, that all these relationships were so powerful in conditioning the minds of the leaders that they almost automatically fitted into the patterns of behavior demanded by the patriotic interests. While a few of the men in the Council seem to have consciously recognized the conflict between ideals and practice, the group in control of the policies were caught in the same war psychosis that dominated the mass of the population. When winning the war by killing Germans became the paramount consideration, to have spent time on conscientious objectors and on going to Sweden to pray for peace with our enemies would have been to divert attention and energy from the real problem set before the nation.

CHAPTER VIII

THE COLLAPSE OF THE PEACE SOCIETIES

"AS MISSIONARIES TO THE GERMANS"

We must help in the bayoneting of a normally decent German soldier in order to free him from a tyranny which he at present accepts as his chosen form of government.

We must lend our help in widowing a good-hearted and kindly German woman in order to save her and her children from the evils of a government which she identifies with fatherland and which she otherwise little understands.

We must aid in the starvation and emaciation of a German baby in order that he, or at least his more sturdy little playmate, may grow up to inherit a different sort of government from that for which his father died.

The Advocate of Peace, May, 1917.

CHAPTER VIII
THE COLLAPSE OF THE PEACE SOCIETIES

THE WORLD'S OLDEST PEACE SOCIETY

THE popularity of peace societies in this country in 1914 led many observers interested in that movement to believe that the Golden Age of Man was just ahead. Michael Clune, addressing the annual meeting of the New York Peace Society in May of that year, reflected the spirit of optimism. "Ambition," said he, "will never again drench a continent in blood. A higher civilization than war's is appearing."[1]

At the outbreak of the European War, the American Peace Society, through its president, Senator Theodore E. Burton, and Arthur D. Call, the secretary, issued a statement to the people of the United States, declaring the causes of the conflict to be military preparedness in Europe, and asked our citizens to unite "in prayer and supplication today and tomorrow, and . . . on each succeeding day until world peace is restored."[2]

Andrew Carnegie even went so far as to blame England for Germany's increased navy, for, stated he, the race for bigger navies had been started by the British.[3]

The world's oldest peace society looked very much as if it would weather the stormy preparedness era for awhile. Despite its history of timid policies during the Civil War and its earlier vacillation of purpose,[4] under the guiding hand of Benjamin F. Trueblood, secretary since 1892, a number of the members of the Society had finally stood out against the Spanish-American War.[5] And though Dr. Trueblood had resigned in 1913 on account of ill health,* the Society retained some of his spirit for a time.

After the sinking of the *Lusitania*, while a number of the peace workers expressed the spirit of retaliation, the editor of *The Advocate of Peace*, the official journal, asked what would be gained by going to war with Germany. "War," he avowed, "would simply compound the felony a thousandfold and get us

---

* Dr. Trueblood continued to edit *The Advocate of Peace* up to the spring of 1915. He died in 1916.

nowhere the while. . . . There will be no war between the United States and Germany."⁶ Even a year later, Arthur Deerin Call, successor to Dr. Trueblood, was led to exclaim that Jesus had been opposed everywhere to the use of force. "The supreme fact of the Christian ethic was then, and ought to be now, that Jesus Christ was a pacifist."⁷

Howbeit, complaints began to pour in from the more radically minded members that the peace societies were "side-stepping and watchfully waiting," and were "parties to a conspiracy of silence."⁸ As if to substantiate these claims, various branches of the Society told of backsliding members. The president of the Derry Peace Society of New Hampshire complained because the leading members of the State organization had "joined the great preparedness army just now sweeping the country."⁹

It was not long before the headquarters of the American Peace Society had swung into line. On the eve of our declaration of war, the Society declared the rather obvious fact that the decision to enter or refrain from entering the war had "to be made by the United States government," since the American Peace Society could not "decide this question."¹⁰ On the last day of March, 1917, the Springfield *Republican* had already congratulated the organization on being such "a good loser."¹¹

Thus when Congress declared what seemed the inevitable, the peace society was ready to take the oath of fealty and say, "the time for discussion is past. The time for action has come."¹² Pledges were distributed to the members calling upon them to sign on the dotted line to support their government "in this war for freedom and democracy," and thus prove that " 'pacifist' means 'patriot,'—'patriot,' 'pacifist.' "¹³

Quite within reason some of the members objected to what they considered high-handed methods and an abdication of the ideals of the historic peace society.¹⁴ But to all of these men and women the editor advised that we were now "fighting for a Governed World," that the "sole aim" of the Society had simply been all along to promote the necessary "international machinery" to establish peace. The ideals of the past as portrayed by Dr. Ladd were being carried out to the letter, it was said. Furthermore, the Society was refusing to "embarrass" the government by "fault-finding even in such matters" as " 'conscription,' 'conscientious objection,' 'taxation,' and the like."¹⁵

Charles F. Dole wrote to express the shock he received at finding the peace society actually advising the support of the war, for he "had not thought of a peace society as an adjunct of the War Department of a fighting nation."¹⁶ The editor replied that it was the "duty of healthy-minded men to put their consciences . . . to work in the interest of . . . the United States Government." For, warned Mr. Call, "to embarrass the United States at this time would be folly, if not treason."[17]

In December, 1917, *The Advocate of Peace* appeared with such a patriotic editorial on "Win and End the War," that it placed the editor and the American Peace Society on the list of leaders in the struggle to save the world. Germany was shown to be a destroyer of all civilization. "Deluded pacifists" in the People's Council and other organizations were indicted for bringing "serious injury" to the cause of international peace; and every man, woman, and child was called upon to join in ending the war "by winning it."[18]

So impressed was the Committee on Public Information with the editorial that Mr. Call received a request from the Committee to prepare a pamphlet setting forth the views of the peace societies regarding the present struggle.* The brochure, distributed widely in this and foreign countries, met with great favor. It proved that all the peace societies of note in this country were solidly behind the government in the prosecution of the war.[19]

That some criticism of the war-time policies of the patriarchal peace society should have been forthcoming is not surprising. The Delaware Society, largely Quaker, withdrew.[20] But the great rank and file of the members appear to have been pleased with its demonstrations of loyalty. Papers from Maine to California praised its efforts,[21] while the notables joined in, William Jennings Bryan among them, of course.[22] W. H. P. Faunce, the president of Brown University, a member of several peace societies, wrote:

> I like very much the way in which you have led the American Peace Society to work in complete harmony with the government. Your position has been exceedingly difficult, and I think you have solved the problem with tact and wisdom and without loss of conviction.[23]

If one is tempted to inquire into the pressures that were exerted upon the American Peace Society, socio-economic and otherwise, a glimpse at the annual reports of the organization will prove of value. For the year ending June 30, 1917, it re-

---

* The editor was a four-minute speaker, and conducted a class in public speaking in Washington, D. C., for the benefit of the "Four-Minute Squad." He also represented the Peace Society on the Advisory Committee of the Speaking Division of the Committee on Public Information. (*The Advocate of Peace*, Vol. LXXX, No. 6, June, 1918, p. 171.)

ceived a subvention from the Carnegie Endowment for International Peace of $25,000 or 70 per cent of its total receipts,[24] and for the following year $20,000.[25] Could the Society have afforded not to have supported the war?

Peace Through Force

The chronicle of the foregoing society during those years is representative of all the peace organizations. One may go down the list and check nearly all of them off on the credit side of the ledger of war.

An organization which helped remarkably in the orientation of the mind to the new day, and assisted in the preparation of the various stages of adjustment by which the efforts for peace gradually became welded to military sanctions, was the League to Enforce Peace, founded in Philadelphia, June 17, 1915, with the prominent preparedness leader, William Howard Taft, as its president. This new group, with its platform proposing arbitration of international difficulties on the one hand and going to war to "enforce peace," if necessary, on the other, gathered into its fold pacifists and militarists without discrimination.

Hamilton Holt had said at the first birthday of the new society, "I believe the League to Enforce Peace furnishes the common ground on which pacifists and the preparationists can unite."[26] He also believed that an international police force was "almost wholly good," for it meant "the enthronement of reason, if necessary, by force."[27] Nehemiah Boynton gave his testimony in behalf of resorting to force, "in order to secure those larger rights of peace. . . ."[28]

With this psychological approach, the League to Enforce Peace simply swept the field, and incidentally gutted the vitality of the older peace societies. With such men as Hamilton Holt, Theodore Marburg, and A. Lawrence Lowell pushing the organization, results soon were in evidence.

The New York Peace Society, founded just one hundred years before, in December, 1915, by a unanimous vote, decided not only to approve the platform of the infant League to Enforce Peace but to expend its energies in promoting the ideas of the new enterprise, with a joint office at 70 Fifth Avenue, New York.[29] About this time the directors of the New York Peace Society had a discussion over the policy. It was reported that they were "not willing to lose . . . either those who are opposed to all preparedness for war or those who believe in the necessity of increased preparedness."[30]

The World Peace Foundation, with the coming of the League to Enforce Peace, turned its attention and much financial support to its activities, its headquarters in Boston being used for the League in its nation-wide "peace and preparedness" campaign in that section.[81]

The League's popularity was in evidence at once. Its membership could boast of prominent leaders from the defense societies and the security leagues, together with many of those active in the old-line peace societies. This process of conversion to the idea of the use of force to enforce peace had been going on within the peace societies themselves during the preparedness era. The accusation of Henry W. Pinkham, that the influence of the League to Enforce Peace had been to promote "militarism in our country," seems to have been based on fact.[82]

Whatever else may be said, the new organization had felt the need of the hour. The widespread approval was sufficient proof of that. Men of peace had been troubled to know what to do. America wanted peace, but Germany did not. With one ruffian loose in the world, peace looked to be a far-off dream. But peace there must be. And enforced peace was better than none at all. The League thus served to resolve the mental perplexities of thousands of earnest and loyal pacifists. It was the bridge that enabled them to cross from the old attitude and world to the new.

With the declaration of war the League was able to say, "We are engaged with our allies in precisely the kind of a war the League's program holds to be both justifiable and necessary."[33] At its Annual Meeting in Philadelphia in May, 1918, the program sounded more like a security league affair than a peace society. The Prussian power should be crushed and we should "by arms enforce a freeman's peace."[34] But, surprising as it may seem, *The Advocate of Peace* estimated that the 3,500 officially accredited delegates present had listened to platitudes and nothing more. The editor was disappointed that nothing constructive had come out of the meeting, which he was ready to rate as a failure, if not a tragedy. The disappointments of Versailles were not far away.[85]

Fighting for Peace

Space does not permit going down the list of the thirty-five organizations devoted to peace activities in April, 1917. All, in fact, according to Devere Allen, save a few "non-violent sects and a little remnant of the Universal Peace Union," decided to join with the majority point of view.[86]

The Lake Mohonk Conferences were given up due to lack of interest.[87] The World Peace Foundation, operating with some strength before the war, succumbed like the others, calling no directors' meeting after November, 1914.[88] The Trustees of the Carnegie Endowment for International Peace, with Elihu Root as president, called for the subjugation of Germany and appealed to "the lovers of peace to assist in every possible way in the effective prosecution of the war."[39]

The Woman's Peace Party, having opposed our entrance into the war, and then in turn conscription, gave in to these policies when Congress acted. Further criticism was not considered in keeping with the best interests of the Society.[40] But some of the women, like Jane Addams, Lucia Ames Mead, and Anna Garlin Spencer did not change their fundamental convictions. The Church Peace Union and its offspring, the World Alliance for International Friendship Through the Churches, the American School League (changed to the American School Citizenship League), all sang the same song, "Peace Through Victory."[41]

The shifting in the policies of the peace societies was due also to another factor in addition to the mere acceptance of pro-Ally propaganda. There was a counter-propaganda going on and some of the efforts for peace came to be labeled "pro-German," which was more obnoxious than "pacifist" or "disloyal." William Bayard Hale had been partially successful in getting the ear of some of the societies and movements before we declared war.[42*] In the Northwest, particularly, pro-Germanism came in the public mind to be allied with the old-line peace societies, and thus all peace movements entered the shadow of suspicion.[43]

With the approach of April, 1917, the leaders in the peace societies found themselves working for the same ends as the pro-German propagandists—to keep the United States out of the war. In seeking to deny the charge of pro-Germanism, they were compelled to repudiate the charge that their aims were identical. Hence real efforts for peace on the part of the old-time societies came to a standstill long before we entered the

---

* Count von Bernstorff on November 1, 1916, telegraphed Berlin (in part), as follows: "At the beginning of the war things were undertaken by the Dernberg Propaganda which would never have been undertaken if we could have seen that the war would be so long; because nothing can for long be kept secret in America. Since the Lusitania case we have strictly confined ourselves to such propaganda as cannot hurt us if it becomes known. The sole exception is perhaps the *Peace Propaganda* which has cost the largest amount, but which also has been the most successful." (Brewing, etc., II, p. 1494.)

war, partly because of their fear of being regarded as centers of pro-Germanism.

The change in the attitude of the peace societies and even those members who were most active in the cause of peace may be illustrated by a study of David Starr Jordan. His reputation as a pacifist was international, and in the years just prior to our entrance into the war he appeared as the principal speaker at mass meetings for peace all over this country.* The American Union Against Militarism and the Emergency Peace Federation staged him as a special feature on their programs. He fought up to the last moment and against great odds in an effort to keep us out of war. But, upon the declaration of war, Dr. Jordan wired the San Francisco *Bulletin*, April 6, while on his way back to California, that, since the United States was now in the war, we must stand together in the hope that in some way we could contribute to the cause of democracy and a quick and lasting peace. "The only way out is forward," said he.[44]

The end of May he came back East, held "Courses of Instruction" for Congressmen on advisable legislation—repeal of the Conscription Act, restating the meaning of treason under the Constitution, and insuring constitutional guarantees in war time, et cetera. Among those who attended these "classes" were Senators Borah, La Follette, Norris, Johnson, Vardaman, Smoot, Curtis, New, and various Representatives.[45]

Dr. Jordan helped to frame the program for the People's Council and became the treasurer of the organization. However, he soon withdrew, for the leaders were getting too radical for him. They continued to use his name for publicity purposes long after permission had been withdrawn.[46]

When, in May, 1918, twenty-five members of the class of '73 of Cornell demanded that the trustees revoke degrees granted him, Dr. Jordan reassured them that he "had been supporting the President since the day we entered hostilities," for "once the die was cast, I believed the whole-hearted prosecution of the war should receive the active support of every loyal American."[47]

---

*For Dr. Jordan's peace activities from August 2, 1914, to January 19, 1921, see his autobiography, *The Days of a Man*, Vol. II, Book VI. On the evening of March 26, 1917, Dr. Jordan had gone to Princeton to speak on peace. A great war demonstration had been held on the Sunday evening preceding, but President Hibben refused permission for a peace meeting. The assemblage gathered in the Presbyterian Church. At the Academy of Music in Baltimore, Sunday night, April 1, an audience of 5,000 packed the building. A mob attempted to break up the meeting. (D. S. Jordan, *op. cit.*, Vol. II, pp. 722 and 727-730.) A few years later the young man who led the mob apologized to Dr. Jordan.

Like the peace societies themselves, he had come to the conclusion that "peace could not be secured by mere submission. To lie down before aggression is to accept the doctrine that might makes right."[48]

It is quite evident that the societies had been working for peace to be brought about by the building up of a body of international law and other machinery, together with sentiment for peace itself. When war actually came it was no longer possible or expedient to believe that war was altogether an evil, for it could be utilized as "the war to end war." Through this means it was believed the aim of the societies to bring perpetual peace into the world would be achieved.

CHAPTER IX
THE Y. M. C. A. IN KHAKI

We could not win this war without the Young Men's Christian Association; for even though our armies reached Berlin, our souls would lose their way.

> Daniel Alfred Poling in *Huts in Hell*, p. 87.

Every dollar given to the Y. M. C. A. is a dollar given toward winning the war.

> Major General Leonard Wood in *Service with Fighting Men*, Vol. II, p. 634.

CHAPTER IX
THE Y. M. C. A. IN KHAKI

THE RED TRIANGLE

NO CONSIDERATION of the later days of the Christian Epic would be complete without chronicling the important part played by one organization in the adjustment of the Protestant religion to the world of business affairs and modern capitalism. I refer to the Young Men's Christian Association. This body has helped to tone down the Calvinism and severities of the Protestant dogmas and to mellow its teachings in such a way as to render it acceptable to the average business man. Religion became practical with an emphasis on activity rather than belief. Serving this purpose, it was nevertheless looked upon with suspicion by many a Christian as teaching but a diluted gospel.

Yet, when the war arrived, Protestantism was able to bless and support the Y. M. C. A. as the only organization equipped to provide religion and support the morale of the boys in the service. It was regarded as accomplishing a creditable piece of work, not only by the Protestants but by the leaders of our armies. General Pershing endorsed it in these words:

> There is no one factor contributing more to the morale of the Army in France than the Y. M. C. A. The value of the organization cannot be overestimated. Give me 900 men who have a Y. M. C. A. rather than 1,000 men who have none, and I will have better fighters every time.[1]

Richard Hooker of the Springfield *Republican*, after a thorough and searching survey of the Y. M. C. A. activities at Camp Devens, Ayer, Massachusetts, said, "If, as Wellington averred, the Battle of Waterloo was won on the playing fields of Eton, then it may be safely said that this war will be won in the Y. M. C. A. buildings." To this thesis the celebrated Dr. Odell, critic of the lukewarmness of the clergy, subscribed.[2] In view of his personal acquaintance with Camp Hancock, Georgia, he could say "deliberately" that he "would rather entrust the moral character of my boy to that camp than to any college or university I know."[3]

The clergy and church laymen were attracted to the "Y" in those days because they saw in it the saving of the manhood of America that would be otherwise destined to moral ruin when exposed to the temptations of life in the army. Henry Sloane Coffin observed: "In our army camps, where one felt how weak were the moral restraints that checked brute lusts, the Christian Associations and the chaplains were turned to as the only stays to bestial demoralization."[4]

Nevertheless, according to the authoritative statements of the Y. M. C. A., the real purpose of these Christian solicitations was to make better fighters. All else was secondary:

> A specific military function was assigned to the Y. M. C. A. Its duty was to assist in maintaining and promoting morale. It had been proved in the Spanish war and on the Mexican border that Y. M. C. A. service made better fighters. That was the justification for allotting space and privileges in the congested camps and lines of communication all the way to the battle line.[5]

Whatever else the Red Triangle may have symbolized, its record fits into the picture for what it really was—a big machine organized to promote the business of killing Germans. Its secretaries were as much a part of the scheme to overthrow the Central Powers as were the officers and men in the trenches. In fact, the "militarizing of the Y. M. C. A." in France became a reality under orders from the Adjutant-General's office in Paris, July 28, 1917.[6]

Yet the organization did not lose sight of its Christian motivation. Its pattern of behavior was essentially related to the forms and ritual of its religion. The International Committee explained this religious purpose under the title, "Religion and Citizenship—the Crusade for God and Country." The Y. M. C. A. "in all its activities, whether in entertainment, athletics, education, or in any other phase of helpfulness to the armies, was actuated at all times by the teachings and the spirit of Christ."[7]

Thus it was discovered that "athletics increased the agility of the men . . . to leap a trench or strand of barbed wire. . . ." Athletics "stimulated the fighting spirit," and

> When the English and French officers brought to the camps new methods of training, especially in bayonet practice, the discovery was made of the very close relationship between boxing and bayonet movements. This gave great impetus to the promotion of the "manly art." [8]

While it was not necessary for the mass of Protestants back home to comprehend all the details of the Christian Crusade, yet it was imperative that the relationship between the "Y" and the Protestant evangelical churches be kept as close as possible. John R. Mott, the general secretary of the International Committee, recognized this: "A cooperating Committee of the Churches with the 'Y' War Work Council" came into being with a membership of seventeen leading men from clergy and laity.[9]

Through the aid of "the best men in the profession"—Bruce Barton, Nolan R. Best, Charles H. Towne, Frank Presbrey and others—the "Y" found a favorable reception in the columns of the dailies and religious publications of the country. Practically all of the religious editors praised the consecration with which the Red Triangle had gone about its task and the remarkable results achieved. Thus in those days of exalted spiritual living, the bulk of the Protestants took a keen interest in what Dr. Kelman called one of the "most important departments of the church."[10] When Gypsy Smith, the evangelist, came to this country to participate in a campaign for the benefit of a Y. M. C. A. drive, he felt qualified, after four years with the British army, to call the "Y" "the communcation trench between the church and the army."[11]

As evidence of the generous attitude the people had toward this relationship the American citizens poured into this "communication trench" a sum of $167,000,000 for war work,[12] making a grand total of over $170,000,000 raised by the Y. M. C. A. for war service.[13] There was employed a total personnel of 25,926, about "equally divided between home and overseas service."[14]

With such a machine geared to the War Department, grinding out publicity, training secretaries, building huts, running canteens, holding religious services, teaching Bible classes, promoting recreation, and supporting the morale of the troops, results were bound to follow. William Howard Taft, head of the editorial board that wrote up the war record of the "Y" (1924), appraised its work as "one of the greatest achievements of peace in all the history of human warfare."[15] The Young Men's Christian Association "served between four and five millions of American soldiers and sailors at home and overseas," and, according to General Pershing, "conducted nine-tenths of the Welfare Work among the American Forces in Europe." Moreover, "alone among American welfare societies, this organization ministered to not less than nineteen millions of the soldiers of the Allied Armies and extended its helpful activities to over five millions of prisoners of war."[16]

The "Y" was proud of its service in spite of the onslaught of criticism it received at the hands of the members of the A. E. F. *The Damn Y* written by Katherine Mayo helped to answer and neutralize the charges of malfeasance in office, thereby assisting the organization in the recovery of its temporary loss of prestige.

An examination of the official literature published during the days of the conflict in behalf of its enterprises and compared with that of later years covering much the same field reveals a marked change of attitude. In the massive work of two volumes, *Service with Fighting Men,* the emphasis is placed on the spiritual side of the service. There is a noticeable toning down of the martial spirit of the "holy war" and "better fighters" theme. One looks in vain for the phrase, "For God and Country." All this is kept in the background while the spiritual ministry to the boys is given the center of the stage.

The Ministry of the Y. M. C. A.

Precisely of what had this spiritual ministry to the troops consisted? According to one eye-witness, some "Y" secretaries talked to the men about a "God with Guts," and then prayed, "Oh God, we men in the depot brigade are lonely tonight and homesick for mother. We'd give a lot to see her and eat a piece of the good old home-made pie once more." This same author, writing to *The Churchman,* claimed he had seen "prayer meetings tacked to the end of stunt-nights with no intermission," and singing meets "where 'Nearer, My God, to Thee,' was sung between 'The Henry Clay' and 'Katie.'" This apparently did not astonish some of the secretaries who, "far from thinking this sort of thing objectionable, delight in it as 'showing how religion and life are bound together.'"[17]

William T. Ellis, Presbyterian clergyman, and writer of expositions of the Sunday school lessons distributed in syndicated form through the medium of the daily press, told of the typical varied Sunday of the Protestant Episcopal Bishop of Erie, Pennsylvania, at the front. It consisted in administering the communion service in the morning and in the afternoon selling "cigarettes and candy over the counter of the 'Y'. And everybody who knows the conditions here believes that the latter action was also a Christian ministry."[18]

For Dr. Ellis the function of the Y. M. C. A. workers was "to stand in the stead of mother and father and home and church to an entire army of boys."[19]

Since the "Y" employed no pacifist secretaries,[20] the government was assured that the moral attributes of the war and the pure aims of the Allies would be explained and receive the proper recognition; that the secretaries had the proper attitude toward the slacker and the conscientious objector and Germans on the one hand and the welfare of the boys on the other.

Secretaries exhibited the Bible as the greatest of all war books, and Jesus as the Happy Warrior going before into battle, thrusting his bayonet through the body of the Hun as an example to others.[21] Literature abounds telling of secretaries enticing men to enlist, settling their doubts and fears about the war, blessing the battle line, bolstering up the courage of the troops, and converting them to Christ just before they went out to their death.

Daniel Alfred Poling's high estimate of the services thus rendered enabled him to write an account, *Huts in Hell,* dedicated to the men and women of the Red Triangle—"they also fight who help the fighters fight." The front picture in this work of appreciation is a copy of one popular in Paris showing "an American soldier standing with French orphans by the grave of their father, slain in battle," with the title, *I Swear to Avenge Your Father.*

This vengeance was to be carried out, according to Dr. Poling, by "modern knights," who were on a crusade more worthy than any since men "fought to free the sepulcher of Christ" and search for the Holy Grail. The author had rationalized the conflict in terms of high idealism. He tells of the *"moment when the American Army was baptized by fire into the sacrificial comradeship of democracy's international Calvary."*[22]

He was proud of the Christian Endeavorers in the service—140,000 young men from the churches of the United States who had not "failed to hear the call of the highest patriotism."[23] To this clergyman, now president of the International Society of Christian Endeavor, it was glorious to realize that "the mightiest soldiers since Christianity became a factor in the affairs of men," had been "worshipers of the Nazarene, followers of Him, who, being the Prince of Peace, was not afraid to die for the Truth."[24]

Harold C. Warren, "Y" Secretary and pastor of the First Presbyterian Church of Walla Walla, Washington, reminisced about his experiences with the "Y". He would never forget the first soldier he found dead upon the field of battle:

> The breeze was gently tossing his glinting hair. The honest blue eyes were wide open. . . . His faithful rifle still clutched

in his hand . . . he lay gazing into the westward sky where the sun was slipping below the crests of the hills. And westward he sent his message to the dear ones at home, . . . "I have fought the good fight. I have finished my course, I have kept the faith." [25]

Ministering to the living men consisted often in saving them from sin by exhibiting a picture of his wife and telling of their courtship days, of bringing "cheer and satisfaction" to the well and wounded, "whom I heard calling in Christ's name for cigarettes and chocolates."[26]

William L. Stidger tells of deeds of heroism in his *Soldier Silhouettes* and *Star Dust from the Dugouts*. Sherwood Eddy wrote *The Right to Fight*, wherein is portrayed "the necessity of war in the defense of righteousness, for the high end of the extension of the Kingdom of God. . . ."[27] A "Y" Secretary, A. E. Marriott, wrote a manual for the army, on *Hand-to-Hand Fighting*.

There were hundreds of books and pamphlets published in those days by the Association Press, the publication department of the organization, written by men connected with the "Y". They were all dedicated to the common purpose of winning the war. Even after the hostilities had ended, a book for high school boys was published teaching them why we fought. "Ours is a victory not only of our Allies," wrote the author, "but also of the principles of Christianity."[28]

It is perhaps needless to point out that the "Y" secretaries rivaled the clergy in their condemnation of conscientious objectors. In one of the home camps, the captain ordered the C. O.'s to file into the mess hall for a lecture, where, according to Ernest L. Meyer, the "Y" men "heaped reproaches" on their heads "for being too Christian and not going to war."[29]

In the work of saving the troops for a higher living, other organizations did their part. The Y. W. C. A., with its message of cheer through the camps, qualified fully as well in its moral enthusiasm for the war as its brother organization.[30]

The Knights of Columbus, while doing their work on a smaller scale than the Red Triangle, nevertheless rendered an important service to the government and to the troops.[31]

The Salvation Army joined the armies of the Allies and promoted the war by feeding doughnuts to doughboys.[32]

The Christian Scientists in this country, believing that "only those nations which had some understanding of principle, as revealed in Christian Science, were adequately armed and equipped to carry a righteous cause to its victorious conclusion," promoted enterprises of relief and healing in America, England, and on the western front.[33]

CHAPTER X

GROUPS OF IRRECONCILABLES

Every man should have the privilege, unmolested and uncriticized, to utter the real conviction of his mind. . . . I believe that the weakness of the American character is that there are so few growlers and kickers among us. . . . Difference of opinion is a sort of mandate of conscience. . . . We have forgotten the very principle of our origin if we have forgotten how to object, how to resist, how to agitate, how to pull down and build up, even to the extent of revolutionary practices, if it be necessary to re-adjust matters.

Woodrow Wilson, "Spurious vs. Real Patriotism," School Review, Vol. 7, p. 604.

CHAPTER X
GROUPS OF IRRECONCILABLES

THOUGH to the casual observer public opinion in this country during the war seemed to have been solidly behind the administration and in favor of crushing all individual sentiment, nevertheless there was quite a body of dissenters who sought to voice their protest. Among them were some of the clergy. Inasmuch as the voice of the church had become the echo of commands from Washington and the church organizations the ready agents for the spreading of propaganda from the Committee on Public Information, the few clergy and laity who differed sought refuge in minority groups for the freer expression of their dissent.

It is not my purpose to go into the history and activities of these various organizations—that would be a book in itself—but to point out their existence as arising out of social conflict.

The People's Council

The People's Council seems to have gathered more into its fold than any other national organization of that kind. This organization grew out of the First American Conference for Democracy and the Terms of Peace held in New York, May 30, 1917, with a mass meeting attended by 15,000 people. Its ambitious program for upholding the rights of labor, the first amendment, repeal of the conscription law, the immediate declaration of war aims by our government, an early peace, and the formation of an international organization for the prevention of all future wars, appealed to the imaginations of hosts of people all over the United States.[1]

The organization itself contained a strange mixture, but most of the members were Socialists: men like Eugene Debs, James H. Maurer, Morris Hillquit, Victor Berger, Louis P. Lochner; women such as Mary Ware Dennett, Crystal Eastman, Elsie Clews Parsons, Emily G. Balch.

The clergy attracted to this magnet included Bishop Paul Jones of Utah, Richard W. Hogue of Baltimore, Jenkin Lloyd Jones of Chicago, Judah L. Magnes of New York, Sydney Strong of Seattle, Irwin St. John Tucker of Chicago, Norman Thomas of

New York, Howard Melish of Brooklyn, Fred A. Moore of Chicago and Lindley Gordon of Louisville.

Meetings were held in the majority of the States of the North in the summer of 1917. A big mass meeting of delegates planned for Minneapolis for the first week of September, 1917, received the unqualified disapproval of Governor Burnquist of Minnesota, who forbade its coming because it "would result in bloodshed, rioting and loss of life." Finally a chartered train of delegates, who had been wondering where they could eventually land, stopped at Chicago. Meetings on September 2 were broken up by the police and threatened by approaching troops.

The People's Council gradually drops out of print, though not out of existence. It continued to function in a quiet way.

Needless to remark, the churches and the religious press regarded this movement as concocted in Germany by the "Potsdam Gang." Rabbi Stephen S. Wise, for instance, seeking to expose the organization, charged its leadership with total incomprehension of Wilson's aims, of being Socialist of the "basement and cellar type," who from the beginning of the war had "served the interests of Germany." Their main interest, according to Dr. Wise, was a peace made in Germany. In criticizing the ideal of the People's Council—"no forcible annexations" of territory—the Rabbi frankly admitted his belief in the annexation of territory, since there could be no peace "until the shameful deed of 1871 be undone" and Alsace-Lorraine be returned to "the arms of France." Yet he would unquestionably have repudiated the idea that America enter the war in April, 1917, to help France regain Alsace-Lorraine.[2]

The Advocate of Peace took, in general, the same point of view as Rabbi Wise, whose lengthy exposures of the leaders of the Peace Council it published.[3]

The Churchman, Episcopalian journal of comparatively restrained tone, in writing about some of the minority groups produced by the war, called a pamphlet issued by the People's Council in July, 1917, "A Shameful Document," with the warning that Episcopalian clergymen aiding this organization evidently did not realize "in what treasonable camps the sentiments" of the Council were bred.[4]

The general state of mind of those against the radical organization may be further appreciated from the nature of the replies which followed a defense of the Council in the columns of *The Churchman* by Bishop Paul Jones. The Bishop had claimed that practically all the expressed objects of the organization had been endorsed by "the General Convention of the Church or in the words of President Wilson." And, he continued, "If those are treasonable camps they should be reported."[5]

This letter did not increase the popularity of Bishop Jones, for Episcopalian clergy and laity started to "report" him. A letter to *The Churchman* from a Henry F. Peake of New York, who referred to him as "this man Jones," and the printing of his article as "an intolerant outrage," maintained:

> This communication contains seditious language, as has recently been clearly set forth by the Department of Justice of the United States. I wish to notify you that if any more such seditious language is published I shall take steps . . . which I hope will lead to the barring of the United States mails to the circulation of *The Churchman*.[6]

Unity seems to have been about the only religious weekly that defended with vigor the People's Council. The editor, Jenkin Lloyd Jones, a member of the outcast group, accused the governors of the States forbidding the meeting of "denying the rights of free speech," and "bringing reproach upon great States." "They humiliate the nation," said he.[7]

Peace Programs in War Time

There were a few religious organizations that tried to keep up their work for peace. In Boston, The Association to Abolish War, founded by Charles F. Dole, retired Unitarian minister, and Wilbur Thomas, executive secretary of the Friends' Service Committee, in November, 1915, attempted to bridge the gap made by the major peace organizations that went over to preparedness. Following the events of April, 1917, many members withdrew from the Association, but meetings continued all through the war. The organization took an active interest in conscientious objectors and political prisoners.[8]

The Fellowship of Reconciliation, organized largely through the instrumentality of John R. Mott, who brought Henry Hodgkin here in 1915, carried on right through the war. In January, 1918, it started a monthly publication, *The New World* (later changed to *The World Tomorrow*), "to proclaim anew the faith that the common life of mankind can and should be ordered in accordance with the spirit and principles of Jesus." The issue of September, 1918, was barred from the U. S. mails by the government. It later was released.

The Fellowship stood by the conscientious objectors. A number of its members were imprisoned. Its secretary for a time, Edward W. Evans, a Philadelphia Quaker, and a later secretary, Norman Thomas, worked prodigiously in their behalf.

Among the ministers actively connected with this group were John Nevin Sayre, Richard Roberts, A. J. Muste, John Haynes Holmes, Noble S. Elderkin, Paul Jones, Sydney Strong, Harold Rotzel, and Harry F. Ward. L. Hollingsworth Wood and Rufus Jones, among the Quakers, found this fellowship congenial.[9]

In Los Angeles in October, 1917, a meeting of Christian Pacifists, largely an F. O. R. gathering, was mobbed by the Home Guards.[10] Three members served terms in jail for their attendance.*

THE RUSSELLITES

An obscure sect which rose to prominence during the war was the Russellites, or the International Bible Students' Association, followers of Pastor Charles Taze Russell. A delineation of their war-time history illustrates many of the psychological phenomena arising in a society bent on killing off members of another civilization. Frustrated desires to kill Germans found an outlet in attacking unpopular minority groups at home.

Before the war the sect was "the thorn in the flesh" of the larger groups, for it had the habit of drawing away members from their congregations. Then along came the war. During the early part of 1918 members of this "pestilential persuasion" were objects of great concern in this country and in Canada as well, because of the circulation of a posthumous book of Pastor Russell's called *The Finished Mystery*. The group itself had supplied the third largest number of the conscientious objectors in the United States. Persisting in pacifist teaching, raids and arrests were made in all parts of the country.

In Los Angeles, after one of these proceedings, the ministers were reported as thanking God and preaching on the theme, "Is the End of Russellism Near?" One of the more prominent in his sermon is quoted as saying, "Thank God, Russellism is now doomed forever."[11] In Worcester, Massachusetts, B. F. Wayland secured space in the *Daily Telegram* for an article under the headline, "Hun Propaganda Is Being Pushed in Worcester."[12] The society with its headquarters in Brooklyn was believed to be financed with German gold if one takes the reports literally. However, Russellite books were as unwelcome in Germany as in the United States.[13]

---

* *Vid.* Chapter XI, *infra*, for further details.

Finally the affair got into the courts. On June 21, 1918, Judge B. B. Howe of the United States Circuit Court of Brooklyn, after a jury trial of two weeks, sentenced seven Russellites, including Judge Joseph F. Rutherford, the successor to Pastor Russell, to twenty years each in the Federal penitentiary in Atlanta. An eighth member was later sentenced to ten years. The offense was the circulation and teaching of the doctrines of Pastor Russell as recorded in *The Finished Mystery.* This had been found to violate the provisions of the Espionage Act of June 15, 1917. The passage found to be particularly objectionable reads:

> Nowhere in the New Testament is patriotism (a narrowly minded hatred of other peoples) encouraged. Everywhere and always murder in its every form is forbidden. And yet under the guise of patriotism civil governments of the earth demand of peace-loving men the sacrifice of themselves and their loved ones and the butchery of their fellows, and hail it as a duty demanded by the laws of heaven.[14]

The trial had been played up in the papers everywhere and the verdict met with general approval. In printing and circulating the above condemned excerpt from the forbidden book, the press did the very thing the Russellites had been sentenced to twenty years for doing, and gave it more publicity than the followers of Russell could possibly have given it.

An analysis of the whole case leads to the conclusion that the churches and the clergy were originally behind the movement to stamp out the Russellites. In Canada, in February, 1918, the ministers began a systematic campaign against them and their publications, particularly *The Finished Mystery.* According to the Winnipeg *Tribune,* the attention of the attorney general had been called to the Russellites, and the suppression of their book was believed to have been directly brought about by the "representations of the clergy."[15]

In Worcester, Massachusetts, B. F. Wayland called upon the authorities to arrest the International Bible Students and prevent them from meeting in their halls.[16] Following this and similar pleas by the hierarchy of the orthodox churches, the Russellites began to be arrested in various centers.

When the news of the twenty-year sentences reached the editors of the religious press, practically every one of these publications, great and small, rejoiced over the event. I have been unable to discover any words of sympathy in any of the orthodox religious journals. "There can be no question," concluded Upton Sinclair, that "the persecution . . . sprang in part from the fact that they had won the hatred of 'orthodox' religious bodies."¹⁷ What the combined efforts of the churches had failed to do the government now seemed to have succeeded in accomplishing for them—the crushing of these "prophets of Baal" forever.

Quoth *The Western Recorder* (Baptist) of Louisville, Kentucky:

> It is a matter of small surprise that the head of this cantankerous cult should be incarcerated in one of the retreats for recalcitrants. The pity is that Russell's perpetrations were not published in his lifetime, so that he might have received the punishment instead of his less deserving satellites. The really perplexing problem in this connection is whether the defendants should have been sent to an insane asylum or a penitentiary. Certainly, the average Russellite would come to his own in the former rather than the latter, though perhaps much at home in either place.¹⁸

Because the Baptists had suffered more than most of the other denominations at the hands of the Russellites, it is not surprising to read variations on the above theme in all the Baptist journals. *The Watchman-Examiner,* having "always believed" the sect "a curse rather than a blessing," thought the convicted men got just what they deserved.¹⁹ *The Baptist Record* of Iowa agreed.²⁰ Periodicals in other denominations voiced similar convictions.²¹

One year later, after the condemned men had spent the twelve months in the Federal Penitentiary at Atlanta, the Court of Appeals reversed the decision and the men were free.²² This verdict was greeted with silence in the churches.

The Russellites accused the larger and more powerful groups of vested interests of spying upon and persecuting them because they were a smaller and despised religious minority. Members of the sect claimed that under the guise of patriotism the actual motives for raids and court prosecutions were covered up. Certainly as one examines the available evidence there seems to be much truth in their contention. That is not to say that the parties engaged in the suppression always recognized the mixed motives which made them eager to help to send the Russellites to jail. Witness the statement of the editor of *The Watchman-Examiner,* above, that he had *"always believed"* the sect "a curse rather than a blessing." It is significant that so many clergymen took an aggressive part in trying to get rid of the Russellites. Long-lived religious quarrels and hatreds, which did not receive any consideration in the courts in time of peace, now found their way into the courtroom under the spell of war-time hysteria.

Friends of the Conscientious Objector

The most conspicuous non-conformist organization operating continuously during the war was the Civil Liberties Bureau. It served as the outpost of what liberal thought and activity remained, challenging every infringement of rights guaranteed by the first amendment to the Constitution, and working unsparingly to maintain a semblance of freedom of thought and action.

The Military Intelligence Bureau of the War Department started an investigation which resulted in its accusing the Civil Liberties Bureau of organized resistance to military service, inasmuch as the Bureau had defended the objectors. In September, 1918, it participated in a raid on the office of the accused organization but no indictments were ever brought. Later the charges made by the Civil Liberties Bureau of brutal and inhuman treatment suffered by objectors in the camps and prisons were proved to be correct and admitted by the War Department.[23]

Of the ministers most active in this organization mention should be made of Norman Thomas, John Haynes Holmes, John Nevin Sayre, and W. G. "Bill" Simpson.

Practically all the other groups of dissenters that carried on during those days were small ones cooperating in some measure for the securing of rights of objectors. The clergy were sparsely represented. After the war fever came to be general, to belong to such a group of irreconcilables was generally regarded as an admission of treasonable tendencies.

There were a few others. In Boston, there was the League for Democratic Control, with A. J. Muste as chairman, and Harold L. Rotzel of the Friends' Church as organizing secretary.[24]

There was also the American Friends' Service Committee in Philadelphia; the Young Democracy of New York, whose executive secretary was Devere Allen; the New York Bureau of Legal Advice; the Young People's Socialist League of Chicago—and a few others, but not many.[25]

In Chicago, the American Liberty Defense League contained a comparatively large number of clergymen. This group enlisted Jenkin Lloyd Jones of the Abraham Lincoln Center and editor of *Unity,* Norman B. Barr of the Olivet Institute, Fred A. Moore of the Universalist Church of the Redeemer, Noble S. Elderkin of the Second Congregational Church of Oak Park, Herman Newman of the Indiana Avenue Friends' Meeting, and Irwin St. John Tucker, minister and journalist.[26] Various meetings were held in Chicago in the interest of free speech and the C. O.'s. Ministers of that vicinity were circularized in July, 1917, with requests that speakers be invited to present from their pulpits the case of the conscientious objectors.[27] This met with no response.

When E. E. Hastings, pastor of the Central Presbyterian Church of Joliet, received his letter he wrote back to the organization heads that their propaganda was "pure treason," and he would place it in the hands of the Federal authorities. His attitude may be regarded as typical of the majority of the parsons:

> What have I done to suffer the insult of such a proposal at this time? Why should my son offer himself to protect the man who will use his conscience to evade his duty? My son is at the front. He left Princeton University to enlist in the navy in recognition of the debt to his country.[28]

Friends, Mennonites, and Dunkards

Among the groups of irreconcilables were a number of religious sects which, holding to a pacifist tradition, reaffirmed their faith in their ancient ideals. The Friends, Mennonites, and the Brethren (Dunkards) and a few others come into this category. Their total number, as compared with the great bodies of Christendom, is very small and, therefore, their attitudes not at all representative of Christian feeling in this country, which, as we have observed, was practically a unity in supporting our arms.

The various Friends' Meetings testified again to their adherence to the teachings of their founder, George Fox, and the testimony of the forefathers in 1660. "We utterly deny all outward wars and strife, and fightings with outward weapons, for any end, or under any pretense whatever; this is our testimony to the whole world."[29]

According to the government regulations, the men of draft age belonging to the Society of Friends, Mennonites, the Church of the Brethren, and a few others having a long-established record against war, were exempt from combatant service and were allowed to take some form of alternate service. These groups supplied a large number of the conscientious objectors.

The American Friends' Service Committee gave unceasing attention to the rights of objectors, and in the summer of 1918 was given by the War Department charge of furloughed objectors waiting to go to France for reconstruction work,[30] et cetera.

The Mennonites and Dunkards also stood back of their young men, the former working jointly with the Friends in behalf of their C. O.'s.

While the majority of the Quakers were opposed to the war, this attitude was by no means universal among them. Some of the young men joined the service and went to the front. In one section, fifty-seven out of eighty-nine local Meetings reporting, there were "787 men of draft age, 370 of whom had either been drafted or had volunteered, 324 of these accepted combatant service, 41 had accepted non-combatant service and 5 refused any service under military direction."[31] Friends' records for all areas are not complete.

As far as can be determined none of the men who shouldered arms were "read out of meeting," which was supposed to have been done according to good Quaker tradition.

Another indication of the division of opinion may be gained from a statement signed by 120 Friends in the Philadelphia area. They were against war on principle but believed that there were "unusual and extraordinary circumstances of infrequent occurrence," like the World War, which were so different that they could not remain neutral. Jesus' teaching had been addressed to men in normal times, and even he, if living in the present, would be "against organized savagery." They were reconciled, therefore, to bearing arms against Germany.[32]

Thus it is seen that while a separatist group, such as the Quakers, can maintain its principles in time of peace, when group pressure to conform to another set of standards becomes sufficiently intense, a considerable number of the members of the "unworldly" group succumb to the pressure of public opinion and accept the majority view. The excitement of war being an unusually severe test of loyalty to minority opinions, it was but natural that, in a growingly standardized America, the attachment to separatist ideals in 1917-18 proved to be less binding than in previous centuries. Even in the Civil War in this country, however, many Quakers either joined the forces or came out definitely for the side of the North.[33]

The record of the Mennonites and the Church of the Brethren during the war is in many respects similar to that of the Friends. The Mennonites, in the estimation of Commission VII of the All

Friends Conference, "held more uniformly to the peace testimony and suffered more for it than did the Society of Friends."[34]

The Mennonites in their attitude toward the purchase of bonds and contributions to the various campaigns differed according to the particular branch of the church and the locality.[35] This group contributed large sums to relief work and works of mercy, but suffered persecution in many areas. In South Dakota, where there were thirty-eight incorporated colonies with several thousand members holding property in common and living in central community houses, the Council of Defense of Yankton County took a herd of cattle and a flock of sheep, put them up at auction and realized $18,000. This sum was invested in war bonds and deposited in the local bank to the credit of the colony, which refused to accept the bonds.[36] In Central Illinois, a number of church buildings were painted yellow and in other sections tar and feathers were freely applied.[37]

The government was quite lenient toward the Mennonite publications, but at least one Mennonite editor got into trouble and was fined $500 for printing an objectionable article.[38]

I have already indicated that they furnished the largest number of conscientious objectors of any religious group in the United States.

The Church of the Brethren in its official pronouncements deplored the war and as a group remained steadfast to the ancient testimony against the use of carnal weapons. But, as with the Friends, many of their young men bore arms, some of them becoming officers in the army. While sections varied a number of Dunkard ministers advised their people to purchase Liberty Bonds.[39]

There were, in addition to the above, several dozen smaller groups, sects, and cults that objected to the war on religious grounds. Among them were the Molokans, Adventists, et cetera. While all these stand out in their attitude toward the war by contrast to the larger church bodies, the total influence of these minorities on the mass of American opinion was practically negligible.

An extensive inquiry into the factors and circumstances which may account for the attitudes shown by the irreconcilables would lead to detailed case studies of personalities. The few organizations and church groups that refused to bless the war, thereby assuming the position of the dissentient minority, simply demonstrated that there are always some individuals in any society who will vary from the norm. No given stimulus, be it ever so powerful, meets with universally identical or even similar responses. Hence, one always discovers differences and a range in pluralistic behavior.

A few of the reasons why the government failed in the complete regimentation of its citizens are: Some individuals saw behind the smoke-screen of propaganda; others were so strongly inhibited against the use of physical force that they responded to the war-time stimuli in a negative manner; a number lived in a comparatively inaccessible sacred society—like the Mennonites and the Molokans, where their own group teachings and pressures were still supreme; a few citizens were almost completely individuated from their surroundings and emancipated from crowd control; some were frankly or secretly pro-German.

CHAPTER XI

THE NON-CONFORMIST CLERGY

As for us we must continue [to declare], so far as we are permitted under the flag, that war is a monstrous crime. . . . We will continue to deplore any efforts to raise an army for invasion by conscription. We will continue to believe in free speech and advocate the same.

> Jenkin Lloyd Jones, Editor, *Unity*, April 26, 1917.

CHAPTER XI
THE NON-CONFORMIST CLERGY

DESPITE the affinity between war and religion there have been discovered in every war a few members of the priesthood who refused to accept the mandates of kings or the decisions of the people as manifested through their legislatures. The last great conflict again verified historical experience, for there was a handful who, reserving the right of private judgment, failed to rally to the national battle cries. These recalcitrants became an object of deep concern and the source of much distress to the churches, many of whose founders, nevertheless, had suffered martyrdom for the right of the individual to follow the dictates of his own conscience.

The Iron Hand of the Hierarchy

The spirit of 1917-18 may be illustrated by a resolution passed by the American Unitarian Association, April 9, 1918, which, after reaffirming its loyalty to the support of the government and the war, voted, ". . . that any society which employs a minister who is not a willing, earnest and outspoken supporter of the United States in the vigorous and resolute prosecution of the war cannot be considered eligible for aid from the Association."[1]

The number of aided churches, and therefore churches that might be affected by this resolution, was 49 in the year 1918.[2] Most of them were able to pay their ministers only through the money given to them by the Association. It is evident that in the Unitarian Church the vested interests used their economic power to maintain control over the expressed opinions of ministers dependent upon the Association for their salaries, and in so doing departed from the historic tradition of allowing each congregation to choose its own minister.

There is evidence of suppression in other denominations where overhead control was possible. Speaking before the Methodist Episcopal Conference in Philadelphia, Bishop Theodore S. Henderson of Detroit is reported as saying: "If there is any preacher in the Methodist Episcopal Church who doesn't see his way clear to espouse the cause of the Allies, if we can't regenerate him, we will eliminate him, and then turn him over to the Department of Justice."³

At another Methodist Conference in New York, E. F. Weise of Bridgeport, Connecticut, tried to inject a pacifist note into the meeting: "I don't want to lose my soul. If I have to choose between my country and my God, I have made up my mind to choose God. I am an American, but I am a Christian first." His fellow-clergymen shouted, "Sit down!" "Shame on you," and cries of "Traitor!" were heard from every part of the room.⁴

Dean Shailer Mathews, apparently exercised over the loyalty of some of his fellow-ministers, wrote a special editorial for *The Biblical World* on "Are Ministers Slackers?" Said the dean: "Exemption from military service means a draft into spiritual service, and a real man will be as ready to die from overwork as from an enemy's bullet."⁵

In general the ministers appeared to agree with Theodore Roosevelt that "the clergyman who does not put the flag above the church had better close his church and keep it closed."⁶

The Number of Pacifist Clergy

The question is frequently asked, "How many pacifist ministers were there during the war?" While no one knows exactly, from various indications probably several hundred ministers were either out-and-out non-conformists or were strongly inclined toward pacifism in their preaching. Yet there is no means of determining, with any degree of preciseness, the total number. And, of course, there are various degrees and shades of pacifism.

However, while recognizing the impossibility of discovering how many clergy did not conform to the war schedule, the present writer has compiled a list of names of alleged pacifists from a variety of sources and, by means of correspondence and interviews, has checked up on its accuracy. The final list, while in no sense offered as a complete enumeration, represents a group of men who were bona fide pacifists and stood by their position all during the war.* Those who put their trust for source material in the famous Lusk report, or the list of pacifists drawn up and presented to the Senate committee investigating German propaganda by Archibald E. Stevenson,⁷ will be relying upon the

---

* In this part of the study I have not attempted to incorporate any facts about the attitudes of clergymen in the Lutheran groups or among the Dunkards and the Mennonites. It would be impossible in these, for instance, to differentiate between the pacifists who were controlled by a pacifistic motivation and those opposed to the war because it was against Germany.

most inaccurate and biased information. Furthermore, it must be remembered that a number of those who started out as pacifists or were such as late as April 6, 1917, had climbed aboard the band wagon by November 11, 1918.

No claim is made here to submitting a complete list of the pacifist clergy. Out of a total of ninety on a doubly checked list, many men, whose addresses have changed, cannot be found; a few have failed to answer correspondence, and a few, whose records are uncertain, are dead. Out of the ninety, I have been able, after a lengthy research, to vouch for seventy. In this search, I have been aided by pacifist organizations, like the Fellowship of Reconciliation, and by individuals who have informed me about themselves as well as others. Because the non-resisters were a minority group and because of the very nature of pacifism operating in war time, the individual pacifist would be driven to seek fellowship with those of like mind. Hence, one man would probably have been known to several others. After this rather detailed explanation as to method of procedure, the following conclusions may be presented.

The most significant thing about the results of the investigation is the paucity of the data itself.* The second observation to be made is that the distribution is entirely over the Northern States, with New York and New York City, New England, Illinois, and California (around Los Angeles) as concentration areas. The fundamentalism of the South does not provide fertile soil for non-conformity in religion.

DISTRIBUTION BY STATES
OF PACIFIST MINISTERS, 1917-18

New York	15
California	11
Massachusetts	10
Illinois	9
New Jersey	5
Maine	3

---

* None of the men on the list of the ninety lived in the South. No Southern minister to whom I have written can recall a single pacifist minister during the war. In fact, even in the North, with the exception of a very few, all the denominational leaders, outstanding clergymen, and denominational secretaries with whom I corresponded or had interviews, could not recall a pacifist minister of 1917-18. As a state secretary (Baptist) remarked, "If they were pacifists, they kept their mouths shut."

Ohio	3
Vermont	3
Pennsylvania	2
Washington	2
Connecticut	1
Maryland	1
Michigan	1
Minnesota	1
Nebraska	1
New Hampshire	1
Utah	1
Total	70

The assortment by denominations shows that the Unitarians, Congregationalists, and Universalists, three of the smaller denominations, contributed thirty-seven out of seventy, or more than fifty per cent of the total. These churches themselves comprise but approximately four per cent of the total membership of the Protestant groups (exclusive of the Lutherans, Mennonites, Dunkards and Friends).*

DISTRIBUTION BY DENOMINATIONS

OF PACIFIST MINISTERS, 1917-18

Denominations	Total Pacifist Clergy	No. Occupying Pulpits
Unitarians	16	15
Congregationalists	13	11
Universalists	8	8
Baptists	8	5
Episcopalians	7	5
Presbyterians	7	6
Methodists	4	3
Reformed	3	3
Hebrews	3	2
Non-denominational	1	1
Total	70	59

* In 1916, the membership of the Unitarians was 82,515, the Universalists 58,566, and the Congregationalists 791,274.

DISTRIBUTION BY DENOMINATIONS AND STATES
OF PACIFIST MINISTERS, 1917-18

Unitarian		Congregationalist		Universalist		Baptist		Episcopalian	
Mass.	5	Cal.	3	Ill.	3	Cal.	3	N. Y.	3
Cal.	3	Mass.	2	Mass.	2	Pa.	2	Ill.	1
N. Y.	2	Wash.	2	Maine	1	Vt.	1	Md.	1
Ill.	1	Conn.	1	N. Y.	1	Mich.	1	N. J.	1
Maine	1	Ill.	1	Vt.	1	N. Y.	1	Utah	1
Minn.	1	N. H.	1						
Neb.	1	N. Y.	1						
N. J.	1	Ohio	1						
Ohio	1	Vt.	1						
Total	16	Total	13	Total	8	Total	8	Total	7

Presbyterian		Hebrew		Methodist		Reformed		Non-denominational	
N. Y.	4	N. Y.	2	Cal.	2	N. J.	2	Ohio	1
Ill.	2	Ill.	1	Maine	1	N. Y.	1		
N. J.	1			Mass.	1				
Total	7	Total	3	Total	4	Total	3	Total	1

The pacifist clergy in the Episcopalian group were nearly all Socialists—Bishop Paul Jones, Irwin St. John Tucker, A. L. Byron-Curtiss, John Nevin Sayre, all members of the Church Socialist League.

The Presbyterians, with Norman Thomas, W. G. Simpson, Edmund B. Chaffee and William A. Fincke, were centered in the New York district.

While the Reformed Church had a strong militarist element, a few, believing in the literal interpretation of Christ as a Man of Peace, refused to side with the majority.

That the largest Protestant denominations, the Methodist and the Baptist, should have contributed but twelve, all told, is significant in that it shows the negative correlation between the strong evangelistic spirit of these groups and pacifism or radicalism. The Methodists and Baptists have always emphasized the emotional element and distrusted the rational in religion. These two largest Protestant bodies had had up to 1917 no liberal tradition or broad social philosophy to speak of.

Among the Jews, in time of war, radicalism cannot very well express itself against the overwhelming mass of Gentiles. Fear of anti-Semitism is a strong factor in the social control of their behavior. The Catholics, with a discipline of obedience, give no room for non-conformity.*

---

* I am informed that there were one or two Catholic priests who were pacifists during the war, but I have been unable to find them.

When further account is taken of the pacifist clergy who occupied pulpits during the war and they are divided into two groups, those who were able to retain their pulpits, and those who were compelled to leave, the array is as follows: *

DISTRIBUTION BY DENOMINATIONS
OF PACIFIST CLERGY, 1917-18, WHO REMAINED IN PULPITS AND THOSE WHO WERE FORCED OUT

Denomination	Remained in Pulpits	Left Pulpits
Unitarians	6	9
Congregationalists	6	5
Universalists	5	3
Baptists	3	2
Episcopalians	3	2
Presbyterians	3	3
Reformed	3	0
Methodists	1	2
Hebrews	1	1
Non-denominational	1	0
Total	32	27

ADVENTURES IN NON-CONFORMITY

I shall not attempt a sketch for each of these men, but shall simply relate some of the experiences of a few of them, since, after all, they do not represent any more than a tiny minority of Christian and Jewish opinion during the war.

The most notable case was that of John Haynes Holmes, who had come to the Church of the Messiah in New York as a young Unitarian minister, just a couple of years after having been graduated from Harvard. It has been said that the Encyclopedia Britannica changed him into a radical. In the 1910 edition, he found Socialism defined as "the economics of Christianity." It set him to thinking. By 1914 when the war came he was thoroughly prepared to deplore it from the economic as well as the Christian pacifist point of view. Between August, 1914, and April, 1917, he participated in nearly all the existing peace movements which tried to prevent our entrance into the war.

His congregation, comprising a mixed popular audience,

---

* I have deducted from the list those who did not occupy pulpits during the war and those who preached to Friends' Churches. Under those who left their pulpits I have listed those who were compelled to resign or did so because the continuance of their pacifist ministry would probably have split the church.

representing all classes of the community, heard him denounce war week after week in the manner of William Ellery Channing. But he was allowed the utmost freedom.

Then America came up to pause a moment before crossing the Rubicon. The Sunday before (April 1), Dr. Holmes stood up before his congregation and preached a sermon, entitled, "A Statement to My People on the Eve of War." In this he reaffirmed his position that "war is never justifiable at any time or under any circumstances." He said he was opposed to all war in general and to this one in particular. "War is an open and utter violation of Christianity," he announced, and "if war is right, then Christianity is wrong, false, a lie. . . . There is not a question raised, an issue involved, a cause at stake, which is worth the life of one bluejacket on the sea or one khaki coat in the trenches. . . . When, years hence, the whole of this story has been told, it will be found that we have been tragically deceived, and all our sacrifice been made in vain. . . . Other pulpits may preach recruiting sermons; mine will not. Other parish houses may be turned into drill halls and rifle ranges; ours will not. Other clergy may pray to God for victory for our arms; I will not. In this church, if nowhere else in all America, the Germans will still be included in the family of God's children." He proposed to stand for free speech, serve as a "minister of reconciliation" to strive to keep alive the spirit of good-will, and to serve his country by "serving the ideals of democracy, preparing the way for the establishment of peace" and the dream of universal brotherhood.[8]

The board of trustees held a meeting the next day. The chairman was a Wall Street financier; the treasurer, a corporation director; and other members included a judge on the Supreme bench and a vice-president of the New York Central Railroad. They disagreed with the minister but voted, according to the Unitarian tradition, that the man in the pulpit should remain and express his views. And he did.

But as the weeks advanced, and the hysteria created by the war increased, the contrast between the accepted beliefs of the majority and Dr. Holmes's preaching became too alarming for many of the old-line congregation. They quietly departed, never to return. In their place came a strange assemblage of men and women from the remote places of the earth. Germans and Americans, Mohammedans and Hindus, Greeks and Jews and Gentiles, Believers and Infidels—all drawn to the Church of the Messiah because they hated war. His "Christian" Church had walked out on him.[9]

The sermons of this minister, while not compromising in any way with the war system, carried the note of hope for a new day after the war. In such a hope Dr. Holmes afterward suffered disillusionment. In the meantime, this militant socialist pacifist kept on with his radical activities, supporting the American Union Against Militarism, the Civil Liberties Bureau, the Fellowship of Reconciliation, the People's Council, and so on. The conscientious objectors had in him one of their strongest supporters. His chief sounding-board, outside of the pulpit, was the pages of *Unity*.

In some way, unknown to him, his sermon, "On the Eve of War," was carried to Germany, copies printed and dropped by the Germans along the Allied lines, much to the discomfiture of the British.

While, no doubt, the government would have liked to have placed this man behind the bars (Secret Service men were in the congregation each Sunday during the war), to have attempted to suppress this voice would probably have reacted against the government officials and created too much of a disturbance.

Furthermore, in a big city like New York, where citizens are not able to pry into the details of their neighbors' lives, a man like John Haynes Holmes was free from the impediments which were so evident in the small towns, which contributed much of the grist for the Espionage Act.

The spiritual affairs of the State of Utah, since December 16, 1914, as far as the Episcopalians were concerned, had been guided by the young Bishop Paul Jones. He was a socialist and immediate successor to Bishop Spalding of the same political persuasion. In 1916, Bishop Jones became president of the Church Socialist League. A year later the war broke out. The League took no official position in the matter, but its president, while not antagonizing the government, made a pronouncement against war:

> . . . as I love my country, I must protest against her doing what I would not do myself because it is contrary to our Lord's teaching. To prosecute war means to kill men, bringing sorrow and suffering upon women and children. . . . No matter what principles may appear to be at stake, to deliberately engage in such a course of action that evidently is unchristian is repugnant to the whole spirit of the gospel.

The vested interests of Utah that had harried but not silenced Bishop Spalding now saw their opportunity, under the guise of patriotism, to get rid of Bishop Jones. Though the government had never taken or apparently contemplated any action against the bishop, certain leading Episcopalians asked him to resign. Bishop Jones transferred the whole matter to the House of Bishops.

This ecclesiastical body received the charges that Bishop Jones had been affiliating with "seditious organizations," and had "persistently promulgated unpatriotic doctrines." It was alleged that his conduct had injured the life of the church; that he had "exceeded his prerogatives" in his expression of views with regard to war and Christianity. These charges referred, in part, to the notoriety Bishop Jones had achieved by his participation in the Christian Pacifist meetings in Los Angeles in September of 1917.

On December 12, 1917, the commission appointed by the House of Bishops to investigate the charges issued its report. It disagreed with Bishop Jones's contention that war is unchristian, for: "This church in the United States is practically a unity in holding that it is not an unchristian thing. In the face of this unanimity it is neither right nor wise for a trusted bishop to declare and maintain that it is an unchristian thing." Moreover, "if the compelling force of conscientious conviction requires such utterances, fairness demands that it not be made by a bishop of this church."

Though no real indictment could be filed against the Bishop of Utah, the commission believed that an end had come to his usefulness in that region, and recommended that he accede to the wishes of the patriots of Utah and resign. They did not wish this to be regarded as a precedent, this listening to the voice of criticism, but it seemed necessary in view of "an excited condition of public opinion."

Bishop Jones, rather than create a further commotion, resigned. Episcopalians, hundreds of them, conservatives and liberals alike, protested this action against this "Catholic and Christian Bishop of America, two hundred seventy-fourth in the Anglo-American succession."

The House of Bishops, in session in April, 1918, expressing itself as unwilling to accept the resignation of any bishop "in deference to an excited state of opinion," therefore rejected the report of the commission, *but accepted* the resignation of Bishop Jones in view of his impaired usefulness to the Christians of Utah.

The Churchman, in commenting upon this action, told the House of Bishops that they had acted "wisely," "fearlessly," had shown no "pacifist leanings," and had defended the right of free opinion and speech in civic matters "insofar as such freedom is consonant with the law of the land. . . ."[10]

The Bishop without a diocese now devoted himself to work with the Fellowship of Reconciliation. Since the war he has come back into popular favor, actually supplying the diocese of Southern Ohio for the greater part of a year. He is at present the college pastor at Antioch College in Ohio.

On the Pacific Coast, at Seattle, Washington, existed another uncompromising spirit in the person of Sydney Strong, pastor of the Queen Anne Congregational Church, active in labor and social movements and an early member of the Municipal League, a local civic organization.

On his way to speak at the National Council of the Congregational Churches to be held in Columbus, Ohio, in October, 1917, Dr. Strong decided to take in the Christian Pacifist conference at Los Angeles. This conference was broken up by the home guards. The Seattle papers reported that their radical Congregational clergyman had been arrested and jailed. This was untrue, but when Dr. Strong arrived in Cleveland, Ohio, the Federal district attorney, having received news of the approaching suspect, held him up as a possible dangerous character.

At the Columbus meeting, speaking on "The Church and Industry," the representative from Seattle advised the churches to get acquainted with labor organizations, including the notorious I. W. W., whose ideals and practices he explained with a sympathetic and sociological touch. The press now painted Dr. Strong an "I. W. W. sympathizer" in speech and in action. On the Monday following, the Municipal League in Seattle ousted him from its membership. The Ministerial Federation, about to take similar action, was stayed in its haste by a friend who advised waiting until the prisoner at the bar had a chance to get back to Seattle and explain his conduct. The ministers finally compromised by severely reprimanding their erring brother.[11]

Jenkin Lloyd Jones, Unitarian minister to the Abraham Lincoln Centre, Chicago, a Civil War veteran, pacifist editor of *Unity* since 1880, leader in peace organizations, member of Henry Ford's Peace Ship party, held to his convictions undeviatingly throughout the war. He said that he hated war, he was opposed to this one, there being a "better way."[12] He would continue to maintain that war was a "monstrous crime."[13]

Unity proved to be the lone star for the radical Christians, as far as the religious journals were concerned, until the appearance of *The World Tomorrow* (at first *The New World*), in January, 1918. In the spring of that year the postmaster at Chicago began to hold up editions of *Unity*. The government barred from the mails all the July and August issues.¹⁴ Most of the last days of Jenkin Lloyd Jones were devoted to securing readmission to the mails of his publication.* The sadness and disappointment of the war years, which cost him many friends, closed to him familiar pulpits and involved *Unity* with the government, helped to bring on his death, September 12, 1918.¹⁵

Charles Fletcher Dole, a retired Unitarian minister, continued his pacifist teaching throughout the war. He was largely responsible for the endurance of the Association for the Abolition of War through the years 1917-18. "Killing Germans," said he, "is wrong—just as wrong if we kill millions of them in war as if we murdered them one by one with pistols and knives. Furthermore it can accomplish no possible good for France, or Britain, or ourselves, or the world; but only evil, evil, evil to everybody." ¹⁶

Norman Thomas, at that time a Presbyterian minister in New York, joined in all the radical movements to aid in preserving what he regarded as the essential liberties that seemed fast disappearing in the battles on the home front. He was tremendously interested in the rights of the C. O.'s, and in free speech; he helped to found *The World Tomorrow,* and the National Civil Liberties Bureau.

John Nevin Sayre, Episcopalian minister at Suffern, New York, retained his pulpit all during the war, at the same time promoting the work of the Fellowship of Reconciliation, taking a leading part in defending Bishop Jones, and joining in efforts on behalf of the conscientious objectors, freedom of speech, et cetera.

A fellow-Episcopalian clergyman, Leigh R. Urban, was compelled to leave his parish, the Church of the Redeemer, Astoria, Long Island. On a Saturday night, April 13, some small boys broke into the church and hung an American flag. The next day

---

* Most of the issues were later readmitted to the mails. *The World Tomorrow,* issue of September, 1918, was barred under the Espionage Act, but later admitted to the mails.

Mr. Urban removed the flag, in which act he was upheld by the vestry. The newspapers expressed patriotic indignation. Mr. Urban's resignation became acceptable "with regrets." [17] He later joined the Friends' Service Committee for work overseas.

The so-called "firebrand" in the Unitarian Church, Henry W. Pinkham, who failed to see an iota of good coming out of the war, lost his pulpit at Melrose, Massachusetts, in June, 1917. He has been blacklisted from practically all the Unitarian pulpits ever since. Shortly after the beginning of hostilities, one parish with a vacant pulpit in which he was interested informed him that they would prefer to see "the church closed and rot" before opening it to men of Pinkham's type. "Ex-ministers of your ilk," reasoned the pulpit committee, "should be employed at hard labor in the government prisons or be subject to a commission *lunatio inquirendo.*" [18]

At the Greenwich Presbyterian Church, New York, William A. Fincke and his associate, Edmund B. Chaffee, now of the Labor Temple, decided that Mr. Fincke should on April 29, 1917, present their joint views in a sermon to be entitled, "A Ministry of Reconciliation." The congregation that day learned of the refusal of the ministers to turn the church into a recruiting station or to offer up prayers for the success of the arms of the United States. Instead, said Mr. Fincke, they proposed to work for the "peace of the world" through understanding. The two clergymen soon joined the ranks of the unemployed.[19]

Paul Harris Drake, minister to the Christ Church (Unitarian), Dorchester, Massachusetts, announced that he would preach on "The Conscientious Objector," at the Sunday morning service, June 3, 1917. On Saturday night he was summoned before the governing board of the Church, and requested not to preach that sermon. Thereupon, he read to the board a prepared statement of his views:

> "War is hell," and hell has no more place in the human order of things than in the Divine order. If I, as a minister of God, am unable to believe in a hell hereafter, I certainly cannot bring myself to believe in the wisdom or righteousness of a hell here and now. . . . War orators may sing the praises of America with her hands red with the blood of my fellow-men—but I shall not! [20]

Mr. Drake was barred from the pulpit the next day and told that if he could not support the war his resignation would be expected. He resigned.

A. J. Muste, pastor of the fashionable Central Congregational Church, Newtonville, Massachusetts, continued with his pacifist sermons in spite of April 6. His congregation, perceiving the increasing embarrassment of a pacifist preacher in war times, tried to prevail on Mr. Muste to take a leave of absence as a "Y" secretary. Considering this an evasion of the issue, he resigned, leaving the first day of the year, 1918.[21] * Mr. Muste was, until recently, chairman of the faculty of the Brookwood Labor College.

In Summit, New Jersey, the Unitarian-Universalist pastor, Frank C. Doan, who had said that he "would rather be right with Jesus Christ than with Woodrow Wilson,"[22] resigned, shortly after the entrance of the United States into the war, because he feared that his church would not take to his continued pacifism. A rare phenomenon occurred, in that his trustees refused to accept his resignation, and issued a series of resolutions. It was pointed out that the greater part of the congregation absolutely disagreed with Mr. Doan on his views of peace and war; nevertheless, he had uttered nothing "capable of being interpreted as treason or disloyalty to his country." The trustees did not believe in the suppression of "honest opinion" and the "free expression of pacifism":

> Let us not see the ghost of Benedict Arnold in every phrase which is not sufficiently warlike to suit our emotions. Let us rather respect an honest man whether he agrees with us or not. In short, while fighting one form of tyranny, let us beware lest we build up another.[23]

From this position the trustees never receded.

Harry F. Ward, Methodist, professor of social science in Boston University, opposed our entrance into the war and refused to have anything to do with efforts expended in furthering the cause of our arms. He turned to attempts at transforming conditions in America, particularly in the industrial field. Dr. Ward's strategy and influence were chiefly responsible for the incorporation of the statement on behalf of conscientious objectors into the Federal Council Declaration in May, 1917.[24]

---

* Mr. Muste was one of the few radical ministers whose congregation defended him from outside attacks and accusations that he was pro-German. Several of the ministers now confess that their parishes were as fair as could be expected under the circumstances.

Among the Jews, Rabbi Judah L. Magnes stands out as the most prominent pacifist. Because of his activities he was thoroughly repudiated by the mass of the members of his race because they regarded him as the *enfant terrible* who was constantly causing trouble by "casting doubt upon Jewish loyalty." Consequently Rabbi Magnes had a most uncomfortable time, despised by his own people on the one hand, and covered by the agents of the Department of Justice on the other, who were watching all the while for some "damning phrase" which might be used against him. Nevertheless he did not seem to be deterred, for he was active in the work of the People's Council, the Civil Liberties Bureau and other projects which were designed to defend the last barricade of free speech and civil liberty.[25]

In the end, out of the war which Dr. Magnes had so hated, grew the hope of a restored homeland for the Jews in Palestine and the actual migration of thousands of them to that country. In 1924, the Hebrew University in Jerusalem, which Judah Magnes had planned and helped to build, was dedicated by Lord Balfour. Magnes became the chancellor.

There was one pacifist who was generally believed to have renounced his views and to have become a convert to the holiness of Allied war aims. That was Walter Rauschenbusch, pioneer of the social gospel, professor in Rochester Theological Seminary.

In the summer of 1918, there was released to the press a letter which Dr. Rauschenbusch had sent to Cornelius Woelfkin. It was a personal letter to explain that he was not a pro-German, for he hoped that "out of all this suffering" would come "the downfall of all autocratic government in the Central Empires." Yet he was not at all certain that the victory of the Allies "would of itself free the world from imperialism." The religious press gave the letter wide publicity. The editors were relieved to know that at last the questions which Dr. Rauschenbusch's acquaintances had been asking "one another privately" were satisfactorily answered. He was a patriot. He wanted to see Germany beaten.

As a matter of fact they were mistaken. Dr. Rauschenbusch never recanted, never accepted the war, or sought to justify any of its high moral pretense. He remained a pacifist to the very end, dying July 25, 1918, mainly, it is said, as a result of acute mental suffering over the war. This was accentuated by the criticism of his German birth and a haunting sense, due to his acute deafness, of being cut off from the world and completely ostracized.[26]

The further recital of the experiences of the pacifist ministers would include stories of those who were able to remain in their pulpits, as did John Haynes Holmes, but who flung no flags, celebrated no victories, made no appeals for the purchase of Liberty Bonds, did not permit the singing of "The Star-Spangled Banner," or give favorable mention of the war. Some of them, aside from being called into the office of the local district attorney, suffered no serious difficulty. Others were cast, rather unceremoniously, out of their pulpits. They were despised, for no other reason than refusing obeisance to the tribal gods. Most of them were barred from all pulpits for the remainder of the war period. Some never were able to locate again, due to continuance of prejudice against pacifist ministers. Many recovered in spirit from their experience and can now view matters with a high degree of objectivity. Yet there are numbers of them who are still suffering from the shock of disillusionment. None has quite the same faith in the church that he had before. A few, who tried the pastorate again after 1918, gave up, as they said, "in disgust," and are now at other occupations.

CHAPTER XII

THE ESPIONAGE ACT, MOB VIOLENCE, AND THE CLERGY

The district attorneys are instructed to make it clear that the complaints of even the most informal or confidential nature are always welcome and that citizens should feel free to bring their information or suspicions to the attention of the nearest representative of the Department of Justice; or if that is not convenient, communicate with the department at Washington.

> From statement issued by Attorney General Gregory. New York *Tribune*, May 12, 1918.

CHAPTER XII
THE ESPIONAGE ACT, MOB VIOLENCE, AND THE CLERGY

Grist for the Espionage Acts

IN A DAY of social upheaval the "in-group" tries to enforce its will upon the outsiders by sundry devices for social control. One of the sternest forms of pressure was exerted by the passage of Espionage and Sedition Acts, which measures were resorted to in both the Federal and State governments during the war. While these laws had a powerful effect in curbing the expressed opinions of individuals and groups, thousands of individuals, including some of the clergy, were arraigned on charges of violating the war-time statutes.*

Among the religious groups placed in an embarrassing position, due to the general state of affairs, were the various German Lutherans scattered over the country. From August, 1914, to April, 1917, it was but natural that in hundreds of Lutheran churches "the continuous preaching was in favor and hope of German victory." [1] The churches were filled with German propaganda as the churches of Anglican and other groups were with Allied propaganda.

But, according to the sworn statement of Captain George B. Lester of the Army Intelligence Service, "even among those who were pro-German, when the question of conscription came, there was no evidence, except in isolated cases, of any attempt on the part of the Lutheran Church, to persuade the young men to evade military service." [2]

During the war, however, there were other opinions about the loyalty of the Lutherans. The Nebraska Council of National Defense in July, 1917, charged that "the conspicuous representatives of the Lutheran Church" had "almost universally refused to cooperate" in efforts for the support of the government and had "discouraged the American cause," showing thereby the utmost partiality to Germany.[3]

---

* The Attorney General, alone, reported nearly 2,000 cases commenced in 1917-19. There were additional State prosecutions and many unrecorded cases. (*Vid.*, Z. Chafee, Jr., *Freedom of Speech*, Harcourt Brace, N. Y., 1920, Appendix II.)

The above statement is reported to have raised a storm of indignation in the Lutheran ranks and to have brought forth stout denials mingled with extravagant claims of loyalty.[4] Some time later, a prominent Lutheran, J. W. Miller of Fort Wayne, Indiana, exclaimed that he had recently visited Lutheran churches in every part of the United States and found unquestioned loyalty, with members of this group "doing more than their share in sacrificing for this country." In fact, said he, "there is no group of citizens as loyal to the Republic, there is no body of citizens as vitally necessary to the success of this land as are the Lutheran people."[5]

At this point difficulties caused by the German element in the Methodist Episcopal Church are of interest. There was a paper, *Der Christliche Apologete,* owned by the Methodists and published by the Methodist Book Concern for the German conferences in the United States. This paper came under the eye of the Department of Justice, which made some complaints. The publishers accused the editor, Albert J. Nast, of having been pro-German prior to April, 1917, and of now maintaining a negative patriotism which, "if universal, would doom the United States and her Allies to defeat." Such a condition seemed "intolerable." So arrangements were made to secure an associate editor who would have charge of all matters touching on the war. The publishers made the editor and his assistant sign a statement admitting that the paper had not been up to the standard of loyalty expected but that in the future it would be one hundred per cent patriotic.[6]

A few months later the bishops of the Methodist Episcopal Church, "with pride in the historic loyalty of the Church in every crisis in the nation's history," passed resolutions in which they "rejoiced" in "the evidence that an overwhelming majority of German Methodists in the United States are loyal to our country in this crisis of world war."[7]

The operations of all German leaders, including clergymen, were watched by government sleuths. Inasmuch as the ministers were in a position to mold public opinion, "suspect" members of this profession soon came under the shadow of the investigators. The Department of Justice, investigating into the records, past and present, of Lutheran clergymen under surveillance, conferred with representatives of Lutheran synods, and "active measures" were taken to curb the offenders. In this procedure, "two or three prominent Lutheran clergymen" assisted the government in getting information.[8] Altogether, 1,200 individual cases of Lutheran clergymen were investigated. Some of these men were convicted under the Espionage Acts and sent to Atlanta.[9]

A search through all the available material from a variety of sources gives a total of fifty-five ministers of the gospel from various denominations and sects arrested for alleged violation of one or more of the espionage and sedition laws.* In addition, there were several dozen Russellites, some of whom suffered severe penalties.†

The fifty-five cases are distributed over the United States from Massachusetts to California, from Michigan to Texas and Florida. Most of them are from the central part of the United States. The German Lutheran, and Reformed (often confused in the newspapers) composed merely fifteen of these.‡ Not all of these cases represent convictions. Other denominations in the list were Pentecostal, Catholic, Congregational, Presbyterian, Methodist, Church of Christ, Church of the Living God, Episcopalian, Baptist, and Mennonite. Several of the men were Negroes. The penalties ranged from fines of small amounts up into the thousands of dollars, and sentences from a short term in jail to ten, fifteen, and twenty years in prison. One Mennonite bishop was fined $500 by a Federal judge for writing to a Mennonite paper criticizing the purchase of Liberty Bonds.[10] Judge Kenesaw Mountain Landis sentenced a clergyman of the Church of the Brethren to ten years in Leavenworth for advising people not to buy Liberty Bonds and attacking the activities of the Red Cross.[11]

Irwin St. John Tucker, Episcopalian clergyman, and Victor Berger, together with other socialists, were sentenced by Judge Landis to twenty years in Leavenworth. The principal evidence introduced for conviction in this trial was the anti-war proclamation of the Socialist party and a pamphlet written by Mr. Tucker,

---

* There are no accurate records of all the individuals who were convicted under the various Espionage Acts. The available reports, et cetera, together with the cases, are listed in Zechariah Chafee, Jr., *Freedom of Speech*, Appendices I-V. Other source material, in the form of several thousand newspaper clippings, is to be found at the New York Public Library, New York City. These were collected and arranged by the National Civil Liberties Bureau during the war.

† For the Russellites, *Vid*. Chapter X *supra*.

‡ The Department of Justice does not have available information in regard to the number of the clergy indicted under the Espionage and Sedition Acts. Various bulletins and newspaper accounts from all over the country comprise the only index. The above number (55) is, doubtless, incomplete.

entitled, "The Price We Pay," of which some 5,000,000 copies were distributed. The United States Supreme Court threw out the decision on the ground that Judge Landis had no right to preside, after a change of venue had been demanded alleging that Judge Landis had been prejudiced.[12] The trial and indictment, however, did not deprive Mr. Tucker of his pulpit. He kept on preaching even while under sentence.

A case which merits attention because of several factors and principles involved, is that of Clarence H. Waldron, pastor of the First Baptist Church of Windsor, Vermont. On the 21st day of October, 1917, Liberty Loan Sunday, Mr. Waldron, believing that the church was not the place to introduce such matters, did not appeal from the pulpit for the support of the Loan. That evening, the news having spread, a large group of people, most of them factory workers, assembled in front of the church, and demanded that the minister sing "The Star-Spangled Banner," which he did, having draped himself in the American flag.

The clergyman's alleged lack of patriotism brought severe criticism and resulted in a quarrel within the church. The matter came to the attention of the Federal authorities, there was a Federal grand jury indictment and a trial set for January 8.

In the meantime other events had developed. Mr. Waldron, who had had Quaker training, and whose wife was a Mennonite, was a literalist in his interpretation of the Scripture, a non-resister, and inclined toward the Pentecostal point of view with emphasis on the physical manifestation of the Holy Spirit among Christians. In a series of Pentecostal meetings held in Windsor, Mr. Waldron had shown considerable interest, and later some of the Pentecostal converts were taken into the Baptist Church. This alarmed the Baptist officials of the state; among other reasons, they had been granting aid to the church. The general spirit of intolerance toward Mr. Waldron, which had been furthered by the vigilantes, became "augmented by the Baptist State officials who came to believe that Mr. Waldron was unworthy to continue as pastor of the Baptist Church because of his conversion to the Pentecostal faith."[13]

Yet he was determined to remain in Windsor. Accordingly, his opponents threatened to use the courts in securing his removal from the Windsor Baptist Church. Under this pressure, he resigned, and part of the congregation, particularly the Pentecostal element, withdrew with him. The Federal indictment followed shortly thereafter.

Then the secretary of the Vermont Baptist State Convention, William A. Davison, "worked with the district attorney in obtaining witnesses and in preparing the case for the government."

Dr. Davison, who had "remonstrated with Mr. Waldron several times for his attitude," [14] advised him to promise to leave Windsor and to plead guilty to the charge of violating the Espionage Act, for "the attorneys hoped this would lighten his sentence."

At this trial the jury, after twenty-four hours deliberation, failed to agree and were dismissed without rendering a verdict. However, the government retried the case. Among other witnesses, all the ministers in Windsor appeared on the stand. "The Methodist minister at the trial gave damaging testimony for the prosecution and the Unitarian minister was equally positive for the defense." [15]

Mr. Waldron was charged with handing to five persons, among whom were the Methodist minister, B. B. Hanscom, two men and a woman, all above military age, a pamphlet, entitled, *The Word of the Cross*.[16] This literature Mr. Waldron had ordered from a large advertisement in D. L. Moody's *Christian Worker Magazine,* a Northfield publication of the Moody interests which was printed and published at Brattleboro, Vermont. The pamphlets were printed in Pennsylvania and distributed up into the thousands of copies. The judge, in his charge to the jury, quoted the following statements from the pamphlet:

> Surely, if Christians were forbidden to fight to preserve the Person of their Lord and Master, they may not fight to preserve themselves, or any city they should happen to dwell in. Christ has no kingdom here. His servants must not fight.
>
> The Christian may not go to "the front" to repel the foe— for there he is required to kill men.
>
> They [referring to the Twelve Apostles] knew the force of the Lord's example, and whether to save themselves or to save others—never, never use the sword.
>
> Better a thousand times to die than for a Christian to kill his fellow.
>
> I do not say that it is wrong for a nation to go to war to preserve its interests, but it is wrong to the Christian, absolutely, unutterably wrong.
>
> Under no circumstances can I undertake any service that has for its purpose the prosecution of war.

Mr. Waldron was convicted for causing insubordination and obstructing recruiting, and sentenced to fifteen years in the Federal prison at Atlanta.[17] *

The Waldron case furnishes another instance of the way in which the Espionage Act gave people the opportunity to get rid of those to whom they had taken a dislike. In this particular case it was the Baptist State officials, led by Dr. Davison, who, being out of accord with Mr. Waldron's "fanatical" religious views, supplied evidence to the government which helped in the sending of Mr. Waldron to Atlanta.

It is probably true that these officials were convinced of their fellow-clergyman's disloyalty. But that simply substantiates the thesis that the majority of the ecclesiastical hierarchy had no patience with freedom of speech, the C. O.'s, and the pacifist clergy, whom they regarded, for the most part, as citizens too dangerous to be at large.

How do the Vermont denominational officials regard the Waldron case now? In answer to a request from the present writer for a statement about the Waldron affair, William A. Davison, executive secretary of the Vermont State Baptist Convention, writes: "I can see nothing good whatever by answering your questions or stirring up this matter, regarding the Rev. C. H. Waldron, up [sic] again." (July 18, 1930.)

Popular Justice

The fury of the courts and Christian justice in those days of mental and emotional confusion again is seen in the case of the Christian Pacifists who met in Los Angeles, California, September, 1917. About seventy-five pacifists from that section of the country had met together to express their opinions about the "militaristic interpretation of Christianity," and to voice a protest "against the attitude of the Christian Church, . . . and not to oppose the government of the United States." Robert Whitaker, Floyd Hardin, and Harold Storey, three of the leaders, were arrested, and then released on bail. At the last of the ses-

---

* *The Christian Register*, commenting on the verdict, said: "The thing of which he was convicted was disloyal action of the darkest kind, and the ugliest word of two syllables comes more nearly to fit the situation. The penalty took into account the important influence of a minister; and we might add, of a preacher in a church whose members are blindly devoted to queer religious ideas. They make susceptible subjects in a time of stress. . . . The forces of religion, in general, are marshaled invincibly, we pray, behind the arms of a divine cause, a crusade that marches forth to win the world." (Vol. 97, No. 13, March 28, 1918, p. 294.)

Mr. Waldron was pardoned a year later.

sions the home guards of Pasadena broke in and mobbed the participants. They had been spurred on by business men and ministers. George Davidson, rector of St. John's Episcopal Church, had assured the Loyalty League that "the name 'pacifist' is just a veneer to shield a traitor. We must fight fire with fire and stamp out all pacifism in Los Angeles." Billy Sunday is reported to have been more specific: "The Christian Pacifists ought to be treated as Frank Little was at Butte and then let the coroner do the rest."

The trial of the three defendants came on November 14. Having been charged with unlawful assembly, refusal to disperse when ordered to do so, and of having disturbed the peace, the trial proceeded. The jury brought in a verdict of guilty. Judge White charged the defendants:

> Duty to country is a duty of conscience, duty to God. For country exists by natural divine right. It receives from God the authority needful for its life and work. . . . The religion of patriotism was not sufficiently considered by you three defendants. . . .

Whitaker, Hardin and Storey were then sentenced to pay fines of $1,500 each and to serve six months in jail. On appeal to the Superior Court this judgment was affirmed without opinion.[18]

In addition to the immense number of people who were spied upon, arrested, and brought to trial, there are other cases resulting from the fact that this country during the war became impatient with due process of law and took justice into its own hands. There were numerous lynchings, a phenomenon not confined to war times, of course, and hundreds of recorded cases of mob violence. Tar and feathers were used in abundance on women as well as men, the students at Rutgers preferring molasses and feathers when applying it to a fellow-student. If one is to credit reports, tons of yellow paint were consumed in decorating homes, painting fences and cattle, thereby designating the residences and hang-outs of local "cowards." The Socialist headquarters in Boston was wrecked, race riots broke out in various sections of the country, the one at East St. Louis being among the most violent. Near Elizabeth, New Jersey, a man of German birth is reported to have been compelled to kiss the American flag sixty-one times, each star and each stripe. Meetings were suppressed in all sections. Members of the Non-Partisan League, on whose ticket the Honorable Charles A.

Lindbergh ran for governor in the State of Minnesota in 1918, were "hounded like rats." The I. W. W. suffered worst of all and in Bisbee, Arizona, hundreds of miners, most of them "Wobblies," were forcibly deported from their homes out into the desert by the members of the loyalty league organized by their employers.[19]

Toward this display of pioneer spirit, the churches and the religious press were for the most part quite silent, and, in attempting to explain the violence and crimes, more often condoned them.*

Some members of the clergy suffered as victims of mob violence during those days of hysteria. There was the wellknown case of Herbert Bigelow, pastor of the People's Church, Cincinnati, who, about to address a meeting in Newport, Kentucky, was seized by a band of masked men, taken into the woods and, "in the name of the poor women and children in Belgium," beaten with a horse-whip.[20]

On Easter morning of 1917, Charles R. Joy, minister to the Unitarian Church in Portland, Maine, referred to the war with Germany as "unrighteous" and most deplorable. That night Mr. Joy was burned in effigy in front of his church. "On the bosom of the dummy effigy, which was committed to the 'flames' there was hung a huge placard with the inscription, 'The patriotic people of Portland resent your speech. Get out!'" Mr. Joy's resignation was demanded by the trustees, and their wishes were acceded to.[21]

That same evening in Melrose, Massachusetts, a peace meeting was broken up by a mob composed of "the best citizens" as the audience was being addressed by Henry W. Pinkham, minister of the Unitarian Church.[22]

Several ministers in various states were reported to be the victims of tar and feathers. In Iowa, one was saved from being hanged only by the interference of the sheriff. At least one min-

---

* Woodrow Wilson and Attorney General Gregory protested against mob violence, but the government must take upon itself a part of the responsibility for the mob spirit. Under the inspiration of the Department of Justice officials, who, in a "slacker raid" in two days of September, 1918, in and around New York, for instance, "arrested" about 75,000 men, with the assistance of soldiers and sailors and patriotic organizations impressed for that purpose, "fewer than 3 per cent of those arrested were found to be actually 'slackers.' That meant that over 70,000 citizens who had discharged their duty in the first selective draft were rudely seized . . . bundled into trucks and improvised patrol wagons . . . exposed in a helpless manner to the hoots and jeers of the populace, detained, . . . and at last released without possibility of redress." (New York *Tribune*, quoted in the *Nation*, Vol. 107, No. 2776, September 24, 1918, p. 282.)

For the government point of view, vid. Second Report of the Provost Marshal General, p. 202.

ister (colored) was lynched for alleged opposition to the draft, that event occurring in South Carolina. In the state of Arkansas, another colored minister received, according to the report, a beating by a mob of three dozen white men. For refusal to participate in a Liberty Loan drive, a Nebraska clergyman saw his house painted yellow by the patriots.[23]

The Russellites, especially marked for attack by the publicity they had received, suffered raids on their headquarters in a large number of the states. It was reported that in Galveston, Texas, 45,000 copies of *The Finished Mystery* were confiscated.[24]

All of these demonstrations against the minority groups and individuals who failed to conform was an attempt on the part of the majority to preserve its solidarity in time of crisis. Fear of the enemy without produced fear of undue variations from the norm within. Group friction and antagonism which expressed itself in times of peace in verbal denunciation, in time of war, when the ordinary controls are relaxed, led to mob action.

CHAPTER XIII

WAR BRINGS A REVIVAL OF RELIGION

There is no denying that up until this year, at least, modern America had become a coddler of the carcass. . . . Pain was the King of Terrors.

. . . One of the blessings of the peace which lies ahead of us is that we shall rebreed from a race of men who have subordinated the body and have jauntily flung it over the top in the teeth of destruction.

> William T. Ellis, *The Outlook*, April 24, 1918.

CHAPTER XIII
WAR BRINGS A REVIVAL OF RELIGION

THE ecclesiastical mind, like that of the entrepreneur, thinks of all new movements and events of import in terms of the total probable effect upon its particular enterprise. Thus the effect of the war upon the state of religion was a constant source of concern to the clergy.

THE RETURN OF THE LORD

Few there were who could view affairs with the abiding trust displayed by George F. Pentecost. "Only the Christian," said he, "can contemplate war with undisturbed mind, for he knows that God is over all, making the wrath and wickedness of man to praise Him." [1]

There existed, however, a small group, the premillenarians, who took that point of view. For them the war was the fulfilment of age-old prophecy, the Kaiser was the anti-Christ, and the Battle of Armageddon, foretold in the Book of Revelation, 16:16, was at hand. The "imminent return of the Lord," for which they had been hoping and praying, would soon take place.[2] In common with all religions of escape, premillennial teaching received a tremendous acceleration from the pessimism of the war period, and, much to the alarm of the liberals in the fold, seemed about ready to capture huge blocs in the denominations.[3]

The strength of the premilliennial movement may be inferred from the amount of interest manifested in a series of meetings in Philadelphia, May 28-30, 1918, called The Philadelphia Bible Conference on the Return of the Lord. There is reported to have been an aggregate attendance of at least 25,000 people. The supporters of this conference included leaders from among the most prominent in the Presbyterian and Baptist folds.[4] Prayer was offered daily "for the speedy return of the Lord."

This type of devotion to the literalisms of the New Testament and eschatological doctrine received the condemnation of the liberal leaders in the churches, not only because the interpretation of its New Testament, and the Book of Revelation in particular, was viewed as exegetically askew, but because it was a complete denial of the efficacy of fighting for righteousness. As J. J. Vichert, dean of the Colgate Theological Seminary, pointed out, in the face of such doctrines, "soldiers cannot be expected to preserve their morale."[5] To pray for the imminent return of the Lord would weaken all men's faith in the necessity of fighting Germany to a finish. The premillenarians hoped for a new world through the bodily return of Christ and the ultimate destruction of this wicked mundane sphere, since all efforts of man were unavailing to improve it.[6]

The New Day

Other disciples saw the dawn of a new day through the destruction of German militarism. Was all the sacrifice of blood and tears to go for naught? No! for as an outcome of the war a great religious revival was to sweep the earth. "As a woman forgets her travailing pains in the joy that comes with the birth of a son, so will mankind rejoice in the rebirth of the world as the result of this war."[7]

One of the primary items of consideration was patriotism. *The Christian Century,* which acclaimed Belgium as "the savior of our civilization," because she "interposed" the German advances, declared: "The war will give us a new and nobler patriotism. The love of country had ceased, ten years ago, to have large place in the average American's heart. Patriotism was languishing, just as were culture and spiritual religion."[8]

In this new world after the war, "the most important factor in its shaping," according to the editor of *The Universalist Leader,* "will be the Christian minister."[9] Francis Greenwood Peabody, speaking at Tuft's College, prophesied that "the signs of the times" pointed to "a new revival of religion and a new approach to God,"[10] while the editor of *The Congregationalist* affirmed: "Already one effect of the war has been the discovery of God."[11] Joseph Fort Newton believed that the war had also been a revelation of the "soul of man, its wonder, its power, its incredible strength, its incredible daring," and that man had learned that his soul was "akin to God and deathless."[12]

The verbalization by Bishop Lawrence of the conviction that the war would certainly "bring the churches closer together," was joined in by thousands of others.[13] This cherished hope, partially realized during the World War, became crystallized by the Protestants in the New World Movement, the final fiasco of which is known to all.[14]

The corresponding secretary of the Northern Baptist Convention, William C. Bitting, in August, 1917, was "almost ready to forgive the Kaiser some of his many sins," when he contemplated "the blessings God is now pouring out and will pour out when our boys in France have sacrificed for the common good." [15]

One of the problems the churches had to prepare to face at the close of the struggle with German militarism was the probable lack of interest in institutionalized religion on the part of the returning troops. Much concerned about the spiritual welfare of the boys who fought, the "Y" had put forth its best efforts. It was believed that they had learned to pray, had a richer experience with God, and had become truly religious,[16] that they would come back "better than they went." [17] But that they would be content to worship and work in the churches was a matter of speculation and deep concern. Many believed, however, that these boys would bring back a definite contribution to religion in America.

In order to ascertain the actual effect of the war on religion, the Y. M. C. A. appointed a committee on The War and the Religious Outlook, which presented its report, written by Robert E. Speer, the chairman. "The net result," estimated Dr. Speer, "will probably be found to have been good." Among other blessings the pressure of life had forced men to pray—"There was more praying in America among all classes of people than ever before in our history." The war had taught us that we were saved by Christ's life, poured out on the cross and through men.[18]

In short, the Kingdom of God of spiritual ideals was to be brought in by men of violence and by methods which in themselves were directly opposed to the spiritual values which ministers always rated as belonging to that Kingdom. William Adams Brown rationalized it: God had a social and religious purpose in history and this He realizes "in spite of evil, yes, even with and through it." [19]

Gold Stars

The manner in which Christian leaders attempted to give comfort to those who had lost their sons in the "holy war" is of interest here because it indicates how firmly they believed that the death of these boys was for great religious values and had insured the coming of the millennium.

A Protestant family had lost two sons in the service of their country. A clergyman, head of the denominational war commission wrote, after the death of one of the sons:

> ... Well, the boy did his Christian duty and died to set the world free from the slavery of military power ... and it won't be long when we shall again look upon the faces of our dear ones, who are but a step or two ahead of us.

The devout headmaster of a large boys' preparatory school in the East extended his sympathy:

> ... such a death as your boy died brings great glory, not only to the boy himself, but to all of his friends. Your boy died for Liberty and all the members of your family have made the great sacrifice. His death also sheds glory upon every one of you. The long days and years to come will bring you many heartaches as you think of him, leaving home high with hope, like the Crusaders of old on a Holy Quest. He has left you all a sweet memory and a very powerful inspiration.

The pastor of a leading church in the denomination said after the death of the second son:

> I know that you feel the great pride which is necessarily present in the heart of one who has made such a great sacrifice for one's country.

The chaplain who had charge of the funeral in France sent his consolations:

> I saw him [the son] with wards full of others as I passed through, but it was not until I came to care for the bodies in the morgue that I really was near the poor chap. ... We had no caskets, but each man was carefully sewed in his own blanket. With a tender heart I tried to see that each face was as the loved ones at home would have tried to have it. ..
> There was always a service which was growingly tender for the chaplain. ... From my own funds I purchased an American flag made in Paris. It is the most precious remembrance I have of those hard days. It was floated over the grave of every American laid away. ...
> May God himself give you comfort ... through the knowledge that your two lads gave their lives for the greatest cause the world has known in war.

And thus did the leaders in the churches try to bring comfort to those who mourned. In Homeric phraseology, "the rosy-fingered dawn" of a new day was to appear through their sacrifice.

CHAPTER XIV
VICTORY AND POST-ARMISTICE DISILLUSIONMENT

MEMORIAL ODE TO PRINCETON'S HEROIC DEAD

* * *

III Now the vile sword
     In Potsdam forged and bathed in hell
     Is beaten down, the victory given
     To the sword forged in faith and bathed in heaven.
    . . .

VI . . .
     And He who died for all on Calvary
     Has welcomed you, brave soldiers of the Cross,
        Into Eternal Peace.

                      Henry Van Dyke.

CHAPTER XIV
VICTORY AND POST-ARMISTICE DISILLUSIONMENT

The Pre-Armistice Mind

BY THE summer of 1918, the National Security League, George Creel's propaganda bureau, the secular press, and the forces of righteousness had worked the citizens of this country up to such an emotional pitch that the American scene represented what has been called "a nation drunk with hate." Never before in the history of warfare had such a phenomenon been observed wherein whole populations became consumed with the desire for revenge on their enemies.

There is no appreciable difference between the pronouncements of the security leagues, the propaganda bureaus, and the edicts of the Christian leaders. And many of those who at the beginning had counseled against yielding to the temptation to curse led the multitudes in doing so now. The editor of *The Churchman* threw all casuistry aside and said it was much better for each one to renounce his hypocrisy and admit he'd like to "put an end once and for all to the whole Potsdam coterie, and he would like to do it personally and with violence." The editor declared: "We are not called upon by our religion to love these people. They are the enemies of God."[1]

The logical outcome of such a point of view was to hold up before the American people the ideal of an absolute crushing of the Germans. In order that the morale of the people would not weaken, various devices to keep alive the spirit of vengeance were resorted to by men of prominence.*

---

* The American Rights League advertised their anti-peace views in the papers in March, 1918, and requested citizens to write to the President expressing the same.

"I. We are opposed to peace negotiations with an unbeaten and unrepentant Germany.

"II. We believe that the war can only be won by *fighting*.

"III. We believe that peace discussions while Germany is consolidating her successes will prolong the war by encouraging Germany and weakening America's will to fight. . . .

"We respectfully urge the President . . . to prosecute the war to final victory, which alone can secure an assured peace—peace with justice."

(This was signed by eighteen prominent citizens, including Lyman Abbott, James M. Beck, Samuel Hardin Church, William Gardiner Hale, John Grier Hibben, Theodore Roosevelt, George Haven Putnam, Randolph H. McKim.)

Only one attitude toward peace seemed possible. In the words of Mark A. Matthews, "Germany shall be crushed and made to submit to terms of peace dictated to her by America and her Allies. It is right to destroy a mad dog; you would not negotiate with him, would you?"[2] Howard Duffield, Presbyterian chaplain of the Ninth Coast Artillery, announced that the war could not come to an end until "the black eagles of the Hapsburgs and the Hohenzollerns have their necks wrung. There must be no peace without victory and without penalties against those who began hostilities."[3]

The total effect of this worship of the tribal war god of American nationalism and the intense hatred of all his enemies promoted a desire to silence, if not annihilate, all those who proposed a peace founded on sanity. In the early fall of 1918 Germany made certain proposals of peace. These came up for discussion all over the country. An incident in the life of a peace-minded professor in a Quaker college illustrates the state of mind of a part of the American public at that time.

Henry Joel Cadbury of Haverford College wrote a letter to the Philadelphia *Public Ledger,* the first week in October, 1918, protesting "as a Christian and an American" against "the orgy of hate" indulged in by the press and people upon the receipt of peace overtures from the enemy. He indicated that our nation was "the greatest obstacle to a clean peace and the least worthy of it." "Never in the period of his greatest arrogance and success did the German Kaiser and Junkers utter more heathen and bloodthirsty sentiments than appear throughout the newspapers today." He asked for a peace founded on "the assurance of a safer and saner international fellowship" and in the spirit of fair play. "A peace on any other terms or in any other spirit will be no peace at all, but the curse of the future."[4]

This open expression of opinion, members of the Board of Managers of Haverford, and prominent alumni of the college, repudiated. They went further and called for Dr. Cadbury's dismissal. In the midst of the controversy, Dr. W. W. Keen, internationally renowned surgeon, and one of the leading spirits in the First Baptist Church of Philadelphia, listing a number of the German "outrages" in the columns of the *Public Ledger,* contended:

> Their treatment of the women and girls of Belgium cannot even be described in print . . . they are now debauching their own women by enforcing promiscuous polygamy, in order to re-

cruit their population. The next generation of Germans, therefore, will consist largely of "official" bastards. That our own wives and daughters have not so suffered we owe chiefly to the splendid, silent, but ever-watchful British fleet.

Then he renewed his vow:

When the war is over Germany disappears from my horizon. I formulated my creed to an English friend early in 1916 as follows:

I will never set foot on a German ship or on German soil again.

I will never eat, drink, wear, buy, or even touch anything which has been polluted by a German hand.

What the government may do I do not know, but these are my firm resolves. Fortunately no government can compel me to eat, drink, wear, or buy what I am firmly resolved not to touch.

Mr. Cadbury dubs this "insane hysteria" forsooth. I call it calmly reasoned out, just assessment of what is due such a country and such a Kaiser.[5]

There were other similar letters in the *Ledger,* including one written by John Archibald MacCallum, pastor of the fashionable Walnut Street Presbyterian Church, Philadelphia. He rebuked Dr. Cadbury for calling himself "a Christian and a patriot," and said the man "whose blood does not boil in righteous anger" at the outrages perpetrated by the Germans "is the victim of a delusion and has no right to be regarded as either Christian or patriotic." According to Dr. MacCallum, "the Christians and patriots of the United States are those who rigorously insist upon the unconditional surrender of the enemy."[6]

In the meantime, the Secret Service agents reported Dr. Cadbury. He was called into the office of the United States District Attorney, Francis Fisher Kane. After a conference a statement was issued indicating that Mr. Kane was satisfied with the loyalty of the Haverford professor.[7] In the light of similar experiences on the part of other suspects, it was fortunate for him to have come under the purview of a district attorney who gave a liberal interpretation to the Espionage Act and believed in the right of free speech even in war time.

Dr. Cadbury left Haverford at the end of the school year to accept a position at Harvard. The administration at Haverford is unwilling to make any statement about the affair.

The Victory

Finally the day of the Armistice arrived.* The followers of Jehovah saw in the victory an answer to prayer, and with one accord thanked Him for the success of our arms. William Adams Brown said that God had given us a victory "beyond our fondest dreams." [8] † The National Lutheran Council, representing most of the Lutheran bodies in America, rendered "thanks unto Almighty God, who has given our just cause such magnificent victory."[9] The readers of *Christian Work* were informed by the editor, Dr. Lynch, that "the whole civilized world" rejoiced because "the enemies of Serbia had been driven from her borders. . . ."[10] Moreover, "the Lord hath done great things for us, for surely it was the Lord's doing . . . so swiftly, so marvelously, so unexpectedly did it all come."[11]

The editor of *The Christian Century* thought we were right in thanking Him for the outcome of the war, since it was God who had "aroused the conscience of the world against our enemies, . . . had brought us into the conflict, [and] . . . helped preserve the most wonderful morale in our soldiers and keep them fit for their duties."[12]

Joseph Fort Newton, with the approach of a mystic, sensed the meaning of God in the hour. It was a "spiritual victory," for "swiftly, terribly, God made bare his holy arm, hurling throned iniquity to the ground, making the vanity of man pitiful . . . God reigns and those who defied him are fallen!"[13]

After the exultations following the day of the Armistice, the nation set its face toward the Peace Conference. There seems to have been a general agreement that there should be a peace with justice and one that would insure no more war. However, though the principle itself was sound enough, there was a wide disagreement as to the details. So-called justice might be but the expression of the spirit of revenge. A few of the leaders in civic and religious life were far-sighted enough to detect the dangers of punitive justice. But they were rare. *The Christian Century*, which was representative of a great portion of Chris-

---

* Henry Van Dyke was reported as saying: "Can there be any armistice in such a war against crime? Can there be any parley with active criminals? No! To enter a parley while the crime continues would be to smear our country's face with shame." (New York *Times*, September 14, 1918.)

† In an address at the meeting of the General War-Time Commission in Washington, D. C., September 24, 1918, Dr. Brown said: "Never before, I believe, in the history of the world has a War Department entered upon a great war with such a moral ideal as has inspired those who have directed our American Army." (*The Record of a Year*, a pamphlet.)

tendom, believed in the thorough chastisement of Germany so that she would never forget her lesson. In commenting on the terms of peace, the editor emphasized that Germany was "a criminal," and the acts which she had committed were of such a nature as to have placed her "outside the pale of respectable citizenship in the social order of the world." The editor insisted: "We do not hate the cannibal, cruel and vicious as he is."[14]

Alva Taylor hoped that the German people would learn to be truly civilized, and demanded that the men responsible for "plunging" the world in the "horrible maelstrom of blood and destruction" and designing such *schrecklichkeit* be personally tried and punished for their crimes together with the army officers who at any time had ordered "barbarities executed."[15]

According to the editor of *The Congregationalist*, "Germany is not a nation overwhelmed in an ordinary war. She is a criminal at the bar of justice."[16] *Zion's Herald*, which had established a record for itself in the intensity of its war spirit, said after the Armistice: "Those who have brought this terrible scourge upon humanity must feel the heavy hand of justice. . . . How different this, however, from a bitterness of spirit that would wreak vengeance."[17]

The Churchman observed that Germany had met defeat and recommended that she be made to suffer retribution "so far as retribution can be made by any terms of peace."[18]

From the recital in past chapters and the above expressions of opinions of religious journals that took some pride in the spirit of tolerance in ordinary days, it might well be said that the Treaty of Versailles was exactly the type of treaty for which the churches had been clamoring in the months prior to and following the day of the Armistice.

Finally, in order to promote the benefits derived from the outcome of the war unto the far ends of the earth, the Methodist Episcopal Church launched its huge Centenary program in 1919, to carry the blessings of "love and peace and helpfulness and true democracy" won by the Allied victory to all the peoples of all the *Allied* countries, including China, India and Japan. The last-named was informed, for example, that the ideals for which she had been fighting, "though Japan could not identify them as [such]—were the Ideals of the New Testament." Moreover that "Big Fellow-Feeling that helped win the war was but another expression of the Spirit of Christ."

In spite of the secret treaties and other revelations and exposures in the Allied camp, this, the largest single Protestant denomination in America announced: "The published notes exchanged between the Allies, the speeches of America's great men—all made clear to the world that we were engaged in a righteous war, in which greed and national aggrandizement never figured." [19]

DISILLUSIONMENT AND REPENTANCE

What happened to the hopes of this new world order, the spiritual values to be derived from the results of the war, the coming of the Kingdom of God upon earth, and the new and vital religion of the returning troops? One feels a spirit of disillusionment in the air. Those spiritual values and moral aims of the war never reached fruition. As for the religion of the boys whose names were enshrined upon the honor rolls, those who were fortunate enough to return have been, for the most part, a total disappointment to clergy and laity alike. The new religion of the trenches failed to function in ways acceptable to the church. The "new political heaven and a regenerate earth at the close of this war," which Bishop Samuel Fallows of the Reformed Episcopal Church and others hoped to witness, did not arrive.[20] With the complete collapse of the New World Movement in the Protestant churches came the simultaneous loss of faith in many of those ideals which had prompted men to fight and which the churches had hoped would be achieved in their midst.

If an inventory were to be made of the disillusionment that took possession of the minds of the leaders in the churches, it probably could not be better expressed than in the words of one who believed the New Jerusalem would arise out of the ashes of the war, Frederick Lynch:

> Our people—government and all—were shouting wonderful things that were going to come to pass as the result of this war. It was a war to end war. It was to make the world safe for democracy. It was to make a new world order where Christian principles were to reign among nations. There is no denying that we are in a disappointed world—a world that looks back upon the men who were at Paris as betrayers of their words and promises. We got no world safe for democracy, no new world order, no Christian era of international good-will.[21]

In what is now referred to as the "post-war reaction," the churches began passing resolutions in renunciation of war. In the year 1924, alone, these were passed by the hundreds in all the major denominations and most of the smaller ones.[22] The Chicago Federation of Churches, representing 650 churches and fifteen denominations, went on record: "In humble penitence for past mistakes and sincere repentance for our want of faith and devotion to the ideals of the Kingdom of God . . . we declare ourselves as unalterably opposed to war."[23] In the Garrett Bible Institute, Evanston, Illinois, of the 125 faculty members and students, 124 declared that under no circumstances would they participate in war in the future.[24]

Among the peace societies is observed the same phenomenon. The World Alliance for Friendship Through the Churches, in session in 1923, pronounced that unless the church took a clear and consistent stand against the war system "she will merit the contempt of men and the judgment of God," for "the war system and the Gospel of Jesus Christ are diametrically and irreconcilably opposed."[25]

This movement, however, did not sweep all the denominations. There are right and left wings in each today. Occasionally comes a reminder that some groups are not renouncing war. In June, 1930, at the annual meeting of the General Synod of the Reformed Church in America, resolutions were proposed by the Committee on Education for World Peace. The Synod adopted the statement that "war is contrary to the spirit of Jesus Christ," but turned down a resolution expressing the "conviction that American citizens should be free and unhampered to follow the dictates of conscience in determining their course of action relative to bearing arms for the nation."[26]

In January, 1918, Charles F. Aked, responding to a questionnaire distributed by Sydney Strong, had listed among the items which he wished to see after the war: "The repentance in sackcloth and ashes of ten thousand ministers of Christ who have howled for blood and raved the ravings of the jingo-press."[27]

The list of penitents increases daily.

Reinhold Niebuhr, professor in Union Theological Seminary, a pastor during the war, confesses: "Every soldier, fighting for his country in simplicity of heart without asking many questions, was superior to those of us who served no better purpose than to increase or perpetuate the moral obfuscation of nations. . . . The times of man's ignorance God may wink at, but now he calls us to repent. I am done with this business."[28]

Harry Emerson Fosdick has made a similar declaration: "I do not propose to bless war again, or support it, or expect from it any valuable thing."[29]

Sherwood Eddy has become an absolute pacifist, refusing to have anything whatsoever to do with any future war between nations.[30]

Samuel McCrea Cavert, general secretary of the Federal Council of Churches, announces:

> I am disillusioned as to the causes of war. I now see that the war arose chiefly as the result of deep-rooted economic competition to control the raw materials and markets of the world. . . . I have come slowly but clearly to the conclusion that the Church, in its official capacity, should never again give its sanction to war or attempt to make war appear as holy.[31]

Eliot Porter, a Presbyterian clergyman who served as a captain in the British army on the firing line (Dr. Porter is an American), writes from Lincoln, Illinois: "If another war comes, I shall not, I think, be sure enough there is any sense in it to fight in it until fifteen years after it is all over. No chaplaincy, either!"[32]

Joseph Fort Newton, while not a pacifist in the sense that he refuses to fight in *any* war (for he thinks wars of defense may be necessary), says that men of state have "declared war to be a crime," and "it is surely time for the church to . . . declare war to be a sin in religion—the supreme social sin of mankind . . . even though it rebuke our past. Already some of us wear crepe on our hearts and sackcloth on our souls, if so God may be merciful to our repentance. . . ."[33]

On Sunday, April 18, 1932, Stephen S. Wise celebrated his twenty-fifth anniversary as rabbi of the Free Synagogue in New York. As a climax to his sermon he asked forgiveness of his congregation for his attitude during the World War, said he viewed his record with "everlasting regret" and pledged "without reservation or equivocation" never to bless or support war or "any war whatsoever" again.[34]

William Pierson Merrill, another convert to Allied war aims, now explains, in an Armistice Day sermon, that "war and the religion of Jesus Christ are incompatible. That means, to a Christian, that war must go!" He maintains that "religion alone can end war."[35]

Perhaps the most famous chaplain during the war who went over with our troops was Father Francis Duffy of the Rainbow Division. Five years after the Armistice he is saying:

> As I look back, I see no occasion for the ordinary man to have had religious experiences whilst in service. War is something so opposed to God! It is so full of the Satanic. . . . Most men have seen in war-experience nothing but evil in its nakedness. . . . Forever stand these words over war which Dante placed over the entrance to Hell—"All hope abandon, ye who enter here!"[36]

Douglas Clyde Macintosh, professor of theology in Yale Divinity School, wholeheartedly supported the Allies in the war, serving as a chaplain. He believed we were "fighting on the side of God," and that "enough religion of the right sort" would create enough morale to insure victory—"a victory by the grace of God." [37] Dr. Macintosh, a Canadian, in applying recently for citizenship in this country, refused to promise to fight in a war which his conscience did not approve.[38]

Charles Clayton Morrison, who as editor of *The Christian Century* had pronounced his blessing upon the war, has now for several years been calling upon the churches to renounce war forever, and advises that "the preachers repentantly resolve that they will never again put Christ in khaki or serve as recruiting officers or advisory enforcers of conscription laws!" In the event of another conflict *The Christian Century* believes, "Leavenworth will have to be enlarged and the apostolic succession will be demonstrated at a point where not many have been willing to assert it."[39]

Another religious periodical, *Zion's Herald*, has changed editors since the feverish days of 1917-18, and also its viewpoint about war. The present editor, L. O. Hartman, is absolutely opposed to the war system. In July, 1931, in an editorial against the war-makers, he issued a call to his fellow-Christians: "Let us be honest and courageous. We know that the men and women of good-will throughout the world could end war tomorrow if they would stand up in their boots, face the truth, and declare themselves unequivocally against this awful iniquity."[40]

In addition to those already mentioned as renouncing war for all time, there are others, among them: Bishop Brewster, Ralph W. Sockman, W. S. Abernethy, Albert Parker Fitch, Ernest F. Tittle, William L. Stidger, W. Russell Bowie, W. Brook Stabler, Bishop E. C. Seaman, James M. Stifler, Halford E. Luccock, J. H. Dietrich, Bernard Iddings Bell.[41]

The World Tomorrow, May, 1931, gives the result of a questionnaire distributed to 53,000 clergymen over the United States.* There were 19,372 replies, and of these ninety-one per cent "expressed a willingness to have their names and replies made public." Ten thousand four hundred twenty-seven clergymen, or

---

* "The replies do not reflect the attitudes of several important religious bodies. The Jews, Roman Catholics, Lutherans, Southern Baptists, and Southern Methodists are not represented in the returns. The total number of clergy in the country exceeds 100,000, and it was necessary on the grounds of expense to limit the inquiry to 53,000." (*The World Tomorrow*, Vol. XIV, No. 5, May, 1931, p. 138.)

fifty-four per cent, stated it was their "present purpose not to sanction any future war or participate as an armed combatant." The detailed figures are as follows:

Summary of all responding	10,427
Total not including seminaries	9,635
Methodist Episcopal	3,598
Presbyterian	1,192
Congregational	1,039
Protestant Episcopal	648
Baptist	804
Disciples of Christ	862
Reformed	345
United Brethren	247
Evangelical Synod	261
Unitarian and Universalist	199
Miscellaneous	440

Why are thousands of ministers renouncing war? Largely for the same reasons that lead others to do so. The facts about the World War, with its propaganda, intrigue, secret treaties, and the Treaty which followed it contradict "holy war" aims. The writings of Fay, Barnes, Gooch, and others about the origins of the recent war, which dispose of the theory of the sole guilt of Germany, have had a positive effect upon the thinking of multitudes of churchmen. *The Christian Century,* in publishing a series of articles by Harry Elmer Barnes on the genesis of the World War, introduced the revisionist point of view to its thousands of readers. *The Christian Century* is, among liberal Christians, the most widely read religious journal in America. Its clear and unwavering stand for the outlawry of war and the promotion of peace has been a powerful factor in leading the clergy to pledge themselves in such numbers never to bless another war. *The World Tomorrow, Unity,* The Methodist Federation for Social Service, through *The Social Service Bulletin,* the Fellowship of Reconciliation, and the National Council for the Prevention of War have also made important contributions to peace sentiment.

Other reasons for the present wave of pacifism going through the churches are: The return to the traditional peace attitude of the churches; the susceptibility of religiously motivated people to an emotional reaction against the horrors of war—now that it is over; repentance is a form of compensation for a feeling of guilt; and a younger generation of ministers trained in history, economics, sociology and psychology, are being graduated from the more radical seminaries and divinity schools that emphasize the social gospel and the relation of the church to the social order.

While a formidable array of names of prominent clergymen who denounce the god Mars for all time can be produced, it would be conveying the wrong impression to let the matter rest there. Peace sentiment just now is popular and the militaristic clergy are rather inclined to keep quiet. But that thousands of ministers are as ready to bless war as ever no one doubts who is acquainted with the range of sentiments among the clerics. For instance, in Baltimore, Maryland, T. Andrew Caraker, pastor of the Universalist Church of Our Father, in addressing an American Legion banquet, denounced pacifism as "a reactionary state of emotion growing out of the war." He said that if Jesus Christ had lived in 1917 he would have been the first to have volunteered in the American Army. Jesus, according to Dr. Caraker, "would have been the first to wear a gas mask, shoulder a rifle and enter the trenches."[42]

CHAPTER XV

CONCLUSION

It had been said that a war could not be conducted on the principles of the Sermon on the Mount. It might also be said that a war could not be carried on according to the principles of Magna Carta.

> Lord Justice Scrutton in Ronnfeldt v. Phillips, 35 T.L.R. 46 (1918, C.A.).

CHAPTER XV
CONCLUSION

THE reader who has followed thus far the record of the churches and the clergy during the World War will probably find himself assuming one of several possible attitudes.

He may have become hostile and concluded that, since he cannot perceive any possible good arising out of these pages, the story might better never have been told. It is possible that he may have seen again, or been reminded of, words uttered in those years of national hysteria which he had long forgotten and now regrets. Or he may be proud of the record of the churches and its leaders during the war. On the other hand, the reader may be so depressed by the display of what he regards as barbaric utterances on the part of the pious folk that he now concludes the clergy and the churches are unworthy of their calling. Or he may maintain that, while the record is unsavory, at the same time he trusts the religious people will never repeat their mistake by blessing war again. The perhaps rarer individual may have been interested in the data presented from the point of view of the social scientist, who, eliminating moral praise and blame, endeavors to study all social phenomena as objectively as the chemist views the reaction of two elements placed together in a test tube in the laboratory.

In any event, upon reflection, it should be apparent to even those who have not been in the habit of studying society and human behavior in a detached fashion that there is really nothing very surprising about the attitudes and activities of the religious groups and the ministers during the war. A great social upheaval like the World War simply reveals the power of fundamental biological and social forces ever at work in society but rarely demonstrated in their fulness during days of peace. The social behavior manifested by the church people and all other groups was not an accident but the result of a perfectly natural process. The naturalistic science of society makes clear that the laws of social causation back of social phenomena are as much a part of the natural order as those behind the summer shower or the earthquake. Since this is so, given the particular situations, factors and individuals involved, nothing else could possibly have occurred other than exactly that which did occur when the forces of religion were called upon to react and interact with all the subtleties and tides of 1914-18.

Of course it should be borne in mind that religions are not separate streams of thought and doctrine giving rise to institutions which have been unchanged and uninfluenced by the rest of the world. Doctrines and speculation do not develop *in vacuo*. They echo the established order. Religious institutions, as others, are social products and are in a reciprocal relationship to the other forces molding society. All combined and integrated give us our total culture pattern.

The World War laid bare the framework of our society and illuminated the basic relationship of institutionalized religion to the social order itself. Thus certain conclusions inevitably present themselves.

The first is the intimate connection between religion and capitalism. The spirit of Protestantism has been credited by Max Weber, R. H. Tawney and others with giving the impetus and driving force to modern capitalism. Since the days of Calvin and coming on through Puritanism, Protestantism has increasingly approved of wealth and the getting of it. The triumph of economic virtues is now supreme. Our modern capitalism is the resultant of several factors, to be sure, but the interaction of the Protestant ethic and the spirit of modern capitalism is significant. For today, with few exceptions, all institutionalized religion in the West is tied up with the prevailing economic order. Our society based upon bookkeeping economy and the sacred right of private profits has been blessed and upheld by the churches as well as by the bankers and big business. While there is some criticism by the clergy of the capitalist system in an era of economic depression and unemployment, during the war and in times of prosperity the churches have been uncritically bound up to the capitalist arrangement which they helped to create.

Hence, being part and parcel of the whole acquisitive society, it was inevitable that, during the war, the churches should have conformed in their judgment and should have been controlled by the will of the vested interests. The statements, for instance, that it was "a capitalistic war" brought on by trade rivalries or conflicting economic interests, were repudiated by the majority of the clergy, after we got into the conflict, because both they and the churches were so closely wedded to the economic order that such remarks sounded to them like slander if not treason. It seemed disloyal to the religious people, and was so pronounced by the courts, to say that the war was the result of capitalism and the bankers in this country had loaned so much money to the Allies that they, the interested bankers, "dragged" us into the war.[1]

Regardless of the exact truth or error of these "unpatriotic" assertions, the leading historians dealing with the World War now point out that capitalism, the race for world markets, foreign investments, and resulting imperialistic policies, were important factors in bringing on the late war, and had their part in leading us in on the side of the Allies.

The matter for consideration here is, that inasmuch as national policies arising out of modern capitalism are major causes leading to war, and institutionalized religion blesses and promotes the spirit of modern capitalism, together with the idolatry of wealth, the churches are not going to be critical of the economic causes and the righteousness of a war when it is once upon us. The churches in such a crisis cannot disentangle themselves from the very fabric of society of which they are a part any more than they can do so in ordinary times when the whole economic and imperialistic system and the will of the vested interests receives their benediction.

Another vital relationship is that which exists between the religion of Christianity and the religion of Nationalism. The churches were consistent in the record of supporting all popular wars and proved, what had long been suspected, that Christianity has been becoming increasingly nationalistic, while the god of Nationalism is more powerful in his ability to command obedience and devotion unto death than is Jehovah himself. Nationalism came to the fruition of its development during the late war. Christianity and Judaism in this country became its servants. The symbols, dogmas, creeds, and precious shibboleths of Nationalism overshadowed and eclipsed those of Christianity, particularly, and by a process of syncretism, absorbed the elements of Christianity which fitted its purposes. Before the war many Protestant churches displayed the American flag in the pulpit, and in 1917-18 practically all the synagogues and churches carried out this symbolic alliance. There were thousands of appropriate flag-raising services in the houses of God. In fact, in some places of Christian worship, as in the First Baptist Church of New London, Connecticut, for example, the pastor, a chaplain during the war, preached in his uniform with a machine gun and an American flag on the platform beside him.

Nationalism means a reversion to the days of tribal gods with the doctrine of henotheism supreme. A Christian minister, George Dowling, assured the people that barbarism could not triumph "over a civilization which it has taken twenty Christian centuries to upbuild." Furthermore, "the United States has thus far never lost a war, and we are not going to lose this one."[2]

The situation may be summarized in the words of Professor C. J. H. Hayes: ". . . it is manifest to us who live in the West that Christianity for enormous numbers of people has become an adjunct to Nationalism."[3]

The facts of the years 1914-18 point to another conclusion, namely, that the members of the cloth and their followers were susceptible to war psychology and crowd-thinking in the same manner as were the other citizens. They possessed no prophylactic against the mob mind.

In time of hostilities a whole nation becomes a homicidal crowd, subordinating every interest—save that of profit-making—to crushing the enemy. Everett Dean Martin describes the crowd as a "device for indulging ourselves in a kind of temporary insanity by all going crazy together."[4] The usual social controls are relaxed, a temporary social environment is produced where "unconscious impulses may be released with mutual approval."[5] The object of hatred is the enemy whom the crowd cannot paint black enough or kill off too soon. Those who cannot or do not march to the front, compensate by displaying their venom through wild talk, or the persecution of suspects, slackers, or personal enemies at home. The mob mind (not to be thought of as a separate entity) is in complete control, brooks no opposition, while individuals under the spell of it say and do things which in their more rational moments would be quite impossible and totally inconsistent with their general behavior.

The record of the parsons during the war amply illustrates the manner in which they were the victims of this crowd mind. In fact the speeches and activities of numbers of them would ordinarily be regarded as symptomatic of highly disorganized personalities. In the light of all the data it may be concluded that, whereas all elements of the population, both high and low, became members of the war-time mob, were controlled by mass psychology, and "went crazy," the clergy were no more inoculated against the current hysteria than others. As a class they shared the common characteristics of the crowd mind, suffered from all its obsessions, delusions, phobias, megalomania and paranoia, persecuted and hated with the others. A comparison of random samples of war-time attitudes and emotional responses of the clergy with a similar collection of reactions of leaders in other professions reveals the same range of attitudes, and if arranged in a frequency distribution, shows a similar attitudinal curve.

What is of equal if not of more significance is the fact that Christians, while claiming to be motivated by the teachings of Jesus and superior humanitarian desires, did not in general demonstrate any different code of ethics or type of behavior from the unbelievers. This is also true for those who idolized the prophet Jeremiah. If there be such a thing as a special discernment of ethical values on the part of a privileged group, like the clergy, the priests, and the professors of ethics, they failed to show, in a practical or even theoretical way, adherence to any different ideals from the security leagues or the chambers of commerce in the years 1917-18. As a result of the ecclesiastical war record, in these days of double disillusionment, hosts of people have lost their faith in the leadership and guidance of the clergy and the churches. They have renounced the men of the cloth as being swayed by mob passions and prejudices, blind leaders of the blind, absolutely unfit to be trusted in a time of great moral crisis.

Whether the above attitude toward the presumed ethical guides of our society be justified or not, it is evident that as long as governments wage war by propaganda as well as by force of arms the citizens will rarely be able to formulate judgments based upon facts. Even in ordinary times it may well be said that public opinion is formed not by the presentation of authenticated evidence, but by the building up of stereotypes, what Walter Lippmann has so aptly called the "pictures in our heads."[6] These pictures may represent an approximation of or be in direct contradiction to the truth. Since a war cannot be run by giving the correct estimate of the situation or the enemy, it is necessary to distort the evidence, tell deliberate lies, and implant in the heads of the people the most effective pictures. Hence public leaders, together with the members of the proletariat, unless they have access to the inside facts denied to others, are compelled to form opinions on news which is most highly controlled. Ministers, as well as business men, are, by necessity, painting pictures and rendering moral verdicts which their governments wish them to.*

But the clergy, by the very nature of their profession, are obliged to be members of a school of thought which subscribes to the spiritual interpretation of history. Every incident has a divine import and a part in the progress toward that goal, the far-off divine event "toward which all creation moves." One must be spiritually minded and in tune with the Almighty to discern His manipulation of current events. During the war thousands of spiritual leaders did not hesitate to declare that they could perceive the divine will in the catastrophic upheaval. Under the fascination of the spell of spiritualizing the war, God's hand was seen in the struggle on their side. The very stars in their courses, we were told, fought on the side of the Allies. Christian righteousness was the palladium of the nation.

Yet, now that all this spiritual philosophy of history can be viewed objectively in the calm of post-war years, it is seen that the clergy as a class, much to the chagrin of some penitents, took the verdicts of the Administration and proclaimed them as the judgments of Almighty God. Their moral pronouncements simply reechoed the voices from Washington and the headlines of the press. In the language of *The Churchman*, written three years after the Armistice, "we [the churches] hated as our Governments bade us hate. We spread lies about our enemies as those lies were meted out to us in official propaganda. We taught unforgiveness even as our rulers and diplomats inspired us to do."[7] (In June, 1918, it will be remembered, the editor of *The Churchman* had said, "We are not called upon by our re-

---

* Consider, for example, the Anglo-American Newspaper Mission to the War Areas as a means of influencing religious opinion in this country by the governments of the United States and Great Britain. Early in the fall of 1918 a group representing religious journalism in this country sailed at the invitation of the British Government, whose guests they were to be during the entire period of absence. They were to observe at first-hand "religious and social conditions" in England and France, the great munition plants of England, the British fleet, and the battle front in France. Thus it was reported they were "likely to have access to many important and exceptional sources of information." Those in the group included Ernest Hamlin Abbott, of *The Outlook*, Robert W. Gammon, of *The Congregationalist*, Clifton D. Gray, of *The Standard*, W. Douglas Mackenzie, President of Hartford Theological Seminary, Dan B. Brummitt, of the *Epworth Herald*, Guy Emery Shipler, of *The Churchman*, Will R. Moody, of the *Record of Christian Work*, Jackson Fleming, of *Asia* and *Harper's*, Philip E. Howard, of the *Sunday School Times*, and Charles Clayton Morrison, of *The Christian Century*. (*The Christian Century*, Vol. XXXV, No. 48, December 12, 1918, p. 5; *The Congregationalist*, Vol. CIII, No. 34, August 22, 1918, p. 207; Vol. CIII, No. 43, October 24, 1918, p. 423.)

ligion to love these people [the Germans]. They are the enemies of God.")[8]

This confession from the editor of a leading Episcopalian journal is a recognition of the sweeping power of the propaganda of war, and the well-nigh irresistible contagion of the crowd mind, examples of which have been furnished in abundance in previous chapters. It is an acknowledgment of the way in which individuals were controlled in their behavior and society directed during those years.

The essential principles of the problem of social control, particularly in war time, were set forth in the introduction and illustrated in their practical application in various chapters. As has been shown, the concept of social control is one of the great master keys to an understanding and adequate interpretation of the pluralistic behavior manifested in those days. Since the field of study, with all its wealth of detail, is so immense, the range of related social forces so wide, and the social phenomena so singular, no single treatment can do more than sketch the broad outlines of the picture with a few parts filled in. An exhaustive treatment would require volumes. The further the social forces at work in American life are studied, together with the changes that have taken place and the devices for social control which our society has evolved, the more comprehensible the whole war period becomes.

In comparison with the Civil War era, for example, by 1914 the American scene represents a highly mechanized culture. A few of the social changes that had taken place in the fifty years following the Civil War may be noted. By the time of the World War society is vastly more organized and closely integrated. Whereas individuation in general is on the increase, social rigidity in several important particulars is likewise growing and social change being feared. Practically all the valuable free land has been used up by 1890, the spirit of the frontier is fast becoming a tradition. The various idealistic and communistic societies, the small experimental groups and the religious movements which characterized what Gilbert Seldes calls "The Stammering Century" are dying out. Many of the little isolated sacred societies are breaking up, thereby becoming accessible and secular in their patterns. As the nation achieves more of a unity, certain types of behavior become standardized. In many academic circles, where freedom of thinking is supposed to prevail, regimentation of ideas (particularly in the economic field), seems to be the ideal. In the America of 1914 group pressure toward conformity can be more easily exerted and rendered effective than in 1861. Because of the shift from an agrarian to an industrial society, an increasing number of people are dependent upon the goodwill of others for the opportunity to earn their daily bread. Due to this relationship of employer to employee, economic pressure can be readily used to suppress minority opinions. People are forced to conform or starve on account of their undesirable views. The first amendment to the Constitution is being narrowed in its interpretation, civil rights to minorities more apt to be denied. Christianity, though divided into denominations, sects, and a caste system, evidences more toleration among the various groups. At the same time the bigger denominations, especially, are losing many of their distinctive characteristics and minimizing doctrines that have kept them apart. All of our institutions, particularly our educational system with its nationalistic history texts, have so magnified the importance and sung the praises of our wars that students think of battles as the most important events in the American Epic. Generals and military heroes are continuously extolled as the finest and greatest products of any age, their sacred personalities above criticism. (Consider the Napoleonic and the Washington legends.) Though "generals die in bed," the death of a soldier upon the field of battle is the most glorious imaginable. We have been taught that every war in which the colonies or the United States fought was one of defense and for the sake of humanity—righteous to the nth degree. The schools teach a narrowed patriotism, propound the outworn isolationist theories, Europe and its affairs seem afar off and of no particular present-day importance. The point of view of the state and the church reenforced the teachings of the school. The press promoted it to perfection. They were all interwoven together. In the meantime the intellectuals here as elsewhere had deserted the abstract love of learning, truth and justice, had become swayed by popular passions, descending into the marketplace as protagonists and in some cases as ranters. The concentration of wealth in the hands of a few is going on at an accelerated rate. The press is under the control of this group, and in case of necessity the channels of communication and the dissemination of news can be brought under their domination and censorship.

The above may be regarded as but a few of the significant changes to be taken into consideration for a complete analysis of the immediate background of American life in 1914. These may aid in understanding the behavior of the churches and the clerics during the war years.* In the presence of the picture of our acquisitive society, the record of the great mass of the churches and their leaders ceases to be, if it has been hitherto, a cause for wonder or surprise. The drama of 1914-18 was but a logical sequence to what had gone before.

There is a final question which logically arises from the material in this volume. It is, "in the event of another war, what will the churches and their leaders do?" Whatever be one's predictions in this matter, the following set of facts at least must be kept in mind.

First, how fortunate (or unfortunate) it has been for western civilization, which resorts to war to settle its major difficulties, that it possesses a great war book, familiar to all the people, to support the gospel of force. I refer, of course, to the Bible. It is perhaps the greatest war book known to man. It is a part of our literary and religious heritage and revered as a sacred authority, occupying a unique place in our culture.

The New Testament is easily interpreted as favoring a just war (and what war is not just?), but it is the Old Testament which contains a veritable arsenal of proof-texts, bristling with the spirit of the fight. Boys and girls in the average Sunday school have never been taught to question the ethics and justice of Yahweh's commands to the Israelites to burn the city of Ai and destroy all the inhabitants, including the innocent women and children (Joshua, ch. viii). The slaughter of the Amalekites and the fact that Samuel, the prophet, "hewed King Agag in pieces before the Lord in Gilgal" (I Sam. ch. xv) seem perfectly proper to the average child. Christians have all but universally accepted the Old Testament teachings at their face value, believ-

---

* For a fuller appreciation of the changes which had taken place since the Civil War, nothing perhaps is more instructive than a comparison of the range and types of attitudes expressed by civilians in 1861-65 with those of 1917-18. Such a study shows a more independent spirit and vigorous individualism persisting during the Civil War years. This is evidenced, for instance, by the attitude and strength of the Copperhead newspapers, the anti-administration editorials of even loyal journals, open and what may be called "scurrilous" criticism of Lincoln, the draft riots, et cetera. While Lincoln's lenient and inconsistent policies had something to do with the amount of variation of opinion, the press of that day was far more free and outspoken. Editors expressed adverse opinions with impunity during the Civil War which, if even approximated in the late war, would have been the cause of the complete suppression of the offending newspaper and a jail sentence for the editor. (*Vid.* James G. Randall, *Constitutional Problems Under Lincoln*, Appleton, N. Y., 1926, Chp. XIX, and an article by the present author, "The Jeffersonian, Copperhead Newspaper," in the *Pennsylvania Magazine of History and Biography*, Vol. LVII, July, 1933.)

ing that all the cruelty administered by the Israelites upon their enemies was justified because Yahweh was on their side, and they were his chosen people conquering the promised land.

A. Edwin Keigwin, pastor of the West End Presbyterian Church, New York, said in 1918 that he usually took his texts for his war sermons out of the Old Testament, "for the very good and sufficient reason that the Old Testament is the book of God's dealings with nations, while the New Testament is the book of God's dealings with individuals."9

It may safely be predicted that as long as Christian ministers and Sunday school teachers continue, as the majority of them now do, to defend the crude ethics in parts of the Old Testament, the Bible will continue to be used as the greatest defense of war in history. While it is true that liberals have adopted the point of view that the barbarous procedures of the battle-scarred Israelites were not approved by the Lord, that these practices were the common custom of the day, and that the Almighty was endeavoring to lead them to a higher plane of ethics and conception of himself as revealed through Jesus Christ, it is to be remembered that when the war was actually upon us the majority of these same liberal leaders dressed Jesus in khaki, interpreted his words of the Sermon on the Mount to justify the fullest Christian participation in the hostilities.*

The basic reason for all this is apparent. Christians and Jews have simply used the Bible to aid in rationalizing any practice or idea which they were carrying out and believed to be justified. It is thus a commonplace that the Bible has been quoted to justify nearly every practice and belief known to man: war and peace, slavery and anti-slavery, child labor, polygamy and monogamy, celibacy, the burning of witches and the torture of heretics, capital punishment, woman suffrage (pro and con), communism, capitalism, the charging of interest (pro and con), temperance and absolute prohibition, faith healing, Christian Science, the erection of hospitals and the furtherance of medical science and missions, standard (as opposed to daylight-saving) time. It was quoted in opposition to Benjamin Franklin's lightning rod.

Secondly, it is not an accident or a mere coincidence that religion has in ages past been the handmaiden of Mars and in America the churches have blessed and participated in all popu-

---

* General Foch stated, "The Bible is certainly the best preparation that you can give an American soldier about to go into battle to sustain his magnificent ideal and his faith." (*Christian Work*, Vol. 14, No. 14, Oct. 5, 1918, p. 390.)

lar wars. Love of country still exceeds love of mankind. In the late combat at arms, the tribal gods proved superior to the ideal of the brotherhood of man which had been so ardently acclaimed prior to that time, the priests in each country accusing those in the enemy nations of worshiping false gods. The very phrase, "the brotherhood of man," in those days came to be used as a slogan to justify the bayoneting of the alienated brother, in order, as the journal of the American Peace Society phrased it, "to free him from a tyranny which he at present accepts as his chosen form of government."[10]

Again it is a question for debate whether in time of war the impulse to fight, which in most people is only inhibited by the conventions and the necessities of every-day life, can be so restrained as to keep the citizens from enlisting. It will necessitate years of education with the reconditioning of almost the entire population, including the church members and the parsons, before there can be any assurance that this country will not go to war again. For war appeals directly to the basic drives of man, the so-called "primitive impulses." Can a whole society be so changed that the symbols of patriotism, the trappings of war, and the sound of martial music will finally lose their power to elicit a positive response? The question cannot be asked more effectively than in the words of Richard Le Gallienne in his poem, *The Illusion of War*.

> War
> I abhor,
> And yet how sweet
> The sound along the marching street
> Of drum and fife; and I forget
> Wet eyes of widows, and forget
> Broken old mothers, and the whole
> Dark butchery without a soul.
>
> Without a soul—save this bright drink
> Of heady music, sweet as hell;
> And even my peace-abiding feet
> Go marching with the marching street,
> For yonder goes the fife,
> And what care I for human life! [11]

The present wave of pacifism has led some observers to state that there is already going on a fundamental change in attitude toward war—both in the school and the church, that education for peace is increasing in popularity. They point to the thousands of anti-war resolutions, and the repentant leaders who have pledged themselves never to bless another war. How much importance should be attached to these phenomena it is difficult to say, but certainly many of the souls who are now prostrated because of their past conduct give every appearance of undergoing an emotional rather than a rational aversion to war. The pendulum is very apt to make an extreme swing, for "the greater the sin the greater the remorse." Some individuals are thoroughly ashamed of the way in which they expressed their hatred of Germany and must find compensation.

How little we have learned from the World War, and how easy it is for our war-like passions to become quickly inflamed, may be illustrated from the current American reaction to the rise to power of the National Socialist Party in Germany, March 5, 1933. Our newspapers are again filled with flaming headlines and atrocity stories which remind us of what we were told about the cruelty of the Hun, 1914-18. Here, it is said, is further proof that the Germans are a barbaric, untamed people, utterly devoid of compassion and refinement. Deluged by propaganda and counter-propaganda, we are prepared to believe the worst. Hitler is a fiend from hell, and Germany has gone mad. Then we damn Hitler and call the Germans idiots for having anything to do with him. Thousands join in mass meetings and street parades and cry out, "We want Hitler with a rope around his neck."[12] There is a strong movement started by Samuel Untermeyer and others to boycott all German goods and German ships.[13] William H. Cohen, vice-president of the American Jewish Congress, announces that "any Jew buying one penny's worth of merchandise made in Germany is a traitor to his people."[14] Others suggest that the conduct of the Hitler government justifies the breaking off of diplomatic relations. Germany is again the destroyer of all that is usually identified with civilization. Bainbridge Colby says that Germany stands "revealed to the world today as the ally of evil and the enemy of good" in contrast to America, whose rise to greatness has been due to always "shaping its policies" and "directing its conduct with due regard to the approval and support of enlightened world opinion."[15]

Heywood Broun, well-known columnist and liberal, writes damning paragraphs against the Nazis and doesn't realize how far his fervor has carried him until a friend "tips him off" that his column has been "pretty bad" and that "we're living 1914, '15, '16 and '17 all over again." Broun looked back at what he had been writing about Hitler, and found that, by substituting "the Kaiser" in every place where "Adolph Hitler" appeared, the material was almost a carbon copy of what was being written when America was preparing for the World War.[16]

Another interesting sidelight upon the effect of the current hysteria upon the human mind is to be seen in the attitude toward Hitler shown by some of the fundamentalists of the premillenarian variety. It will be recalled that during the last war it was said by them that the Kaiser corresponded to the "little horn" in Daniel, and the "beast" whose number is 666, foretold in the book of Revelation, 13:18:

> Here is wisdom. He that hath understanding, let him count the number of the beast; for it is the number of a man: whose number is six hundred and sixty-six.

Now, it appears, Hitler has taken the place of the Kaiser in this prophecy (a miscalculation must have been made during the war!). According to one "authority" the letters of *Adolph Hitler* or *Herr Hitler,* either one, if the Greek system of using the numerals that correspond to the letters of the alphabet be used and added up, the sum is 666. Hitler, therefore, was foretold in the book of Revelation; he is the "Anti-Christ" and

> as the supreme human embodiment of demonic wickedness and power, a veritable Nero incarnated, this European ruler is to endure three and one-half years. He will be a great persecutor of the Jews. At the end of that period, the Jewish Messiah (the Christ of the Gentiles) will appear at Jerusalem to set up His righteous kingdom, and the "Beast" will be taken and destroyed. (Rev. 19: 19.)[17]

Thus does the campaign of hatred go on.

That there has been excessively cruel and heinous treatment of Jews, Communists, and other groups in Germany seems to be amply verified. But is persecution in one country remedied by stirring up hatred and vilification in another? Instead of laying all the blame on Hitler, might it not be more reasonable to try to understand and account for the present German situation?

For nearly fifteen years the Germans have been held down and driven to despair by the provisions of the Treaty of Versailles—a treaty conceived in hatred and forced upon Germany at the point of a gun—and the repressive policies pursued by the Allies since the war. It was inevitable that the day of reckoning should come. The dragons' teeth have been sown and the world is now reaping the harvest. Sixty-three million Germans cannot be held down forever. Hitler is the symbol of their desperation and revolt. That the Jews are being persecuted is symptomatic of deeper unrest. Minority groups serve as scapegoats for a nation's troubles.

Of all the tons of newspaper pulp devoted to the present situation in Germany very little, comparatively, is given over to a study of the underlying causes. Moreover, the church leaders in America, with a few exceptions, have been hurling anathemas at Hitler and the Germans, paying slight attention to the fundamental social, economic and political factors which have produced Hitler and all that is going on in Germany. John Grier Hibben, president of Princeton (now deceased), and H. A. Atkinson, secretary of the Church Peace Union, both declared that Hitler is a menace to the world, as if by getting rid of Hitler the world could get rid of the "menace"; or, by analogy, by executing criminals we could solve the problem of crime. The present unrest and turmoil in Germany goes much deeper than Hitler. The basic question is: Why do millions of Germans worship and follow him?

A few religious writers have attempted to be objective and see the German crisis in its proper perspective, without minimizing the cruelty of the present wave of anti-Semitism. W. A. Visser't Hooft, general secretary of the World Christian Student Federation, writes of the utter lack of

> patience and self-restraint with which not only journalists and politicians, but also pacifists and Christian leaders, judge the recent developments in Germany. A new mob psychology has appeared, expressing itself in damning the German nation without even trying to find out what sins it has exactly committed, and without making a deeper attempt to inquire into the deeper reasons for its present actions and reactions.[18]

The general secretary of the Federal Council of the Churches of Christ in America, Samuel McCrea Cavert, pleads for "a less superficial appraisal of the Nazi movement" and asks us to treat Germany as "a patient and not a criminal."[19] The editors of *The Christian Century, The World Tomorrow* and *Unity* have taken much the same point of view.

Under the spell of the current wave of hysteria over Hitler, which reveals the war spirit and plays directly into the hands of the war mongers, it is difficult to believe that the churches have become immune to hatred and could not again engage in a "holy war."

Furthermore, if any forecast of the actions of the clergy in the next war be attempted, an historical fact of supreme importance cannot be overlooked. In this country, at least, many of the ministers have repented after every big war and sworn never to bless another. As Devere Allen has pointed out, in between wars anti-war resolutions have been prevalent and exceedingly popular.[20] Yet when the country called upon its yeomanry to battle for Old Glory, the parsons led the attack.

Any unbiased and candid judgment or prediction about the future relationship of the churches and their leaders to war cannot ignore the facts of history, particularly the record of the institutions of religion during 1914-18 and other periods of similar social upheavals. There must also be taken into account the interpretations of this data and the general contributions on the subject made by the other social sciences—together with a consideration of the integral relationship of the forces of religion to the whole structure and pattern of our society at the present hour.

CHAPTER XVI

THE CHURCHES AND THE CLERGY IN WORLD WAR II

CHAPTER XVI
THE CHURCHES AND THE CLERGY IN WORLD WAR II

When the armies of Hitler started their triumphal march into Poland on September 1, 1939, Americans, after they had partially recovered from their initial shock, gave immediate attention to trying to keep the United States out of the European conflict.

There was a widespread belief that the Neutrality Acts passed between 1935 and 1937 would help to keep this country out of another European or world war. The President on September 5, 1939, issued a proclamation of neutrality, and by a second proclamation made necessary by the Neutrality Acts—in which an embargo was placed on the shipment of war material to belligerents—travel of Americans on belligerent ships in the war zones was banned.

FROM NEUTRALITY TO BELLIGERENCY

As the war progressed in Europe it seemed evident to many Americans that a defense of the Western Hemisphere was necessary. Canada and Latin America were virtually unprotected. We could not permit the invasion and conquest of these areas. In 1941 the United States occupied Greenland and Iceland, the two governments involved having given consent. In September 1940 Great Britain received fifty "over-age" destroyers from the United States and in return granted us the right to lease naval and air bases in Newfoundland, Bermuda, Bahamas, Jamaica, St. Lucia, Trinidad, Antigua, and British Guiana. By the end of 1941 the construction of these bases had proceeded rapidly.

In the meanwhile the conviction was growing in this country that Great Britain was our "first line of defense." "The British Navy alone stands between us and Hitler"—that was the phrase one heard.

Congress was called into session soon after war started, and the Neutrality Act of 1937 was revised so that the Allies might obtain arms and munitions from this country. Belligerents could purchase arms and munitions here, but on a "cash and carry" basis. By January 1941 the famous Lend-Lease Acts were introduced. After two months of heated debate the President's proposals were passed with certain amendments.

It would seem that most Americans had never really been neutral, and it was not long before the majority came to believe that the "Allied cause" was our cause. The Neutrality Acts were weakened and we were virtually in the war as a partner to the Allies except in terms of armed conflict. Dunkerque, the fall of France, and the threatened invasion of England began to frighten large sections of the population when they contemplated the consequences in the event of the fall of Great Britain. Rational and influential citizens were predicting that Hitler would be over here in three weeks.

During 1940 a total of $17,692 billion was appropriated for national defense. A two-ocean navy was in the making. Furthermore the Selective Training and Service Act of 1940 brought in compulsory military training in peacetime. We began to mobilize all our resources for war.

Our four-year attempt to check Japanese expansion in the Pacific had been a failure. The supposedly unexpected attack of the Japanese on Pearl Harbor, December 7, 1941, gave them an initial success in the "shooting war." But this "treachery" united the people of this country as probably nothing else could have done. On Monday, December 8, the Senate voted to declare war against Japan 82 to zero, and in the House of Representatives the vote was 388 to 1. (Only Jeannette Rankin voted "no.")

On December 10 Germany and Italy declared war against the United States, and the next day Congress, without a dissenting vote, passed resolutions to the effect that a state of war with these countries existed.

President Roosevelt in his war message of December 8 said: "No matter how long it may take us to overcome this premeditated invasion, the American people in their *righteous* [italics mine] might, will win through to absolute victory."

POSITION OF THE CHURCHES, 1940-41

Keeping in mind this brief résumé of some of the major trends in this country between the time that war broke out in Europe and the Pearl Harbor attack, what were the churches and the forces of organized religion doing with respect to the war in those twenty-seven months prior to December 7, 1941?

A survey of the religious periodicals and literature, of many sermons preached in that period, and of material based on interviews with religious leaders indicates that the churches and the clergy were hopelessly divided in their attitudes toward the war in Europe. Moreover, there was a great deal of confusion over the causes of the war, the role that the United States should play, and what the churches should or should not do. Like the historians, the economists, the political scientists, and the political leaders of the time, the men of the cloth were to be found in many diverse camps. The editors of *Fortune* in January 1940 complained in an article on "The Failure of the Church":

> We are asked to turn to the church for our enlightenment, but when we do so we find that the voice of the church is not inspired. The voice of the church, we find, is the echo of our own voices. And the result of this experience, already manifest, is disillusionment.

They even said that "so far as the record goes, the American people would do as well by their souls to follow the advice of the industrial leaders [with reference to the war] as to follow the advice of the spiritual leaders."

Pacifism

At first the pacifist and near-pacifist groups took the spotlight. In September 1939 great peace rallies and parades were held over the country. Resolutions were passed calling for an absolutely neutral policy. The statement of a religious reporter at the time seemed to express the general sentiment: "Today the voice of the churches is almost unanimously against American intervention."

Dr. George H. Buttrick, then the president of the Federal Council of the Churches of Christ in America, broadcast a plea in early September 1939: "We must be neutral from high and sacrificial motives— not for physical safety . . . because we know that war is futile and because we are eager through reconciliation to build a kindlier world."

In October of that year the executive committee of the Federal Council passed a resolution by unanimous vote of the fifty representatives of the various denominations present, calling upon the churches "to repent" and denouncing war "as an evil thing contrary to the mind of Christ."

The National Peace Conference, which included nearly all the peace organizations of the various Protestant churches, sent to President Roosevelt a six-point program for this country in which they asked him to "keep the United States out of war," to "initiate a continuous conference of neutral nations to procure a just peace," and to work for a "permanent world government as the basis for peace and security."

In those early days of the war the religious forces for the most part fought to keep the Neutrality Acts intact and avoided taking sides as much as possible. Religious propaganda designed to keep us out of war was based on several factors. First, the terrific disillusionment that followed World War I had had a profound effect upon the general population and especially upon the churches and the clergy. Thousands of clergymen and laymen had pledged themselves never to endorse or have anything to do with another war. Practically every Protestant church in America had passed resolutions in the thirties branding war as a "sin"; and they would have nothing to do with sin. According to Dr. Walter Van Kirk in his *Religion Renounces War:*

> When the Federal Council of Churches in 1932 declared that the Church as an institution should neither sanction nor bless war there were only one or two dissenting voices among the four hundred delegates representative of the twenty-five communions adhering to the council.

Conscientious objectors—past, present, and future—were considered heroes in many communions. Churches went on record that in the event of war the conscientious objectors would receive the backing of the denomination. The historic position of the Friends, the Mennonites, and the Church of the Brethren was regarded with great favor in other and larger Protestant bodies.

Again, there had been a great deal of repentance on the part of thousands of clergymen for words spoken in World War I. There were memories of bellicose and hateful pronouncements against the Kaiser and the Huns. This time there was more caution. In the words of Stanley High, there was the fear lest they make another "holy war and someone, some day" would rise up "to write another *Preachers Present Arms."*

There was certainly a widespread belief that organized religion could no longer afford to bless war, which was regarded as a complete denial of the teachings of Christ.

The religious press

In this pre-Pearl Harbor period, of all the influential Protestant weeklies the *Christian Century* seems to have been among the most outspoken of the noninterventionist journals. The aims of President Roosevelt's administration were denounced in practically every issue. Dr. Charles Clayton Morrison, the editor, opposed any revision of the Neutrality Acts, the "destroyer deal," Lend-Lease, Selective Service, and so forth. By January 1941 Dr. Morrison was talking about "the President's war" and maintaining that "the President has gone on the assumption that Great Britain is fighting America's war." In October of the same year he wrote:

> ... the obsession of our statesmen with the weird illusion that this is in any true sense America's war must be broken. America's only genuine and rational responsibility in this war is to mediate for peace—not the peace of a mere armistice, but the peace of justice.

As late as the first week of December 1941, in the last editorial before that fatal Sunday, December 7, Dr. Morrison wrote, "Every national interest and every moral obligation to civilization dictates that this country shall keep out of the insanity of war which is in no sense America's war." He declared, "The romanticists are the interventionists. In general they pride themselves on taking a realistic view, and charge that noninterventionists are star-gazing romantics. . . ."

Other equally honest, sincere, and conscientious Christians were convinced that the *Christian Century* and those who supported its positions were naïve romanticists and misguided Christians.

Perhaps somewhat to counteract the influence of the *Christian Century*, a new religious periodical started up under the name of *Christianity and Crisis* with Reinhold Niebuhr, a professor in Union Theological Seminary, as the chief editor. Here was expounded the interventionist position and the "Aid to Britain" program. Niebuhr frankly stated that the Neutrality Act was "one of the most immoral laws that were ever spread upon the Federal statute book." "The essence of immorality," wrote he, "is the evasion or denial of moral responsibility." According to him, "misguided idealism" was "evoked in its support" at the time of passage.

That the clergy were divided in their appraisal of the merits of the war and the part that the United States should play is further evidenced by innumerable group resolutions and recommendations of one type and another.

Before our entrance into the struggle of the nations for survival, the Fellowship of Reconciliation announced that over two thousand clergy from every state in the Union had signed a statement of "unalterable opposition to America's present threatened belligerency" and pledged themselves never to use their ministry to "bless, sanction or support war." Early in February 1941, 648 churchmen signed a statement calling for "peace without victory now." Many eminent ministers were on this list.

The files of the religious periodicals are filled with articles and letters on both sides of the fence. Clergymen had a perfect field day in writing letters and engaging in endless discussions over finespun theological questions about religion and war.

For ten weeks beginning in early December 1940, the *Christian Century* ran a series on "If America Enters the War What Shall I Do?" Prominent clergy took opposite sides in the debate.

Preparedness propaganda

Gradually, however, the social forces which were to bring America into World War II became stronger and more dynamic. Events proved much stronger than philosophical reasoning. The isolationist groups, the "America First" and "Keep America Out of the War" committees, were being offset by those who gathered around the banners of "Aid to Britain," "Defend America by Aiding the Allies," and similar organizations. Leading churchmen took an active part in several of these important propaganda groups.

In the early days of 1940 a manifesto was issued by a rather large number of influential clergymen for an "enlistment of our moral and material resources in support of the Allied nations." They believed, in general, that if "the American people are determined to take effective action toward the establishment of peace, one and only one course opens to them—the enlistment of their full national resources in assistance to Great Britain." During the next year similar and stronger statements and resolutions appeared with signatures from the clergy from practically all over the country and from the leading denominations.

In World War I, during the "preparedness era," the Episcopalians and the clergy with British and Canadian ancestry were the most conspicuous among the religious groups in arousing sympathy for Britain and promoting preparedness propaganda. To a certain extent this was true in World War II (though more research is needed on this point to determine how widespread the phenomenon was). Of the Episcopalians, Bishop William T. Manning was probably the most outspoken and seemed to be much in the limelight of publicity. He had been active before 1917 in World War I on behalf of the mother country. In World War II he followed the identical pattern. In the summer of 1941 at the convention of his diocese the Bishop announced:

> Speaking as an American, as a Christian, and as a bishop of the Christian church, I say that it is our duty as a Nation to take full part in this struggle, to give our whole strength and power to bring this world calamity and world terror to an end, and to do this now while Great Britain still stands.

This statement, it should be said, aroused considerable discussion within Episcopalian ranks. Sixty-four Episcopalians issued a pronouncement in the New York *Times* which seems to have been directed at their Bishop, repudiating the notion that the conflict across the Atlantic Ocean was a "holy war."

Adjustment to War

Up to December 7, 1941, then, the forces of organized religion were divided into several camps ranging all the way from the absolute pacifists to the interventionists who wanted us to declare war at once. Each, however, appealed to the same authorities—the Bible and Jesus of Nazareth—to support his position. (The Catholic and Jewish groups will be discussed later.)

The seemingly surprise Japanese attack on Pearl Harbor settled, for the time being at least, many of the finespun theological and philosophical arguments that had been going on for over two years. War was no longer a possibility. It was a reality.

Correspondence with nearly all the editors of the leading Protestant and Catholic religious periodicals reveals that they accepted the war as a fact and did not attempt to hinder the all-out war effort. Most of these journals seem to have supported our Government, and some quite actively. A few stood idly by and watched the process of events.

In the case of *Unity,* a comparatively small but influential liberal religious periodical, a novel situation arose. Dr. John Haynes Holmes, who was the editor (and continued to be up to 1946), was in opposition to the war. The managing editor, Dr. Curtis W. Reese, supported the war. So each of these gentlemen wrote signed editorials and each approved articles for publication. For the most part, both the editor and the managing editor were in agreement on the matter of conscientious objectors.

It will be observed that several types of adjustments or readjustments were possible for the Christian group. Confronted with a shooting war, religious institutions are called upon to shift, for the time being, patterns of thought in a manner that is not characteristic of any of our other institutions. One example of this is furnished in an editorial in the *Living Church* (Episcopalian), December 17, 1941: "May we seek always, not that God may be on our side, but that we may be on His side, so that the victory may in the end be His."

The guilty necessity

The editors of the *Christian Century,* while not absolute pacifists, nevertheless had so consistently decried all preparation for war that for them Pearl Harbor must have been a terrible psychological blow. In the first editorial written after the fatal December 7, entitled "An Unnecessary Necessity," we read:

> Our Government has taken a stand. It is our Government. It spoke for us as the voice of national solidarity. It is *our* voice. The President is *our* President, all his official acts, even those which we disapprove, are our acts. . . .
> We stand with our country, we cannot do otherwise. We see no alternative which does not involve national self-stultification. Our country is at war. Its life is at stake. . . .

In a later, more detailed analysis the editor stated that the war was "the judgment of God" and "the terrible fruit of disobedience." Said he:

> It is our necessity, an unnecessary necessity, therefore a guilty necessity. . . . Our fighting, though necessary, is not righteous. God does not command us to fight. His condemnation, written with our own hands, is that we must slay our human brothers and be slain by them. This condemnation, we now affirm, is hell.

The shifting policies of the paper and the above type of reasoning did not appeal to a great many of the brethren. Pacifists did not like it, interventionists ridiculed it. The collected editorials of Dr. Morrison were reviewed by Reinhold Niebuhr with what the editors of *Fortune* called "scornful rigor." The editor of the *Christian Leader* commented on the *Christian Century:*

> The erratic editorial policy of that paper, first isolationist and then would-be isolationist, first pacifist and then "wants to be pacifist," first against the Government and then for the Government but pulling back on the halter, has destroyed much of its influence.

Considerable attention has been devoted to the *Christian Century* and the opposition to it because nothing portrays so clearly the controversy that raged through Protestantism during those war years. Some day, perhaps, a psychoanalyst will write up the underlying processes at work and there will be laid bare the struggles of religious souls as they grappled with the problem of war. From the institutional point of view, the rationalizations that were resorted to in order to make war more acceptable are worthy of far more space than is herein provided.

The holy war

One example of this is with respect to the use of the phrase "holy war." In 1917-18 the struggle had frequently been referred to as "the most holy war of all the ages." However, with the events that had intervened between the two wars, the phrase had fallen into thorough disrepute. Karl Barth, the distinguished Swiss theologian, had shocked a great many of the faithful when, addressing the Christians of Great Britain, he declared the war "is a righteous war which God commands us to wage ardently."

The Archbishop of York, Dr. William Temple, solved the theological dilemma by stating: "We are fighting for Christian civilization. I cannot use the phrase 'holy war,' for war in its own nature is always an expression of the sin of man. But without hesitation I speak of this as, for us, a righteous war."

The theological frame of reference is very important. Hence among the theologians (and in one sense every clergyman *must* be a theologian) it is important to know what God thinks about the war. Once having discovered the "mind of God" on this subject, the major premise can be stated. The rest of the syllogism, or line of logic, is comparatively easy, particularly for a master dialectician. This helps immensely to reassure religious folks that God is still on His throne and is greatly concerned with the triumph of righteousness.

Wartime Trends

After the United States entered the war as an active belligerent the following major trends seem to be significant as far as the churches are concerned.

When compared with 1917-18, the population in World War II took the conflict and the horrors of war more in its stride. Twenty-four years before there had been a great deal of hysteria. This time, while there was plenty of denunciation of the "Japs" and of Hitler *et al.*, far less real excitement prevailed. One heard and saw less of the wild-eyed patriot. The clergy in their utterances reflected the same differences. A few bellicose warmongers, yes, but they were not outstanding, certainly. In general, the clergy were calm about the struggle. and, in fact, in their sermons seem to have paid relatively less attention to the current problems of the war than one might have supposed. The generalization is based on data gathered from all over the United States. The war was a grim necessity—something to be gotten over as soon as possible.

Again, a greater toleration of diverse opinions was demonstrated. The Jehovah's Witnesses fared badly, it is true. Yet, the record of civil liberties appears better this time than for the previous war. The churches regarded the pacifist or near-pacifist clergymen with more urbanity than in 1917-18. No one knows how many preachers were pacifists, but they undoubtedly numbered several thousand. A few of them were exceedingly prominent.

The conscientious objectors were more highly regarded than in World War I, when they were damned or spurned by the clergy in general. The pacifist movement of the twenties and the thirties carried right on through the war with remarkable strength. On this point Dr. F. Ernest Johnson comments: "The number of objectors has been extremely small in view of the strength of the pacifist movement, but they constitute a symbol of religious freedom, and the churches in general seem so to regard them."

Approximately 12,000 conscientious objectors served in the Civilian Public Service and in the alternate service to war. About 6,500 spent an average of thirty months in prison for their violation of the Selective Training and Service Act of 1940. They came from 240 religious denominations and sects. The Mennonite group numbered 4,665; the Church of the Brethren, 1,353; the Society of Friends, 951; the Methodist, 673; the Jehovah's Witnesses, 409; and the remainder was distributed through various denominations and small sects.

The furnishing of chaplains to the armed forces was one of the outstanding contributions of the religious bodies. The Army and the Navy recognized the importance of chaplains in maintaining the morale of the men in the service.

Since this paper is primarily concerned with attitudes rather than activities of the churches and the clergy during the war period, no attempt will be made to appraise the many ways in which the religious people contributed their support to the war effort.

The Roman Catholic Position

So far little has been said with reference to the Catholic and Jewish groups. More space has been given to the Protestant wing of Christendom because it was in that sector of the religious world that the greatest intellectual and spiritual difficulties arose over the war. The Protestant institutions—the established way of doing things—could not meet the impact of the war as readily or as easily as the Catholics and the Jewish organizations did.

While the Roman Catholic Church in this country had for the most part been isolationist prior to that day when our battleships were destroyed at Pearl Harbor, nevertheless the shift from peace to war in a few brief minutes did not constitute a theological nightmare for the Catholics. The hierarchy took care of the role that the church would play. Among the pronouncements of the Catholic bishops was a letter addressed to President Roosevelt on December 23, 1941, by the Administrative Board of the National Catholic Welfare Conference (NCWC), pledging full support of the Nation in the war effort and placing at the President's disposal, in the country's service, "our institutions and their consecrated personnel." The bishops promised to lead their priests and people in the prayer that God "may strengthen us all to win a victory that will be a blessing not for our nation alone but for the whole world." The Roman Catholic hierarchy directed all Catholic churches to pray on December 8, 1942, for "a victory and a peace acceptable to God."

With reference to the question of the conscientious objectors, no official statement of the Catholic bishops as a group or of the Administrative Board of Bishops of the NCWC was issued. A Catholic editor writes that as far as he is able to learn no individual bishop commented on this topic. He continues:

> It is my personal view that the attitude of the Catholic press generally was not sympathetic. However, the Catholic group in New York that publishes *The Catholic Worker* came out strongly in support of conscientious objectors and formed an organization on their behalf.

The role of Pope Pius XII in the war constitutes a study in itself. His statements about the struggle and the various attempts to bring about a peaceful settlement greatly impressed Roman Catholics in this country. Protestants were suspicious. That the Papacy had a most difficult set of problems can scarcely be denied.

Roman Catholic influence in the White House has always been a matter of grave concern for the Protestants. Therefore, when the Roosevelt administration virtually resumed diplomatic relations with the Vatican after a break of seventy-two years, Protestants became indignant.

Thus the war not only called for new adjustments on the part of specific organized religious groups, but frequently complicated their relations to each other in an intense interaction pattern. In the struggle for power, prestige, and the preservation of what was regarded as essential values and institutions within the framework of American culture, historic cleavages, rivalries, and suspicions were intensified.

Jewish Interventionism

The Jewish groups—Orthodox, Conservative, and Reform—were able, on a religious plane at least, to accept the war without much difficulty. Dr. F. Ernest Johnson points out that the Jewish community "is too closely bound by its sense of peoplehood to the democratic cause to experience any such shock in the outbreak of war as has come to the Protestant churches."

For the Jewish people in this country there was a more dynamic reason for hoping that some good would come out of the war. The Jews in Germany had suffered such extreme cruelty and torture under Hitler that, for the most part, members of that group in the United States had long hoped to see the Nazis completely defeated. The Allied cause was in a real sense their cause.

A thorough analysis of sermons preached by leading rabbis in the New York area before we were catapulted into the war shows that a considerable proportion of them were definitely preaching against the

Nazis and suggesting that something should be done about this "menace." That is not to suggest they were advocating that the United States should declare war, but they were pleading for some form of interventionist policy. On the other hand, there was the haunting fear among them that the Jews in this country would be accused of trying to start a "Jewish war." Of course, that is exactly the accusation which the extreme rightist groups made. As Lavine and Wechsler phrased it in their *War Propaganda in the United States* (1940):

> William Pelley, leader of the Fascist Silvershirts, was the most bellicose exponent of this creed; Father Coughlin said essentially the same thing in more devious ways; and both of them derived most of their ideological inspiration from the propaganda ministry in Berlin. These slogans were not suddenly fashioned. They were the keynotes of the anti-Semitic drive which had begun many months before in America. It did not matter that the "Jewish conspiracy" was imaginary. . . . The fact that the bulk of American Jewry supported the Allied cause was invoked to sustain the cry of "Jewish war."

It would seem that after the United States got into the war, the Jewish community was about as loyal and active as any cultural-religious group in the country in working for Allied victory.

A "Righteous" Cause

While it has been possible only to point out relatively a few of the high lights on the broad canvas of the relationship of the churches and the clergy to World War II, it is clear that the forces of organized religion played an important part in the struggle of the ideologies. In the dark hour of war most Christians could not follow or understand those who, like A. J. Muste of the Fellowship of Reconciliation, reaffirmed their sincere belief in "nonviolent non-cooperation with the enemy." The great mass of believers in and followers of Jesus were more interested in national survival than in issuing continual statements to the effect that war is a sin.

One fact, however, was characteristic of nearly all the religious groups, pacifist and nonpacifist. They talked and planned for a just and durable peace and some kind of federation of nations. The Delaware Conference which met in Ohio in March 1942, composed of 377 delegates from twenty-seven American Protestant communions, drafted a statement on "The Bases of a Just and Durable Peace." This proved to be but one of many attempts in various quarters to bring about an end to all wars by planning for permanent peace.

A Dilemma

It was a Christian soldier of three hundred years ago, Miles Standish, who is credited with saying:

> War is a terrible trade;
> But in the cause that is righteous
> Sweet is the smell of powder. . . .

Cromwell and many other stalwarts of bygone days would have agreed with the soldier of Plymouth. It is doubtful, however, whether today many followers of Jesus of Nazareth really relish war or enjoy the sweet smell of powder even in a righteous cause.

Thus times have changed—but how much? As has been observed, when groups of Christians believe that their country is fighting for its life, the attempt by force of arms to preserve its institutions becomes at least a "righteous" cause. Prayers for victory are heard over the land. The soldier dead are buried with the blessing of the Almighty. Yet between wars many of these same groups of believers in the Prince of Peace have declared that for them war is a colossal sin.

Here, then, is one of the great dilemmas of the Christian church. In time of peace, war is against God. In time of war, except for the absolute pacifists, there comes the intellectual and emotional necessity of making the war acceptable in terms of some kind of moral objective. Though war is recognized as a tragedy, fighting to preserve a Christian civilization against the "paganism" of the Axis is essentially waging war to defeat the enemies of Christ. When it became apparent that World War II was a fight to the finish, not many of even the pacifists could honestly say that it made no difference to them which side won.

Why is there often this hesitation on the part of those who believe in a sovereign God to ask Him to bless their cause? Why are all manner of circumlocutions resorted to in the use of words and phrases (that in the end mean practically the same thing) to avoid labeling our cause as righteous or just? To answer that the pacifist movement has had a sobering effect upon the thought of the churches is only a step in the direction of the answer. Whatever cultural factors have been involved, the final answer must be sought in the understanding of the basic human motivations.

There is clear evidence that some of the institutional patterns that have developed to resolve the conflict within Christendom have a schizophrenic quality. An analysis of the theological arguments over war would seem to indicate that frequently the emotions and the intellect are split off from each other. Furthermore, many of the rationalizations that are used to cover up the real underlying motives are symptomatic of the unresolved conflicts and emotional turmoil within individuals themselves. For example, repressed hostility, frustrations, feelings of guilt, sadistic and masochistic tendencies, the fear of death, attachments to love objects on an infantile level, and dozens of other psychological and psychoanalytic phenomena may often lie behind attitudes developed toward war. The conflict over the relationship of the church to the god Mars may often be a projection of these more personal and emotional difficulties. Moreover, not infrequently debates regarding the nature of war from the Christian point of view were carried on as if in a vacuum, with little reference to reality. That fact also is diagnostic.

There is nothing new in the above statements. They are emphasized again because frequently men become so engrossed with the more dramatic aspects of the death struggle of civilizations that these primary considerations are forgotten.

How much longer the forces of organized religion will continue to serve the gods of nationalism is perhaps a moot question. At least it is evident that many drastic changes will have to be made in man's social institutions before he can enjoy the warless world envisioned by Isaiah: ". . . and they shall beat their swords into plowshares, and their spears into pruning hooks; nation shall not lift up sword against nation, neither shall they learn war any more."

CHAPTER XVII

CONCLUSION, 1969

CHAPTER XVII

CONCLUSION, 1969

At this writing in early 1969, representatives from Hanoi and the United States are meeting for peace talks in Paris. Whether this conference will bring an end to the war in Vietnam is a matter of conjecture. By the time this book is off the press, the reader will know and obviously be in a better position to view the war in perspective than is possible at the moment. He will have the advantage of hindsight. The best histories of wars and crises are usually written years later, though one may still attempt to view the present with some degree of insight and objectivity amid the tumult itself.

Such an attempt will be made to describe briefly the relationship of organized religion in this country to the Vietnamese War. Only the highlights will be presented. There will be no survey in detail as was done in *Preachers Present Arms* of the attitudes and activities of the churches and the clergy in World War I. Rather, here is a suggested random sample of the range of such phenomena. Illustrations from the contemporary scene are intended to shed a little light and sharpen the focus rather than cover the universe.

Many interesting comparisons and contrasts can be made with World War I. In general, the clergy and the churches reflect as well as help to make up public opinion. In World War I, the religious groups in their almost complete endorsement of our participation in the war were talking and acting in exactly the same manner as a cross section of the population. The same is true today. The people in the United States are seriously divided in their support of the war; so are the clergy and the churches. As a social institution organized religion is not an independent social force, but is interwoven with other movements and social forces beyond its control. Dynamic social change affects the old order and in subtle ways forces even the entrenched Establishments to adjust though the time lag may be long indeed.

Massive criticism of our part in the war in Vietnam on a scale scarcely contemplated has been mounting in the past three years particularly. By comparison, the pursuit of our objectives in World Wars I and II met with little opposition on the home front. They were conceived as life and death struggles to preserve civilization itself. The future of our country was at stake. From the point of view of propaganda, to unite the people was relatively easy. The accumulation of incidents that led up to the declaration of war against Germany, April 6, 1917, seemed to leave no alternative. The atrocity stories, the memory of the sinking of the Lusitania, the image of the Kaiser, all these and thousands more kept us at fever heat during the war. It was a field day for the propaganda machines. On Sunday, December 7, 1941, the "day of infamy," the attack on Pearl Harbor united this country in an instant. We had been wary of the "Japs" for years; now we knew the truth about their "treachery." As for Hitler and the Nazis, by the fall of 1941 we had been thoroughly briefed and were already hating the German leadership.

By contrast, our entrance into the war in Vietnam was anything but dramatic. No great crises presented themselves; no events really united us. Even today it seems like some far-off struggle removed from reality and taking place on the periphery, unless we have a son or daughter or relatives in the services. There is no sense of feeling that civilization is at stake. There are no Kaisers or Hitlers to serve as objects of hatred. By comparison, Ho Chi Minh is at his worst merely an old, obstinate, Asiatic "gentleman." We cannot get too stirred up about him.

The war has provided little emotional appeal or given rewards or satisfactions for most of the populace. Its very frustrations have served to open the sluice gates of criticism and the torrents of opposition to our continuation of the struggle in Vietnam. Nearly every day we read about some incident in which there is a demonstrated denunciation of our participation in behalf of saving the South Vietnamese from the North.

In contrast to World War I, when the most innocuous statements of criticism of the war brought prison sentences of fifteen and twenty years in the Federal Prison in Atlanta, today thousands of provocative and inflammable statements and actions go unchallenged. The "true patriots" are shocked, naturally, at the petitions which pull no punches, the peace marchers, the antiwar organizations and speeches. The opposition to the war has been manifested within the halls of Congress itself. Many of our Senators have made remarks and criticisms of our conduct of the war that unquestionably would have resulted in a jail sentence for a civilian in World War I.

A couple of examples from 1917-18 may suffice to indicate the climate of opinion back in those halcyon days.

D. H. Wallace, an ex-British soldier, was sentenced to twenty years for saying:

> That when a soldier went away he was a hero and that when he came back flirting with a hand organ he was a bum, and that the asylums

will be filled with them; that the soldiers were giving their lives for the capitalists, that 40 percent of the ammunition of the allies or their guns was defective because of graft.

Wallace went insane and died in jail.[1]

The Reverend Clarence H. Waldron of Windsor, Vermont, distributed a pamphlet to five adults which stated that since Jesus would never fight in a war, therefore, Christians should not fight. He did not deny the right of a nation to go to war "to preserve its interests," but it was "wrong to the Christian."

Mr. Waldron was convicted "for causing insubordination and obstructing recruiting." His sentence was for twenty years in Atlanta.[2]

It is doubtful that cases of this type would come to the courts today. Opposition to the draft for one reason or another is too widespread, vocal, and demonstrative.

No doubt such opposition is a part of a wider pattern of revolt. This war is being fought at a time when our society is being "torn asunder" by all manner of dissent: civil rights, open housing, marches, hippies, the sexual revolution, "far out" literature, plays, and movies, campus riots, crime in the streets, violence of all types, and the burning of our cities. Opposition to authority is not new, but today it is being channelized into a great variety of expressions.

The academic and religious communities have shown the greatest amount of verbal opposition to the war and on certain occasions marches and demonstrations as well. The New York *Times* has published from time to time a considerable number of statements signed by thousands of professors and teachers in the colleges and universities calling for a quick end to the "immoral" war.

Bishops and church organizations, large and small, have passed resolutions, or made extensive statements about the war in Vietnam. In general, there is a call for a "quick end" to the war with a blueprint spelling out all of the steps. The bishops of the Methodist Church pleaded, "In the name of God and in the name of humanity, we insist that both sides cease their mutual destruction and seek peace." The Catholic bishops have called attention to the pleas of the pope and asked for peace on earth, though recognizing that self-defense in wars is sometimes necessary. The Synagogue Council of America has made itself known, and many of the Jewish leaders have spoken out against the war. The groups of Mennonites, Church of the Brethren, the Society of Friends have, of course, condemned the war.[3] This is far from a coverage of the church bodies, but will serve as a small sample of attitudes and opinions about our participation in Vietnam.

The clergy have called meetings in various cities to consider what attitudes to take toward our participation in the conflict and have on several occasions condemned our part in the war. According to a report from the National Council of Churches of Christ in the U.S.A.,

> On January 31 and February 1, 1967 some twenty-four hundred clergymen, seminarians, nuns, church women, and laymen gathered in Washington, D.C., from 47 states in the union. Their purpose was to protest the role of the United States in the war in Vietnam.
>
> This major event organized by the National Emergency Committee of Clergy and Laymen Concerned About Vietnam was generally underplayed by the American press. In particular, the classic statement of conscientious concern approved and issued by the **Executive Committee** at that time received only passing reference.
>
> * * *
>
> The Committee is drawn from all faiths and includes many outstanding churchmen. It has as its co-chairmen, Dr. John C. Bennett, Rabbi Abraham Heschel, Father John McKenzie, and Mr. Philip Scharper.

The report is condemnatory of the war as being "immoral." On the other hand, it calls for a negotiated peace with many details that must be considered. The organization, the National Emergency Committee of Clergy and Laymen Concerned About Vietnam, has been extremely active. Their book, *In the Name of America,* a well-documented exposé of the crimes committed in the war in Vietnam in the name of democracy, is a contribution to a realistic consideration of a part of the war that the average person would never know about.[4]

The clergy on numerous occasions have created picket lines and shown up in demonstrations against the war. In the winter of 1968 they picketed the home of Dean Rusk, the Secretary of State.

There would appear to be a real connection between the activist clergy who participated in the march on Selma, for example, and forthright opposition to the war in Vietnam. The patterns or syndromes of operation in civil rights and opposition to the war are similar, as Dr. Martin Luther King pointed out and tried to unite. In previous wars there was no such bridge or proving ground whereby religious and civil rights groups could become articulate to the degree which is possible today. *Action* is the watchword of the hour.

A random sample of ecclesiastical opinion as expressed by the editors of various religious journals, reveals a wide variety of attitudes, The editor of *The Lutheran*, "the magazine of the Lutheran Church in America," in January 1968 declared, "The great unfinished business in 1968 is the war in Vietnam. This war is miserable, cruel, and pointless adventure of the U.S. on the world stage. The disaster that has been wreaked on the South Vietnamese by American military power is far more terrible than any other fate that might have befallen them." The editor accuses the United States of prosecuting the war for purely national self-interest.[5]

In the same issue a young professor of ethics in the Lutheran Seminary in Chicago wrote under the title, "What Is a Just War?" After quoting Paul, the Augsburg Confession, and Martin Luther, he arrives at the conviction that "Under certain circumstances, therefore, the Christian may find that he can take part in a just war. . . . And even when it is so justified, war is still not to be considered 'righteous,' but rather a tragic necessity."[6]

Another professor of Christian social ethics at Wesley Theological Seminary in Washington, D.C., maintains that we should not be in the war in Vietnam, because it is immoral. But he adds, "At the very least, war in all its forms must bear the burden of proof before the Christian conscience."[7]

The Christian Century, an ecumenical weekly, said to have the largest circulation of any nondenominational weekly, has long been against our participation in the war and has considered it to be "immoral" on all counts.

Catholic opinion, while divided, has been often openly and bitterly antiwar. The Roman Catholic *Critic,* speaking of our participation, declared, "Rather, it is a moral question which American citizens as individuals must resolve for themselves. To us only one conclusion seems valid: the United States should get the hell out of Vietnam."[8]

Jesuit theologian, Daniel O'Hanlon, maintains that the anti-communist policy of the United States is "the holy-war theory, and it has been specifically rejected by the church."[9]

The U.S. Catholic, published by the Clarentian Fathers, has declared that the war in Vietnam is "immoral," "unjust," and "wrong."[10]

The Commonweal at least as far back as December 1966 said: "The U.S. should get out of Vietnam; it should seek whatever safety it can for our allies, it should arrange whatever international face-saving is possible; and even at the cost of a Communist victory, the U.S. should withdraw. The war in Vietnam is an unjust one, a crime and a sin."[11]

By contrast, Cardinal Spellman of New York, on his visit to Vietnam, pictured the war as "one for civilization. . . . Less than victory is inconceivable."[12]

United States policies have been endorsed by the Episcopal diocese of New Jersey and the state Baptist conventions of New Mexico and Tennessee. The Episcopal statement declared that those who fight in Vietnam "demonstrate their courage and their defense of their nation's tradition of faithfulness to its pledged word and to its international responsibility. They have responded to the call of duty despite those who, by word and gesture, defy the government under which they have freedom for such defiance." Both the Baptist statements pledged complete support of the United States in Vietnam.[13]

The Southern Baptist Convention, with a membership of 11,000,000, is reputed to be the largest Protestant body in the country. In the spring of 1967, meeting in Miami Beach, the convention "voiced solid support for a continuation of the Vietnam War until 'an honorable and just peace could be achieved.'" A year later, June 1968, meeting in Houston, Texas, the delegates or "messengers" expressed a somewhat different point of view. They "urged leaders on all sides of the Vietnam War to seek an immediate cease-fire, a termination of all hostile activities and no further buildup of military power."[14]

At this same meeting the Reverend Billy Graham, the evangelist, "predicted the return to earth of Jesus Christ, at which time," he said, "peace will be restored to the world." Under heavy security guard, Mr. Graham explained he was "ready to die at any time, and that if being shot or killed would glorify God," he would "accept death unflinchingly."[15]

While church bodies have been busy passing resolutions of one kind or another about the war, some of the service-minded Christians have been trying to relieve the suffering in Southeast Asia. This is an old story for the small pacifist segments of Christianity, particularly the Mennonites, the Friends, and the Church of the Brethren. The Lutherans, the third largest Protestant body, have also manifested much concern and given substantial contributions. (It is impossible to list all the church groups that have attempted to provide relief.)

The Mennonites who have had years of experience in conducting such programs in various parts of the world, and particularly in Vietnam where they have been for more than twelve years, supervise the program for the Lutherans who work with the Church World Service. The Mennonite Central Committee, at least up to a couple of years ago, was the only Protestant agency handling government surplus commodities in Vietnam. In 1966 alone, it received 4,250,000 pounds of dried milk powder, flour, bulgur, cornmeal, beans, and vegetables. Supplies of drugs are sent in from the Interchurch Medical Assistance.[16]

The Roman Catholic Church has been active in relief services in Vietnam. The United States Catholic Conference through one of its committees has been involved in undertaking all possible services to the suffering people in that country, as well as other parts of the globe.

In an all-out war that calls forth the patriotic enthusiasms of the citizens, the newspapers usually whip up sentiment and help to boost morale. In the last year or two many of our most powerful dailies have taken issue with the government in general and the President in particular. The New York *Times* and the *Washington Evening Post* (not to mention dozens of others) have tried to take apart our foreign policy and to show many of its inconsistencies.

A considerable number of our top flight columnists have been most incisive in their criticisms. Tom Wicker of the New York *Times* maintains that the temperament and the mistakes of LBJ have gotten us into trouble. He points out that in a conference with Henry Cabot Lodge in November 1963 Johnson said, "I am not going to be the President who saw Southeast Asia go the way China went." In September 1964 Johnson in a public address declared. "We don't want our American boys to do the fighting for the Asian boys. We don't want to get involved in a nation with 700 million people and get tied down to a land war in Asia."

Wicker's conclusion is, "No bombing campaign to bring the North to its knees was planned or intentionally started. The bombing began because Lyndon Johnson, in the ebullience of his power and in the fatal grip of an irrelevant experience, wanted to strike and thought he needed to strike and found in the rationale of retaliation the political stance required to fit his lifelong method of operation. The result was the fourth bloodiest war in American history."[17]

The above paragraphs concerning the attitudes of the press toward this war have been introduced to show that the forces of organized religion have not been unusual or exceptional in their criticism of the war in Vietnam. It is to a great extent a part of the temper of our times, the cultural milieu in a broad sense.

The dissent among the clergy as individuals has been significant in contrast to World War I. Perhaps the most prominent was Dr. Martin Luther King, Jr. Since his death there is no voice among the Negroes or whites so loud, clear, and compelling.

The cases of the Reverend William Sloane Coffin, Jr., Dr. Benjamin Spock, along with three others, have received the most publicity perhaps because of their indictment by the Federal government for a "conspiracy to counsel evasion and violation of the Universal Military Training and Service Act."

The press and the public are greatly divided over these cases. The religious press is inclined to side with these men. Many maintain that the testing of these laws is not unconstitutional; it is not sedition or treason. Norman DePuy in *Mission* magazine (Baptist) wrote that the testing of the validity of laws is traditionally American; "Our whole judiciary system of checks and balances of our governmental organization are designed for testing, trials, judgments—these are the stuff of American freedom. . . . If anything is going to create destructive anarchy, it is the denial of due process, or what's worse, ignorance on the part of the people as to what it is."[18]

Coffin has maintained that he has not told men to accept or resist the draft, but to follow the dictates of their own consciences.[19] In a sermon delivered at the Riverside Church in New York City, April 1, 1968, he is quoted as having said that young men who turn in their draft cards are in a nonviolent way taking a stand that does not infringe on the rights of anyone. He declared, "It is in the best American tradition not to surrender one's conscience to the state."[20]

In a printed sermon of two and one-half pages, Coffin used the word "conscience" twenty-one times.

In January 1968 the national governing board of the American Civil Liberties Union had voted that it would not give legal aid to those who counseled noncooperation with the draft. In April, because of grass roots pressures from the regional affiliates, the board reversed its former decision. It will now furnish aid to the accused in such cases.

On June 14, 1968 (by coincidence, it was Flag Day), Dr. Spock, the Reverend Mr. Coffin, and two others were convicted in Boston by an all male jury of being guilty in a conspiracy to defeat the operation of the draft. The cases are being appealed.

Never before in modern times has so much support been given to the right of conscientious objection to war. The Mennonites, Society of Friends, Church of the Brethren, the Amish, and related groups have always been concerned about their young men of draft age and have supported the right of these youth to be conscientious objectors. In fact, in several of these religious groups it is expected that their young men will not bear arms but accept some form of alternate service. In World War I the "C.O.'s" were almost universally scorned by the larger denominations but in World War II more often respected and helped. No longer were they a thorn in the flesh. The churches during the thirties, especially, had gone on record against war as "a colossal sin"; they could not go back on their young men who had taken those manifestos seriously. At the present time support comes from a variety of quarters. Several universities such as Yale and Chicago have announced that if any of their students go to jail rather than submit to the draft, they may come back and continue their studies after their sentence is served. As indicated above, Yale's chaplain, the Reverend William Sloane Coffin, Jr., has set an example of objection to the war, and, apparently, the administration of the University has upheld his right to object.

More than 9,300 faculty members from colleges and universities all over the country have signed a statement supporting the five who had been indicted by the government for advocating resistance to the draft. The statement reads in part:

> Technically, Dr. Spock and his four associates will be the defendants, but it is our government's Vietnam policy that will be on trial. . . . Strong support by the American people for the defendants' cause will make it clear that the opposition to the war will not be intimidated, that dissent cannot be suppressed.
>
> * * *
>
> As members of the academic community, and as private citizens, we believe that every American has both the right and the duty to protest this wasteful and illegal war that threatens every segment of our society. Active opposition to oppression or immoral acts of government is in the finest tradition of our Constitutional history.[21]

Legal opinion, as usual, is divided on the merits of the case. One of the professors in the Yale Law School. Joseph W. Bishop, Jr., who has been critical of Coffin's logic, has said, "I personally believe that Dr. Spock and the Reverend Mr. Coffin have not exceeded those freedoms which the First Amendment allows them."[22]

For the religious community the great symbol of the right to object to war is the age-old appeal to *conscience*. This duty to follow the dictates of one's own conscience has for many individuals an honored mystical appeal. Even the United States government has conceded that under certain circumstances, conscience stands supreme. Young men who are drafted who belong to religious groups that have a historic objection to war, such as the Mennonites, the Quakers, Church of the Brethren, and the Amish, may be exempt from the draft. They are privileged to elect alternate service, such as working in mental hospitals, medical corps, and the like.

However, in the last half of the twentieth century, the simple faiths of the past get entangled with new questions and philosophies. One of the questions is, "Does conscience object to all wars or merely to specific wars?" Also, though the larger churches and denominations have made no historic stands against war as have some of the sects, why is not the objection to war on the part of a Unitarian, a Congregationalist, or a Baptist just as valid? Why must one always believe in the teachings of the Bible (interpreted through the eyes of a pacifist) to be a genuine conscientious objector? An atheist who argued before a draft board or a judge that all wars are wrong on humanitarian grounds would not stand a chance of being seriously considered. However, his sincerity would be as deep as any other objector—the Mennonite or Amish lad.[22a]

If the religious folk would look at some of the facts of history, they would probably change their perspective with respect to the question, "What is conscience?" In the name of conscience, many of the worst crimes known to man have been committed, such as the religious wars, persecutions, burnings at the stake, the Salem witchcraft trials and hangings, and the outrages perpetrated by the Ku Klux Klan. Those who burned John Huss and Savonarola and Joan of Arc—they too were people of conscience. It is easy to say that they were wrong, but not so easy to say who is always right. Even our Supreme Court, with its five to four decisions, has its troubles trying to decide.

Abraham Lincoln suspended the writ of *habeas corpus* and was most inconsistent in his treatment of the opposition, all in the name of good conscience.

Senator Joseph McCarthy in 1954 "argued that a higher patriotism obligated government employees to disregard the law and turn over to him the loyalty and security files of other employees whom they thought subversive."[23] In the army hearings, McCarthy, under oath to tell the truth, the whole truth, and nothing but the truth, refused to answer certain questions put to him by the attorney, Mr. Welch, on the grounds that he had a higher loyalty to his informers.

In the opinion of Joseph W. Bishop, Jr.,

> Conscience is certainly a worse guide to conduct than the Constitution of the United States, it may even be worse than Congress. It is practically impossible to say that A, but not B, should have the right to be guided by his conscience and thus to practice civil disobedience whenever the conscience points in one direction and the law in the other.[24]

In the religious community it is generally assumed that loyalty to one's conscience, loyalty to one's religious beliefs, and loyalty to God are more or less one and the same. In the struggle between the church and the state, now of many centuries' duration, the question still persists, "Which is the highest loyalty?" Obviously, there can be no final answer because of the nature of the question. However, in wartime, the populace votes for loyalty to the state. To refuse draft service, save under conditions described above, is an insult to one's country and the flag. Jail sentences await certain types of objectors, draft card burners, and those who protest too vociferously.

The right of dissent in a democratic society is essential for its survival. Dissent in wartime appears to most people to be tantamount to sedition or treason. The power of nationalism is so great that the emotional tide sweeps away basic reason and common sense. If, as Alvin Johnson has pointed out, "the main forces making for war in the successive historical epochs consist in general conflict of interests, material or ideal, actual or traditional,"[25] it can scarcely be argued that patriotism is one hundred percent pure.

When, however, the state allows itself to be trapped in an unpopular war (one that it cannot sell to the people), there is trouble ahead. Its propaganda and techniques of persuasion (often to the point of desperation) fail to bring enthusiasm or unite the people sufficiently to suppress the dissenters or effectively carry on the role of leadership. In the United States at the present time, the leader of the Establishment, the President himself, thought it wise to announce his retirement from public life rather than risk further unpopularity and perhaps ruin his party's chances at the next election. To be able to bring about peace through negotiations rather than hope for a final victory by pouring more and more troops into Vietnam has seemed the wiser part of valor.

The glory of victory in a war becomes an obsession in the religion of nationalism. Eisenhower, the successful general, became a president of the United States. Many observers of the political scene think that he could have run on either ticket and won. By contrast, what chances would a known pacifist have (who had yielded to his conscience in wartime) to be elected to any major public office, such as mayor, governor, congressman, senator, or president? Our society is not geared to accept those who take the teachings of Jesus this seriously, at least they would not be trusted in public office. Hence, unless the religious community can change the current feeling about war objectors, or bring Jesus down to earth as a human being (not just a Savior and the Son of God in the clouds), there is no hope that pacifism or resistance to war has any chance of being anything in the social milieu but playing the role of a gadfly to the government. The personal satisfaction that may be derived from following one's conscience is another matter completely. After all, the state cannot deprive a person of the euphoria that may accompany his listening to and following the dictates of his own conscience—doing the right rather than the wrong.

It would seem that wars are going to be with us for some time to come. The vested interests in such are too powerful to dislodge at present. The military-industrial complex is an integral part of our society. The forces of "righteousness" as represented by the religious objectors, pacifists, and dissenters among the intellectuals, are dealing with powers that they may try to understand and expose, but with which it is most difficult to cope or defeat. Billions are at the disposal of the war machine. War is sociological phenomena that can no longer be rationally defended, yet it serves for millions as a means of ego gratification and an outlet for an emotional binge. There is little chance of deflating its glamour, its nobleness of purpose or objectives. The men out there giving their lives for us, the flag-draped coffins, the crosses row on row, the medals of honor, the purple hearts, the mighty war machines, the uniforms and military parades, the flags floating in the breeze—these are the symbols of nationalism. It is a religion and the failure to do obeisance, worship its gods, is the greatest of all heresies.

The Christian Science Monitor, in whose pages no one ever dies, except by inference (since Christian Scientists do not believe in evil, disease, or death), praises the valor of the men in Vietnam. They are not like those who protest at home, who march against the draft, "the collegian who burns his draft card," or the "young fellow who migrates to Canada to escape military service." This phenomenon does not mean "that the United States forces in Vietnam are anywise weak in morale or minus in guts." There follows a comment from one of the generals as to the splendid performance of our boys in Vietnam and praising their bravery and ability to stand up to hardship. An army chaplain is quoted as saying he had been "disgusted with the modern American teen-agehood." He thought they were "the lost generation, but they are redeeming themselves in Vietnam."[26]

One will accept all that is said about the bravery of our boys in Vietnam. Let us hope that they will not have died in vain. The concept and philosophy of *The Christian Science Monitor* and the chaplain are that the reputation of this generation of youth is being redeemed on the battlefields of Southeast Asia. The dissenters at home are not true Americans according to them.

Sections of organized religion in this country are again at the crossroads. For the Christians the question is, "Shall they continue to endorse the gods of nationalism and the kind of statecraft that continually thinks in terms of war as a national policy, or shall they reevaluate the whole business on different terms?" It is all related to the meaning of life itself. Is it the noblest thing one can do to give his life for his country? Nathan Hale thought so. He and millions of others have given their lives in many a righteous cause.

For nearly two thousand years Christians have idolized and worshiped a man who gave His life for what He regarded as a righteous cause. *The Man on the Cross* and all of its implications is the central theme in Christian thinking. The question rephrased is, "How can a Christian reconcile the life of Christ, the Man of Peace, and the meaning of His death on the cross, with an endorsement of or participation in a war?" Again, "What would Jesus do if He were here today?"

To change the topic completely, there is a subject rarely mentioned in religious circles, and that is the fascination with death that is deep in the unconscious of many people. The scientific literature abounds with studies and writings on the subject. It is quite clear that for millions of individuals (based on samples), the wish for death is a most powerful force in their own psyche. There is a certain tropism, an allurement, an inescapable compulsion, and enchantment with the mystery and state of death, particularly one that is tragic. Much of this, of course, is in the unconscious and has never been brought to the surface. The point here is that war provides these people with a legitimate gratification for this fascination. Every night for several years the TV sets have been bringing the battlefield right into our living rooms. We are there. Death on the field of battle or in the air becomes quite normal and relatively acceptable. Often the pictures for the average mortal are revolting—corpses treated as cordwood, lifted up in the air by bulldozers and thrown into a common trench, or piled high to be carried off by a helicopter to their last resting place. The dead and the dying are all around us, within a few feet, optical wise. For many there is a morbid pleasure in watching the performance. If there were enough complaints, the TV networks would discontinue such intimate pictures of death. War is not a game of ping-pong as we now know. Perhaps a part of the protest in this war stems from watching TV newscasts. For sensitive people this is difficult to take.

While pictures and news about the war provide a daily diet for those members of our society who are strongly motivated in the direction of death, our culture has provided dozens of other sources of satisfaction, such as plays, novels, and movies where horror and violence and death reign supreme. The detective stories usually wind up with a first-class murder. One of the best sellers recently was Capote's *In Cold Blood*.

Without delving into the psychiatric and psychoanalytic aspects of this psychological phenomenon, it is quite obvious that war does furnish much allurement and emotional gratification for large segments of the population. Condemned on the one hand, it is enjoyed on the other. Many people thoroughly enjoy fires, but they would condemn the arsonist if he were responsible for a particular conflagration. There seems to be a kind of schizophrenic pattern—life and death battling for ascendancy within the individual as well as on the battlefield. The assumption, "No one really wants a war," should be reevaluated.

The social phenomenon of violence in various forms that is taking place in so many societies is often allied to the love of violence just for the sake of violence and destruction. The veneer of "civilization" is thin indeed, as Freud pointed out in his *Civilization and Its Discontents*. Universities all over the world are experiencing riots as expressions of discontent, the like of which has never been known before on such a wide scale. Granted that complaints lodged against the administrations and faculties often have merit, the fact is that in the name of reconstructing the universities which the left have come to label as "immoral and stupid" the "hell-raisers" take advantage of the mood of discontent, exploit the situation, and move in to take over. The chain reaction of hysteria and violence is out of all proportion to the nature of the complaints. This is evident in the Japanese universities, the Sorbonne, Columbia, Berkeley, and dozens of others.

War, perhaps the greatest form of violence man has ever witnessed that is created by himself, furnishes a perfectly acceptable and socially approved pattern of activity for acting out aggression. The more of the enemy killed, the better. Exterminate him and the war is over. Those who remain at home may live with their fantasies and/or watch television. This is not to suggest that all men in the service are thus motivated. It is only to point out that, *if* an individual possesses a personality pattern characterized by a sadistic desire to inflict punishment and suffering or is bent on destroying things or people, a uniform may be of considerable help and fortification.

Almost one hundred and fifty years ago, Alexis de Tocqueville wrote in *Democracy in America* that democratic nations were developing deterrents to war. However, as Jules Henry has recently pointed out,

> American industry expands and unemployment declines in the presence of war atmosphere, the usual economic and emotional deterrents to war do not exist for us. Thus since *fear of war is anesthetized by heightened economic well-being, we become accustomed to living comfortable under conditions of impending annihilation.* That is why the decision to go to war or to the "brink" can be accepted much more readily than if the economy were placed in jeopardy by war. . . . The fact that war-*fear* is partly narcotized by consumption-*euphoria* habituates us to living with the Great Fear. (Italics are the author's.)[27]

From what has been said about the myriads of forces and motivations in war, the road to peace on a permanent basis would seem to be both lonesome and long.

It was Pareto, the Italian sociologist, who pointed out that while we erect monuments to the dead or dying soldier, we do not build monuments depicting our soldiers engaged in the act of killing the enemy outright—plunging the bayonet into his vitals. We would cringe in the presence of such realism. We romanticize the dead soldier who gave his life for his country; inscriptions for the unknown soldiers who "died for God, for king and country" or similar epitaphs abound. Yet this is not what the soldier was trained to do—not to die but to kill as many of the enemy as possible and remain alive in the meantime. We train men to be great killers. If all the men laid down their lives on the battlefield, there could scarcely be a victory. Yet the "passive" qualities of the warrior are thus emphasized and cherished. Here again is the ambivalence which war creates. It is hated and glorified at the same time.

NOTES AND REFERENCES

NOTES AND REFERENCES

Explanation of Symbols

C.L. refers to bound volumes of news clippings, letters, et cetera, of the American Civil Liberties Union now available at the Public Library, New York City.

CHAPTER I

THE CHURCHES OF AMERICA IN THE REVOLUTION, THE CIVIL, AND SPANISH-AMERICAN WARS

[1] Van Tyne, C. H., *The Cause of the War for Independence*, Chp. XIII.
[2] Baldwin, A. M., *The New England Clergy and the American Revolution*, Chps. VI, VII, VIII.
[3] *Ibid.*, p. 171.
[4] Sweet, W. W., *The Story of Religions in America*, p. 256.
[5] Baldwin, *op. cit.*, p. 164.
[6] *Ibid.*, p. 164.
[7] Humphrey, E. F., *Nationalism and Religion*, pp. 82-104.
[8] Sparks, Jared (Ed.), *The Writings of George Washington*, Vol. XII, pp. 154-55.
[9] Humphrey, *op. cit.*, pp. 114-116.
[10] O'Gorman, Thomas, *A History of the Catholic Church in the United States*, 3d Edition, 1895. Pub. 1900, pp. 255-256; Shea, J. G., *Life and Times of Archbishop Carroll*.
[11] Sweet, *op. cit.*, pp. 269-271. Sharpless, Isaac, *A History of Quaker Government in Pennsylvania*, Vol. II, p. 94.
[12] Sweet, *op. cit.*, pp. 272-273.
[13] *Ibid.*, p. 256
[14] Wesley, John, *Works*, American Edition, Vol. VI, pp. 300-321; Humphrey, *op. cit.*, p. 173.
[15] McPherson, Ed., *The Political History of the United States of America During the Great Rebellion*, Appendix, "The Church and the Rebellion," pp. 461-554. Edition, 1882.
[16] Sweet, *op. cit.*, p. 449.
[17] Nicolay, J. G. and Hay, John, *Abraham Lincoln, A History*, Vol. VI, p. 324.
[18] McPherson, *op. cit.*, p. 514.
[19] *Ibid.*, p. 514.
[20] Sweet, *op. cit.*, pp. 454-455.
[21] McPherson, *op. cit.*, p. 519.
[22] *Ibid.*, p. 521.
[23] Sweet, *op. cit.*, p. 465.
[24] McPherson, *op. cit.*, p. 521.
[25] Sweet, *op. cit.*, p. 462.
[26] Nicolay and Hay, *op. cit.*, p. 337.
[27] Rudd and Carleton, *Fast Day Sermons*, pp. 152, 139.
[28] *Ibid.*, pp. 299, 308.
[29] Stanton, R. L., *The Church and the Rebellion*, pp. 569, 559, 561.
[30] McPherson, *op. cit.*, p. 514.
[31] Sweet, *op. cit.*, p. 466.
[32] *Ibid.*, p. 466.
[33] Sweet, W. W., *The Methodist Episcopal Church in the Civil War*, pp. 154-159.
[34] Van Dyke, Henry, *The Cross of War*. (Pamphlet.)
[35] *The Presbyterian*, Vol. LXVIII, No. 27 (June 29, 1898), pp. 8-10.
[36] Quoted in, Allen, Devere, *The Fight for Peace*, p. 39.
[37] *The New Republic*, Vol. XI, No. 141 (July 14, 1917), p. 297.
[38] Allen, *op. cit.*, pp. 482-483.

⁸⁹ Lynch, Frederick, *Personal Recollections of Andrew Carnegie*, p. 156.
⁴⁰ *The Christian Century Pulpit*, Vol. II, No. 11 (Nov., 1931), p. 2.
⁴¹ Macfarland, C. S., *The Churches of Christ in America and International Peace*. (Pamphlet.)
⁴² *Ibid*.
⁴³ Report of the 18th Annual Lake Mohonk Conference in International Arbitration, 1912, p. 197.
⁴⁴ For a summary of the peace activities just prior to the World War vid. Charles and Mary Beard, *The Rise of American Civilization*, pp. 532-537; 612-615.
⁴⁵ Lynch, Frederick, *The Peace Problem*, pp. 30, 96.
⁴⁶ *Ibid.*, pp. 60-61.
⁴⁷ Lynch, Frederick, *Through Europe on the Eve of War*, passim.
⁴⁸ *The Advocate of Peace*, Vol. LXXVI, No. 7 (July, 1914), p. 152.
⁴⁹ *Ibid.*, Vol. LXXVI, No. 9 (Sept., 1914), p. 207.

CHAPTER II

Europe Starts a War and America Prepares

¹ Russell, B., in *These Eventful Years*, Vol. I, p. 380.
² Grattan, C. H., *Why We Fought*, p. 44.
³ *Harper's Magazine*, Vol. CXXXVI, No. DCCCXIV (March, 1918), pp. 521-531.
⁴ Willis, Irene, *England's Holy War*, Chp. 3.
⁵ *Ibid.*, p. 87.
⁶ *Ibid.*, p. 88.
⁷ *The New Republic Book*, p. 36.
⁸ Brewing, etc., Vol. II, p. 1913.
⁹ Hayes, C. J. H., *Brief History of the Great War*, Macmillan, N. Y., 1928, p. 208. Quoted by permission of the publishers.
¹⁰ Lasswell, H., *Propaganda Technique in the World War*, p. 199.
¹¹ Viereck, G. S., *Spreading Germs of Hate*, p. 118. For story of German propaganda in the United States vid. Part II.
¹² Bernstorff, J. von, *My Three Years in America*, p. 15.
¹³ Czernin, O., *In the World War*, p. 79.
¹⁴ Kaiser's *Memoirs*, p. 332.
¹⁵ Viereck, *op. cit.*, p. 114.
¹⁶ For full discussion of this paragraph, vid. Grattan, C. H., *Why We Fought*, Chp. XII; and Barnes, H. E., *The Genesis of the World War*, Chp. IX.
¹⁷ Dunn, *American Foreign Investments*, p. 4; and Barnes, H. E., *World Politics in Modern Civilization*, p. 360.
¹⁸ Grattan, *op. cit.*, pp. 159-160.
¹⁹ *Ibid.*, pp. 160-161.
²⁰ *The New Republic*, Vol. XI, No. 143 (July 28, 1917), p. 358.
²¹ *New York Times*, Sept. 20, 1914.
²² *Ibid.*, Aug. 21, 1914.
²³ *Ibid.*, Oct. 5, 1914.
²⁴ *Ibid.*, Oct. 5, 1914.
²⁵ *Ibid.*, Dec. 28, 1914.
²⁶ *Ibid.*, Oct. 12, 1914
²⁷ *Ibid.*, Oct. 5, 1914.
²⁸ *Ibid.*, Nov. 20, 1914
²⁹ Nelson, Arthur, in *The Progressive*, Vol. XI, No. 8 (June, 1928), p. 6.
³⁰ *New York Times*, Dec. 2, 1914.
³¹ Grattan, *op. cit.*, pp. 117-118.
³² Hapgood, Norman, *Professional Patriots*, pp. 21-23.
³³ Nelson, *op. cit.*, p. 8.
³⁴ *New York Times*, June 10, 15, 1915.
³⁵ *Ibid.*, Dec. 2, 1915.
³⁶ *Ibid.*, Dec. 28, 1915.
³⁷ *Ibid.*, Dec. 19, 1915.
³⁸ *Ibid.*, Oct. 4, Dec. 3, 1914.
³⁹ *Ibid.*, March 7, 1915.
⁴⁰ *Ibid.*, March 2, 1915.
⁴¹ *Ibid.*, March 7, 1915.
⁴² *Ibid.*, April 26, 1915.
⁴³ *Ibid.*, May 31, 1915.
⁴⁴ *Sixty American Opinions on the War*. p. 120.
⁴⁵ *Ibid.*, p. 148.

46 New York *Times*, May 10, 1915.
47 Lawrence, D., *True Story of Woodrow Wilson*, pp. 197-198.
48 New York *Times*, Nov. 13, 1916.
49 *Ibid.*, May 10, 1915.
50 *Ibid.*, May 11, 1915.
51 *Ibid.*, June 7, 1915.
52 Sneath, E. H. (Ed.), *Religion and the War*, pp. 82-83.
53 *The Independent*, Vol. LXXXIV, No. 3487 (Oct. 4, 1915), p. 1.
54 New York *Times*, Oct. 18, 1915.
55 *Ibid.*, Nov. 26, 1915.
56 *The Advocate of Peace*, Vol. LXXVIII, No. 4 (April, 1916), p. 116.
57 New York *Times*, April 28, 1916.
58 *Ibid.*, Jan. 26, 1916.
59 Cleveland *Leader*, Feb. 21, 1916.
60 New York *Times*, April 3, 1916.
61 *Ibid.*, Jan. 22, 1916.
62 *Ibid.*, Jan. 9, 1916.
63 *Ibid.*, May 4, 1916.
64 *Ibid.*, May 8, 1916.
65 *Ibid.*, Jan. 24, 1916.
66 Broughton, L. G., *Is Preparedness for War Unchristian?* p. 169.
67 *The Advocate of Peace*, Vol. LXXVIII, No. 5 (May, 1916), p. 137.
68 New York *Times*, Jan. 9, 1916.
69 Grattan, *op. cit.*, p. 63.
70 New York *Times*, Feb. 6, 1916.
71 Tumulty, J. P., *Woodrow Wilson as I Know Him*, p. 247.
72 New York *Times*, March 8, 1916.
73 *Ibid.*, May 14, 1916.
74 *Ibid.*, May 15, 1916.
75 *Ibid.*, May 15, 1916.
76 *Ibid.*, May 16, 1916.
77 Manning, W. T., *The Present Crisis in the Nation's Life.* (Pamphlet.)
78 *The Advocate of Peace*, Vol. LXXVIII, No. 11 (Nov., 1916), p. 287.
79 Viereck, G. S., *op. cit.*, p. 241.
80 New York *Times*, Oct 31, 1916.
81 *Ibid.*, Oct. 19, 1916.
82 Viereck, G. S., *op. cit.*, pp. 249-254.
83 Hibben and Grattan, *The Peerless Leader: William Jennings Bryan*, pp. 353-354.

84 New York *Times*, Nov. 9, 13, 19, 1916.
85 *Ibid.*, Dec. 19, 1916.
86 Passelecq, F., *Déportation et travail forcé des ouvriers et de la population civile de la Belgique occupée*, pp. 293-297.
87 Grattan, *op. cit.*, pp. 387-388.
88 Hendrick, B. J., *The Life and Letters of Walter Hines Page*, Vol. II, p. 207.
89 *The Churchman*, Vol. CXV, No. 2 (Jan. 13, 1917), p. 37.
90 *The Independent*, Vol. LXXXIX, No. 3544 (Jan. 15, 1917), p. 92.
91 New York *Times*, Jan. 27, 1917.
92 *Christian Work*, Vol. CII, No. 4 (Jan. 27, 1917), p. 102.
93 *Unity*, Vol. 78, No. 22 (Feb. 1, 1917), p. 143.
94 New York *Times*, Jan. 22, 1917.
95 *The New Republic*, Vol. X, No. 12 (Feb. 17, 1917), p. 82.
96 McKim, R. H., *For God and Country*, p. 9. (Pamphlet.)
97 *Ibid.*, p. 21.
98 McKim, R. H., *America's Stewardship*, p. 12. (Pamphlet.)
99 New York *Times*, Feb. 4, 1917.
100 *Ibid.*, Feb. 5, 6, 1917.
101 *Ibid.*, Feb. 5, 1917.
102 *Ibid.*, Feb. 4, 1917.
103 Lusk Report, Vol. I, p. 998.
104 *Unity*, Vol. 78, No. 25 (Feb. 22, 1917), p. 462.
105 *The Advocate of Peace*, Vol. LXXXIX, No. 4 (April, 1917), p. 116.
106 New York *Times*, April 3, 1917.
107 *Ibid.*, March 26, 1917.
108 Boston *Herald*, Feb. 26, 1917.
109 Pinkham, H. W., *Was Jesus a Pacifist?* (Pamphlet.)
110 Boston *Herald*, Feb. 19, 1917.
111 *The Literary Digest*, Vol. 54, No. 12 (March 24, 1917), pp. 820-821.
112 *The Congregationalist*, Vol. CII, No. 11 (March 15, 1917), p. 338.
113 Boston *Transcript*, March 5, 1917.
114 New York *Times*, April 2, 1917.
115 *The Literary Digest*, Vol. 54, No.

12 (March 24, 1917), p. 821; *The Christian Century*, Vol. XXXIV, No. 5 (Feb. 1, 1917), p. 17.
[116] *New York Times*, April 6, 1917.
[117] Brooklyn *Eagle*, March 19, 1917.
[118] *New York Times*, April 23, 1917.
[119] Hankins, Frank, *Introduction to the Study of Society*, p. 371.

CHAPTER III

The Holy War

[1] Springfield (Mass.) *Times*, April 15, 1917.
[2] *The Lutheran*, Vol. 21, No. 28 (April 12, 1917), p. 2.
[3] Indianapolis *Star*, May 7, 1917.
[4] *Deseret Evening News*, April 2, 1917.
[5] *Ibid.*, April 2, 1917.
[6] *Ibid.*, April 2, 1917.
[7] *Ibid.*, April 16, 1917.
[8] *Ibid.*, May 14, 1917.
[9] *Ibid.*, April 9, 1917
[10] *Ibid.*, April 9, 1917.
[11] Benda, Julian, *The Treason of the Intellectuals*, Chps. II, III.
[12] *The New Republic*, Vol. X, No. 27 (April 7, 1917), p. 279.
[13] Bourne, Randolph, "Twilight of Idols" in *Untimely Papers*.
[14] Bourne, Randolph, *Untimely Papers*, pp. 22-23.
[15] Creel, George, *How We Advertised America, passim*.
A few of the better known professors were: Historians—William Roscoe Thayer, James T. Shotwell, Albert Bushnell Hart, Robert McElroy, Charles D. Hazen, Carl L. Becker. Economists—E. R. A. Seligman, Henry W. Farnum. Sociologists—Franklin D. Giddings, Albion W. Small. Philosophers—John Dewey, Josiah Royce, Arthur O. Lovejoy, Richard C. Cabot.
Vid. Angoff, Charles, "The Higher Learning Goes to War," *The American Mercury*, Vol. XI, No. 42 (June, 1917), pp. 177-191; Grattan, C. H., "The Historians Cut Loose," *The American Mercury*, Vol. XI, No. 44 (August, 1927), pp. 414-430.
[16] *The Advocate of Peace*, Vol. LXXXI, No. 1 (Jan., 1918), pp. 14-18.
[17] *New York Times*, Oct. 22, 29, 1917.
[18] Lynch, Frederick, *The Church and the New World Order*, p. 74.
[19] *Christian Work*, Vol. 105, No. 8 (Aug. 24, 1918), p. 214.
[20] *New York Times*, March 4, 1918.
[21] *Christian Work*, Vol. 105, No. 10 (Sept. 7, 1918), p. 271.
[22] *Vid.* *The Commoner*, Aug., Sept., Oct., 1917; *Sante Fe Magazine*, Dec., 1917; National Security League, *Patriotism Through Education Series*, No. 26 (Nov. 1, 1917).
[23] McKim, R. H., *For God and Country*, pp. 116-117.
[24] Barton, W. E., *The Heritage of Humanity*. (Pamphlet.)
[25] Lasswell, H. D., *Propaganda Technique in the World War*, p. 73.
[26] *Christian Work*, Vol. 102, No. 20 (May 19, 1917), p. 616; Newton, J. F., *The Sword of the Spirit*, p. 15.
[27] *The Biblical World*, Vol. L, No. 6 (Dec., 1917), p. 351.
[28] Quoted in, Allen, Devere, *The Fight for Peace*, p. 40.
[29] *The Congregationalist*, Vol. CIII, No. 14 (April 4, 1918), p. 418.
[30] Meyers, W. B., *America at War*. (Pamphlet.)
[31] *New York Times*, May 13, 1917.
[32] *Federal Council Bulletin*, Vol. 1, No. 3 (March, 1918), p. 12.
[33] Squiers, A. L. (Ed.), *One Hundred Per Cent American*, p. 156.
[34] Lansing, I. J., *Why Christianity Did Not Prevent the War*, pp. 242-243.
[35] Bell, B. I., *What Has God to Do with War?* (Pamphlet.)
[36] Hughes, E. H., *The Preacher and the War*. (Pamphlet.)

37 Wilson, Luther, *America — Here and Over There*, pp. 44; 35-36.
38 Stires, E. M., *The Price of Peace*, pp. 4, 7, 9.
39 *Ibid.*, p. 172.
40 *New York Times*, July 22, 1915.
41 Rihbany, A. M., *Militant America and Jesus Christ*, pp. 8-9.
42 Stidger, W., *Soldier Silhouettes*, pp. 111, 50.
43 Kelman, J., *The War and Preaching*, p. 89.
44 Plater, Charles (Ed.), *Catholic Soldiers*, pp. 9, 11.
45 *The Watchman-Examiner*, Vol. 6, No. 47 (Nov. 21, 1918), p. 1434.
46 American Tract Society, *Manual of Devotion for Soldiers and Sailors*, pp. 8-9; 94; 95; 97; 101-102.
47 Fosdick, H. E., *The Challenge of the Present Crisis*, p. 26.
48 *Ibid.*, p. 27.
49 *The Biblical World*, Vol. LIII, No. 5 (Sept., 1919), pp. 453, 456.
50 King, H. C., *The Way to Life*, Macmillan, N. Y., 1918, p. 128. Quoted by permission of the publishers.
51 *Christian Work*, Vol. 103, No. 26 (Dec. 29, 1917), p. 807.
52 Pell, E. L., *What Did Jesus Really Teach About War?* pp. 99, 47, 50, 78.
53 *Ibid.*, p. 54.
54 Rihbany, *op. cit.*, p. 64.
55 *Ibid.*, p. 66.
56 *New York Times*, May 13, 1917.
57 Rihbany, *op. cit.*, p. 35.
58 Hough, L. H., *The Clean Sword*, p. 12.
59 *Ibid.*, pp. 128-129.
60 Wright, H. B., in *The American Magazine*, Vol. LXXXV, No. 2 (Feb., 1918), p. 56.
61 Mackenzie, W. D., *Christian Ethics in the World War*, pp. 187, 189.
62 *The Biblical World*, Vol. LI, No. 3 (March, 1918), pp. 137, 138.

63 *The Congregationalist*, Vol. CII, No. 39 (Sept. 27, 1917), p. 390.
64 *Unity*, Vol. 93, No. 20 (Aug. 7, 1924), p. 322.
65 Bosworth, E. I., *The Christian Witness in War*, pp. 8-9; 9-10.
66 Quoted in, Thomas, Norman, *The Conscientious Objector in America*, p. 272.
67 Pittsburgh *Gazette Times*, Nov. 12, 1917.
68 Boston *Herald*, Oct. 22, 1917.
69 *The Christian Register*, Vol. 97, No. 33 (Aug. 15, 1918), p. 775.
70 *The Advocate of Peace*, Vol. LXXIX, No. 5 (May, 1917), p. 138.
71 Kelman, *op. cit.*, p. 55.
72 Poling, Dan, *Huts in Hell*, p. 159.
73 *The Biblical World*, Vol. LII, No. 2 (Sept., 1918), p. 162.
74 Stewart and Wright, *The Practice of Friendship*, p. 13.
75 *Ibid.*, pp. 22-24.
76 *The Churchman*, Vol. CXVI, No. 7 (Aug. 18, 1917), p. 198.
77 *Ibid.*, Vol. CXVI, No. 13 (Sept. 29, 1917), p. 299.
78 Naumann, F., *Briefe über Religion* (Fifth Edition), 1910, pp. 69, 71, 72, 86.
79 *The Biblical World*, Vol. LIII, No. 5 (Sept., 1919), p. 454.
80 Pentecost, G. F., *Fighting for Faith*. pp. 42-43; 77, 103, 52, 72,
81 *The Lutheran*, Vol. 21, No. 27 (April 5, 1917), p. 12.
82 Wagner, J. F., *War Addresses*, p. 11.
83 *Ibid.*, p. 27.
84 *New York Times*, May 14, 1917.
85 *Ibid.*, Nov. 30, 1917.
86 Mackenzie, *op. cit.*, pp. 48-49.
87 Dennett, Tyler, *A Better World*, p. 99.
88 *Religious Education*, Vol. XIII, No. 2 (April, 1918), p. 140.

CHAPTER IV

The Church as Servant of the State

1 Lasswell, H. D., *Propaganda Technique in the World War*, p. 74.
2 Federal Council, *War-Time Agencies of the Churches*, p. 152.
3 Macfarland, C. S., *The Progress of Church Federation*, p. 170.
4 Federal Council, *op. cit.*, p. 153.
5 *Ibid.*, pp. 149-176.
6 Brown, W. A., *The Allies of Faith*. (Pamphlet.)
7 Federal Council, *op. cit.*, pp. 154-155.
8 *Ibid.*, pp. 277-337.
9 *Handbook of the National Catholic War Council*, p. 8.
10 Federal Council, *op. cit.*, pp. 50-52.
11 Tippy, W. M., *The Church and the Great War*, p. 22.
12 Boston *Transcript*, April 2, 1917.
13 New York *Times*, April 16, 1917.
14 Stone, J. T., *That Friday Night: An Easter Incident*. (Pamphlet.)
15 *The World Tomorrow*, Vol. I, No. 2 (Feb., 1918), p. 43.
16 Liberty Loan Committee, Second Federal Reserve District, "Material for Clergy in Third Liberty Loan."
17 New York *Times*, April 4, 1917.
18 *The Biblical World*, Vol. LII, No. 1 (July, 1918), p. 13.
19 First and Second Liberty Loan Pamphlets for the Clergy.
20 *Unity*, Vol. 79, No. 15 (June 7, 1917), p. 229.
21 Laidlaw, Walter, *The Moral Aims of the War*, pp. 14-15.
22 *Ibid.*, p. 95.
23 This and all quotations immediately following are taken from the official pamphlet issued by the Third Liberty Loan Committee, Second Federal Reserve District, "Material which may be helpful to clergymen in promoting the Third Liberty Loan."
24 *Federal Council Bulletin*, Vol. I, No. 9 (Oct., 1918), p. 2.
25 *The Christian Advocate*, Vol. XCIII, No. 14 (April 4, 1918), p. 423.
26 *Utah's Loyalty and War Record* (pamphlet); *Deseret Evening News*, Oct. 7, 1918.
27 *Christian Work*, Vol. 105, No. 15 (Oct. 12, 1918), p. 447.
28 Philadelphia *Public Ledger*, Oct. 13, 1918.
29 U. S. Food Commission, "Bulletin for the Clergy," Religious Press Section, Vol. I, No. 2, Jan., 1918.
30 Federal Council, *op. cit.*, p. 13.
31 U. S. Food Commission, *op. cit.*
32 *Unity*, Vol. 81, No. 9 (May 2, 1918), p. 144.
33 Tippy, *op. cit.*, Appendix II.
34 Committee on Public Information, *National Service Handbook*, July 30, 1917, pp. 47, 49.
35 Letter George Creel to the author.
36 *Federal Council Bulletin*, Vol. I, No. 3 (Mar., 1918), p. 12.
37 Federal Council, *op. cit.*, pp. 194, 196.
38 *Ibid.*, p. 197.
39 *Federal Council Bulletin*, Vol. I, No. 6 (June, 1918), pp. 13-14.
40 *Ibid.*, p. 7.
41 *Ibid.*, Vol. I, No. 3 (Mar., 1918), p. 12.
42 Federal Council, *A War-Time Program for Country Churches*, p. 7, (pamphlet).
43 *Federal Council Bulletin*, Vol. I, No. 1 (Jan., 1918), p. 6.
44 Federal Council, *op. cit.*, p. 322.
45 *Unity*, Vol. 80, No. 11 (Nov. 15, 1917), p. 175.
46 *The Churchman*, Vol. CXVI, No. 23 (Dec. 8, 1917), p. 729.
47 *Federal Council Bulletin*, Vol. I, No. 1 (Jan., 1918), pp. 12-13.
48 *Ibid.*, Vol. I, No. 6 (June, 1918), p. 16.

CHAPTER V

THE CHURCHES CONTRIBUTE TO WAR-TIME HYSTERIA

1 *Vid.* Ponsonby, A., *Falsehood in War Time;* Allen, W. C., *War! Behind the Smoke Screen;* Viereck, G. S., *Spreading Germs of Hate.*
2 *New York Times,* Oct. 5, 1914.
3 Hillis, N. D., *Studies of the Great War, passim.*
4 *New York Times,* Dec. 22, 1914.
5 *Ibid.,* Dec. 28, 1914; Jan. 29, 30, 31, 1915.
6 *Ibid.,* Sept. 20, 1915; Jan. 27, 1916; Aug. 2, 1918.
7 *Current Opinion,* Vol. 59, No. 5 (Nov., 1915), pp. 335-336.
8 *Brooklyn Eagle,* Mar. 26, 1917.
9 *Ibid.,* Feb. 19, 1917.
10 *New York Times,* April 25, 1917.
11 *Ibid.,* May 22, 1917; June 13, 1917.
12 *Ibid.,* July 7, 1917.
13 Ms. from a witness in possession of the author; Cf. Hillis, N. D., *German Atrocities,* pp. 32-34.
14 Hillis, N. D., *German Atrocities,* p. 56.
15 *Ibid.,* p. 16.
16 *New York Times,* Oct. 15, 1917.
17 *Ibid.,* Dec. 24, 1917.
18 *The Churchman,* Vol. CXVII, No. 2 (Jan. 12, 1918), p. 44.
19 *The Christian Century,* Vol., XXXIV, No. 39 (Sept. 27, 1917), p. 6; No. 43 (Oct. 25, 1917), pp. 16-17.
20 *Christian Work,* Vol. 104, No. 4 (January 26, 1918), p. 20.
21 *Ibid.,* Vol. 103, No. 13 (Sept. 29, 1917), p. 369.
22 *The Literary Digest,* Vol. 59, No. 3 (Oct. 19, 1918), p. 28.
23 Squiers, A. L. (Ed.), *One Hundred Per Cent American,* p. 159.
24 *The Biblical World,* Vol. LIII, No. 5 (Sept., 1919), p. 453.
25 *New York Tribune,* June 11, 1918.
26 Quoted from Chicago *Herald Examiner* in *Unity,* Vol. 81, No. 25 (Aug. 22, 1918), p. 390.
27 *Ibid.; The Nation,* Vol. 107, No. 2769 (July 20, 1918), p. 55.
28 Grattan, C. H., "The Historians Cut Loose," *The American Mercury,* Vol. XI, No. 44 (Aug., 1927), pp. 415-430.
29 Sneath, E. L. (Ed.), *Religion and the War,* p. 185.
30 Thompson, W. O., *The Church After the War,* "Introduction" by W. F. Anderson.
31 Laidlaw, Walter, *The Moral Aims of the War,* p. 62.
32 *The Biblical World,* Vol. LII, No. 1 (July, 1918), pp. 58-65.
33 *The Independent,* Vol. 91, No. 3588 (Sept. 8, 1917), p. 373.
34 *Ibid.,* Vol. 91, No. 3589 (Sept. 15, 1917), p. 407.
35 *Ibid.,* Vol. 92, No. 3598 (Nov. 17, 1917), p. 350.
36 *The Literary Digest,* Vol. 59, No. 3 (Oct. 19, 1918), p. 28.
37 Quoted in Hicks, Granville, "The Parsons and the War," *The American Mercury,* Vol. 10, No. 38 (Feb., 1927), p. 137.
38 *The Congregationalist,* Vol. CIII, No. 50 (Dec. 12, 1918), p. 658.
39 Hicks, *op. cit.,* p. 139.
40 Maurer, J. M., in Davis, Jerome, *Labor Speaks for Itself on Religion,* Macmillan, N. Y., 1929, pp. 31-32. Quoted by permission of the publishers.
41 *Zion's Herald,* Vol. XCV, No. 26 (June 27, 1917), p. 807.
42 Van Dyke, Henry, *Fighting for Peace,* pp. 105-106.
43 Peabody, F. G., in *The Soul of America in Time of War,* p. 7.
44 *Brooklyn Eagle,* Dec. 3, 1917.
45 *New York Times,* Feb. 19, 1918.
46 War Committee, Chapel of the Comforter, N. Y. C., "War Paper No. 4," (Sept. 1, 1918).
47 *The Biblical World,* Vol. LII, No. 2 (Sept., 1918), p. 187.
48 *The Forum,* Vol. 60, No. 4 (Oct., 1918), p. 471.
49 *New York Times,* April 8, 1918.

50 *The Literary Digest*, Vol. 59, No. 9 (Nov. 30, 1918), p. 30.
51 *The Congregationalist*, Vol. CII, No. 34 (Aug. 23, 1917), p. 231.
52 Boston *Transcript*, May 7, 1917.
53 New York *Times*, Oct. 1, 1917.
54 *Ibid.*, April 1, 1918.
55 *The Nation*, Vol. 107, No. 2776 (Sept. 14, 1918), p. 294.
56 Philadelphia *Public Ledger*, Mar. 17, 1918.
57 Hillis, N. D., *The Blot on the Kaiser's Scutcheon*, pp. 57-59.
58 *The Congregationalist*, Vol. CIII, No. 33 (Aug. 15, 1918), p. 178.
59 *Ibid.*, Vol. CIII, No. 35 (Aug. 29, 1918), p. 227.
60 *The Outlook*, Vol. 119, No. 3 (May 15, 1918), p. 99.
61 New York *Times*, Feb. 23, 1918.
62 Speer, Robert, *The Christian Man, The Church, and the War*.
63 New York *Times*, Feb. 23, 1918.
64 *Ibid.*, Feb. 27, 1918.
65 *Ibid.*, Mar. 7, 1918.
66 *The Congregationalist*, Vol. CIII, No. 10 (Mar. 7, 1918), pp. 293-294.
67 *The Watchman-Examiner*, Vol. 6, No. 22 (May 30, 1918), p. 690.
68 New York *Times*, Feb. 24, 1918.
69 *Ibid.*, Feb. 26, 1918.
70 *Ibid.*, Feb. 26, 1918.
71 *The Advocate of Peace*, Vol. LXXX, No. 3 (Mar., 1918), p. 89.
72 New York *Times*, May 4, 1917, Feb. 19, 1918.
73 *The Watchman-Examiner*, Vol. 6, No. 16 (April 18, 1918), p. 503.
74 New York *Times*, Jan. 7, 1918.
75 Manners, J. H., *Hate with a Will to Victory*, pp. 54, 59.
76 New York *Tribune*, Feb. 14, 1918.
77 *The Atlantic Monthly*, Vol. CXXII, (Oct., 1918), p. 464.
78 *Ibid.*, Vol. CXXII (Dec., 1918), (Contributor's Column).
79 War Committee: Chapel of the Comforter, *op. cit.*, p. 37.
80 *The Nation*, Vol. 107, No. 2791 (Dec. 28, 1918), p. 803.
81 *The Literary Digest*, Vol. 58, No. 9 (Aug. 31, 1918), p. 32.

82 *The Outlook*, Vol. 118, No. 5 (Jan. 30, 1918), p. 180.
83 *The Presbyterian*, Vol. 88, No. 31 (Aug. 1, 1918), p. 10.
84 Jones, D. H., *German Culture and American Christianity*. (Pamphlet.)
85 Lansing, I. J., *Why Christianity Did Not Prevent the War*, p. 153.
86 *Zion's Herald*, Vol. XCV, No. 36 (Sept. 5, 1917), p. 1126.
87 *The Biblical World*, Vol. LI, No. 5 (May, 1918), p. 257.
88 Squiers, *op. cit.*, p. 226.
89 Boston *Herald*, Jan. 14, 1918.
90 *The Nation*, Vol. 107, No. 2791 (Dec. 28, 1918), p. 803.
91 Viereck, G. S., *Spreading Germs of Hate*, pp. 188-189.
92 *The New Republic*, Vol. 14, No. 174 (Mar. 2, 1918), p. 146.
93 American Defense Society. (Pamphlet.)
94 Philadelphia *Public Ledger*, Mar. 17, 1918.
95 New York *Times*, April 1, 1918.
96 *Ibid.*, Mar. 16, 1918.
97 *Ibid.*, Mar. 20, 1918.
98 *Ibid.*, May 21, 1918.
99 Merrill, W. P., *War Time Hymns*.
100 New York *Times*, Mar. 14, 1918.
101 *Ibid.*, Mar. 13, 1918.
102 *Ibid.*, Nov. 27, 1917.
103 *Ibid.*, Nov. 27, 1918.
104 *The New Republic*, Vol. 13, No. 169 (Jan. 26, 1918), p. 380.
105 New York *Times*, Nov. 27, 1917.
106 New York *Times*, Nov. 22, 1918; Second Report of the Provost Marshal General up to Dec 20, 1918, p. 200 ff.
107 New York *Times*, Nov. 22, 1918.
108 United States *Bulletin*, Dec. 19, 1918.
109 New York *Tribune*, July 22, 1918.
110 Philadelphia *Public Ledger*, Mar. 17, 1918.
111 Baltimore *Sun*, Mar. 16, 1918, Philadelphia *Public Ledger*, Mar. 16, 1918.
112 New York *Times*, Mar. 12, 1918.
113 *Ibid.*, Feb. 14, 1918.
114 *Ibid.*, May 17, 1918.

115 Brooklyn *Eagle*, Nov. 26, 1917.
116 *The New Republic*, Vol. 13, No. 164 (Dec. 22, 1917), pp. 213-214.
117 Beard, Chas. and Mary, *The Rise of American Civilization*, Macmillan, N. Y., 1930, p. 643. Quoted by permission of the publishers.
118 *The Atlantic Monthly*, Vol. CXXI, (April, 1918), pp. 521-525.
119 *The Outlook*, Vol. 118, No. 8 (Feb. 20, 1918), pp. 280-281.
120 *The Congregationalist*, Vol. CIII, No. 6 (Feb. 7, 1918), p. 167.
121 *Ibid.*, Vol. CIII, No. 9 (Feb. 28, 1918), p. 263.
122 Squiers, *op. cit.*, p. 154.
123 *The Christian Register*, Vol. 97, No. 31 (Aug. 1, 1918), p. 727.

CHAPTER VI

The Churches Interpret the First Amendment

1 Lowell, A. L., *Public Opinion in War and Peace*, p. 222.
2 Macfarland, C. S., *The Churches of Christ in Time of War*, p. 136.
3 *Unity*, Vol. 81, No. 8 (April 25, 1918), p. 28.
4 *The Watchman-Examiner*, Vol. VI, No. 11 (Mar. 14, 1918), p. 330.
5 *Catholic World*, Vol. CVI, No. 635 (Feb., 1918), pp. 577-588.
6 Wagner, J. F., *War Addresses*, pp. 14-15.
7 *The New Republic*, Vol. XII, No. 150 (Sept. 25, 1917), pp. 175-177.
8 *The Survey*, Vol. 39, No. 3 (Oct. 20, 1917), p. 75.
9 Boston *Herald*, Jan. 7, 1918.
10 *Zion's Herald*, Vol. XCV, No. 31 (Aug. 1, 1917), p. 963.
11 *Ibid.*, Vol. XCV, No. 40 (Oct. 3, 1917), p. 1252.
12 *Ibid.*, Vol. XCV, No. 29 (July 18, 1917), p. 903.
13 *The Christian Register*, Vol. 97, No. 23 (June 6, 1918), p. 533; Chafee, Z., *Freedom of Speech*, p. 58.
14 *The Outlook*, Vol. 118, No. 13 (Mar. 27, 1918), pp. 478-479.
15 *Ibid.*, Vol. 117, No. 15 (Dec. 12, 1917), pp. 590-592.
16 *Ibid.*, Vol. 117, No. 11 (Nov. 14, 1917), pp. 411-412.
17 *Ibid.*, Vol. 117, No. 2 (Sept. 12, 1917), p. 43.
18 *Ibid.*, Vol. 119, No. 1 (May 1, 1918), p. 11.
19 Mathews, S., *Patriotism and Religion*, Macmillan, N. Y., 1918, p. 39. Quoted by permission of the publishers.
20 *New York Call*, April 2, 1918.
21 Wilson, Luther B., *America—Here and Over There*, pp. 61-62.
22 Chafee, *op. cit.*, p. 57.
23 *Ibid.*, Chapter II.
24 *The Churchman*, Vol. CXVI, No. 8 (Aug. 25, 1917), p. 229.
25 *Christian Work*, Vol. 102, No. 9 (Sept. 1, 1917), p. 225.
26 *The Christian Century*, Vol. XXXIV, No. 34 (Aug. 23, 1917), p. 14.
27 *New York Times*, Oct. 22, 1917.
28 *Ibid.*, Aug. 16, 1917.
29 *The Literary Digest*, Vol. 55, No. 10 (Sept. 8, 1917), p. 32.
30 Lansing, I. J., *Why Christianity Did Not Prevent the War*, p. 128.
31 *New York Times*, Mar. 8, 1918.
32 Sneath, E. H. (Ed.), *Religion and the War*, pp. 59, 60.
33 *The Congregationalist*, Vol. CIII, No. 43 (Oct. 24, 1918), p. 424.
34 *Unity*, Vol. 79, No. 14 (May 31, 1917), p. 212.
35 *Ibid.*, p. 212.
36 *Christian Work*, Vol. 105, No. 11 (Sept. 14, 1918), p. 311.
37 Steele, David, *Papers and Essays for Churchmen*, pp. 21-22.
38 *Unity*, Vol. 70, No. 9 (Nov. 1, 1917), p. 131.
39 Detroit *Free Press*, Mar. 4, 1918.
40 Fosdick, H. E., *The Challenge of the Present Crisis*, p. 31.
41 Mathews, *op. cit.*, p. 100.

⁴² For a discussion of this psychological phenomenon, *vid.* Menninger, Karl, *The Human Mind,* Chapter IV. I have, in part, followed Dr. Menninger's use of terminology.
⁴³ Thomas, Norman, *The Conscientious Objector in America,* p. 14.
⁴⁴ *Vid. Second Report* of the Provost Marshal General to the Secretary of War on the operation of the Selective Service System to December 20, 1918, pp. 199 ff.
⁴⁵ Thomas, *op. cit.,* p. 15.
⁴⁶ *Ibid.,* p. 31.
⁴⁷ *Vid.* Thomas, *op. cit.;* Meyer, W. L., *Hey! Yellowbacks,* and Jones, Rufus, *A Service of Love in War Time.*
⁴⁸ Playne, C. E., *Society at War,* pp. 277, 281.
⁴⁹ Thomas, *op. cit.,* p. 266, ff.
⁵⁰ Philadelphia *Record,* June 17, 1918.
⁵¹ Wilson, *op. cit.,* p. 63.
⁵² *The Christian Advocate,* Vol. XCII, No. 30 (July 26, 1917), p. 748.
⁵³ Pittsburgh *Gazette Times,* Nov. 12, 1917.
⁵⁴ Anthony, A. W., *Conscience and Concessions,* p. 175.
⁵⁵ *The Literary Digest,* Vol. 57, No. 6 (May 11, 1918), p. 31.
⁵⁶ *The Independent,* Vol. 92, No. 3593 (Oct. 13, 1917), p. 77.
⁵⁷ Douglas, G. W., *The Treatment of the Conscientious Objectors.* (Pamphlet.)
⁵⁸ *The Baptist Courier,* Vol. 49, No. 19 (May 9, 1918), p. 4.
⁵⁹ Bridges, Horace, *As I Was Saying,* p. 159; 172-173; 175-176.
⁶⁰ Thomas, *op. cit.,* p. 270.
⁶¹ For a description of the role played by the chaplains and the Y. M. C. A. secretaries in the camps, *vid.* Meyer, *op. cit.,* p. 54.
⁶² Letter Norman Thomas to John R. Mott, C. L. Vol. XXIX, Sept. 24, 1918, pp. 69-73.
⁶³ C. L., C. O. General, Vol. IV, p. 2145.
⁶⁴ Thomas, *op. cit.,* pp. 265-266.
⁶⁵ Allen, W. C., *War! Behind the Smoke Screen,* p. 129.
⁶⁶ C. L., C. O. General, Vol. III, p. 20.
⁶⁷ C. L., Vol. XXIX, p. 181.
⁶⁸ *Ibid.,* p. 197.
⁶⁹ For further details on this point *vid.* Allen, W. C., *op. cit.,* Chapter XIII; Thomas, *op. cit.,* p. 261 ff., Graham, John W., *Conscription and Conscience.*
⁷⁰ Allen, W. C., *op. cit.,* p. 123.
⁷¹ Kellogg, Walter G., *The Conscientious Objector,* p. v. For data on the conscientious objectors and the intelligence tests in which they rated very well, *vid.* articles by Lane, Winthrop in *The New Republic,* Vol. XXII, No. 280 (April 14, 1920), pp. 215 217; May, Mark, in *American Journal of Psychology,* Vol. XXXI, No. 2 (April, 1920), pp. 152-165.

CHAPTER VII

THE FEDERAL COUNCIL OF THE CHURCHES OF CHRIST IN AMERICA, 1917-18

¹ Macfarland, C. S., *Progress of Church Federation,* p. 56.
² Macfarland, C. S., *The Churches of Christ in Time of War,* p. 131.
³ Pritchard, J. W., *Soldiers of the Church,* pp. 122-128.
⁴ *Pacific Baptist,* Vol. 42, No. 22 (June 1, 1918), p. 3.
⁵ Cavert, Samuel, *The Churches Allied for Common Tasks,* p. 73.
⁶ Federal Council, *War-Time Agencies,* p. 213.
⁷ *Ibid.,* p. 213.
⁸ Macfarland, C. S., *The Churches of Christ in Time of War,* p. 136.
⁹ Committee on War-Time Work in the Local Church, "War-Time Program for Local Churches." (Pamphlet.)

10 Macfarland, C. S., *The Churches of Christ in Time of War*, p. 136.
11 Thomas, Norman, *The Conscientious Objector in America*, p. 265.
12 Federal Council, *op. cit.*, p. 58.
13 Jones, Rufus, *Service of Love in War Time*, p. 97, ff.
14 Letter Norman Thomas to Roger Baldwin, C. L., C. O. General, Vol. IV, June 20, 1917, pp. 2149-2151.
15 *Ibid.*
16 Thomas, *op. cit.*, Chapter XI.
17 C. L., Vol. XXIX, p. 133.
18 *Ibid*, p. 134. Professor R. C. McCrea of Columbia University was a kind of civilian commissioner under Assistant Secretary of the War Department, F. P. Keppel.
19 *Ibid.*, p. 141.
20 *Ibid.*, p. 135.
21 *Ibid.*, p. 144.
22 New York *World*, Nov. 21, 1918.
23 Thomas, *op. cit.*, p. 195.
24 *Evening* (Philadelphia) *Public Ledger*, Jan. 10, 1919.
25 *Federal Council Bulletin*, Vol. II, No. 3 (Mar., 1919), pp. 52-53.
26 *The New Republic*, Vol. XVIII, No. 228 (Mar. 15, 1919), pp. 217-218.
27 *Ibid.*, Vol. XVIII, No. 232 (April 12, 1919), p. 351.
28 Committee on War-Time Work in the Local Church, *op. cit.*
29 *Federal Council Bulletin*, Vol. I, No. 1 (Jan., 1918), p. 1.
30 *Ibid.*, Vol. I, No. 5 (May, 1918), p. 4.
31 *Ibid.*, Vol. I, No. 8 (Sept., 1918), p. 6.
32 Macfarland, C. S., *Progress of Church Federation*, p. 172.
33 Macfarland, C. S., *The Churches of Christ in Time of War*, p. 190.
34 *The World Tomorrow*, Vol. I, No. 7 (July, 1918), p. 166.
35 The American Council of the World Alliance and the Commission on International Justice and Goodwill of the Federal Council have a joint executive committee, so they act practically as one body. (Charles Macfarland, *Progress of Church Federation*, p. 154.)
36 *Federal Council Bulletin*, Vol. I, No. 5 (May, 1918), p. 5.
37 *Ibid.*, p. 5.
38 *The World Tomorrow*, Vol. I, No. 7 (July, 1918), p. 166.
39 *Ibid.*, p. 166.
40 *Federal Council Bulletin*, Vol. I, No. 7 (July, 1918), p. 7.
41 Cavert, *op. cit.*, p. 85.
42 *The Nation*, Vol. 107, No. 2783 (Nov. 2, 1918), p. 499.
43 *Ibid.*, p. 499.
44 *The World Tomorrow*, Vol. I, No. 7 (July, 1918), p. 183.
45 *Federal Council Bulletin*, Vol. II, No. 2 (Feb., 1919), p. 32.
46 *Ibid.*, p. 32.

CHAPTER VIII

The Collapse of the Peace Societies

1 *The Advocate of Peace*, Vol. LXXVI, No. 5 (May, 1914), p. 111.
2 New York *Times*, Sept. 13, 1914.
3 *Ibid.*, Jan. 29, 1915.
4 Allen, Devere, *The Fight for Peace*, Chapter 18; Curti, Merle, *The American Peace Crusade*, *passim*.
5 Allen, *op. cit.*, pp. 483-493.
6 *The Advocate of Peace*, Vol. LXXVII, No. 8 (Aug., 1915), p. 186.
7 *Ibid.*, Vol. LXXVIII, No. 10 (Oct., 1916), pp. 287-288.
8 *Ibid.*, Vol. LXXVIII, No. 7 (July, 1916), p. 197.
9 *Ibid.*, p. 215
10 *Ibid.*, Vol. LXXIX, No. 4 (April, 1917), p. 99.
11 *Ibid.*, Vol. LXXIX, No. 5 (May, 1917), p. 137.
12 *Ibid.*, p. 134.
13 *Ibid.*, p. 160.

14 *Ibid.*, Vol. LXXIX, No. 6 (June, 1917), pp. 220-221.
15 *Ibid.*, p. 166.
16 *Ibid.*, Vol. LXXIX, No. 8 (Aug., 1917), p. 242.
17 *Ibid.*, p. 231.
18 *Ibid.*, Vol. LXXIX, No. 12 (Dec., 1917), p. 320.
19 The Committee on Public Information, *The War for Peace*, No. 14, March, 1918.
20 *The Advocate of Peace*, Vol. LXXX, No. 6 (June, 1918), p. 173.
21 *Ibid.*, Vol. LXXX, No. 3 (Mar., 1918), p. 94.
22 *Ibid.*, Vol. LXXX, No. 8 (Aug., 1918), p. 253.
23 *Ibid.*, Vol. LXXX, No. 3 (Mar., 1918), p. 94.
24 *Ibid.*, Vol. LXXX, No. 6 (June, 1918), p. 179.
25 *Ibid.*, p. 170.
26 League to Enforce Peace, *Proceedings*, May, 1916, p. 51.
27 *Ibid.*, p. 53.
28 *Ibid.*, pp. 187-188.
29 New York *Times*, Dec. 25, 1915.
30 *Ibid.*, Jan. 28, 1916.
31 *The Advocate of Peace*, Vol. LXXVIII, No. 5 (May, 1916), pp. 148-149.
32 *Ibid.*, Vol. LXXVIII, No. 9 (Sept., 1916), p. 264.
33 Allen, *op. cit.*, p. 506.
34 League to Enforce Peace, *Win the War for Permanent Peace*, p. 11.
35 *The Advocate of Peace*, Vol. LXXX, No. 6 (June, 1918), pp. 166-167.
36 Allen, *op. cit.*, p. 504.
37 *The Advocate of Peace*, Vol. LXXIX, No. 5 (May, 1917), p. 156.
38 Jordan, D. S., *The Days of a Man*, Vol. II, p. 292.
39 *The Advocate of Peace*, Vol. LXXX, No. 7 (July, 1918), p. 222.
40 *Ibid.*, Vol. LXXX, No. 1 (Jan., 1918), p. 20.
41 Allen, *op. cit.*, p. 508.
42 Viereck, G. S., *Spreading Germs of Hate*, p. 97.
43 *The Advocate of Peace*, Vol. LXXIX, No. 5 (May, 1917), p. 152. For the manner in which pro-German periodicals played up the activities of peace societies, etc., *vid.* various numbers of *Issues and Events*.
44 Jordan, *op. cit.*, Vol. II, p. 735.
45 Lusk Report, Vol. I, pp. 1088-1099.
46 Letter Mrs. David Starr Jordan to the author.
47 New York *Times*, May 20, 21, 1918.
48 Jordan, D. S., *Democracy and World Relations*, p. v.

CHAPTER IX

The Y. M. C. A. in Khaki

1 International Committee of Y. M. C. A., *Summary of World War Work*, p. vi.
2 Odell, J. H., *The Spirit of the New Army*, p. 86.
3 *Ibid.*, p. 63.
4 Coffin, H. S., *In a Day of Social Rebuilding*, p. 7.
5 International Committee of Y. M. C. A., *op. cit.*, p. v.
6 Y. M. C. A., *Service with Fighting Men*, Vol. II, p. 498.
7 International Committee of Y. M. C. A., *op. cit.*, p. 179.
8 Y. M. C. A., *op. cit.*, Vol. I, pp. 321, 328.
9 Members of the Committee were: Bishop Luther B. Wilson, Chairman, J. Ross Stevenson, Peter Ainslee, Clarence A. Barbour, Charles R. Brown, William A. Brown, Bishop Charles S. Burch, S. Parkes Cadman, Bishops Earl Cranston, Eugene R. Hendrix and William Lawrence, W. Douglas Mackenzie, William H. Roberts, Robert E. Speer, John Timothy Stone, George W. Truett, James I. Vance.

(Y. M. C. A., *op. cit.*, Vol. II, p. 494.)
10 Kelman, J., *The War and Preaching*, p. 178.
11 Rowell, W. A., *Patriotism and the Christian Life*, p. 46.
12 Y. M. C. A., *op. cit.*, Vol. II, p. 527.
13 *Ibid*, Vol. I, p. 243.
14 *Ibid.*, Vol. I, pp. 248-249.
15 *Ibid.*, Vol. I, p. vii.
16 *Ibid.*, Vol. I, p. vii.
17 *The Churchman*, Vol. CXVIII, No. 14 (Oct. 5, 1918), pp. 382-383.
18 Boston *Transcript*, June 1, 1918.
19 *Ibid.*, June 1, 1918.
20 International Committee of Y. M. C. A., *op. cit.*, p. 113.
21 Stewart and Wright, *The Practice of Friendship*.
22 Poling, D., *Huts in Hell*, pp. 9, 44.
23 *Ibid.*, pp. 138-139.
24 *Ibid.*, p. 150.
25 Warren, H. C., *With the Y.M.C.A. in France*, p. 40.
26 *Ibid.*, pp. 124-126; 89-90.
27 Eddy, Sherwood, *The Right to Fight,* p. 30.
28 Adams, O. M. and Baber, E. M., *The Task that Challenges*, p. 1.
29 Meyer, E. L., *Hey! Yellowbacks*, p. 107.
30 Y. W. C. A.—War Work Council, *War Work Bulletin*
31 Williams, Michael, *American Catholics in the War*.
32 Booth, Evangeline and Livingston, Grace, *The War Romance of the Salvation Army*.
33 Christian Science War Relief Committee, *Christian Science War Time Activities*, p. 21; *passim*.

CHAPTER X

Groups of Irreconcilables

1 Lusk Report, Vol. I, pp. 1051-1076; *The New Republic*, Vol. XII, No. 149 (Sept. 8, 1917), pp. 157-159; *Unity*, Vol. 79, No. 18 (June 28, 1917), p. 287; Vol. 79, No. 25 (Aug. 16, 1917), p. 399.
2 *The Advocate of Peace*, Vol. LXXX, No. 1 (Jan., 1918), pp. 14-19.
3 *Ibid.*, Vol. LXXIX, No. 11 (Nov., 1917), p. 320.
4 *The Churchman*, Vol. CXVI, No. 3 (July 21, 1917), p. 69.
5 *Ibid.*, Vol. CXVI, No. 6 (Aug. 11, 1917), p. 183.
6 *Ibid.*, Vol. CXVI, No. 15 (Oct. 13, 1917), p. 481.
7 *Unity*, Vol. 79, No. 1 (Sept. 6, 1917), p. 5.
8 Letter from H. W. Pinkham to the author.
9 Int. Fellowship of Reconciliation, "Towards a Christian International"; Files of *The World Tomorrow*, 1918.
10 National Civil Liberties Bureau, *The Case of the Christian Pacifists*. (Pamphlet.)
11 *The Kingdom News*, April 15, 1918.
12 *Ibid.*, April 15, 1918.
13 *Ibid.*, April 15, 1918.
14 New York *Times*, June 22, 1918; Bulletin of Dept. of Justice, No. 119.
15 *The Kingdom News*, April 15, 1918.
16 *Ibid.*, April 15, 1918.
17 *The Appeal to Reason*, Mar. 22, 1918.
18 *The Western Recorder*, 93rd Year, No. 39 (July 4, 1918), p. 8.
19 *The Watchman-Examiner*, Vol. 6, No. 26 (June 27, 1918), p. 819.
20 *The Baptist Record* of Iowa, Vol. XIX, No. 27 (July 6, 1918), p. 8.
21 *Vid. The Presbyterian*, Vol. 88, No. 27 (July 4, 1918), p. 5; *Christian Work*, Vol. 105, No. 3 (July 20, 1918), p. 60.
22 U. S. 258 Fed. 855.
23 *Vid.* Files of National Civil Liberties Bureau, N. Y. Public Library.
24 C. L., C. O. General, Vol. III

25 C L., C. O. General, Vol. IV.
26 *Unity*, Vol. 80, No. 6 (Oct. 11, 1917), p. 95; C. L., C. O. General, Vol. III.
27 C. L., C. O. General, Vol. III.
28 Chicago *Tribune*, July 16, 1917.
29 *Friends' Intelligencer*, Vol. LXXV, No. 14 (Fourth Month 6, 1918), p. 220.
30 Jones, R. M., *A Service of Love in War Time*, Chapter IX.
31 Hunt, Leigh, *Quakers in Action*, p. 16.
32 *The Advocate of Peace*, Vol. LXXX, No. 5 (May, 1918), pp. 146-147.
33 Wright, E. N., *Conscientious Objectors in the Civil War*.
34 Hirst, M. E., *The Quakers in Peace and War*, p. 519.
35 Smith, C. H., *The Mennonites*, Chapter XVIII.
36 *Christian Science Monitor*, Oct. 30, 1918.
37 Smith, *op. cit.*, p. 296.
38 *Ibid.*, p. 297.
39 Dove, F. D., *Cultural Changes in the Church of the Brethren*, Chapter VIII.

CHAPTER XI

The Non-conformist Clergy

1 *Unity*, Vol. 81, No. 10 (May 9, 1918), p. 160.
2 Letter J. H. Holmes to the author.
3 Detroit *Times*, Mar. 19, 1918.
4 *Unity*, Vol. 79, No. 13 (May 24, 1917), p. 195.
5 *The Biblical World*, Vol. L, No. 2 (Aug., 1917), p. 66.
6 New York *Times*, June 15, 1917.
7 Brewing, etc., Vol. II, pp. 2782-2785.
8 Holmes, J. H., *A Statement to My People on the Eve of War*. (Pamphlet.)
9 New York *Telegram*, Dec. 31, 1930, "Holmes, Whose Pacifism Lost a Parish. . . ." p. 3; Holmes, J. H., *New Wars for Old;* various articles by Holmes in magazines during the war. I am also indebted to Dr. Holmes for information about his case.
10 *The Churchman*, Vol. CXVII, No. 16 (April 20, 1918), p. 513; *The Social Preparation* (The Bishop Jones Number), Vol. V, No. 2 (April, 1918); *The Literary Digest*, Vol. LVII, No. 4 (April 27, 1918), p. 32.
11 Seattle *Daily Call*, Oct. 10, 16, 1917. I am also indebted to Dr. Strong for further details.
12 *The Christian Century*, Vol. XXXIV, No. 8 (Feb. 22, 1917), pp. 13-14; *Unity*, Vol. 79, No. 17 (June 21, 1917), p. 260.
13 *Unity*, Vol. 79, No. 9 (April 26, 1917), pp. 133-134.
14 *Ibid.*, Vol. 101, No. 1 (Mar. 5, 1928), esp. p. 16; *vid.* also Vol. 82, No. 2 (Sept. 19, 1918), p. 18.
15 *Ibid.*, Vol. 82, No. 3 (Sept. 26, 1918), p. 29.
16 *Ibid.*, Vol. 100, No. 16 (Dec. 26, 1927), pp. 253-254.
17 *The Churchman*, Vol. CXVII, No. 19 (May 11, 1918), p. 631.
18 Letter H. W. Pinkham to the author.
19 Ms. in possession of the author.
20 Letter P. H. Drake to the author.
21 Letter A. J. Muste to the author.
22 *Unity*, Vol. 79, No. 9 (April 26, 1917), p. 133.
23 *Ibid.*, Vol. 79, No. 10 (May 3, 1917), pp. 150-151.
24 Letter H. F. Ward to the author.
25 *The World Tomorrow*, Vol. 14, No. 1 (Jan., 1931), pp. 21-24; Norman Thomas, *The Conscientious Objector in America*, p. 184; Lusk Report, Vol. I, pp. 971 ff.
26 For a copy of the letter *vid.* Chris-

tian *Work*, Vol. 105, No. 5 (Aug. 3, 1918), pp. 135-136. For the facts about Dr. Rauschenbusch's attitude I am indebted to several individuals who knew him intimately up to the time of his death. They all agree that he never wavered from his earlier feeling about the war.

CHAPTER XII

THE ESPIONAGE ACT, MOB VIOLENCE, AND THE CLERGY

1 Brewing, etc., p. 1788.
2 *Ibid.*, p. 1791.
3 New York *Times*, July 12, 1917.
4 *Ibid.*, July 13, 1917.
5 *Ibid.*, April 25, 1918.
6 *The Christian Advocate*, Vol. XCIII, No. 5 (Jan. 31, 1918), p. 132; Vol. XCIII, No. 6, (Feb. 7, 1918), p. 164.
7 *Ibid.*, Vol. XCIII, No. 25 (June 20, 1918), p. 765.
8 Brewing, etc., p. 1788.
9 *Ibid.*, p. 1788.
10 Cleveland *Plain Dealer*, Aug. 6, 1918.
11 Chicago *News*, Nov. 20, 1918; Chicago *Post*, Nov. 21, 1918.
12 Letter I. St. J. Tucker to the author.
13 All quotations, unless otherwise noted, are taken from an account of the Waldron case by Harold L. Rotzel, New York *Evening Post*, Feb. 4, 1918. Mr. Rotzel and others, including a subpœnaed witness at the trial, have kindly furnished additional details.
14 Plainfield (New Jersey) *Courier News*, Nov. 28, 1917.
15 Letter from Burton A. Lucas to the author. Mr. Lucas was the Congregational minister in Windsor at the time.
16 For further details of the trial and the case, *vid.* Newark (New Jersey) *News*, Dec. 26, 1917; Boston *Globe*, Mar. 22, 1918; Troy *Record*, Jan. 16, 1918; Boston *Advertiser*, Mar. 15, 1918; *Christian Science Monitor*, Jan. 10, 1918.
17 Chafee, Zechariah, Jr., *Freedom of Speech*, pp. 61, 62; Bulletin of the Department of Justice No. 79; *Espionage Act Cases* compiled by Walter Nelles (published by the National Civil Liberties Bureau, 1918).
18 *Vid.* pamphlet prepared by Norman Thomas, *The Case of the Christian Pacifists*, Jan., 1918; Walter Nelles, *op. cit.*, pp. 53-55.
19 National Civil Liberties Bureau, *War Prosecutions and Mob Violence*, July, 1918; Mar., 1919; C. L. Vol. I, A. B. (Cases of Mob Violence).
20 National Civil Liberties Bureau, *The Outrage on the Rev. Herbert S. Bigelow of Cincinnati, Ohio; The New Republic*, Vol. XIII, No. 158 (Nov. 10, 1917), pp. 35-37.
21 *Unity*, Vol. 79, No. 9 (April 26, 1917), p. 133.
22 *Ibid.*, p. 133.
23 *Vid.* No. 19 *supra*.
24 *Ibid.*

CHAPTER XIII

THE WAR BRINGS A REVIVAL OF RELIGION

1 Pentecost, G. F., *Fighting for Faith*, p. 20.
2 Gordon, S. D., *Quiet Talks on the Deeper Meaning of the War*, p. 57.
3 *Vid.* articles against the "Activities and Menace of Millennialism" by Herbert Willett in *The Christian Century*, Vol. XXXV (1918); editorials in same, Vol. XXXIV, No. 26 (June 26, 1917); Vol. XXXV, No. 11 (Mar. 4, 1918); Case, S. J., *The Millennial Hope, A Phase of*

War Time Thinking; Cole, S. G., *History of Fundamentalism,* Chapter X.
4 *Vid. Christian Work,* Vol. 104, No. 21 (May 25, 1918); Vol. 104, No. 23 (June 28, 1918); *Christian Work* was opposed to such attitudes and activities.
5 *The Biblical World,* Vol. LIII, No. 1 (Jan., 1919), p. 36.
6 Torrey, R. A., *The Return of the Lord Jesus,* pp. 89, 91.
7 Pentecost, *op. cit.,* p. 186.
8 *The Christian Century,* Vol. XXXIV, No. 44 (Nov. 1, 1917), p. 5.
9 *The Universalist Leader,* Vol. XX, No. 43 (Oct. 27, 1917), p. 719.
10 *Ibid.,* Vol. XX, No. 50 (Dec. 15, 1917), p. 899.
11 *The Congregationalist,* Vol. CII, No. 28 (July 12, 1917), p. 37.
12 *The Christian Century,* Vol. XXXV, No. 48 (Nov. 21, 1918), p. 10.
13 Boston *Herald,* June 24, 1918.
14 For estimate of reasons for failure from the side friendly to it *vid.* Brown, W. A., *The Church in America,* Chapter VII.
15 *The Independent,* Vol. 91, No. 3587 (Sept. 1, 1917), p. 303.
16 Some of the better known popular books on this theme were: Hankey, Donald, *A Student in Arms;* Barres, Maurice, *The Undying Spirit of France;* Dawson, Coningsby, *The Glory of the Trenches;* Tiplady, Thomas, *The Cross at the Front* and *The Soul of the Soldier.*
17 *The Congregationalist,* Vol. CIII, No. 49 (Dec. 5, 1918), pp. 615-616.
18 Speer, R. E., *The War and Religious Outlook.* (Pamphlet.)
19 Brown, W. A., *Christianity and the War,* p. 6.

CHAPTER XIV

Victory and Post-Armistice Disillusionment

1 *The Churchman,* Vol. CXVII, No. 22 (June 1, 1918), p. 705.
2 New York *Times,* Aug. 26, 1918.
3 *Ibid.,* Mar. 31, 1918.
4 Philadelphia *Public Ledger,* Oct. 12, 1918.
5 *Ibid.,* Oct. 14, 1918.
6 *Ibid.,* Oct. 15, 1918.
7 *Ibid.,* Oct. 17, 1918.
8 Federal Council, *Looking Forward.* (Pamphlet.)
9 Brewing, etc., p. 1805.
10 *Christian Work,* Vol. 105, No. 20 (Nov. 16, 1918), p. 572.
11 *Ibid.,* Vol. 105, No. 21 (Nov. 23, 1918), p. 606.
12 *The Christian Century,* Vol. XXXV, No. 46 (Nov. 28, 1918), p. 3.
13 *Ibid.,* Vol. XXXV, No. 50 (Dec. 28, 1918), p. 6.
14 *Ibid.,* Vol. XXXV, No. 43 (Nov. 7, 1918), p. 4.
15 *Ibid.,* Vol. XXXV, No. 45 (Nov. 21, 1918), p. 13.
16 *The Congregationalist,* Vol. CIII, No. 47 (Nov. 21, 1918), p. 534.
17 *Zion's Herald,* Vol. XCVI, No. 47 (Nov. 20, 1918), p. 1478.
18 *The Churchman,* Vol. CXVIII, No. 20 (Nov. 16, 1918), p. 565.
19 Centenary Commission of the Board of Foreign Missions of the Methodist Episcopal Church, *The Methodist Episcopal Church Fighting America's Fight.* (Pamphlet.)
20 *Christian Work,* Vol. 104, No. 5 (Feb. 2, 1918), p. 133.
21 *Ibid.,* Vol. III, No. 19 (Nov. 5, 1921), p. 559.
22 *The Christian Century,* 1924 *passim; Unity,* 1924 *passim.*
23 Eddy and Page, *The Abolition of War,* p. 193.
24 *Unity,* Vol. 93, No. 14 (June 5, 1924), p. 219.
25 World Alliance for International Friendship Through the Churches, *The Churches' Plea Against the War System.* (Pamphlet.)

26 *The Christian Intelligencer,* Vol. CI, No. 25 (June 18, 1930), pp. 402 ff; Report of the Committee on Education for World Peace.
27 *Christian Work,* Vol. 104, No. 5 (Feb. 2, 1918), p. 134.
28 Niebuhr, Reinhold, *Leaves from the Notebook of a Tamed Cynic,* p. 47.
29 *The Christian Century,* Vol. XLV, No. 1 (Jan. 5, 1928), p. 11.
30 Eddy and Page, *op. cit.,* p. 73.
31 *Evening* (Philadelphia) *Public Ledger,* Feb. 6, 1931.
32 *Ibid.,* Feb. 6, 1931.
33 *The Christian Century,* Vol. XLVII, No. 21 (May 21, 1930), p. 651.
34 New York *Herald Tribune,* April 18, 1932.
35 *The Christian Century Pulpit,* Vol. II, No. 11 (Nov., 1931), p. 2.
36 *Unity,* Vol. 92, No. 14 (Dec. 20, 1923), p. 214.
37 Sneath, E. H. (Ed.), *Religion and the War,* pp. 23, 31.
38 Supreme Court of the U. S. No. 504, Oct. Term, 1930 (May 25, 1931); *The Christian Century,* Vol. XLIX, No. 3 (Jan. 20, 1932), *passim.*
39 *The Christian Century,* Vol. XLI, No. 5 (Jan. 31, 1924), p. 134.
40 *Zion's Herald,* Vol. CIX, No. 26 (July 1, 1931), p. 804.
41 *The World Tomorrow,* Vol. XIV, No. 5 (May, 1931), p. 145.
42 Philadelphia *Daily News,* Nov. 13, 1931.

CHAPTER XV

Conclusion

1 Chafee, Zechariah, Jr., *Freedom of Speech,* pp. 62, 63, 81 (note 68), 101-105.
2 *The Churchman,* Vol. CXVII, No. 2 (Jan. 12, 1918), p. 44; Vol. CXVII, No. 4 (Jan. 26, 1918), p. 120.
3 Hayes, C. J. H., *Essays on Nationalism,* Macmillan, N. Y., 1926, p. 119. Quoted by permission of the publishers.
4 Martin, E. D., *The Behavior of Crowds,* p. 37.
5 *Ibid.,* p. 40.
6 Lippmann, Walter, *Public Opinion, passim.*
7 *The Churchman,* Vol. CXXIV, No. 20 (Nov. 12, 1921), p. 5.
8 *Ibid.,* Vol. CXVII, No. 22 (June 1, 1918), p. 705.
9 *The Christian Herald,* Vol. 41, No. 26 (June 26, 1918), p. 770.
10 *The Advocate of Peace,* Vol. LXXIX, No. 5 (May, 1917), p. 138.
11 Le Gallienne, Richard, *New Poems,* John Lane Co., N. Y., 1910 (now Dodd, Mead and Co., N. Y.), p. 16. Used by permission of the publishers.
12 So reports Heywood Broun, Philadelphia *Record,* May 19, 1933.
13 New York *Times,* May 8, 1933.
14 *Ibid.,* March 21, 1933.
15 *Ibid.,* May 11, 1933.
16 Philadelphia *Record,* May 19, 24, 1933.
17 *The Christian Century,* Vol. L, No. 23 (June 7, 1933), p. 759, letter written by Earl H. Pendell.
18 *Ibid.,* Vol. L, No. 18 (May 3, 1933), p. 589.
19 News release from Dr. Cavert. *Vid.* New York *Times,* May 22, 1933.
20 Allen, Devere, *The Fight for Peace, passim.*

Conclusion, 1969

[1] Zechariah Chafee, Jr., *Freedom of Speech* (New York: Harcourt, Brace and Howe, 1920), p. 62.
[2] *Ibid.*, pp. 61, 62.
[3] *Vietnam. A Resource Collection of Statements, Clippings, and Other Documents* (Akron, Pa.: Prepared by Peace Section, Mennonite Central Committee, n.d.).
[4] *Information Service,* Vol. XLVI, No. 6, Mar. 25, 1967. Clergy and Laymen Concerned About Vietnam. *In the Name of America* (New York, Jan. 1968).
[5] *The Lutheran,* Vol. 6, No. 2, Jan. 17, 1968, p. 50.
[6] *Ibid.,* pp. 16-19.
[7] *The Christian Century,* Vol. LXXXIV, No. 1, Jan. 4, 1967, pp. 7-9.
[8] *Time,* Vol. 91, No. 4, Jan. 28, 1968, p. 62.
[9] *Ibid.,* p. 62.
[10] *The Christian Century,* Vol. LXXXV, No. 1, Jan. 3, 1968, p. 6.
[11] Quoted in *United States News and Reports,* Vol. LXII, No. 4, Jan. 23, 1967, p. 71.
[12] *Ibid.,* p. 71.
[13] *The Christian Century,* Vol. LXXXV, No. 1, Jan. 3, 1968, p. 6.
[14] *New York Times,* June 5, 8, 1968.
[15] *Ibid.,* June 8, 1968.
[16] See: *Gospel Herald, Vietnam Issue,* Vol. LIX, No. 4, Jan. 25, 1966 (Mennonite); American Friends Service Committee. *Peace in Vietnam, A New Approach in Southeast Asia* (New York: Hill and Wang, 1967). These groups have published many pamphlets dealing with service, relief, and aid to Vietnam.
[17] *The Atlantic,* Vol. 221, No. 5, May 1968, pp. 69, 75, 84.
[18] Quoted in *The Christian Century,* Vol. LXXXV, No. 16, Apr. 17, 1968, p. 476.
[19] *Ibid.,* p. 477.
[20] *New York Times,* Apr. 1, 1968.
[21] *Ibid.,* Apr. 14, 1968.
[22] *Harper's,* Vol. 236, No. 1416, May 1968, p. 68.
[22a] *The New York Times* has pointed out that while Congress has since World War II extended exemption from combat service to those who are in opposition to war because of "religious training and belief," even though they are not members of the pacifist sects such as the Quakers, Mennonites, etc., draft boards do not always recognize such claims. On Long Island a draft board refused to grant such exemption to a young man of Jewish faith. In 1965 in the Seegar ruling, the Supreme Court had affirmed the right of non-religious objection. However, Congress in the 1967 Selective Service Act attempted to limit the status of the CO to religious objectors. In April, 1969, Federal Judge Charles E. Wyzanski, Jr., in Boston ruled that the 1967 Act of Congress "unconstitutionally discriminated against atheists, agnostics, and men . . . who, whether they be religious or not, are motivated in their objection to the draft by profound moral beliefs which constitute the central convictions of their beings." The *Times* comments, "Even if the Supreme Court should fail to sustain the Wyzanski ruling, it is time for Congress to recognize that formal religious affiliation is not the only test of a sincere conscience." *The New York Times,* May 15, 1969
[23] *Ibid.,* p. 67.
[24] *Ibid.,* p. 67.
[25] *Encyclopedia of the Social Sciences* (New York: The Macmillan Co., 1937), article on "War," Vol. 8, p. 341.
[26] *The Christian Science Monitor,* May 7, 1968.
[27] Jules Henry, *Culture Against Man* (New York: Random House, 1963), p. 102. Reprinted by permission.

BIBLIOGRAPHY

BIBLIOGRAPHY

The following bibliography contains a list of books cited in the foregoing pages with the addition of a few others. It is suggestive rather than exhaustive.

BOOKS

A. The Revolution and Civil Wars

Baldwin, Alice M., *The New England Clergy and the American Revolution*, Duke University Press, Durham, 1928.

Humphrey, E. F., *Nationalism and Religion*, Chipman, Boston, 1924.

McPherson, Ed., *The Political History of the United States of America During the Great Rebellion*. Appendix, "The Church and the Rebellion," pp. 461-554. Washington, D. C., 1882.

Nicolay, J. G. and Hay, John, *Abraham Lincoln, A History*, Vol. VI, Century, N. Y., 1890.

O'Gorman, Thomas, *A History of the Catholic Church in the United States* (3d Edition), The Christian Literature Co., N. Y., 1900.

Rudd and Carleton, *Fast Day Sermons*, Rudd and Carleton, N. Y., 1861.

Sharpless, Isaac, *A History of Quaker Government in Pennsylvania*, 2 vols., Ferris, Philadelphia, 1898-99.

Shea, John G., *Life and Times of Archbishop Carroll*, N. Y., 1888.

Stanton, Robert L., *The Church and the Rebellion*, Derby, N. Y., 1864.

Sweet, W. W., *The Methodist Episcopal Church in the Civil War*, Methodist Book Concern, Cincinnati, 1912; *The Story of Religions in America*, Harpers, N. Y., 1930.

Van Tyne, C. H., *The Cause of the War for Independence*, Houghton Mifflin, Boston, 1922.

Washington, George, *The Writings of*, edited by Jared Sparks, Boston and New York, 1834-47.

Wesley, John, *Works*, 7 vols., Methodist Book Concern, N. Y.

Wright, Edward N., *Conscientious Objectors in the Civil War*, University of Pennsylvania Press, Philadelphia, 1931.

B. History, etc.

Archer, Wm., *Gems (?) of German Thought*, Doubleday, N. Y., 1917.

Bang, J. P., *Hurrah and Hallelujah*, Doran, N. Y., 1917.

Barnes, Harry Elmer, *The Genesis of the World War* (3rd Edition), Knopf, N. Y., 1929.
World Politics in Modern Civilization, Knopf, N. Y., 1930.

Beard, Chas. A. and Mary R., *The Rise of American Civilization*, Macmillan, N. Y., 1930.

Beck, James M., *The Evidence in the Case*, Putnam, N. Y., 1914.
The War and Humanity (2nd Edition), Putnam, N. Y., 1917.

Benda, Julien, *The Treason of the Intellectuals*, Morrow, N. Y., 1928.

Bernstorff, J. von, *My Three Years in America*, Scribners, N. Y., 1920.

Bourne, Randolph, *Untimely Papers*, Huebsch, N. Y., 1919.

Bruce, Andrew A., *The Non-Partisan League*, Macmillan, N. Y., 1921.

Chafee, Zechariah, Jr., *Freedom of Speech*, Harcourt, Brace, N. Y., 1920.

Czernin, O., *In the World War*, Harpers, N. Y., 1920.

Davis, Arthur K. (ed.), *Publications of the Virginia War History Commission*, Richmond, Va., 1925.

Fay, Sydney B., *The Origins of the World War*, 2 vols., Macmillan, N. Y., 1928.

Gaston, Herbert E., *The Non-Partisan League*, Harcourt, Brace, N. Y., 1920.

Giddings, Franklin H., *Studies in the Theory of Human Society*, Macmillan, N. Y., 1922.

Grattan, C. Hartley, *Why We Fought*, Vanguard, N. Y., 1929.

Hankins, Frank, *Introduction to the Study of Society*, Macmillan, N. Y., 1928.

Hayes, C. J. H., *A Brief History of the Great War*, Macmillan, N. Y., 1928.
Essays on Nationalism, Macmillan, N. Y., 1926.

Hendrick, B. J., *The Life and Letters of Walter Hines Page*, 3 vols., Houghton Mifflin, N. Y., 1925.

Hibben, Paxton and Grattan, C. H., *The Peerless Leader: William Jennings Bryan*, Farrar, N. Y., 1929.

Kaiser's Memoirs, Harpers, N. Y., 1922.

Lawrence, David, *The True Story of Woodrow Wilson*, Doran, N. Y., 1924.

Passelecq, F., *Déportation et travail forcé des ouvriers et de la population civile de la Belgique occupée*, Paris, 1928.

Perla, Leo, *What Is National Honor?*, Macmillan, N. Y., 1918.

Roosevelt, Theodore, *Fear God and Take Your Own Part*, Doran, N. Y., 1916.

Sixty American Opinions on the War, T. Fisher Unwin, London, 1915.

Stout, Ralph, *Roosevelt in the Kansas City Star*, 1921.

Seymour, Charles, *Intimate Papers of Colonel House*, 2 vols., Houghton Mifflin, Boston, 1926.

These Eventful Years, article by Bertrand Russell, et al., 2 vols., Encyclopedia Britannica, N. Y., 1924.

Thwing, Chas. F., *The American Colleges and Universities in the Great War*, Macmillan, N. Y., 1920.

Turner, John K., *Shall It Be Again?*, Huebsch, N. Y., 1922.

Willis, Irene C., *England's Holy War*, Knopf, N. Y., 1928.

U. S. Committee on Public Information. Complete Report of the Chairman of the Committee on Public Information, 1917, 1918, 1919, Washington, D. C., 1920.

German War Practices, Washington, D. C., 1918.

C. Propaganda, etc.

Allen, W. C., *War! Behind the Smoke Screen,* Winston, Philadelphia, 1929.
Brewing and Liquor Interests and German Bolshevik Propaganda, Senate Document 62, 65th Congress, 2nd Session, 1919, Washington, D. C., 1919.
Cook, Sir Edward, *The Press in War Time,* Macmillan, London, 1920.
Creel, George, *How We Advertised America,* Harpers, N. Y., 1920.
Hapgood, Norman (ed.), *Professional Patriots,* Boni, N. Y., 1927.
Lasswell, Harold D., *Propaganda Technique in the World War,* Knopf, N. Y., 1927.
Lippmann, Walter, *Public Opinion,* Harcourt, Brace, N. Y., 1922.
Lowell, A. Lawrence, *Public Opinion in War and Peace,* Harvard University Press, Cambridge, 1923.
Lumley, F. E., *Means of Social Control,* Century, N. Y., 1925.
The Propaganda Menace, Century, N. Y., 1933.
Martin, Everett Dean, *The Behavior of Crowds,* Harpers, 1920.
National German American Alliance, U. S. Senate, S. 3529, Washington, D. C., 1918.
New York State Senate. Report of the Joint Legislative Committee—Investigation Seditious Activities, 4 vols., J. B. Lyon, Albany, 1920.
Playne, Caroline E., *Society at War,* Houghton Mifflin, Boston, 1931.
Ponsonby, Arthur, *Falsehood in War Time,* Allen, London, 1929.
Ridder, Herman, *Hyphenations,* Max Schmetterling, N. Y., 1915.
Stuart, Sir Campbell, *Secrets of Crewe House,* Hodder and Stoughton, London, 1920.
Trotter, W., *Instincts of the Herd in Peace and War* (2nd Edition), Macmillan, N. Y., 1919.
Viereck, George S., *Spreading Germs of Hate,* Liveright, N. Y., 1930.
War and Militarism in Their Sociological Aspects, Vol. 10, University of Chicago Press, Chicago, 1916.

D. Religion and War

Abbott, Lyman, *The Twentieth Century Crusade,* Macmillan, N. Y., 1918.
Adams, O. M. and Baber, E. M., *The Task That Challenges,* Association Press, N. Y., 1919.
Albertson, Charles C., *The Pulpits and the War,* Meridan Press, N. Y., 1917.
Anthony, A. W., *Conscience and Concessions,* Revell, N. Y., 1918.
Black, Hugh, *Lest We Forget,* Revell, N. Y., 1920.
Blackstone, W. E., *Jesus Is Coming,* Revell, N. Y., 1904.
Booth, Evangeline and Livingstone, Grace, *The War Romance of the Salvation Army,* Lippincott, Philadelphia, 1919.
Bosworth, E. I., *The Christian Witness in War,* Association Press, N. Y., 1918.
Boynton, Richard W., *The Vital Issues of the War,* Beacon Press, Boston, 1918.

Bradshaw, Marion J., *The War and Religion*, a Bibliography, Association Press, N. Y., 1919.
Brennan, Anthony, *Pope Benedict XV and the War* (Second Edition), King, London, 1918.
Bridges, Horace, *As I Was Saying*, Marshall Jones, Boston, 1923.
Broughton, Len G., *Is Preparedness for War Unchristian?*, Doran, N. Y., 1916.
Brown, William Adams, *Is Christianity Practicable?*, Scribners, N. Y., 1916.
The Church in America, Macmillan, N. Y., 1922.
Carpenter, J. E., (ed.), *Ethical and Religious Problems of the War*, Lindsey Press, London, 1916.
Case, Shirley J., *The Millennial Hope*, University of Chicago Press, Chicago, 1918.
Cavert, Samuel, *The Churches Allied for Common Tasks*, Federal Council of Churches, N. Y., 1921.
Christian Science War Relief Committee, *Christian Science War Time Activities*, The Christian Science Pub. Co., Boston, 1922.
Church of Jesus Christ of the Latter-Day Saints: Nineteenth Semi-Annual Conference, Deseret News, Salt Lake City, 1919.
Coffin, Henry S., *In a Day of Social Rebuilding*, Yale University Press, New Haven, 1918.
Committee on the War and Religious Outlook, Association Press, N. Y., 1921.
Copping, Arthur E., *Souls in Khaki*, Doran, N. Y., 1917.
Davis, Jerome, (ed.), *Labor Speaks for Itself on Religion*, Macmillan, N. Y., 1929.
Davis, Ozora S., *The Gospel in the Light of the Great War*, University of Chicago Press, Chicago, 1919.
Dawson, Coningsby, *The Glory of the Trenches*, John Lane, N. Y., 1918.
Dennett, Tyler, *A Better World*, Doran, N. Y., 1920.
Douglas, G. W., *Christ's Challenge to Man's Spirit in this World's Crisis*, Longmans Green, N. Y., 1918.
Dove, Frederick D., *Cultural Changes in the Church of the Brethren*, a Ph.D. thesis, University of Pennsylvania, Philadelphia, 1932.
Eddy, Sherwood, *The Right to Fight*, Association Press, N. Y., 1918.
Eddy, S. and Page, K., *The Abolition of War*, Doran, N. Y., 1924.
Empey, Arthur G., *Over the Top*, Putnam, N. Y., 1917.
Faunce, W. H. P., *Religion and War*, Abingdon Press, N. Y., 1918.
Federal Council of the Churches of Christ in America. Selected quotations on Peace and War, N. Y., 1915.
Fosdick, Harry Emerson, *The Challenge of the Present Crisis*, Association Press, N. Y., 1918.
General War-Time Commission of the Churches, War-Time Agencies of the Churches, Federal Council of the Churches of Christ in America, N. Y., 1919.
Gladden, Washington, *The Forks of the Road*, Macmillan, N. Y., 1916.
Gordon, George A., *The Appeal of the Nation*, Pilgrim Press, Boston, 1917.
Gordon, S. D., *Quiet Talks on the Deeper Meaning of the War*, Revell, N. Y., 1919.

Goyan, Gorgas, *The Church of France During the War*, Blond and Gay, Paris, 1918.

Gulick, Sidney L., *The Christian Crusade for a Warless World*, Macmillan, N. Y., 1922.

Hankey, Donald, *A Student in Arms*, Dutton, N. Y., 1917.

Hartzler, J. S., *Mennonites in the World War*, Mennonite Pub. House, Scottdale, Pa., 1922.

Hillis, Newell Dwight, *German Atrocities*, Revell, N. Y., 1918.
Studies of the Great War, Revell, N. Y., 1915.
The Blot on the Kaiser's Scutcheon, Revell, N. Y., 1918.

Hocking, Wm. E., *Morale and Its Enemies*, Yale University Press, New Haven, 1918.

Hodges, George, *Religion in a World at War*, Macmillan, N. Y., 1917.

Holland, Henry Scott, *So as by Fire*, Young Churchman, Milwaukee, 1918.

Holmes, John Haynes, *New Wars for Old*, Dodd Mead, N. Y., 1916.
Religion for Today, Dodd Mead, N. Y., 1917.

Hough, Lynn Harold, *The Clean Sword*, Abingdon Press, N. Y., 1918.

Jefferson, Charles E., *Christianity and International Peace*, Crowell, N. Y., 1915.
Forefather's Day Sermons, Pilgrim Press, Boston, 1917.
What the War Has Taught Us, Revell, N. Y., 1919.
What the War Is Teaching, Revell, N. Y., 1918.

Johnston, Mercer Green, *Patriotism and Radicalism*, Sherman, Boston, 1917.

Jones, Lester, *Quakers in Action*, Macmillan, N. Y., 1929.

Jones, Rufus M., *The Faith and Practice of the Quakers*, Methuen, London, 1927.

Jordan, David Starr, *Democracy and World Relations*, World Book Co., Yonkers, 1918.
The Days of a Man, World Book Co., Yonkers, 1922.
Ways to Lasting Peace, Bobbs-Merrill, Indianapolis, 1916.

Kelman, John, *War and Preaching*, Yale University Press, New Haven, 1919.

King, Henry C., *The Way to Life*, Macmillan, N. Y., 1918.

Laidlaw, Walter (ed.), *The Moral Aims of the War*, Revell, N. Y., 1918.

Lansing, Isaac J., *Why Christianity Did Not Prevent the War*, Doran, N. Y., 1918.

Levinger, Lee J., *A Jewish Chaplain in France*, Macmillan, N. Y., 1921.

Loisy, Alfred, *War and Religion*, Blackwell, Oxford, 1915.

Lovell, Murray J., *The Call of a World Task in War Time* (Third Revised Edition), Student Volunteer Movement, N. Y., 1918.

Lynch, Frederick, *The Peace Problem*, Revell, N. Y., 1911.
Through Europe on the Eve of War, Church Peace Union, N. Y., 1914.
The Challenge: The Church and the New World Order, Revell, N. Y., 1915.
The Christian in War Time, Revell, N. Y., 1917.
President Wilson and the Moral Aims of the War, Revell, N. Y., 1918.
Personal Recollections of Andrew Carnegie, Revell, N. Y., 1920.
(Ed.) *Mobilizing for Peace*, Revell, N. Y., 1924.

Macfarland, Charles S., *The Churches of Christ in America and International Peace*, Church Peace Union, N. Y., 1914.
The Churches of Christ in Time of War, Missionary Education Movement, N. Y., 1917.
The Progress of Church Federation, Revell, N. Y., 1922.

Mackenzie, W. D., *Christian Ethics in the World War*, Association Press, N. Y., 1918.

MacPherson, Hector, *The Vatican and the War: Papal Aims and Methods*, Knox Club, Edinburgh, 1916.

Manners, J. Hartley, *Hate with a Will to Victory*, Mitchell Kennerly, N. Y., 1918.

Mathews, Shailer, *Patriotism and Religion*, Macmillan, N. Y., 1918.
The Spiritual Interpretation of History (Third Edition), Harvard University Press, Cambridge, 1919.

Mayo, Katherine, *That Damn Y*, Houghton Mifflin, Boston, 1920.

McCabe, Joseph, *The War and the Churches*, Watts and Co., London, 1915.

McKim, Randolph H., *For God and Country or the Christian Pulpit in War Time*, Dutton, N. Y., 1918.

Merrill, Wm. P., *War Time Hymns*, Revell, N. Y., 1918.

Moomau, D. C., *Christianity versus War*, Press of the Brethren Pub. Co., Ashland, Ohio, 1924.

National Catholic War Council, *Handbook*, Washington, D. C., 1918.

Naumann, Frederick, *Briefe über Religion* (Fifth Edition), Berlin, 1910.

Newton, Joseph Fort, *The Sword of the Spirit: Britain and America in the Great War*, Nisbit, London, 1918.

Niebuhr, H. Richard, *The Social Sources of Denominationalism*, Holt, N. Y., 1929.

Niebuhr, Reinhold, *Leaves from the Notebook of a Tamed Cynic*, Willett, Chicago, 1929.

Odell, Joseph, *The New Spirit of the New Army*, Revell, N. Y., 1918.

Pell, Edward L., *What Did Jesus Really Teach About War?* Revell, N. Y., 1917.

Pentecost, George F., *Fighting for Faith*, Doran, N. Y., 1918.

Plater, Chas. S. J. (ed.), *Catholic Soldiers*, Longmans Green, London, 1919.

Poling, Daniel A., *Huts in Hell*, Christian Endeavor World, Boston, 1918.

Price, Burr, *The World Talks It Over*, Herkle, N. Y., 1927.

Pritchard, John W., *Soldiers of the Cross (Covenanters)*, Christian Nation Pub. Co., N. Y., 1919.

Rihbany, Abraham M., *Militant America and Jesus Christ*, Houghton Mifflin, Boston, 1917.

Roberts, Elder B. H., *Mormons*, Zion's Printing and Pub. Co., Independence, Missouri, 1923.

Rowell, Wilfrid A., *Patriotism and the Christian Life*, Womans Press, N. Y., 1918.

Russell, Chas. T., *The Finished Mystery*, International Bible Students, N. Y.

Smith, C., Henry, *The Mennonites*, Mennonite Book Concern, Berne, Indiana, 1920.

Sneath, E. Hershey (ed.), *Religion and War*, Yale University Press, New Haven, 1918.
Soul of America in Time of War (a collection of war sermons by 15 Unitarian ministers), Beacon Press, Boston, 1918.
Speer, Robert E., *The Christian Man, the Church and the War*, Macmillan, N. Y., 1918.
Squiers, A. L. (ed.), *One Hundred Per Cent Americanism*, Doran, N. Y., 1918.
Steele, David M., *Papers and Essays for Churchmen*, Jacobs, Philadelphia, 1919.
Stevensen, Lilian, *Towards a Christian Internationalism*, The International F. O. R., Vienna, 1929.
Stewart, George, Jr., and Wright, Henry B., *The Practice of Friendship*, Association Press, N. Y., 1918.
Stidger, William L., *Soldier Silhouettes*, Scribners, N. Y., 1918.
Stires, Ernest M., *The High Call*, Dutton, N. Y., 1917.
The Price of Peace, Dutton, N. Y., 1919.
Swift, Judson, *Manual of Devotion for Soldiers and Sailors*, American Tract Society, N. Y., 1918.
Taylor, Joseph J., *The God of War*, Revell, N. Y., 1920.
Temple, Wm., *Christianity and War-Papers for War Time*, Humphrey Milford, Oxford Press, 1914.
Tiplady, Thomas, *Soul of the Soldier*, Revell, N. Y., 1918.
Tippy, Worth M., *The Church and the Great War*, Revell, N. Y., 1918.
Torrey, R. A., *The Return of the Lord Jesus*, Christian Alliance Pub. Co. of N. Y.
Vance, James I., *The Silver on the Iron Cross*, Revell, N. Y., 1919.
Van Dyke, Henry, *Fighting for Peace*, Scribners, N. Y., 1917.
Wagner, John F., *War Addresses—from Catholic Pulpit and Platform*, Wagner, N. Y., 1918.
Warren, Harold L., *With the Y. M. C. A. in France*, Revell, N. Y., 1918.
Williams, Michael, *American Catholics in the War*, Macmillan, N. Y., 1921.
Wilson, Luther B., *America—Here and Over There*, Abingdon Press, N. Y., 1918.
Y. M. C. A., *The Religious Program of the Y. M. C. A. with the A. E. F. in Europe*, Religious Work Department, Paris, 1918.
Service with Fighting Men, 2 vols., Association Press, N. Y., 1924.
Summary of World War Work of American Y. M. C. A., International Committee of Y. M. C. A. (for private distribution), 1920.
For the Millions of Men Now Under Arms, International Committee of Y. M. C. A. (Strictly private, not to be printed.)
Y. W. C. A., *Report of the Social Morality Commission*, War Work Council, National Board of Y. W. C. A., June, 1917, July, 1919, N. Y., 1919.

E. Peace Movement

Allen, Devere, *The Fight for Peace*, Macmillan, N. Y., 1930.
Curti, Merle, *The American Peace Crusade*, Duke University Press, Durham, 1929.
Eliot, Chas., *The Road to Peace*, Houghton Mifflin, Boston, 1915.

Goldsmith, Robert, *A League to Enforce Peace*, Macmillan, N. Y., 1917.
League to Enforce Peace, *Enforced Peace*, N. Y., 1916.
Win the War for Permanent Peace: Addresses Made at the National Convention, Philadelphia, May, 1918, N. Y., 1918.
Mead, L. A., *Law or War*, Doubleday, N. Y., 1928.
Page, Kirby, *National Defense*, Farrar and Rinehart, N. Y., 1931.

F. THE CONSCIENTIOUS OBJECTORS

Graham, John W., *Conscription and Conscience*, Allen, London, 1922.
Hirst, Margaret E., *The Quakers in Peace and War*, Doran, N. Y., 1923.
Hole, Allen D., *Conscientious Objectors and Alternate Service*, Peace Association of Friends of America, Richmond, Indiana, 1917.
Jones, Rufus, *A Service of Love in War Time*, Macmillan, N. Y., 1920.
Kellogg, Walter G., *The Conscientious Objector*, Boni, N. Y., 1919.
Meyer, Ernest L., *Hey! Yellowbacks*, John Day, N. Y., 1930.
Provost Marshal General, *Second Report to the Secretary of War on the Operations of the Selective Service System to December 20, 1918*, Washington, D. C., 1919.
Thomas, Norman, *The Conscientious Objector in America*, Huebsch, N. Y., 1923.

PAMPHLETS, MAGAZINES, ETC.

Since the number of important pamphlet, magazine, and newspaper references would run into the thousands, no list is attempted here. For a collection of pamphlets, sermons, reports of the various war-time commissions, etc., the reader is referred to a remarkably complete collection in the library of Union Theological Seminary, New York City. For important documents, correspondence, and newspaper clippings, see the collection of the American Civil Liberties Union at the New York Public Library.

INDEX

INDEX

Abbott, Lyman, 23, 24, 30, 43, 65, 83, 110, 229 n. *See also Outlook.*
Abernethy, W. S., 237.
Addams, Jane, 10, 44, 166.
Advocate of Peace, 39, 180. *See also* American Peace Society; Chap. VIII.
Aked, Charles F., 55, 110, 235.
Albertson, C. C., 106.
All-Allies Anti-German League, 117 n.
Allen, Devere, 165, 185, 257.
Allen, W. C., 140.
Allies, propaganda in U. S., 16-19; atrocity propaganda, 95-96; effectiveness of propaganda of, 47-48, 247-249; loans from bankers in U. S., 20; blessings of victory of, 224-226, 232-234. *See also* France; Great Britain.
America (Catholic journal), 131.
American Defense Society, 23, 117 n.
American League to Limit Armaments, 24-25.
American Legion, 25.
American Liberty Defense League, 185.
American Peace Society, 8-9, Chap. VIII. *See also Advocate of Peace.*
American Protective League, 119.
American Rights League, 43, 229 n.
American Tract Society, 62.
American Union Against Militarism, 37, 40, 167, 200.
Anderson, Bishop W. F., 103.
Anglo-American Newspaper Mission, 248 n.
Anthony, A. W., 137.
Anti-Yellow Dog League, 119-120.
Ashworth, R. A., 107.
Association to Abolish War, 181, 203.
Atkinson, H. A., 148, 149, 256.
Atrocity stories, 95, 99 ff., 102, 230.
Atwater, G. P., 123-124.
Atwood, Bishop J. W., 70.

Bacon, B. W., 132.
Baker, Newton D., 34, 140, 148, 149, 150.
Bankers, and the war, 21, 43, 244-245.
Baptist Courier, 137-138.

Baptist Record, 184.
Baptists, in Revolutionary War, 4; in Civil War, 5, 6, 7; English background and sympathy for Allies, 31; pacifist clergy, 196, 197, 198.
Barbour, Clarence A., 117.
Barnes, Harry Elmer, 238.
Barr, Norman B., 186.
Barton, W. E., 55-56, 71, 105.
Bayonet, approval of use of, 67 ff., 160.
Beard, Charles A., 53; Charles A. and Mary R., 122.
Beck, James M., 17, 20, 24, 40, 229 n.
Belgian deportations, 40.
Bell, Bernard Iddings, 59, 237.
Benda, Julien, 53.
Bernstorff, Count Von, 19, 166 n.
Bible, the, war declared issue between German writers and, 56; used to give faith to soldiers and sailors, 62; pacifist texts explained, 64 ff., Sermon on the Mount and the war, 66; printing of Sermon on the Mount advised against by agents of Department of Justice, 66; Golden Rule and the war, 66; as a war book, 251-252; used to defend various practices, 252.
Bigelow, Herbert, 218.
Bitting, W. C., 225.
Blanchard, F. Q., 29.
Bosworth, E. I., 66-67.
Bourne, Randolph, 53.
Bowie, W. Russell, 237.
Boynton, Nehemiah, 164.
Brent, Bishop Charles H., 58.
Brewster, Bishop Benjamin, 55, 237.
Bridges, Horace J., 113, 138.
Bridgman, Howard A., 55, 66, 111. *See also Congregationalist.*
Brockman, Fletcher S., 111.
Brotherhood of St. Andrew, 140.
Broughton, L. G., 35.
Broun, Heywood, 254-255.
Brown, Charles R., 103-104, 123, 124.
Brown, William A., 80, 225, 232.
Brummit, Dan B., 248 n.
Brunner, Edmund de S., 89-90.
Bryan, William Jennings, 10, 39, 44, 55, 163.

323

Bureau of Legal Advice, 139, 149, 185.
Burrell, David J., 28, 38.
Burton, Ernest de Witt, 66.
Bustard, W. W., 105.
Byron-Curtiss, A. L., 197.

Cadbury, Henry J., 230-231.
Cadman, S. Parkes, 28, 30, 38, 46, 121, 124.
Call, Arthur D., 161, 162, 163.
Capitalism, and patriotic organizations, 24; not a capitalistic war (Bishop Brent), 58; and religion, 244-245; as a factor in cause of war, 244-245.
Carnegie, Andrew, 9, 24, 161.
Carnegie Endowment for International Peace, 9, 163-164, 166.
Carter, William, 30, 35, 38.
Catholic World, 131.
Catholics, in Revolutionary War, 4; in Civil War, 5; attitude toward Great Britain (1915), 31, 32; faith of Catholic soldiers, 61; philosophy of the state, 73, 74; Pope's peace proposals, 131; conscientious objectors, 135; pacifist clergy, 197.
Cavert, Samuel M., 57, 236, 256.
Chaffee, Edmund B., 197, 204.
Chapel of the Comforter, pronouncements on the war, 106, 113.
Christian Century, 100, 224, 232, 232-233, 238, 248, 256. See also Charles Clayton Morrison.
Christian Register, 129, 216 n. See also Albert C. Dieffenbach.
Christian Scientists, 176.
Christian Work, 100-101, 130. See also Frederick Lynch.
Christliche Apologete, Der, 212.
Church Peace Union, 9, 26-27, 37, 42, 136, 166.
Church, Samuel Hardin, 109, 116, 120, 229 n.
Church (and churches), and social control, xvi-xviii; in previous wars, Chap. I; and pre-war peace movement, 10; pray for peace, 22; abandon neutrality, 30 ff.; national origins of as affecting point of view about the war, 30-32; pass resolutions supporting U. S. in the war, 51; relied upon to bless popular wars, 56; and the state, 70 ff.; and war, Lutheran view of, 73; and pre-millennialism, 223-224; and victory and disillusionment, Chap. XIV; and Nationalism, 245-246. See also Chaps. IV, V, VI, VII, IX.
Churchman, 41, 126, 130, 180, 201, 229, 233, 248-249, 248 n.

Civil Liberties Bureau, See National Civil Liberties Bureau.
Clergy, outline for ecclesiastical defense of war prepared in England, 18; and American Legion, 25; and *Lusitania* disaster, 28-29; cultural background as affecting attitude toward the war, 30-32; vote on preparedness, 33, 37; asked by patriotic societies to preach on preparedness, 33; effect of Theodore Roosevelt upon, 34; and preparedness parade, New York, 37-38; as chaplains of patriotic organizations, 38; and presidential election of 1916, 39; and peace sentiment, 41-42; and patriotic organizations, 43; furnished with sermonic material on war, 83 ff.; used as propaganda agents, 83 ff.; Presbyterian clergy in New York, 91-92; in Harrisburg, Pa., 105; accused of slackness, 122-123, 124; defended, 123-124; suggest method of treatment for conscientious objectors, 136-138; lack of interest in objectors, 139-141; and the Y. M. C. A., Chap. IX; and People's Council, 179-181; and Russellites, 182-185; Chicago clergy and the conscientious objectors, 185-186; and revival of religion, 224-225; give comfort to bereaved, 225-226; as victims of crowd mind, 246-247; basis of ethical judgments about the war, 247-249; in the next war, 251 ff. See also various chapters on the clergy and the churches.
Coffin, Henry Sloane, 28, 172.
Committee on Public Information, 53-54, 88, 146, 163.
Congregationalist, 108, 224, 233. See also H. A. Bridgman.
Congregationalists, in Revolutionary War, 4; in Civil War, 5; English background and sympathy for Allies, 31; pacifist clergy, 196, 197, 198.
Conscientious objectors, 134 ff., 147 ff., 181-182, 185 ff.
Continent, 33.
Conwell, Russell, 29.
Cooke, Bishop Richard J., 107-108, 130, 137.
Copperhead newspapers, 251 n.
Coudon, H. N., 132.
Crane, Frank, 55.
Crapsey, Algernon, 55.
Creel, George, 53, 88, 97 n. See also Committee on Public Information.

Darrow, Clarence S., 55.
Davis, Ozora S., 83.
Davis, W. W., 107.
Davison, William A., 215, 216.
Day, James R., 104.
Department of Justice, 66, 119, 157, 200, 212-213, 231.
Dewey, John, 8, 21, 53.
Dieffenbach, Albert C., 68, 124. *See also Christian Register.*
Dietrich, J. H., 237.
Doan, Frank C., 205.
Dole, Charles F., 32, 162, 181, 203.
Douglas, George W., 38, 137.
Dowling, George T., 100, 246.
Downs, George W., 67, 137.
Drake, Paul H., 204.
Duffield, Howard, 230.
Duffy, Francis, 236.
Dunkards, and preparedness, 31; and conscientious objectors, 135, 147; war-time attitude of, 188.

Eaton, Charles A., 28, 30, 33, 38, 45, 82, 85, 113, 121.
Eddy, Sherwood, 176, 235.
Elderkin, Noble S., 182, 186.
Eliot, Charles W., 23, 36.
Elliott, John L., 149.
Ellis, William T., 174, 222.
Emergency Peace Federation, 44-45, 167.
Episcopalians, in Revolutionary War, 5; in Civil War, 5; English background and sympathy for Allies, 31; and British propaganda, 31 *n.;* and war-time prohibition, 91 *n.;* War-Time Commission, 148; pacifist clergy, 196, 197, 198; and Bishop Paul Jones, 200-202.
Epworth Herald, 248 *n.*
Espionage and Sedition Acts, passed, 128; general approval of 129-130; and Russellites, 183-184; and clergy, Chap. XII.
Ethnocentrism, examples of, 27, 35, 58-59, 62, 106-107, 155, 160.
Evans, Edward W., 141, 182.

Fagnani, C. P., 111, 137.
Fallows, Bishop Samuel, 132, 234.
Farley, John Cardinal, 23, 73, 129.
Faunce, W. H. P., 27 *n.,* 163.
Federal Council of Churches, and prewar peace movement, 9; and prayers for peace, 22; pledges cooperation to win the war, 80; cooperates in war program, 88 ff., polls clergy on attitude toward the war, 91-92; passes resolution favoring free speech, 127-128. *See* Chap. VII, *passim.*

Fellowship of Reconciliation, 139, 181-182, 195, 200, 203, 238.
Fincke, William A., 197, 204.
Fitch, Albert Parker, 237.
Food conservation, 87-88.
Fosdick, Harry Emerson, 54, 61, 62, 63, 72, 102, 110, 113, 124, 133, 235.
France, propaganda in U. S., 19, 153, 155. *See also* Allies.
Francis, James A., 57.
Friends, in Revolutionary War, 4; and conscientious objectors, 135, 147; war-time attitude of, 186-187.
Friends' Service Committee, 139, 185, 187.

Gammon, Robert W., 124, 248 *n.*
Garland, Bishop Thomas J., 136.
Gates, Milo H., 38.
General War-Time Commission, 80-81, 88 ff., 147, 148.
German-Americans, 29, 30, 31, 39-40, 113-114, 116.
Germany, propaganda in U. S., 19-20; loans in U. S., 20; propaganda and the Lutherans, 31; boycott against, 108-109; plot against America, 115; theology, 114-115, 123; language and music, 116-118; propaganda in U. S. through peace societies, 166-167; Adolph Hitler, 254-257.
Gibbons, James Cardinal, 30, 46, 73, 131.
Gilbert, George H., 104.
Goodchild, Frank M., 35, 54.
Goodell, Charles L., 34.
Gordon, George A., 45, 124.
Gordon, Lindley, 180.
Grant, Percy S., 25, 151.
Grattan, C. Hartley, 16, 20-21, 36.
Great Britain, propaganda in U. S., 16-19; loans from bankers in U. S., 20; propaganda and Episcopalians, 31 *n. See also* Allies.
Greer, Bishop David H., 22, 25, 28, 32, 55, 110.
Gregory, Attorney General, 210, 218 *n.*
Griffith, George A., 114.
Grose, George R., 51.
Grose, Howard B., 88.
Gunsaulus, Frank, 132.

Haldeman, Isaac M., 46, 54.
Hall, Frank O., 38, 54.
Hartman, L. O., 237.
Hayes, Carlton J. H., xvi-xvii, 19, 246.
Hebrews, *See* Jews.
Henderson, Bishop Theodore S., 120-121, 193.

Index

Hibben, John Grier, 26, 34, 167 n., 229 n., 256.
Hillis, Newell Dwight, 32, 82, 96 ff., 108, 109, 118, 124.
Hitler, Adolph, 254-257.
Hogue, Richard W., 179.
Holmes, John Haynes, 22, 28, 32, 132, 141, 149 n., 151-152, 182, 185, 198-200.
Holt, Hamilton, 41, 164.
"Holy war," origin of legend of, 17-18; theology of, 55 ff.; clergy suppress their doubts about, 133-134; conscientious objectors mar the legend, 135-136. See Chap. III, *passim;* Chap. XV, *inter alia.*
Hooft, W. A. Visser't, 256.
Hough, Lynn Harold, 65.
Hubbell, W. H., 34.
Hughes, Bishop Edwin H., 59.

Industrial Workers of the World (I. W. W.), 129, 202, 218.
International Bible Students (Russellites), 135, 182-185, 219.
Ireland, Archbishop, 73, 124.

Jefferson, Charles E., 32, 33, 55, 110, 113.
Jenkins, Burris, 82.
Jesus, opinions about his approval of war, 45, 55, 57, 59, 62, 63, 64-65, 66, 68, 69-70, 71-72, 86, 133, 145.
Jewish Welfare Board, 81.
Jews, and preparedness, 32; pacifist clergy, 196, 197, 198; and Judah L. Magnes, 206; persecution under Hitler, 254, 255, 256.
Johnson, Herbert S., 67-68, 115-116.
Johnston, J. Wesley, 63, 132.
Jones, David H., 114.
Jones, Jenkin Lloyd, 32, 42, 141, 179, 181, 185, 192, 202-203.
Jones, Bishop Paul, 141, 179, 180-181, 182, 197, 200-202.
Jones, Rufus, 141, 182.
Jordan, David Starr, 167-168.
Jowett, John Henry, 23, 28, 42, 84, 85.
Joy, Charles R., 218.

Keen, W. W., 230-231.
Keigwin, A. E., 252.
Keller, Frederick, 29.
Kellogg, Walter G., 142.
Kelman, John, 61, 68, 173.
Keppel, F. P., 25, 149 n.
King, Henry C., 50, 63, 124, 154.
Knights of Columbus, 176.
Kreisler, Fritz, 118.

La Follette, Robert, 120, 129, 130, 167.
Laidlaw, Walter, 30, 37, 84.
Lake Mohonk Conference, 9, 166.
Lansing, Isaac J., 58, 114, 115, 131.
Lasswell, Harold D., xv, 19, 56, 95.
Latter-Day Saints, Church of Jesus Christ of the, 21, 52, 86.
Lawrence, Bishop William, 22, 29, 46, 224.
Laws, Curtis Lee, 111. See also *Watchman-Examiner.*
League for Democratic Control, 139, 185.
League to Enforce Peace, 164-165.
Le Gallienne, Richard, 253.
Liberty Loans, 83 ff., 86, 87, 98 ff., 152.
Luccock, Halford E., 237.
Lutherans, in Revolutionary War, 4; in Civil War, 5; and *Lusitania,* 29; and preparedness, 31; and German propaganda, 31 n.; presidential election (1916), 39; pledge loyalty, 51; philosophy of the state, 73, 74; loyalty of, 91, 211; Commission for Soldiers and Sailors Welfare, 147; clergy and Espionage Act, 212-213; and thanks for victory, 232.
Lynch, Frederick, 10, 26, 32, 33, 37, 42, 44, 54, 113, 130, 136, 137-138, 232, 234. See also *Christian Work.*

MacArthur, R. S., 105.
MacCallum, John A., 231.
Macfarland, Charles S., 147-148, 152, 153.
Macintosh, Douglas C., 237.
Mackenzie, W. Douglas, 65-66, 74.
MacLeod, Malcolm J., 22, 28, 45, 108.
Magnes, Judah L., 141, 179, 206.
Mann, Louis L., 55.
Manners, J. Hartley, 111-112.
Manning, Bishop William T., 22, 30, 35, 38, 40, 118, 124, 131.
Marriott, A. E., 67, 176.
Mathews, Shailer, 54, 133, 194.
Matthews, Mark A., 108-109, 129, 230.
Maurer, James H., 105, 179.
McKim, R. H., 43, 55, 229 n.
McPherson, George W., 114.
Melish, J. Howard, 55, 180.
Mennonites, and Revolutionary War, 4; and preparedness, 31; and conscientious objectors, 135, 147; and attitude toward the war, 187-188.
Merle-Smith, W., 38.
Merrill, William Pierson, 25, 32, 33, 35, 117, 236.

Index

Methodists, in Revolutionary War, 5; in Civil War, 5-6; English background and sympathy for Allies, 31; of New England endorse entrance into the war, 51; bishops support Liberty Loan, 86; pacifist clergy, 196, 197, 198; German Methodists, 212; centenary program and Allied victory, 233.
Meyer, E. L., 176.
Meyers, W. B., 58.
Missions, war as enterprise of, 57-58, 66, 85, 160.
Moldenke, A. B., 28-29, 40.
Moore, Fred A., 180, 186.
Morrison, Charles Clayton, 237, 248 n. See also *Christian Century*.
Mothers, Gold Star, 225, 226.
Mott, John R., 55, 173, 181.
Muck, Karl, 118.
Muste, A. J., 182, 185, 205.
Myers, Cortland R., 29, 104.

National Catholic War Council, 81.
National Civil Liberties Bureau (now American Civil Liberties Union), 139, 140-141, 147 ff., 185, 200, 203.
National Security League, 23-24, 33, 36, 130.
Nationalism, and religion, xvi-xviii, 245-246. See chapter headings for various manifestations of.
Naumann, Frederick, 71-72.
Newton, Joseph Fort, 57, 224, 232, 236.
New York Peace Society, 8, 26, 164.
Niebuhr, Reinhold, 235.
North, Frank Mason, 58, 89, 152.

Odell, Joseph H., 123-124, 171.
Oldham, G. Ashton, 30, 43-44.
Outlook, 124, 129-130, 248 n. See also Lyman Abbott.

Pacifists, and preparedness movement, 24 ff.; and election of 1916, 40; and Wilson's speech to Senate, 42; go to Washington, 44; converted to war aims, 54-55; sentiment against, 131 ff.; Christian, 216-217, 230-231. See Chaps. X, XI, XII.
Paradise, Frank I., 27.
Parker, Sir Gilbert, 16-17.
Parkhurst, Charles Henry, 27.
Patriotic societies, See separate organizations.
Peabody, Francis Greenwood, 70, 106, 224.
Peace societies, See separate organizations and Pacifists.
Pell, Edward L., 63-64.

Pentecost, George F., 72-73, 223.
People's Council, 163, 179-181, 200.
Pepper, George Wharton, 24, 41.
Pershing, General John J., 61, 78, 102-103, 171, 173.
Pinchot, Gifford, 90.
Pinkham, Henry W., 32, 45, 141, 165, 204, 218.
Playne, Caroline E., 135-136.
Poling, Daniel A., 69, 78, 170, 175.
Pope Benedict XV., peace proposals, 108, 130-131.
Porter, Eliot, 236.
Premillennialism, 223-224, 255.
Presbyterians, in Revolutionary War, 4; in Civil War, 5, 6; background as affecting attitude toward Allies, 31; clergy of New York in war work, 92; pacifist clergy, 196, 197, 198.
Propaganda, principles of, xiv ff.; effect on the churches and religious leaders, xvi, xvii-xviii, 247-249; of peace movement (pre-war), 8 ff., (preparedness era), Chap. II, *inter alia*; and presidential election of 1916, 39-40; effectiveness of Allied, 47-48; Committee on Public Information, 53-54; use of in case of Edith Cavell, 95; churches and clergy as agents of, Chap. IV, 145-146, 152; and peace societies, 166-167. See also Allies, France, Germany, Great Britain.
Putnam, George Haven, 23, 43, 229 n.

Quakers, See Friends.
Quayle, Bishop W. A., 101.

Rauschenbusch, Walter, 206-207.
Record of Christian Work, 248 n.
Recruiting, by clergy, 73, 81-83.
Reformed Church, censures clergyman relating pleasant experiences with German prisoners, 102; pacifist clergy, 196, 197, 198; clergy and Espionage Act, 213; post-war pronouncements, 235.
Reformed Presbyterians (Covenanters), 145-146.
Rihbany, A. M., 60, 64-65.
Roberts, Richard, 182.
Roosevelt, Theodore, 10, 23, 25, 34, 40, 229 n.
Rotzel, Harold, 182, 185.
Russell, Bertrand, 16.
Russellites, See International Bible Students.
Ryan, John A., 128.

Salvation Army, 176.
Sayre, John Nevin, 141, 182, 185, 197, 203.
Schulman, Samuel, 35.
Schwab, Charles M., 36.
Seaman, Bishop E. C., 237.
Sharp, I. M., 104.
Shipman, Herbert, 38, 39 n.
Shumaker, Ellsworth E., 32.
Simpson, W. G., 141, 148, 149, 185, 197.
Sinclair, Upton, 184.
Smith, Gypsy, 173.
Sneath, E. Hershey, 103.
Social Control, principles of, xiv-xvi; of the churches, xviii. *See also* Church, Clergy, Propaganda. Examples of Social Control (suggestive rather than exhaustive):
   (1) Use of religious symbolism for war purposes, 41, 82, 83, 85, 86, 89, 90-91, 104, 107, 113, 114, 115, 117, 122, 123, 137, 145, 146, 152, 153, 164, 165, 174, 175, 176, 223, 224, 225, 226, 232, 233, 245-246, 252. *See* Chap. III, *passim*.
   (2) Appeal to authorities; Jesus, 62-70, 82-83, 145, 162; symbol of the state, 70 ff.; church, 201.
   (3) Law, 149-150 n., 181, 183 ff. *See also* Chaps. VI, XI, XII.
   (4) Economic pressure, 20-21, 31, 87, 157, 163-164, 244-245.
   (5) Appeal to pride, 51-52, 53, 81, 87, 212.
   (6) Use of epithets, 24, 34-35, 87, 112, 114, 128 ff.
   (7) Appeal to sadism, 67 ff., 86, 96, 99-101, 102, 105, 109, 229.
   (8) Appeal to sex drive, 63-64, 84, 96, 99-100, 101, 230-231.
   (9) Fear of lack of preparedness, 23 ff., 34-35, 46, 115-116.
   (10) Appeal to symbols of friendship, *See* Propaganda, Allies, France, Great Britain.
   (11) Music and patriotism, 85, 116-118.
   (12) Types of group pressures, *See* Table of Contents and various organizations.
   (13) Relaxing of ordinary controls, promoting espionage, hysteria, etc., 246. *See* chap. headings.
   (14) Failure to control minorities, 188-189. *See* Chaps. VI, VII, X, XI, XII.
   For effect of cultural factors in conditioning group behavior, *See* 5, 30 ff., 188-189, 249-251.
Socialists, 130, 156, 179.
Sociology, contribution to understanding of the war period of, Introduction, *passim;* and naturalistic science of society, 243-244; Chap. XV, *passim*.
Sockman, Ralph W., 237.
Soldiers, and the war (statements about): need of Christ, 59; discovering their souls, 60; spiritually reborn, 60; bear the marks of the Lord Jesus, 61; faith in God of Catholic, 61; Christian leadership of, 61; manual of devotion for, 62; can kill enemy in friendship, 67; Catholic addresses to, 73; German, 98, 106, proposed sterilization of, 109; significance of service and death of, 225-226. *See also Chap.* IX.
Speer, Robert E., 32, 55, 80, 110-111, 225.
Stabler, W. Brook, 237.
Standard, 248 n.
State, and church, *See* Church and state.
Steele, David M., 132.
Stelzle, Charles, 91, 152.
Stewardson, Langdon C., 27.
Stewart, George, Jr., 69-70.
Stidger, William L., 60, 176, 237.
Stifler, James M., 69, 237.
Stires, Ernest M., 21 n., 38, 60.
Stone, James S., 132-133.
Stone, John Timothy, 82-83, 139.
Strong, Sydney, 110, 141, 179, 182, 202, 235.
Sullivan, William L., 86.
Sunday School Times, 248 n.
Sunday, William A. (Billy), 79, 106, 112, 129, 217.
Sweden, proposed conference in, 153 ff.

Taft, William Howard, 23, 36, 164, 173.
Taylor, Alva, 130, 233.
Thomas, Norman, 140, 141, 147, 149 n., 179, 182, 185, 197, 203.
Thomas, Wilbur, 141, 181.
Tippy, Worth M., 82, 89, 91.
Tittle, Ernest F., 237.
Trueblood, Benjamin F., 161.

Tucker, Irwin St. John, 179, 186, 197, 213.

Unitarians, English background as affecting attitude toward Allies, 31; 193; pacifist clergy, 196, 197, 198.
Unity, 127, 181, 200, 203, 238, 256. *See also* Jenkin Lloyd Jones.
Universalist Leader, 224.
Universalists, English background as affecting attitude toward Allies, 31; pacifist clergy, 196, 197, 198.
Universal Peace Union, 165.
Urban, Leigh R., 203-204.

Van Allen, William H., 45, 108.
Vance, James I., 50, 153.
Van de Water, George R., 35, 38, 58, 101, 124.
Van Dyke, Henry, 8, 24, 105, 117, 122, 124, 228, 232 *n*.
Van Dyke, Henry (Sr.), 6-7.
Viereck, George S., 19, 31 *n*.

Waldron, Clarence H., 214-216.
War Department, 134, 140, 141, 149, 150-151, 185.
Ward, Harry F., 147, 182, 205.
Warren, Harold C., 175-176.
Washburn, Henry B., 148.
Watchman-Examiner, 128, 184. *See also* Curtis Lee Laws.
Weise, E. F., 194.
Wells, H. G., 17, 18.
Wendte, Charles W., 55.

Western Recorder, 184.
Whitaker, Robert, 216, 217.
Whittlesey, Colonel, 113.
Wilson, Bishop Luther B., 59, 124, 130, 136.
Wilson, Woodrow, 20, 22, 36, 39-40, 42, 178, 218 *n*.
Wise, Stephen S., 32, 37, 38, 54, 86, 180, 236.
Woelfkin, Cornelius, 116, 206.
Woman's Peace Party, 166.
Wood, L. Hollingsworth, 25, 141, 149, 182.
World Peace Foundation, 9, 165, 166.
World Tomorrow, 127, 155-156, 181, 203, 237-238, 256.
World War, theories about origin and nature of, 18, 20, 23, 26, 35, 53-54, 97, 103-104, 105, 107-108. *See* Chap. II; *also* "Holy war."
Wright, Harold Bell, 65.
Wright, Henry B., 69-70.

York, Alvin C., 139.
Young Democracy, 185.
Y. M. C. A., and Dr. Speer, 110-111; criticism of, 130; secretaries and the conscientious objectors, 139; Committee on War and Religious Outlook, 225. *See* Chap. IX.
Young People's Socialist League, Chicago, 185.
Y. W. C. A., 176.

Zion's Herald, 105, 114-115, 129, 137, 233, 237.

INDEX II
For Chapter XVI, World War II

Barth, Karl, 268
Buttrick, George H., 263
Chaplains in war time, 270
Christian Century, 264, 265, 267, 268
Christian Leader, 268
Churches, attitudes toward the war, 262-264
Church of the Brethren, 264, 270
Civil Liberties, 269
Clergy, attitudes toward the war, 262-266
Conscientious objectors, 269, 270
Episcopalians, 266
Federal Council of Churches, 263, 264
Fellowship of Reconciliation, 265, 272

Fortune (magazine), 263, 268
High, Stanley, 264
Hitler, Adolph, 261
Holmes, John Haynes, 267
"Holy War," 266, 268-269, 272, 273
Jehovah's Witnesses, 269, 270
Johnson, Ernest, 269, 271
Judaism, 271, 272
Living Church, 267
Manning, Bishop William T., 266
Mennonites, 264, 270
Methodists, 270
Morrison, Charles Clayton, 264, 265 268
Nationalism, 273, 274

National Peace Conference, 263
Neutrality Acts, 261, 262, 263, 265
Niebuhr, Reinhold, 265, 268
Pacifism, 263-265
Pearl Harbor, 252, 267, 270
Pope Pius XII, 271
Propaganda, preparedness, 265, 266; war-time, 272
Reese, Carter W., 267
Religious Press, 264-265

Roman Catholic Church, 270, 271
Roosevelt, Franklin D., 262, 263, 264, 270, 271
Selective Service Act of 1940, 262
Society of Friends, 264, 270
Standish, Miles, 273
Temple, William, 268
Unity, 267
Van Kirk, Walter, 264
War, declaration of war, 262; see "Holy War"

INDEX III

For Introduction, 1969 and Conclusion (Chapter XVII), 1969

American Civil Liberties Union, 284
Amish, 284, 285
Baptists, 231, 282
 Southern Baptist Convention, 282
Bishop, Joseph W., Jr., 285, 286
Christian Century, 281
Christian Science Monitor, 288
Church of the Brethren, 279, 282, 284, 285
Clergy, opposition to the war; attitudes to the war, 230-282
Coffin, William Sloane, 283, 284, 285
Colleges and Universities, statement re Spock, Coffin, et al, 285
Commonweal, 231
Conscience and the war, 285-286
Conscientious objectors, 234
Copperhead newspapers and Civil War, xxiii
Critic (Roman Catholic), 281
Death, fascination with, 288-289
De Puy, Norman, 283
de Tocqueville, Alexis, 290
Domment, Arthur J., xxvi
Eisenhower, Dwight D., xxii
Episcopalians, 281, 282
Freud, Sigmund, 289
Graham, Billy, 232
Henry, Jules, 290
Johnson, L. B., 283
Judaism, Synagogue Council of America, p. 279
King, Martin Luther, 280, 283
Lincoln, Abraham, xxiii, 286
Lippmann, Walter, xxv
Lutheran, The, 280, 281

Lutherans, 282
McCarthy, Joseph, 286
McIntire, Carl, xxvi
Mennonites, 279, 282, 284, 285
Methodists, 279
Missions (Baptist), 283
National Council of Churches of Christ in the U.S.A., 280.
National Emergency Committee of Clergy and Laymen Concerned About Vietnam, 230
Nationalism and war, 287
New York Times and the war, 283
O'Hanlon, Daniel, 281
Pareto, Vilfredo, 290
Paris Peace Conference, xxvi, 277
Propaganda, techniques in Vietnam War, xxi, xxii
Roman Catholic Church, 282
Society of Friends, 279, 282, 284, 285
Spellman, Cardinal, 281
Spock, Benj., xxiv, 283, 284, 285
United States Catholic, 281
Vallandigham, Clement L., xxiii
Vietnam War, reasons for opposition to, xxiv, cf. to World War I, 277-279
Waldron, Clarence H., 279
Wallace, D. H., 278-279
War and violence, 289
Wars, opposition to: Revolution, xxiii; War of 1812, xxiii; Mexican War, xxiii; Civil War, xxiii
Washington Evening Post and the war, 283
Wicker, Tom, 283

www.ingramcontent.com/pod-product-compliance
Lightning Source LLC
Chambersburg PA
CBHW070011010526
44117CB00011B/1504